Computational Intelligence for Autonomous Finance

Scrivener Publishing
100 Cummings Center, Suite 541J
Beverly, MA 01915-6106

Publishers at Scrivener
Martin Scrivener (martin@scrivenerpublishing.com)
Phillip Carmical (pcarmical@scrivenerpublishing.com)

Computational Intelligence for Autonomous Finance

Edited by

Deepa Gupta

GL Bajaj Institute of Management, India

Mukul Gupta

GL Bajaj Institute of Management, India

Rajesh Kumar Dhanaraj

Symbiosis International (Deemed University), India

Balamurugan Balusamy

Shivnadar University, Greater Noida, UP, India

and

Parth Mukul Gupta

Birla Institute of Technology & Sciences, Pilani, Rajasthan, India

Scrivener Publishing

WILEY

This edition first published 2025 by John Wiley & Sons, Inc., 111 River Street, Hoboken, NJ 07030, USA and Scrivener Publishing LLC, 100 Cummings Center, Suite 541J, Beverly, MA 01915, USA

For more information about Scrivener publications please visit www.scrivenerpublishing.com.

Wiley Global Headquarters
111 River Street, Hoboken, NJ 07030, USA

For details of our global editorial offices, customer services, and more information about Wiley products visit us at www.wiley.com.

Library of Congress Cataloging-in-Publication Data

ISBN 978-1-394-23322-9

Front cover image courtesy of Adobe Firefly
Cover design by Russell Richardson

Set in size of 11pt and Minion Pro by Manila Typesetting Company, Makati, Philippines

Printed in the USA

10 9 8 7 6 5 4 3 2 1

Contents

Preface **xvii**

1 The Role of Autonomous Finance in the Era of Automatic Civilization **1**
Sanjeet Singh, Geetika Madaan and Jaskiran Kaur
1.1 Introduction 2
1.2 The Concept of Autonomous Finance 2
1.2.1 Autonomous Finance: The Technology and Factors Driving Its Widespread Deployment 3
1.2.2 CFO's Function in Autonomous Finance 3
1.2.3 Motives to Switch to an Autonomous Finance Structure 4
1.2.4 What is the Process of Autonomous Finance (How Does it Work)? 6
1.2.5 Advantages of Autonomous Finance 6
1.2.6 Challenges Associated with Autonomous Finance 7
1.3 Autonomous Finance: Prospects and Developments 9
1.4 Key Considerations for Implementing Autonomous Finance 14
1.5 Conclusion 15
References 15

2 Analyzing the Latest Tools and Techniques for Stock Market Analysis **21**
Ochin Sharma, Raj Gaurang Tiwari, Suvarna Sharma and Annu Priya
2.1 Introduction 21
2.2 Need for Trading Softwares 23
2.3 How Software for Technical Analysis of the Indian Stock Market Operates 23
2.4 Helpful Tools to Analyze Stock Market 24
2.4.1 Masterswift 2.0 24

2.4.2 RichLive Trade 25
2.4.2.1 Key Features of RichLive Trade Software 25
2.4.3 MetaTrader 4 25
2.4.3.1 Key Features of MetaTrader4 26
2.4.4 MotiveWave 27
2.4.4.1 Key Features of MotiveWave 27
2.4.5 Spider Stock Market Software 28
2.4.6 Investar 29
2.4.6.1 Key Features 30
2.4.7 eSignal 30
2.4.7.1 Main Properties of eSignal 31
2.4.8 Sharekhan Trade Tiger 31
2.4.8.1 Main Properties of Trade Tiger 32
2.4.9 Trader Guide 33
2.4.9.1 Trader Guide Features 33
2.4.10 NinjaTrader 33
2.4.11 AmiBroker India 34
2.4.12 VectorVest 35
2.4.13 Profit Source Platform 36
2.4.14 Algo Trader 37
2.4.15 Deep Learning Using Python 38
2.5 Conclusion 39
References 40

3 Challenges and Security Issues in Autonomous Finance 43
Mukul Gupta, Deepa Gupta, Nitin Agrawal and Parth Mukul Gupta
3.1 Introduction 44
3.2 A Review of the Literature 45
3.3 Concerns Regarding the Protection of Identity and Privacy in Autonomous Finance 46
3.3.1 The Vulnerability of Data 46
3.3.1.1 The Challenge 46
3.3.1.2 Aspects of Danger 47
3.3.1.3 Various Methods of Risk Reduction 47
3.3.2 Dangers Posed by Cybersecurity 47
3.3.2.1 The Challenge 47
3.3.2.2 Most Frequent Attacks from the Opponent 47
3.3.2.3 Countermeasures 48

3.3.3 The Protection of Personal Privacy 48
3.3.3.1 The Challenge 48
3.3.3.2 The Dangers to Privacy 48
3.3.3.3 Preserving Individual Cofense 48
3.4 Using Algorithms to Make Decisions Can be Biased 49
3.4.1 Understanding Bias in Algorithms 49
3.4.2 Repercussions of Bias in the Financial Sector 49
3.5 Ensuring Fairness in Autonomous Finance 50
3.5.1 Openness and Responsibility for One's Actions 50
3.5.2 Measures of Fairness and Compliance Monitoring 50
3.5.3 The Pre-Processing of Data and the Engineering of Features 50
3.5.4 Modifications to the Model 50
3.5.5 Considerations of Ethical Implications and Diverse Teams 51
3.6 Compliance with Regulations in the Field of Autonomous Finance 51
3.6.1 Navigating Legal Frameworks 51
3.6.1.1 Being Able to Adapt to Rapid Change 51
3.6.1.2 Data Privacy and Security 52
3.6.1.3 Anti-Money Laundering (AML) and Fraud Detection 52
3.6.1.4 Protection of Consumers 52
3.6.1.5 Operations Across Borders 52
3.6.2 Be Open and Honest 53
3.6.2.1 Capacity to Explain and Interpret Information 53
3.6.2.2 Fairness and the Elimination of a Bias 53
3.6.2.3 User Consent and Control 53
3.7 Gaining an Understanding of the Fundamentals of Operational Risk 54
3.8 Risks Encountered in the Operation of Autonomous Finance 55
3.9 Concerns Regarding Ethical Issues in Autonomous Finance 57
3.10 Consumer Trust in Autonomous Finance 59
3.10.1 Establishing Trust in Financial Systems that are Independent 59
3.10.1.1 Recognising the Concept of Autonomous Finance 59

3.10.2 User Education: Filling in the Gaps in Knowledge 60
3.10.2.1 Challenges in Technology and Expectations 60
3.10.2.2 Educating Users 60
References 61

4 Involvement of Artificial Intelligence in Emerging Fintech Industry 4.0: A TCCM Framework 65
Annu and Ravindra Tripathi
4.1 Introduction 66
4.1.1 Literature Review 68
4.2 Data and Methodology 69
4.2.1 Data Collection 69
4.2.1.1 The Source of Data Collection 69
4.2.1.2 Keyword Selection and Refinement Process 70
4.3 Results and Discussion 70
4.3.1 Bibliometric Data Analysis (Descriptive and Network) 70
4.4 Finding, Conclusion, and Research Directions 76
4.5 Summary 77
References 77

5 Robotic Process Automation in the Financial Sector 81
Neha Sonik, Deepa Gupta and Parul Gupta
5.1 Introduction 81
5.1.1 Robotic Process Automation in Banking 82
5.1.2 What is Finance Automation? 82
5.2 How are Financial Institutions Making Use of Robotics and Automation? 83
5.2.1 Importance of Banking in Robotic Process Automation 84
5.3 Major Use Cases of Robotic Process Automation in Banking and Finance 84
5.4 Minding Gaps in Financial Process Automation 91
5.5 The Key Benefits of Finance Automation 92
5.6 A List of Accounting and Financial Services Companies That are Using RPA 95
5.7 Steps to Deploy RPA in Banking and Finance 97
5.8 Conclusion 99
References 99

6 **Integration of Fintech with Data Science (DS) and Artificial Intelligence (AI): A Challenging Footstep** **101**
Ankur Goel, Monisha Awasthi, Anamika Rana and Sushma Malik
6.1 Introduction 102
6.2 Historical Background of Fintech 102
6.2.1 Fintech 1.0 102
6.2.2 Fintech 2.0 103
6.2.3 Fintech 3.0 104
6.2.4 Fintech 4.0 104
6.3 Advantages of Fintech 104
6.3.1 Block Chain and Crypto Currency 105
6.3.2 Insurance (InsurTech) 105
6.3.3 Regulatory (RegTech) 105
6.3.4 Lending (LendTech) 106
6.3.5 Payments (PayTech) 106
6.3.6 Mobile Payments 106
6.3.7 Trading (TradeTech) 106
6.3.8 Robo-Advising and Stock-Trading Apps 107
6.3.9 Personal Finance (WealthTech) 107
6.3.10 International Money Transfers 107
6.3.11 Equity Financing 107
6.3.12 Accounting 108
6.3.13 Banking for Consumers (BankTech) 108
6.4 Role of Data Science and AI 108
6.5 Data Science and AI (DSAI) Making Smart Fintech 111
6.5.1 Complex System Methods 112
6.5.2 Automatic Contact Recognition and Response Synthesis 113
6.5.3 Analytics, Teaching, and Learning Strategies 113
6.5.4 Deep Financial Modeling 114
6.5.5 Techniques for Augmentation and Optimization 114
6.5.6 Smart EcoFin Companies and Services 115
6.5.7 Automated Analytics and Learning 115
6.5.8 Whole-of-Business and Privacy-Preserving Federated Fintech 115
6.6 Use Cases of Data Science in Fintech 116
6.6.1 Fraud Prevention 116
6.6.2 Risk Analysis 117

6.6.3 Customer Behavior Analysis 117
6.6.4 Credit Allocation 118
6.6.5 Predictive Analytics 119
6.6.6 Product Development 119
6.6.7 Algorithmic Trading (AT) 119
6.6.8 Personalized Marketing 119
6.7 Conclusion 119
References 120

7 Evaluation of Fintech: The Techno-Functional Application in Digital Banking 123
Priyanka Verma, Rajesh Kumar Dhanaraj, Deepa Gupta and Mukul Gupta
7.1 Introduction 123
7.2 Overview of Fintech 124
7.2.1 Details of the Working Algorithm 125
7.2.2 Relationship Between FINTECH and Modern Financial Application in Digital Banking 128
7.2.3 Advantages of the Application 131
7.2.4 Barriers in the Implementation Process 133
7.2.5 Details of the Security System Present in the Application 135
7.3 Theoretical Overview 136
7.4 Measurement of the Success Factor of Fintech in Digital Banking 137
7.5 Summary 139
References 139

8 Real-Time Data Visualization and Autonomous Finance: Uses of Emerging Technologies 143
Govind Singh, Lokesh Verma and Anshika Baliyan
8.1 Introduction 144
8.1.1 Industry 4.0 144
8.1.2 Business Process 145
8.1.2.1 Management Process 147
8.1.2.2 Operating Process 147
8.1.2.3 Support Process 147
8.1.3 Finance 147
8.2 Thriving in the Tech Age: How Businesses Adapt to Emerging Technologies 148

8.2.1 Boosting Efficiency and Innovation: The Critical Role of Adapting to New Technologies 149
8.2.2 Navigating the Digital Age: The Current State of Technological Adoption 149
8.2.3 The Driving Force: Why Businesses Embrace New Technologies 150
8.2.4 Top Seven Emerging Technologies Businesses are Embracing 150
8.3 The Future of Work and Innovation: Emerging Technologies Transforming Businesses 151
8.3.1 Actionable Insights at Your Fingertips: The Power of Embedded BI 151
8.3.1.1 Application of Embedded BI 152
8.3.1.2 Embedded BI in Supply Chain Management and Logistic 152
8.3.1.3 Embedded BI in Sales and Services 153
8.3.2 Augmented Analytics 153
8.3.2.1 Importance of Augmented Analytics Prospecting the Opportunity of Big Data 153
8.3.2.2 Benefits and Uses of Augmented Analytics in Business 154
8.3.2.3 Use of Analytics in Business 155
8.3.3 Cloud Computing 155
8.3.3.1 How Cloud Management Works 156
8.3.3.2 Benefits of Cloud Management 156
8.3.4 Artificial Intelligence 157
8.3.4.1 Learning Processes 157
8.3.4.2 Reasoning Process 157
8.3.4.3 Self-Correction Process 157
8.3.5 Current Scenario of Artificial Intelligence in Businesses 158
8.3.6 Application of Artificial Intelligence in Businesses 158
8.3.6.1 Machine Learning 158
8.3.6.2 Cybersecurity 158
8.3.6.3 Customer Relationship Management 158
8.3.6.4 Internet and Data Research 159
8.4 Major Emerging Technologies in Finance 159
8.4.1 Robotics Process Automation (RPA) 159
8.4.2 Blockchain 161

8.4.2.1 Types of Blockchain 161
8.4.3 Autonomous Finance 162
8.4.4 Internet of Things (IoT) 163
8.5 Risk Associated with Emerging Technologies 164
8.6 Conclusion 165
References 166

9 AI and ML Modeling and Autonomous Finance in Microfinance: An Overview 167
D. N. Rao and Maheswaran Mahalingam
9.1 Understanding Autonomous Finance and Microfinance 168
9.1.1 Context 168
9.1.1.1 Application Areas 168
9.1.1.2 Scope 169
9.1.1.3 Significance 170
9.2 Readiness of MFIs for Autonomous Finance Transformation 170
9.2.1 Autonomous Finance and Microfinance—A Prelude 170
9.2.2 Diverged Microfinance Global Market 171
9.2.3 Autonomous Finance as a Turning Point 172
9.2.3.1 Key Components of Autonomous Finance 172
9.2.3.2 Technology Drivers of Autonomous Finance 172
9.3 Solution Drivers in the Life Cycle Journey of an MFI Customer 173
9.3.1 The Life Cycle Journey of an MFI Customer 173
9.3.2 Solution Drivers Across the Phases of the Life Cycle Journey 175
9.3.3 The Impact of Autonomous Finance in the Journey Cycle 177
9.4 Readiness of MFIs for Autonomous Finance Operations 177
9.5 Technology and AI and ML Enablers of Autonomous Finance for MFIs 180
9.5.1 Technology Enabled Autonomous Finance for MFIs 180
9.5.2 Optical Character Recognition (OCR) 180
9.5.3 Robotic Process Automation (RPA) 180
9.5.4 Big Data Driven Automated Approvals 181
9.6 Critical Business Needs of Autonomous Finance 182
9.6.1 Autonomous Receivables 182
9.6.2 Autonomous Treasury 182
9.6.3 Autonomous Accounting 182
9.7 AI and ML Analytical Models for MFIs 182

9.7.1 Logistic Regression 184
9.7.2 Logistic Regression with Ridge Regularization 185
9.7.3 An Examination of Linear Discriminants 186
9.7.4 K-Nearest Neighbor 186
9.7.5 Decision Trees 186
9.7.6 Support Vector Machines 187
9.7.7 XGBoost 187
9.8 Overall Deployment and Suitability 188
9.9 Roadmap for Autonomous Finance in MFIs 188
9.9.1 Transformation Operations for MFI 188
9.10 Stage-1: Operation Moonwalk 190
9.10.1 Stakeholders Vision 190
9.10.2 Prioritize Autonomous Finance Goals 190
9.10.3 Set KRIs and Its Impact 190
9.10.4 Straw Man Project 190
9.10.5 Assess Current State 191
9.10.6 Funding Needs 192
9.11 Stage 2—Operation Sun Shine 192
9.11.1 Setup Governance 192
9.11.2 Other Key Drivers 192
9.12 Stage 3 Operation Bloomsdale 193
9.13 Improvement Opportunities of Autonomous Finance for MFIs 193
9.13.1 Precautions in Adopting Autonomous Finance by MFIs 193
9.13.2 Data Privacy 193
9.13.3 AI and ML Governance 194
9.13.4 More Machine vs Less Human 194
9.13.5 Ethical Considerations 194
9.13.6 Regulatory Compliance 195
9.13.7 Surveillance and Discrimination 195
9.14 Embracing Future AI Agents and Robotics of Autonomous Finance 195
References 196

10 Application of Machine Learning Models in the Field of Autonomous Finance 199
Umesh Gupta, Shriyash Saxena, Sachin Kumar Yadav and Aditya Bhardwaj
10.1 Overview 199
10.2 Introduction 201

10.3 Reinforcement Learning 203
10.3.1 Demerits of Reinforcement Learning Techniques 204
10.3.2 Markov Decision Process (MDP) 204
10.3.2.1 Transition Function 205
10.3.3 Reinforcement Learning and Deep Reinforcement Learning 208
10.3.3.1 Deep Reinforcement Learning 209
10.4 Neural Network Basics 209
10.4.1 Fully Connected Neural Network (FNN) 210
10.4.2 Convolutional Neural Network (CNN) 211
10.4.3 Recurrent Neural Networks (RNN) 212
10.4.4 Deep Value-Based Methods 212
10.5 Management of Information for Credit Risk 213
10.5.1 Management of Information for Fraud Detection 213
10.5.2 Portfolio Optimization Driven by Big Data 213
10.5.3 Management of Information for Assets and Derivative Market 213
10.5.4 Algorithmic Trading 214
10.5.5 Big Data Analysis with the Usage of Text Mining 214
10.5.6 Essence of Convolutional Neural Network 215
10.6 Sentiment Analysis with Data Mining Approach 215
10.6.1 Case Study of Wang 215
10.7 Conclusion 216
References 216

11 Machine Learning Algorithm in Indian Stock Market for Revising and Refining the Equity Valuation Models 221
Nitha K. P., Suraj E. S. and Ranjith Karat
11.1 Introduction 221
11.1.1 Multiple Regression Machine Learning Algorithm 222
11.1.2 Classification 222
11.2 Objectives of the Study 223
11.3 Methodology 223
11.3.1 Softwares Used 224
11.4 Review of Literature 225
11.5 Machine Learning for Equity Valuation Models 228
11.6 Architecture of Refined Equity Models 232
11.6.1 Architecture of Refined Price to Earnings Model (P/E) Using Multiple Regression Machine Learning Approach 232

11.6.2 Architecture of Refined Price to Book Value Model Using Multiple Regression Machine Learning Approach 232
11.6.3 Architecture of Refined Capital Asset Pricing Model Using Multiple Regression Machine Learning Approach 232
11.7 Analysis—Checking the Valuation Accuracy of Revised and Refined Models Using Machine Learning Approach 234
11.8 Conclusion 240
References 240

12 Hyper Automation and its Applicability in Automation Finance 243
Pushpendra Pal Singh, Rakesh Kumar Dixit and Rajesh Kumar Dhanaraj
12.1 Introduction 244
12.2 Background 245
12.3 Hyper Automation: Evolution, Technologies, and Impact in the Digital Era 247
12.4 Automation-(2)-Hyper Automation: Gartner 249
12.5 Could Hyper Automation be a Name for AI Plus RPA? 250
12.6 Sophistication of the Automation 252
12.7 Hyper Automation Process Flow 254
12.7.1 Technologies 255
12.7.2 Robotics Process Automation (RPA) 256
12.7.3 Artificial Intelligence (AI) 256
12.7.4 Machine Language (ML) 257
12.7.5 Optical Character Recognition (OCR) 258
12.7.6 Language Understanding Intelligent Service (LUIS) 258
12.7.7 Hyper Automation Technological Ecosystem 259
12.8 Banking and Finance Applications 260
12.8.1 Marketing 261
12.8.2 Sales and Distribution 261
12.8.3 Regulatory Reporting 262
12.8.4 ICICI Bank 262
12.8.5 Softbank 263
12.9 Conclusions 264
References 265

13 Pre- and Post-COVID Autonomous Finance: Global Perspective **269**
Shikha Singh, Deepa Gupta, Roshan Kumar and Balamurugan Balusamy
13.1 Introduction 270
13.2 Literature Review 271
13.2.1 Objectives 273
13.2.2 Research Design 273
13.2.3 Data Collection 273
13.3 Factors Behind the Digitalization of Financial Services During the COVID Pandemic 273
13.4 Challenges/Barriers for FinTech 279
13.5 Advantages and Disadvantages of Market Structure Modifications Towards the Digitalization of FinTech Services 280
13.5.1 Advantages 281
13.5.2 Disadvantages 282
13.6 Conclusion 283
References 285

14 Emerging Trends and Future Directions in Artificial Intelligence for Next-Generation Computing **289**
Rafael Vargas-Bernal
14.1 Introduction 290
14.2 Concepts of Neuromorphic Computing, Artificial Intelligence, and Memristor 291
14.3 Advantages of Two-Dimensional Materials Used in Neuromorphic Computing 294
14.4 Devices Implemented with Two-Dimensional Materials to Evolve Artificial Intelligence 298
14.5 Future Research Directions 308
14.6 Summary 309
Acknowledgments 310
References 310

Index **313**

Preface

In an era marked by unprecedented technological advancements, the financial sector stands at the cusp of a transformative revolution, propelled by the burgeoning field of computational intelligence. This book serves as a seminal exploration into this dynamic domain, offering a comprehensive examination of how artificial intelligence (AI), machine learning (ML), and robotic process automation (RPA) are redefining the landscapes of finance and banking. This book is designed to navigate the intricate interplay between emerging technologies and financial services, addressing both the profound opportunities and the intricate challenges that lie ahead.

The genesis of this book lies in the recognition of a new age of automatic civilization, where autonomous finance emerges not merely as a possibility but as an imperative for survival and prosperity. Chapter 1 sets the stage by delving into the role of autonomous finance in the era of automatic civilization. This section lays the groundwork for understanding the transformative potential of computational intelligence in finance.

As we progress through the book, each chapter systematically unfolds the multifaceted aspects of this revolution. Chapter 2 provides a deep dive into the cutting-edge technologies shaping stock market strategies today. This is followed by an insightful chapter on the challenges and security issues that are present in autonomous finance, highlighting the paramount importance of cybersecurity in a digitally dependent financial world.

In subsequent chapters, the book expands its purview to explore the symbiotic relationship between AI and the Fintech industry, the pivotal role of RPA in financial operations, and the intricate integration of fintech with data science and AI. Notably, Chapter 4 introduces a TCCM (Theory, Context, Characteristics, and Methodology) framework for understanding AI's role in Fintech Industry 4.0, offering a structured approach to navigating the complex landscape.

Chapters 5 through 8 delve into specific applications and innovations in the field, from robotic process automation in finance to the techno-functional applications in digital banking, and the uses of real-time data visualization in autonomous finance. These discussions underscore the practical implementations of computational intelligence and highlight the ongoing evolution of financial technologies.

Next, our focus shifts toward more specialized applications of AI and ML in finance, with chapters dedicated to autonomous finance in microfinance, the application of ML models in autonomous finances, and the use of machine learning algorithms in the Indian stock market. Each chapter provides a unique lens through which to view the potential for computational intelligence to revolutionize financial models and valuation methods.

As the book nears its conclusion, it addresses the broader implications of these technologies in the context of hyper-automation and its applicability in finance, as well as the impact of the COVID-19 pandemic on autonomous finance from a global perspective. The final chapter offers a forward-looking perspective on the future trajectories of AI in finance, inviting readers to contemplate the vast horizons yet to be explored.

More than just an academic treatise, this volume is a call to action for innovators, policymakers, and practitioners to embrace the challenges and opportunities presented by autonomous finance. It will inspire a new generation of financial technologies that are secure, efficient, and, above all, equitable. As we stand on the brink of this new era, this book serves as a beacon, guiding the way toward a future where finance is not just autonomous but also inherently more human.

The editors are grateful to everyone who has contributed to improving the quality of the book through their constructive comments. We also thank Martin Scrivener and Scrivener Publishing for their support and publication.

1

The Role of Autonomous Finance in the Era of Automatic Civilization

Sanjeet Singh[1]*, Geetika Madaan[2] and Jaskiran Kaur[3]

[1]*Research Centre and Faculty of Management Studies, Marwadi University, Rajkot, Gujrat, India*
[2]*Research Centre, Marwadi University, Rajkot, Gujrat, India*
[3]*Division of Academic Affairs, Lovely Professional University, Phagwara, India*

Abstract
Financial and accounting process management can be demanding in terms of both time and mental energy. Manually performing tasks like data mining and discovering financial facts takes a lot of time and effort. Long hours spent staring at spreadsheets and databases may cause accountants to experience mental fatigue. When automation can simplify the lives of your financial team members, it makes no sense to have them waste their time with inefficient manual operations. If we or our team are still manually copying and pasting information across Excel spreadsheets, then we need to get out of the 1990s as quickly as possible. We have officially entered the era of "automatic civilization." Instead of spending time on commonplace, repetitive chores, organizations can streamline their operations by integrating data-driven insights and cutting-edge analytics into their autonomous financial systems. In the chapter, author aims to uncover the role of autonomous finance in the era of automatic civilization. The term "autonomous finance" refers to a method of handling financial transactions and management based on data or algorithms. Due to the fast-paced and competitive nature of the modern corporate world, innovative strategies have surpassed conventional ones. Enterprises need to be nimbler and more forward-thinking if they are to stay up with the times and enhance their operations. Automation of financial procedures can save a lot of time and effort, as finance is one of the most complex and time-consuming aspects of any firm.

**Corresponding author*: singh.sanjeet2008@gmail.com; ORCID: https://orcid.org/0000-0001-6103-2346
Geetika Madaan: ORCID: https://orcid.org/0000-0001-8141-9935
Jaskiran Kaur: ORCID: https://orcid.org/0000-0002-4452-1807

Deepa Gupta, Mukul Gupta, Rajesh Kumar Dhanaraj, Balamurugan Balusamy and Parth Mukul Gupta (eds.) Computational Intelligence for Autonomous Finance, (1–20) © 2025 Scrivener Publishing LLC

Keywords: AI, autonomous finance, accounting, machine learning, robotics, process automation

1.1 Introduction

The emergence of "automatic civilization," along with other technological breakthroughs [1], has made a huge difference in the way we deal with money in the real world. One of the most significant developments changing this is autonomous finance, which is transforming how budgets are managed in a big way.

The onset of the "automated civilization" period has brought about a significant change in the way individuals around the world manage their money. Free banking is a crucial component of this change [2]. This new technology makes it is easier for people to keep track of their money, transforming the financial world. For the most part, autonomous finance means letting AI along with other computerized decision-making tools handle your money. Managing money involves various tasks, such as automatically investing in the stock market, managing more complex accounts, and selecting the best ways to handle risk [3–5]. Organizations can use the tools for monitoring data and making market predictions that come with autonomous finance to make better, less risky decisions.

Autonomous finance and other AI-based technologies, such as predictive analytics, can help businesses excel in the present-day data-driven market. Autonomous finance has initiated an entirely new phase in financial management. Computers can now perform complex tasks that previously required human assistance.

1.2 The Concept of Autonomous Finance

Autonomous finance refers to the capability to perform routine monetary tasks with little or no oversight from a human operator. It automates financial procedures using AI and machine learning, leading to greater productivity and precision. Budgeting, investing, and managing risks are all part of this [6].

Forrester defines the term as *algorithm-driven financial services that make decisions or take action on a customer's behalf.*

In a nutshell, autonomous technology can perform its intended tasks without any assistance from a human operator. These technologies are like us in that they continually improve by taking in new information from their surroundings and applying it to their decision-making [7].

1.2.1 Autonomous Finance: The Technology and Factors Driving Its Widespread Deployment

Cloud computing, RPA, advanced analytics, NLP, and AI are the engines that propel the field of autonomous banking [8]. Finance analysts' productivity is boosted by the seamless two-way communication between humans and computers enabled by the program. Autonomous technologies are more common, with artificial intelligence (AI) being a prime example. Autonomous intelligence, a more advanced kind of AI, can make decisions and act without any human input.

Finance departments often follow the path shown in the following figure to achieve complete autonomy. Some companies have achieved 80% autonomy with AI-assistance, but the vast majority are in the 0–40% range, moving towards the 60% autonomous mark with RPA, AI, and analytics tools [9]. However, we have not yet reached a point when the department is entirely independent.

1.2.2 CFO's Function in Autonomous Finance

The chief financial officer's responsibilities in an autonomous financial system now extend beyond the conventional realm of finance to include managing and optimizing autonomous financial systems [10]. In autonomous finance, the Chief Financial Officer (CFO) plays a crucial role in making decisions about technology investments, monitoring data quality and integrity, and mitigating risks related to automation.

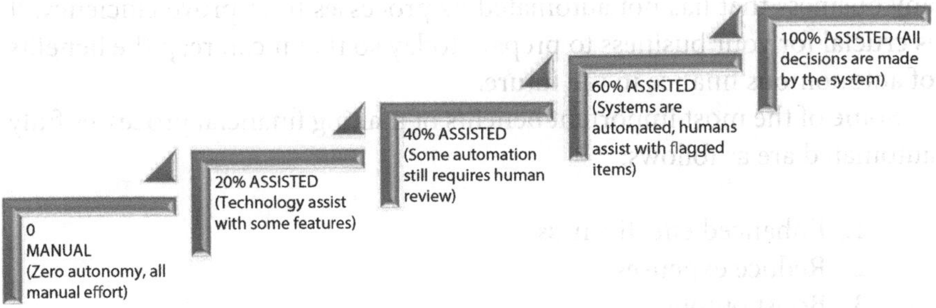

Figure 1.1 Finance transformation journey. (Source: Authors' own compilation). Adapted from [10].

CFOs are responsible for managing risks related to data privacy and security, maintaining compliance with legislation, and implementing and integrating new technology into autonomous finance systems. The CFO also needs to work with other division heads to ensure that the company's financial systems are aligned to achieve its overarching goals and strategy [11].

With the rise of autonomous finance, the chief financial officer's responsibilities are shifting from being a mere custodian of financial data to being an active participant in business strategy. The ability to analyze data in real-time is essential for chief financial officers (CFOs) who want to guide their companies towards strategic growth.

1.2.3 Motives to Switch to an Autonomous Finance Structure

With the advent of autonomous finance, future financial services will be safer and more convenient than ever before. It is a revolutionary new approach to wealth management that offers various advantages over the status quo [3–6].

First, autonomous finance boosts productivity. By automating the analysis of transactions and optimization of investments using artificial intelligence and machine learning, you can potentially save time and effort in budgeting.

It uses state-of-the-art data encryption technology to enhance the security of financial activities. This protects your financial information from unauthorized parties and keeps it secure from harm. Finally, autonomous finance allows you to manage your finances whenever and wherever is most convenient with you [11].

Autonomous finance, as a whole, might usher in an era of "automated civilization" with entirely new standards for the security and convenience of personal banking. Keeping up with the competition will be difficult for any business that has not automated its processes to improve efficiency. It is crucial for your business to prepare today so that it can reap the benefits of autonomous finance in the future.

Some of the most important benefits of making financial processes fully automated are as follows:

1. Enhanced effectiveness
2. Reduce expenses
3. Boost output
4. Superior Assistance to Clients
5. Marketable Distinction

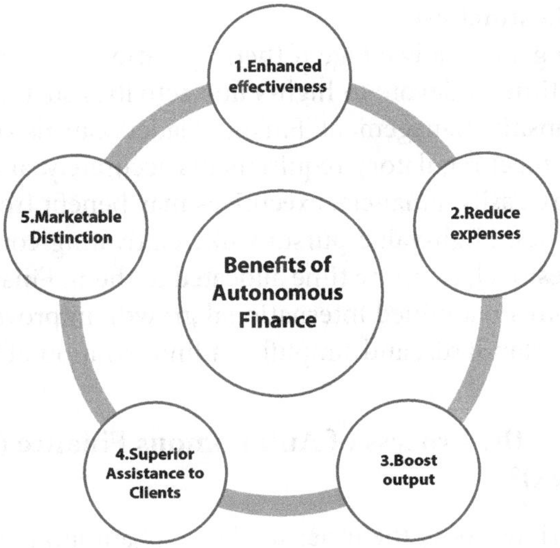

Figure 1.2 Benefits of autonomous finance. (Source: Authors' own compilation). Adapted from [11].

- **Enhanced effectiveness**

Automated solutions expedite operations, free up resources, and reduce human error.

- **Reduce expenses**

Through more efficient use of available resources, autonomous financial technology enables firms to save money in areas like customer service, reporting, and more.

- **Boost output**

Your financial staff will have more time for high-value, strategic work thanks to the automation provided by autonomous finance solutions.

- **Superior Assistance to Clients**

The finance department will have more time to devote to high-value operations and strategic planning thanks to the automation of routine, repetitive work enabled by autonomous finance technology.

Eighty-nine percent of financial service executives surveyed by Salesforce agreed that industry leaders who adopt autonomous finance early would establish new standards for client satisfaction.

- **Marketable Distinction**

CFOs stand to gain an advantage if their operations are fully automated. There is more time to devote to high-value activities such as customer or investor relationship management. Finance leaders can also expand to new markets faster, meet regulatory requirements accurately, and manage taxation rules more easily. Financial executives may benefit from automating all their processes. High-value pursuits like cultivating connections with clients and investors have more time allocated to them. Finance executives also benefit from streamlined international growth, improved compliance with regulatory standards, and simplified administration of tax policies.

1.2.4 What is the Process of Autonomous Finance (How Does it Work)?

You may be curious about the inner workings of autonomous finance and the advantages it offers. The term "autonomous finance" (or "auto finance") refers to a specific type of technology that uses AI and ML to handle financial transactions without any human involvement [10].

Customers' purchasing habits, payment histories, and other financial data are analyzed to determine the best way to manage their money, which is how auto financing works. Budgeting, investing, and debt repayment can all be automated with this newfound knowledge. In car financing, several algorithms are employed to improve the customer experience by providing each client with personalized recommendations on how to best manage their finances.

1.2.5 Advantages of Autonomous Finance

- **Online budgeting software:** One can quickly create a budget with auto finance that considers income and expenses. Rules may be automated for anything from saving to paying off debt [12].
- **Prudent financial decisions:** Autonomous finance takes the guesswork out of investing by automatically assessing the market and ensuring that the portfolio is diversified and risk-appropriate [11].
- **Available in any location:** Customers may log in to their auto finance accounts whenever they choose, from any device. This makes keeping track of one's money simpler than ever [2].

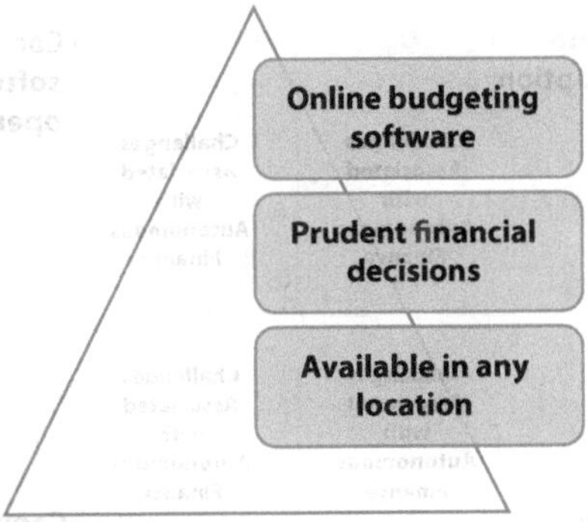

Figure 1.3 Advantages of autonomous finance. (Source: Authors' own compilation). Adapted from [12].

Due to its ability to improve digital banking's transparency, convenience, and client financial decision-making, autonomous finance is swiftly becoming a major player in the industry.

1.2.6 Challenges Associated with Autonomous Finance

There are several issues to consider when it comes to autonomous finance. The reliability of automated systems depends on the accuracy and completeness of the data they use to make decisions. There is also the possibility that people will not trust algorithmic decision-making because they do not understand it [6].

Additionally, there is the problem of who should be held accountable when an autonomous system makes a mistake. Is it the developers? Those responsible for implementing it? Or something completely different? These are crucial issues that must be resolved for the safe and ethical use of these systems [8].

Although there are many unresolved issues regarding autonomous finance, many of them will likely be addressed as technology improves. We can get closer to an automated and easily controlled "automatic civilization" if we establish clear norms and standards now. Financial procedures that are straightforward, effective, and efficient are always preferred over more cumbersome and outdated alternatives [12]. While automation helps in practically all repetitive tasks, some businesses are still hesitant to adopt new technologies for various reasons. The various challenges of autonomous finance are as follows:

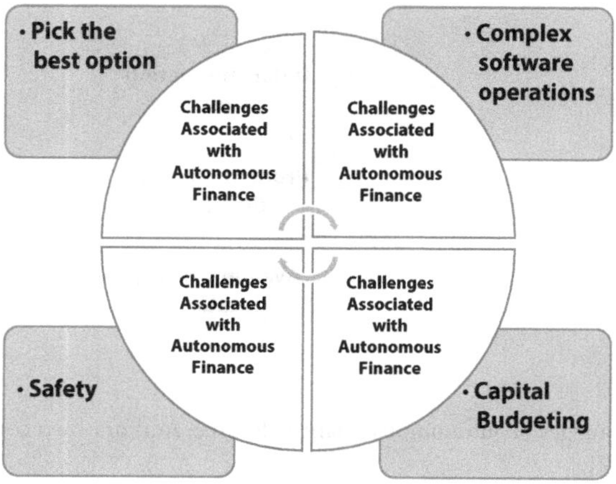

Figure 1.4 Challenges of autonomous finance. (Source: Authors' own compilation). Adapted from [12].

- **Complex Software Operations**

Companies that have been handling their finances entirely manually for years may struggle to learn the intricacies of a newly implemented automated system. One of the most prevalent reasons businesses hesitate to adopt automation is a lack of staff with the necessary technical expertise to use the software [13].

To utilize the automated software, employees may need to devote time to learning how the various financial procedures are implemented. The inability to fully automate tasks due to the learning curve of the software is a significant barrier [9].

- **Capital Budgeting**

Another factor that keeps businesses from switching to automated financial processes is the high cost of making the transition. Decision-makers often worry about spending money on subpar software. There is no way to know in advance which software will integrate seamlessly with their existing manual procedures [14]. It is challenging for company executives to fully deploy automated financial processes since most organisations want their procedures to be repeatable, but not all software providers can achieve this [3].

In the end, a profitable return on investment is the goal of any business. The financial implications of automating processes are a primary concern. To convince key decision-makers that the substantial capital investment required to automate the process is worthwhile, businesses must outline the specific ways in which automation might improve their operations [15].

• Pick the Best Option

Either a stand-alone RPA system or intelligent automation (a mix of AI and ML) can help finance executives transform their financial operations and add a greater degree of refinement to their end-to-end processes [6]. In addition to facilitating process improvement, autonomous finance is essential for maintaining a competitive edge in the market.

Choosing the right automation solution can make short work of the project. When processes are automated, they become more efficient, profitable, reliable, economical, and transparent.

Financial managers need to stop resisting change and start automating routine back-office financial tasks if they want to free up staff time for more strategic work.

• Safety

Another major issue with autonomous banking is safety, as there is a higher risk of theft or hacker involvement as these systems become more complex and operate in multiple locations. If suitable measures are not in place, this could result in monetary losses or data breaches.

1.3 Autonomous Finance: Prospects and Developments

One needs to be on the leading edge to realize the full potential of autonomous finance, which is a whole new field. The possibilities are endless, and so are the changes in trends.

Blockchain technology is important for open financial systems because it acts as a global ledger that records transactions securely and permanently [16]. When this technology is used, central banks and other regulatory bodies do not need to get involved with autonomous banking [17–23]. Blockchain not only makes sharing resources more efficient and secure, but it also opens new ways for companies to collaborate [24].

Decentralized financing (DeFi) is an concept that has become increasingly popular. It is different from traditional centralized banking. By allowing a network of users to determine the amount of money and price of assets [25], DeFi eliminates the need for central bank or government intervention. This results in a decentralized banking system that is more efficient and stable than previous systems [26–29].

Artificial intelligence (AI) is important for autonomous finance because it allows data to be processed in real time. This tool helps detect fraudulent

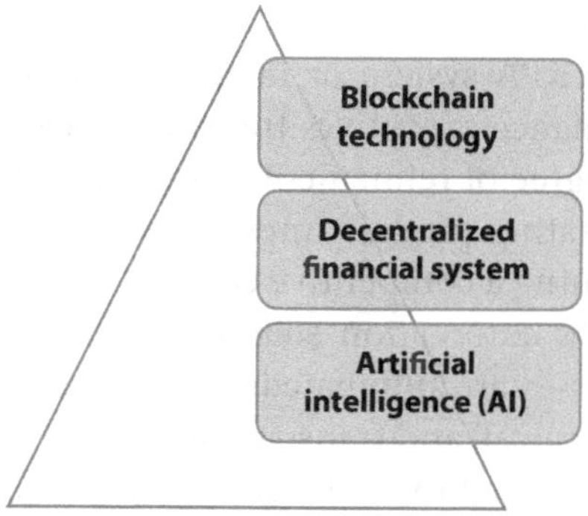

Figure 1.5 Prospects or opportunities of autonomous finance. (Source: Authors' own compilation). Adapted from [16].

behavior and high-risk investments [30+]. AI also helps automate the insights needed to make smart investment decisions [34–38] by using smart contracts that execute predetermined actions.

With blockchain and AI working together, autonomous finance is an exciting new area for businesses that want to cut costs and boost productivity [34, 39, 44]. As we approach the era of autonomous financing, also known as the "Automatic Civilization," banks need to prepare for significant changes. By eliminating the need for people interaction, automation speeds up tasks that used to take a long time to complete [31–33]. It is expected that markets will become fully automated as blockchain technology and AI continue to improve. Smart contracts will enable fully automated trades [6].

Because of this shift towards autonomous finance, the financial system has become more efficient and transparent. Decentralized autonomous finance provides clarity in decision-making, allowing investors to actively manage their investments and make informed choices [7, 8, 12, 13]. As a result of these changes, the banking industry needs to embrace the opportunity for greater efficiency and transparency that comes with blockchain and AI working together in autonomous finance. Autonomous finance also enables new types of collaboration, such working together on larger projects or developing new financial products that leverage the expertise of other markets. Furthermore, trust is enhanced on both sides by the immutability and traceability provided by autonomous finance.

As the financial services industry embraces new technologies, autonomous finance will continue to transform the landscape. As more people learn about the potential of autonomous finance, its importance will grow.

Bank customers are better served by financial organizations that use autonomous finance, as it streamlines and automates processes.

What kinds of tasks within the financial system should be prioritized for automation?

Finance is responsible for a wide variety of tasks, most of which have impact a company's bottom line. Here are some of the most important financial procedures in a company.

- **Accounts Payable**

A company's obligation to pay its suppliers for products and services received on credit is recorded as accounts payable (AP) [45]. Sales orders are received, reviewed, reconciled, routed for approval, conditions are negotiated, payments are processed, and suppliers are paid on time [46]. Late payments cost money and might strain your relationship with suppliers.

- **Accounts Receivable**

Customer payments that have not yet been received are known as accounts receivables. Invoicing clients, following up on overdue payments, and timely closing of open accounts are all aspects of managing accounts receivable [47]. Avoid disrupting your company's cash flow by diligently tracking accounts receivable and collecting payments on time. In most businesses, a DSO of fewer than 45 days indicates a strong sales pipeline.

- **Account Reconciliation**

The month-end and year-end closes are not the only times that account reconciliations are undertaken; they are just the most prominent. Accounts in the general ledger are cross-referenced with information from subsidiary ledgers and external sources, such as bank statements and other evidence of underlying transactions [6]. Accountants investigate the reasons

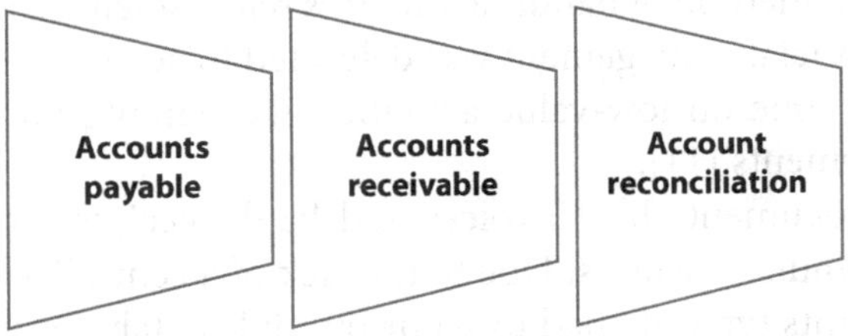

Figure 1.6 How autonomous finance works in financial system. (Source: Authors' own compilation). Adapted from [24].

for any inconsistencies and make adjustments to reflect any missing or incorrect transactions.

Finance managers should emphasize automating reconciliation due to its impact on a company's bottom line. Let us analyze the CAGR for each type of automation solution used in the finance industry.

- Forecasts put the accounts payable automation market's value will reach $7.5 billion by 2030, up from $2.6 billion in 2021.
- The receivables automation industry is projected to expand from its current value of $3.3 billion at a compound annual growth rate (CAGR) of 12.1% between 2022 and 2027.
- In 2019, analysts predicted that the global account reconciliation software market will be worth $1.82 billion. By 2027, that number is expected to increase to $5.38 billion, a CAGR of 14.6%.

As the above numbers show, the three financial procedures are rapidly becoming automated. This suggests that your rivals have likely already deployed the appropriate autonomous finance systems.

When should financial automation be prioritized?
Existing procedures and the finance department need to be digitally transformed if any of the following problems are occurring:

- Excessive routine work
- Too many individuals in everyday activities
- Workflow delays
- Significant interference with other procedures and systems
- Inconsistencies in audit trails and compliance

Reasons why the current financial system could fail?
The traditional method of handling finances relied solely on physical labor. Complete financial management was delegated to accountants, who spent most of their time on low-value activities like sending out invoices and collecting payments [11].

Merging documents like invoices and bank receipts proved difficult, among other mundane tasks. Due to the lack of a centralized data repository, accountants typically had to scour multiple databases to compile the necessary information [40–42].

Furthermore, dependence on several stakeholders slows down procedures that require information or input from various groups. If a key participant is unavailable due to illness or vacation, the entire operation might stall. The risk of failing to meet requirements or deadlines is heightened by these obstacles.

How does autonomous finance use technology?
Listed below are some of the most widespread technologies associated with autonomous finance:

• Robotic Process Automation
Automating low-value, high-volume business processes using RPA frees up workers to focus on higher-value tasks [48]. It helps businesses boost their return on investment (ROI) and speed up their digital transformation efforts.

Rule-based automation, like RPA, is excellent for eliminating the need for humans to perform routine, monotonous tasks. RPA's widespread appeal to medium-sized enterprises can be attributed to the adoption of its most common use cases, such as invoicing and cash processing automation [49].

Remittance aggregation is one example of an important process that can be automated by RPA technology. The system uses web bots to automatically retrieve relevant information, instead of relying on human users entering into and obtain customer-uploaded remittance data from online portals. In this scenario, the effort required to obtain remittance information from online systems is greatly reduced.

While robotic process automation (RPA) is certainly ground-breaking, it cannot be the sole focus. Complex situations can be challenging to address

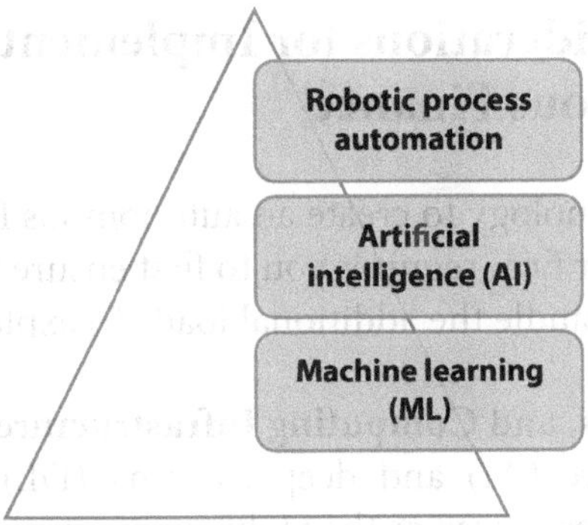

Figure 1.7 Technologies associated with autonomous finance. (Source: Authors' own compilation). Adapted from [49].

using RPA alone. For instance, RPA can parse emails for remittance information, but it cannot verify the data's accuracy or anticipate and fill in any gaps. Therefore, RPA is best seen as a practical tool.

When RPA bots are given organized data and explicit instructions on how to use it, they perform flawlessly. However, they fail to provide the expected outcomes when processing unstructured input.

- **Artificial Intelligence (AI)**

Since RPA is not perfect and cannot do everything by itself, AI is necessary [50–54]. When RPA is used to automate mundane tasks, artificial intelligence can give bots the appearance of human intelligence, allowing for faster data extraction and more informed business choices [49, 55–57].

By preventing the bots from breaking when the underlying rules on other websites change, AI increases the efficacy of RPA [58]. Predictive analysis and identifying trends in previous data are two more areas where AI becomes useful for locating the facts you need to make educated decisions [43, 44, 59–66]. The most advanced RPA software applications use AI to improve exception handling. For instance, they may foresee gaps in remittances [67].

- **Machine Learning (ML)**

By using machine learning technology, automated financial solutions can make more precise predictions with little to no human input [68]. Machine learning algorithms use previously collected data to make predictions about the future [69–72].

ML enables proactive collections in many of the best financial automation applications. Collectors may anticipate future payment dates and be more proactive with dunning by analyzing historical payment data [73].

1.4 Key Considerations for Implementing Autonomous Finance

Investing in AI technology to create an autonomous financial structure to recession-proof your firm requires you to first ensure that your existing IT infrastructure can handle the additional load. To explain how:

- **Storage, Networks, and Computing Infrastructure**

Artificial intelligence (AI) and deep learning (DL) techniques require much more computer power, as they rely on massive data sets and scalable neural networks. Invest in AI and NLP only after you have worked with reputable service providers to improve your IT infrastructure.

- **ProTip**

Get rid of any slow, inflexible, and unscalable outdated systems, and replace them with newer, more capable ones.

- **Safeguarding Information Systems**

Big data fuels AI systems. It is important to use correct and trustworthy data when training AI models. Also, ensure that any personal or financial data used by AI products is encrypted.

1.5 Conclusion

The concept of "autonomous finance" is on the rise, and it might completely alter the financial industry as we know it. It promises to automate financial decision-making, giving individuals who have not had access to financial services before a chance to do so, and giving those who have more control and transparency over their finances. It has the potential to revolutionize the delivery of financial services thanks to blockchain technology.

The field of autonomous finance is in its infancy, and many problems remain unanswered. However, it is evident that this technology has the capacity to usher in a new age of "automated civilization" and radically alter the way we approach financial matters. It is time to investigate how this innovation might improve our economic future.

References

1. Vieira, P.C. and Teixeira, A.A.C., Are finance, management, and marketing autonomous fields of scientific research? An analysis based on journal citations. *Scientometrics*, 85, 3, 627–646, 2010.
2. Verhoest, K., Peters, B.G., Bouckaert, G., Verschuere, B., The study of organisational autonomy: A conceptual review. *Public Adm. Dev.*, 24, 2, 101–118, 2004.
3. Clark, B.Y., The impacts of autonomous vehicles on local government budgeting and finance: Case of solid waste collection. *Natl. Tax J.*, 73, 1, 259, 2020.

4. Oulasvirta, L. and Turala, M., Financial autonomy and consistency of central government policy towards local governments. *Int. Rev. Adm. Sci.*, 75, 2, 311–332, 2009.
5. Wang, S., Money and autonomy: Patterns of civil society finance and their implications. *Stud. Comp. Int. Dev.*, 40, 4, 3–29, 2006.
6. Kristof, A., *Autonomous Finance*, 1st ed., vol. 2, Elsevier Inc, Amsterdam, 2018.
7. Ashcroft, R.E., Personal financial incentives in health promotion: Where do they fit in an ethic of autonomy? *Health Expect.*, 14, 2, 191–200, 2011.
8. Harwick, C. and Caton, J., What's holding back blockchain finance? On the possibility of decentralized autonomous finance. *Q. Rev. Econ. Financ.*, 84, 420–429, 2022.
9. Adler, M.W., Peer, S., Sinozic, T., Autonomous, connected, electric shared vehicles (ACES) and public finance: An explorative analysis. *Transp. Res. Interdiscip. Perspect.*, 2, 100038, 2019.
10. Yusuf, A., Qureshi, S., Feroz Shah, S., Mathematical analysis for an autonomous financial dynamical system via classical and modern fractional operators. *Chaos Solitons Fractals*, 132, 23–27, 2020.
11. Kumar, P., Pillai, R., Kumar, N., Tabash, M., II, The interplay of skills, digital financial literacy, capability, and autonomy in financial decision making and well-being. *Borsa Istanb. Rev.*, 23, 1, 169–183, 2023.
12. Ege, J. and Bauer, M.W., How Financial Resources Affect the Autonomy of International Public Administrations. *Glob. Policy*, 8, 75–84, August 2017.
13. Devaro, J., Teams, autonomy, and the financial performance of firms. *Ind. Relat. (Berkeley)*, 45, 2, 217–269, 2006.
14. Denison, C.A., Real Options and Escalation of Commitment: A Behavioral Analysis of Capital Investment Decisions. *Account. Rev.*, 84, 1, 133–155, Jan. 2009.
15. Fulmer, I.S. and Ployhart, R.E., Our Most Important Asset: A Multidisciplinary/Multilevel Review of Human Capital Valuation for Research and Practice. *J. Manag.*, 40, 1, 161–192, 2014.
16. Anjum, A., Sporny, M., Sill, A., Blockchain Standards for Compliance and Trust. *IEEE Cloud Comput.*, 4, 4, 84–90, 2017.
17. Beninger, P. and Ibara, M.A., Pharmacovigilance and Biomedical Informatics: A Model for Future Development. *Clin. Ther.*, 38, 12, 2514–2525, 2016.
18. Brunese, L., Mercaldo, F., Reginelli, A., Santone, A., A blockchain based proposal for protecting healthcare systems through formal methods. *Procedia Comput. Sci.*, 159, 1787–1794, 2019.
19. Tariq, N., Qamar, A., Asim, M., Khan, F.A., Blockchain and smart healthcare security: A survey. *Procedia Comput. Sci.*, 175, 615–620, 2020.
20. Al-Janabi, S., Al-Shourbaji, I., Shojafar, M., Shamshirband, S., Survey of main challenges (security and privacy) in wireless body area networks for healthcare applications. *Egypt. Inf. J.*, 18, 2, 113–122, 2017.

21. Zhang, J., Xue, N., Huang, X., A Secure System for Pervasive Social Network-Based Healthcare. *IEEE Access*, 4, c, 9239–9250, 2016.
22. Shi, S., He, D., Li, L., Kumar, N., Khurram, M., Applications of blockchain in ensuring the security and privacy of electronic health record systems: A survey Shuyun. *Comput. Secur.*, 1, 1–20, January 2020.
23. Cai, Y. and Zhu, D., Fraud detections for online businesses: a perspective from blockchain technology. *Financ. Innov.*, 2, 1, 132–139, 2016.
24. Chukwu, E. and Garg, L., A systematic review of blockchain in healthcare: Frameworks, prototypes, and implementations. *IEEE Access*, 8, 21196–21214, 2020.
25. Abimbola, S., Baatiema, L., Bigdeli, M., The impacts of decentralization on health system equity, efficiency and resilience: A realist synthesis of the evidence. *Health Policy Plan.*, 34, 8, 605–617, 2019.
26. Schär, F., Decentralized finance: on blockchain-and smart contract-based financial markets. *Fed. Reserve Bank St. Louis Rev.*, 103, 2, 153–174, 2021.
27. Kumar, V. and Jayanta Mishra, A., Healthcare under the Panchayati Raj Institutions (PRIs) in a decentralised health system: Experiences from Hardoi district of India. *Leadersh. Heal. Serv.*, 29, 2, 151–167, 2016.
28. Zarrin, J., Wen Phang, H., Babu Saheer, L., Zarrin, B., Blockchain for decentralization of internet: prospects, trends, and challenges. *Cluster Comput.*, 24, 4, 2841–2866, 2021.
29. Mahal, A. and Rajaraman, I., Decentralisation, preference diversity and public spending: Health and education in India. *Econ. Polit. Wkly.*, 45, 43, 57–63, 2010.
30. Madhavi, Role of AI in business development. *Open J. Soc. Sci.*, 6, 6, 28–33, 2021.
31. Rathi, A. and Asava, T., The role of artificial intelligence in disinformation. *Data Policy*, 3, 01, 175–179, 2021.
32. Palanivelu, V.R. and Vasanthi, B., Role of artificial intelligence in business transformation. *Int. J. Adv. Sci. Technol.*, 29, 4 Special Issue, 392–400, 2020.
33. Roundy, P.T., Artificial intelligence and entrepreneurial ecosystems: understanding the implications of algorithmic decision-making for startup communities. *J. Ethics Entrep. Technol.*, 2, 1, 23–38, 2022.
34. Soni, N., Sharma, E.K., Singh, N., Kapoor, A., Artificial Intelligence in Business: From Research and Innovation to Market Deployment. *Procedia Comput. Sci.*, 167, 2200–2210, 2020.
35. Mishra, S. and Tripathi, A.R., AI business model: an integrative business approach. *J. Innov. Entrep.*, 10, 1, 1–19, 2021.
36. Anute, N., Paliwal, M., Patel, M., Kandale, N., Impact of artificial intelligence and machine learning on business operations. *J. Manage. Res. Anal.*, 8, 2, 69–74, 2021.
37. Jain, V., Impact of Artificial Intelligence on Business. *Electron. J. Bus. Ethics Organ. Stud.*, 24, 2, 302–308, 2019.

38. Enholm, I.M., Papagiannidis, E., Mikalef, P., Krogstie, J., Artificial intelligence and glaucoma: A literature review. *J. Fr. Ophtalmol.*, 45, 2, 216–232, 2022.
39. Leitch, R., Artificial intelligence in engineering. *Comput. Control Eng. J.*, 3, 4, 152–157, 2021.
40. Chalmers, D., MacKenzie, N.G., Carter, S., Artificial Intelligence and Entrepreneurship: Implications for Venture Creation in the Fourth Industrial Revolution. *Entrep. Theory Pract.*, 45, 5, 1028–1053, 2021.
41. Sadiku, M.N.O., Fagbohungbe, O., Musa, S.M., Artificial Intelligence in Business. *Int. J. Eng. Res. Adv. Technol.*, 06, 07, 62–70, 2020.
42. Geisel, A., The current and future impact of artificial intelligence on business. *Int. J. Sci. Technol. Res.*, 7, 5, 116–122, 2018.
43. Yoopetch, C., Nimsai, S., Kongarchapatara, B., Bibliometric Analysis of Corporate Social Responsibility in Tourism. *Sustainability*, 15, 1, 56–59, 2023.
44. Soni, N., Sharma, E.K., Singh, N., Kapoor, A., Impact of Artificial Intelligence on Businesses: from Research, Innovation, Market Deployment to Future Shifts in Business Models. *Open J. Bus. Manage.*, 6, 2, 1–38, 2019.
45. Demirguc-Kunt, A., Klapper, L., Singer, D., *Financial Inclusion and Inclusive Growth: A Review of Recent Empirical Evidence*, World Bank Group, USA, April 2017.
46. Hada, D.B.S., Impact of Internet Banking on the Customer Satisfaction: Evidence from the Indian Banking Sector. *Int. J. Recent Technol. Eng.*, 8, 6, 3833–3841, 2020.
47. Xiong, H., Dalhaus, T., Wang, P., Huang, J., Blockchain Technology for Agriculture: Applications and Rationale. *Front. Blockchain*, 3, 1–7, February 2020.
48. Dirican, C., The Impacts of Robotics, Artificial Intelligence On Business and Economics. *Procedia Soc. Behav. Sci.*, 195, 564–573, 2015.
49. Turkina, E., The importance of networking to entrepreneurship: Montreal's artificial intelligence cluster and its born-global firm Element AI. *J. Small Bus. Entrep.*, 30, 1, 1–8, 2018.
50. Bogachov, S., Kwilinski, A., Miethlich, B., Bartosova, V., Gurnak, A., Artificial intelligence components and fuzzy regulators in entrepreneurship development. *Entrep. Sustain. Issues*, 8, 2, 487–499, 2020.
51. Giuggioli, G. and Pellegrini, M.M., Artificial intelligence as an enabler for entrepreneurs: a systematic literature review and an agenda for future research. *Int. J. Entrep. Behav. Res.*, 2, 112–123, June 2022.
52. Ahmed, A.A.A. and Ganapathy, A., Creation of Automated Content With Embedded Artificial Intelligence: a Study on Learning Management System for Educational Entrepreneurship. *Acad. Entrep. J.*, 27, 3, 1–10, 2021.
53. Miao, Z., The Influence Factors of Psychological Understanding and Behavior Choice for Legal Industry Entrepreneurs Based on Artificial Intelligence Technology. *Front. Psychol.*, 11, 1–10, July 2020.

54. Nuseir, M.T., Basheer, M.F., Aljumah, A., Antecedents of entrepreneurial intentions in smart city of Neom Saudi Arabia: Does the entrepreneurial education on artificial intelligence matter? *Cogent Bus. Manage.*, 7, 1, 42–47, 2020.
55. Obschonka, M. and Audretsch, D.B., Artificial intelligence and big data in entrepreneurship: a new era has begun. *Small Bus. Econ.*, 55, 3, 529–539, 2019.
56. Townsend, D.M. and Hunt, R.A., Entrepreneurial action, creativity, & judgment in the age of artificial intelligence. *J. Bus. Ventur. Insights*, 11, e00126, January 2019.
57. Ughulu, D.J., The importance of AI in starting , automating , and scaling businesses for entrepreneurs Department of Entrepreneurship & Innovation Cornerstone Christian University CCU The role of Artificial intelligence (AI) in Starting , automating and scaling busin. *Open J. Bus. Manage.*, 2, 8, 1–7, 2022.
58. Garbuio, M. and Lin, N., Artificial intelligence as a growth engine for health care startups: Emerging business models. *Calif. Manage. Rev.*, 61, 2, 59–83, 2018.
59. Al-Dalahmeh, M.L., Talent Management: a Systematic Review. *Oradea J. Bus. Econ.*, 5, 115–123, 2020.
60. Sareen, P. and Mishra, S., A Study of Talent Management and Its Impact on Performance of Organizations. *Integr. J. Res. Arts Humanit.*, 2, 4, 56–59, 2016.
61. Hongal, P. and Kinange, D.U., A Study on Talent Management and its Impact on Organization Performance- An Empirical Review. *Int. J. Eng. Manage. Res.*, 10, 01, 64–71, 2020.
62. Sharma, M. and Rathore, B.S., Research Paper on Exploring Talent Management Practices: Antecedents and Consequences. *Int. J. Manage.*, 11, 12, 1332–1363, 2020.
63. Nwanisobi, B.C. and Christopher, I.C., Talent Management: A Conceptual Framework with Practical Approach Talent Management: A Conceptual Framework with Practical Approach. *Open J. Bus. Manage.*, 7, 1–10, March 2020.
64. Liu, M., An Empirical Study on Talent Management Strategies of Knowledge-Based Organizations Using Entrepreneurial Psychology and Key Competence. *Front. Psychol.*, 12, 1–10, October 2021.
65. Pestonjee, D.M., Barot, H., Chhaniwal, P., A Study On Talent Management Practices In India. *Nveo Nat. Volatiles Essent. Oils*, 5, 1, 1–8, 2017.
66. Manthena, S.R.L., Talent Management: Employee Performance and impact on Organizational Performance. *Open J. Bus. Manage.*, 8, 8, 226–229, 2022.
67. (Kevin) Chae, B. and Goh, G., Digital entrepreneurs in artificial intelligence and data analytics: Who are they? *J. Open Innov. Technol. Mark. Complex.*, 6, 3, 21–38, 2020.

68. Huntingford, C., Jeffers, E.S., Bonsall, M.B., Christensen, H.M., Lees, T., Yang, H., Machine learning and artificial intelligence to aid climate change research and preparedness. *Environ. Res. Lett.*, 14, 12, 6–9, 2019.
69. Vollmer, S. *et al.*, Machine learning and artificial intelligence research for patient benefit: 20 critical questions on transparency, replicability, ethics, and effectiveness. *BMJ*, 368, 1–12, 2020.
70. Stocker, S., Csányi, G., Reuter, K., Margraf, J.T., Machine learning in chemical reaction space. *Nat. Commun.*, 11, 1, 1–11, 2020.
71. Pathak, Y., Juneja, K.S., Varma, G., Ehara, M., Priyakumar, U.D., Deep learning enabled inorganic material generator. *Phys. Chem. Chem. Phys.*, 22, 46, 26935–26943, 2020.
72. Wetterich, C.B., Felipe de Oliveira Neves, R., Belasque, J., Ehsani, R., Marcassa, L.G., Detection of Huanglongbing in Florida using fluorescence imaging spectroscopy and machine-learning methods. *Appl. Opt.*, 56, 1, 15, 2017.
73. Zame, W.R. *et al.*, Machine learning for clinical trials in the era of COVID-19. *Stat. Biopharm. Res.*, 12, 4, 506–517, 2020.

2

Analyzing the Latest Tools and Techniques for Stock Market Analysis

Ochin Sharma*, Raj Gaurang Tiwari, Suvarna Sharma and Annu Priya

Chitkara University Institute of Engineering & Technology, Chitkara University, Punjab, India

Abstract
There are various risks associated with the stock market. Since a long, users feel to predict and analyze the stock market movement before head. Apart from the mathematical analysis, in the current technical development, there exists various tools that provide ready to use solution in terms of stock price prediction. This chapter is to provide information for various free and licensed tools to predict and analyze stock market.

Keywords: Traders, prediction, freeware, open source, industry, employability

2.1 Introduction

In this chapter, various tools and techniques are explored that can help analyze and predict the current stock market. Although there are a few well known classical methods that are helpful, new technical findings are extending the analytical part significantly. Therefore, it is useful to explore some new methods and the latest tools and techniques to support stock market analysis.

The Figure 2.1, represents a brief workflow of investment in stock market. The major problem with most of the traders is not understanding the current market scenario, leading to trades that eventually result in the loss of hard-earned money. However, many useful tools are now available that provide virtual money and allow users to simulate their decisions in

**Corresponding author*: ochin.sharma@chitkara.edu.in

Deepa Gupta, Mukul Gupta, Rajesh Kumar Dhanaraj, Balamurugan Balusamy and Parth Mukul Gupta (eds.) Computational Intelligence for Autonomous Finance, (21–42) © 2025 Scrivener Publishing LLC

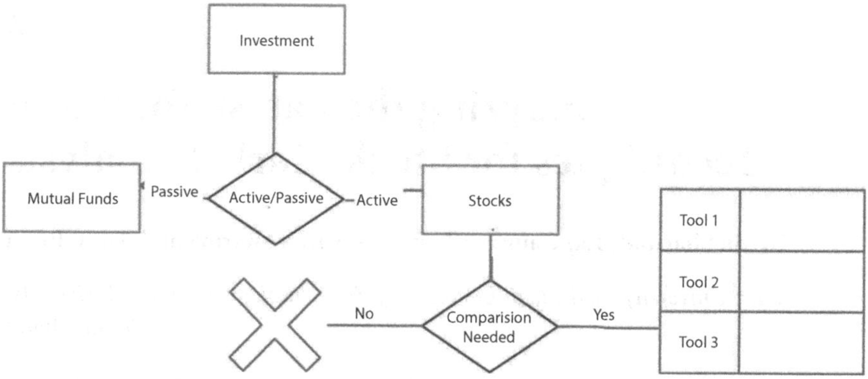

Figure 2.1 Brief workflow of investment analysis.

the real market. Since users are not very aware of these tools, this chapter will share useful information about them. Examples of such tools include Investopedia, Virtual Stock Exchange, and Wealthbase.

These simulations are available at no cost. Some salient features of these simulations are:

1. Virtual currency can be used for trading stocks.
2. Online simulation can be performed.
3. They can be played like a game, allowing you to compare with your performance with friends during the simulation.

In addition to simulations, there are useful and interesting tools for technical analysis that are not only efficient but also easy to use. These tools work based on certain technical indicators. Technical indicators can be broadly divided into two categories:

1. **Overlays:** Technical indicators that are plotted using the same scale and overlaid on a stock chart.
2. **Oscillators:** Examples include the stochastic oscillator, MACD, and RSI. This post will focus mostly on this second category of technical indicators.

When studying a security, traders frequently apply a variety of technical indicators at random. With hundreds of options available, traders need to select the tools and indicators that perform best and become familiar about their workings. To generate trade ideas, traders may integrate technical signals with less objective types of technical analysis, such as looking at chart patterns. Because they are quantitative, trend indicators can be utilized by automated trading systems.

As a result of this knowledge, it is highly important to investigate tools more thoroughly to make a more accurate analysis of the stock market for forecasting reasons.

2.2 Need for Trading Softwares

Because of its automated trading methods and capabilities, trading software is frequently employed by traders and investors. Chat forums, specialized instruments, data visuals, and indications are additional options for performing technical analysis.

The use of technical analysis tools has helped investors and traders better understand the complexity of trading and investing. There are numerous modules for both algorithmic and paper trading.

Conversely, paper trading provides risk-free transaction procedures without using real money, while algorithmic trading ensures that trade-related actions are automated.

2.3 How Software for Technical Analysis of the Indian Stock Market Operates

This intraday trading tool has several main characteristics that assist investors and traders in making informed investment decisions.

- **Tools for Scanning:** This application allows investors and traders to learn more about stock markets and their variations.
- **Customizable Charts:** These charts can be used to forecast stock patterns based on both current and historical data.
- **Up-to-Date Information:** Stock trading software India provides with you the most recent stock market news from reliable sources to keep you informed.

- **Reports:** You can also review third-party research papers and studies on the general and stock markets.
- **Keep an Eye on the Numbers:** The availability of data, such as stock prices, company valuations, quarterly reports, and other relevant information, allows traders and investors to make well-informed decisions about their trading and investment possibilities.

2.4 Helpful Tools to Analyze Stock Market

2.4.1 Masterswift 2.0

This tool's built-in stock research capabilities for tracking derivatives and equities are a unique selling point.

Technical indicators and charting tools are integrated into the Masterswift trading program to assist users in making important trading decisions. Users of the software can access a range of data types, such as market, fundamental, and historical data. It is utilized by professionals including investors, traders, and bankers.

The buy–sell signal program supports interactive dividends, earnings, and splits, as well as graphic charts displaying important financial data, enabling quick trade execution. User can also utilize instruments such as dividend adjustment charts and financial data charts to improve your understanding of pricing trends and stock values [12].

In India, the key features of the Masterswift stock trading software are as follows:

- **Recognizing Patterns:** This tool analyzes data patterns in trade charts to determine market trends.
- **Integration Support**: For semi-automated online trade techniques, third-party platforms like Excel, .Net, Python, and Java can be connected to Masterswift.
- **Buying and Selling Signals:** Expert advisors can assist end users with real-time trading signals.
- **Advanced Charting Techniques:** Trading can be executed with a single click on various chart formats and built-in indicators.
- **Scanners:** Online stock trading scanners help identify the best trading opportunities.

- **Information from the Past:** Use historical data from previous years to make informed stock buying and selling decisions.

2.4.2 RichLive Trade

This is a best stock research tool for the Indian market, covering commodities, currencies, and stocks.

RichLive Trade is the most useful for stock market technical analysis and charting. The buy–sell signal program, created specifically for the Indian market, can be used by traders to analyze the stock, currency, and commodities markets. Choose RichLive Trade's excellent technical signal program if you want a bundle that can help you profit from trading [13].

Use the technical indicators included in the software to analyze the stock market and alter your profit ratio. With the best charting software in India, you can expect a little more.

RichLive has a staff of expert trainers who can assist traders and investors in understanding the market.

2.4.2.1 Key Features of RichLive Trade Software

- **High Accuracy:** For greater accuracy, the buy–sell signal software makes future forecasts based on a stock's past performance.
- **Filters for Advanced Levels:** An advanced filtering technique assists traders in selecting more than 95% correct buy–sell signals with 100% capital protection.
- **Global Markets:** RichLive is a technical analysis program developed by seasoned traders with years of trading expertise. It supports FOREX, All Global Indices, MCX (India), NSE (India), and COMEX (USA).
- **Individualized Advanced Software Training:** The team of specialists and professionals has more than 15 years of experience in the Indian market, forex market, and global market, and they train their customers to help them grow their money.
- **Jackpot Calling Service:** A telephone service is available.

2.4.3 MetaTrader 4

This is an effective stock analysis tool for Forex Trading and technical analysis.

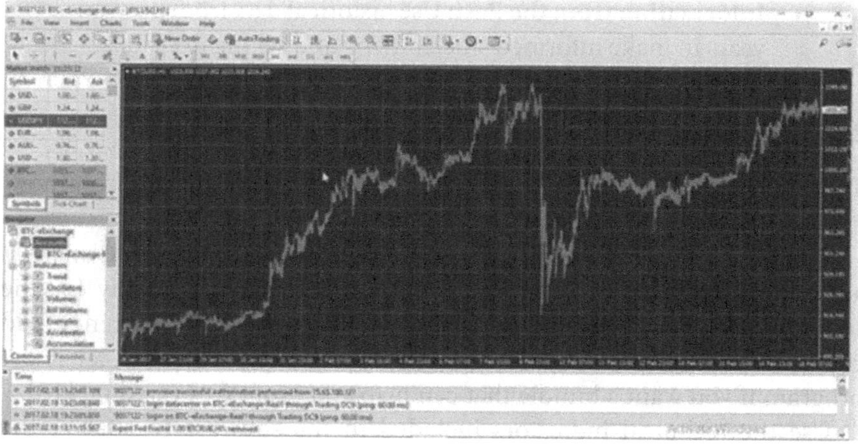

Figure 2.2 MetaTrader 4.

Figure 2.2, displays the screen of MetaTrader4 tool is a popular piece of Forex market software that traders use to analyze financial markets. The numerous functions included in this auto trading system in India benefit traders of various skill levels.

In India, algorithmic trading software is ideal for technical analysis, algorithmic trading, and flexible trading. Other technical analysis techniques for Indian stocks include mobile trading, which is utilized by traders to analyze both financial markets and Forex deals. User can perform technical analysis on currency pairs in the Forex market. This software in India can be used to trade all currency pairings, including major, minor, index, commodity, metals, and minor exotic trades [14].

2.4.3.1 Key Features of MetaTrader4

- **Comprehensive Trading System:** There are two execution modes and four order types in the fully featured trading free trading software in India.
- **Market Meta Trader:** Users can utilize this function to purchase indicators and trading robots.
- **Algorithmic Trading:** It is a type of trading that uses algorithms to make decisions. Expert advice and technical indicators can be created, tested, and used.
- **Analytical Instruments:** Approximately 30 built-in indicators, 2,000 free custom indicators, and approximately 700 premium indicators can be used by traders to analyze markets at different levels of sophistication.

- **Signals for Trading:** Trading signals enable you to imitate other traders' trades.
- **Notifications Sent Automatically:** With the help of MT4 software's SMS and push notification capabilities, you can now stay up to date on the latest happenings as a trader.

2.4.4 MotiveWave

Traders can easily conduct market research using the MotiveWave trading platform. This expert-level trading software also includes tools for analysis using Ratio, Elliott Wave, Gann, and Fibonacci.

Replay mode, trade simulation, walk-forward testing, strategy trading, scanners, optimization, reporting, and are among the key support features offered [15].

2.4.4.1 Key Features of MotiveWave

Figure 2.3, displays the screen of MotiveWave's tool key features include:

- Strategy trading
- Native support for multiple monitors: To display numerous graphs and charts on multiple screens simultaneously, use the "Tile Windows" functionality.

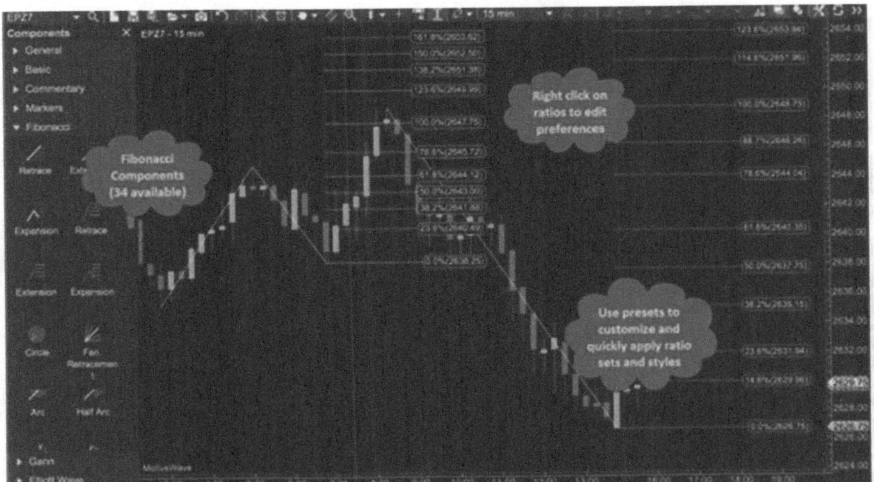

Figure 2.3 MotiveWave.

- Order Entry Using Charts: As a trader, you can use a chart to place, change, and cancel orders, as well as visualize positions.

2.4.5 Spider Stock Market Software

This is real-time technical analysis software.

Spider Software is a popular tool for analyzing current stock market patterns. In addition to stock market charting, the software includes a portfolio management module.

These features are required for the entire trading operation to be lucrative. Built-in indicators and real-time data are available to use the software for precise data predictions and stock movement analysis. Figure 2.4, displays the screen of Spider tool.

Spider Stock Market provides [16]:

- **NSE Data in Real Time:** It delivers real-time NSE data for futures and F&O scripts analysis.
- **Investing in the Stock Market:** With the help of Neat Feed, it is possible to track the stock market in real time.
- **Advanced Charting Techniques:** Spider software manages numerous exchanges and provides extensive technical analysis tools for Indian stocks.
- **Currency Market Surveillance:** It aids in the automatic tracking and analysis of recent currency market changes.

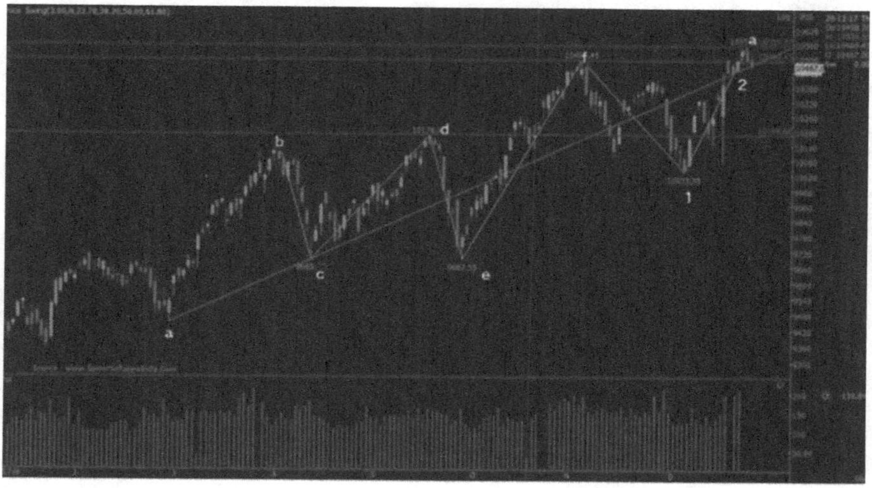

Figure 2.4 Spider tool.

- **NSE Post-Market:** This stock trading software gives end-of-day statistics as well as NSE post-market data, among other things.

Spider Stock Market Technical Analysis Software is available for purchase at the following price: The cost of the Spider Stock market software can be obtained upon request.

Now, let us explore some licensed tools to serve the purpose of stock analysis.

2.4.6 Investar

This tool is very useful for day trading and swing trading for NSE stocks.

For managing portfolios and analyzing Indian stock markets, use Investar stock market software (NCDEX, MCX, NSE F&O, BSE, and NSE). Additional capabilities of the software include mutual fund scans and auto-divergence. This stock trading tool also has multi-time frame inquiry capabilities [17].

Through Investar, you can also trade with reputable online brokers. Transactions from a broker's Trade Book or Contract Note can be easily imported. View accurately where your portfolio stood on any previous date. Figure 2.5, displays the screen of Investar tool.

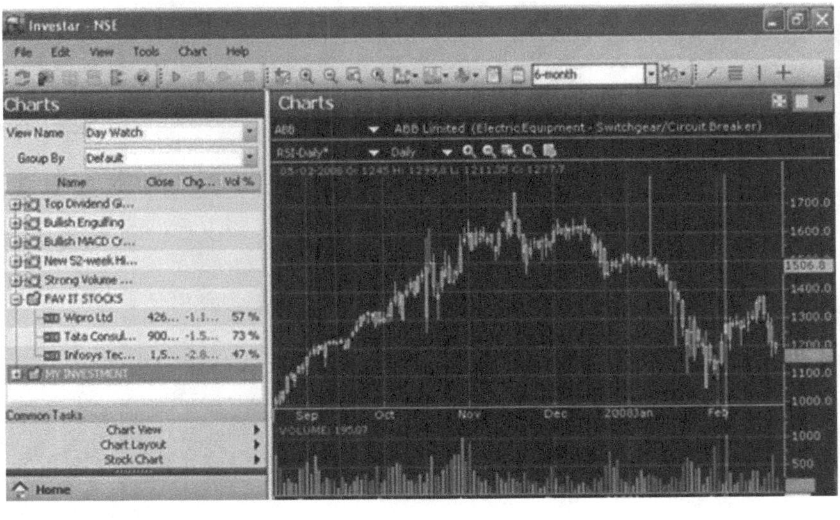

Figure 2.5 Investar tool.

2.4.6.1 *Key Features*

- Auto-Support/Resistance: This function scans high risk/reward stocks, boundary breakouts, and procurement zone breakouts. The software also identifies targets for any stock.
- For Trend Analysis, Auto-Trendlines: This function allows you to spot trend reversals with trendline breakouts. Trendlines are automatically set on the chart to spot trends.
- Technical and Fundamental Analysis: Use fundamental and technical analysis for the best buying/selling times.
- Technical Clues: Investar offers technical indicators for analyzing futures, equities, and options.

Pricing: A yearly subscription to Investar can be purchased for 10,950. Based on user preferences and platforms, there are about seven versions of the software available (mobile, tablet, etc.).

2.4.7 eSignal

eSignal is an effective technical research tool with chart formation for daily traders.

With the help of technical analysis tools and eSignal charting, you can execute trade actions quickly. Tools for backtesting and scanning are also

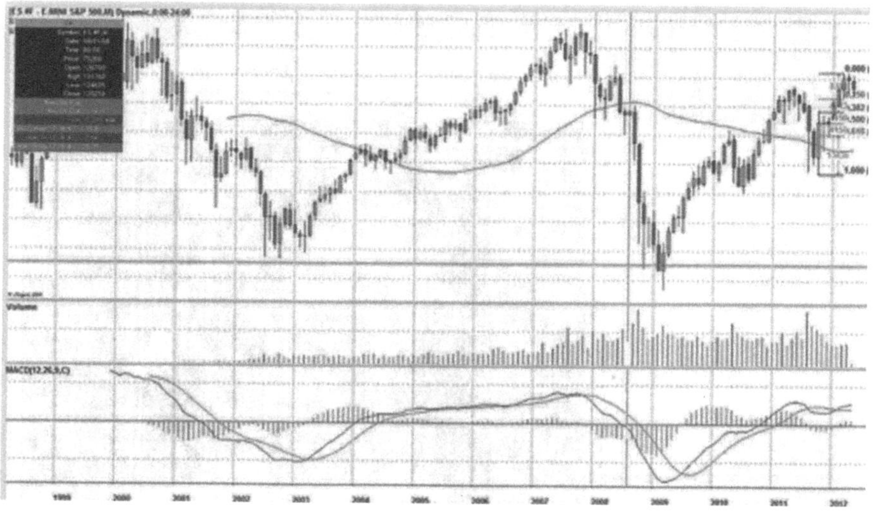

Figure 2.6 eSignal tool.

integrated for assessing the effectiveness of trading strategies. VIRATECH technology is the authorized supplier of e-Signals. Figure 2.6, displays the screen of eSignal tool.

Through the application's real-time data service, users can plan their plans and implement best trade practices by accessing data from numerous foreign markets. With the help of this day-to-day trading application, you can obtain intraday market data for trading decisions. You can utilize customized process generators to gather data with this daily trading application [18].

2.4.7.1 Main Properties of eSignal

- **Business Alerts:** The software enables trading alerts from market professionals using various filters and alerts.
- **Workspace Customizability:** To design a workspace, use keys and attach/detach pages.
- **Direct connections** with more than 50 brokers are made using the Trade Integration Trading/Order Management System.
- **Free Instruction:** Learn about markets by taking a course in advanced technical analysis. This is intended mainly for those who want to develop their trading strategies.

Additionally, Market Screener Without having to search through thousands of different stocks, you can learn about new investing opportunities. Cost of eSignal Technical Analysis Program: The software costs 25,707 per month.

2.4.8 Sharekhan Trade Tiger

This tool has swing trading signals for equities, indices, etc.

Users can obtain data from several markets, such as the NSE and BSE, using the Trade Tiger web platform. Packed with state-of-the-art features like global market monitoring, trade call access, and 24-hour market news, this is one of the best share trading systems available. Figure 2.7, displays the screen of Sharekhan Trade Tiger tool.

Beyond NSE and BSE, the software provides data for IPOs, mutual funds, MCX, and NCDEX. Additionally, accessible are graph studies for typical indicators like MACD, RSI, or Band-Bollinger, and Know Sure Thing. Moreover, user alert options for input price trigger are provided [19].

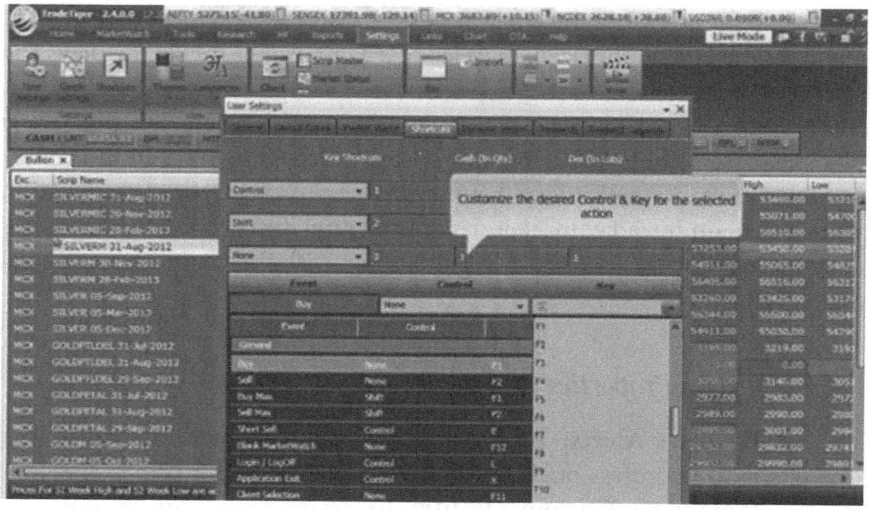

Figure 2.7 Sharekhan Trade Tiger tool.

2.4.8.1 Main Properties of Trade Tiger

Detecting Patterns: Get information on technical facts as well as regular alerts based on chart patterns.

- **Invest in BSE and NSE:** Find opportunities in BSE quickly and easily, then purchase and sell them.
- **Complex Charting Capabilities:** Create charts using mathematical techniques to outline trading rules.
- **Quotes from Live Streams:** Stock values fluctuate with changes in the exchange. You can watch these developments in real time, anytime, anywhere.
- **Commercial Tools:** For determining market trends, other tools are available, including Tick Query, Ticker, Market Summary, Action Watch, and Span Calculation.
- **Investigations & News:** It offers real-time news and suggestions based on research from Sharekhan specialists.
- **Tech-Indicators:** Assists in identifying any new developments in the financial sector.

The cost of the Trade Tiger software is disclosed in the available information.

2.4.9 Trader Guide

Based on stock analysis, this is the best intraday tool available. Trader Guide, an Indian stock trading analysis program, is a dependable source of intraday signals. It identifies reliable buying and selling indications in markets that are trending either way [19].

2.4.9.1 Trader Guide Features

- **Drawing Tools:** Create and save drawings with resistance, support, horizontal lines, and other features.
- **Buy/Sell Automatic:** Generates buy and sell indications for both daily traders and positioning traders.
- **Reports about Future and Options:** With Trade Alert software, you may also monitor the effectiveness of buy/sell signals.

2.4.10 NinjaTrader

This tool is for quickly managing expirations for intraday traders.

NinjaTrader's technical analysis software facilitates trade management by providing established entry and exit points. Consequently, trading can be lucrative and low-stress. It also helps reduce the amount of time required for important market study and trading strategy formulation,

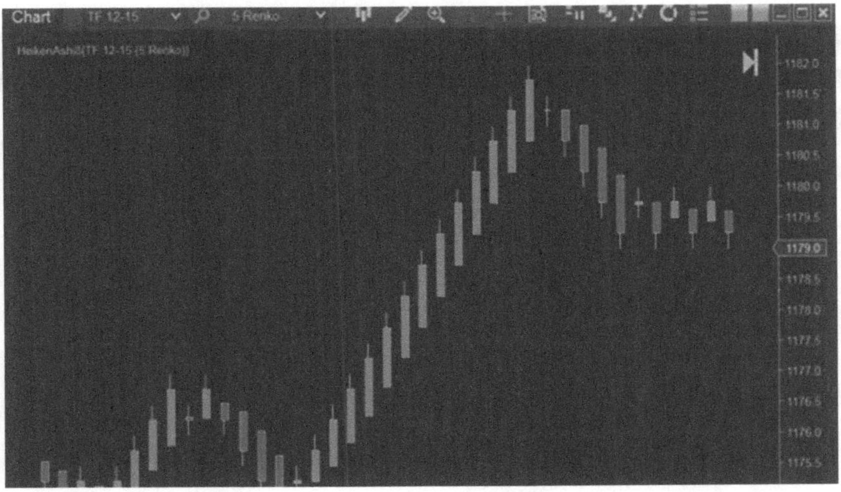

Figure 2.8 NinjaTrader tool.

removing emotion from trading decisions [20]. Figure 2.8, displays the screen of NinjaTrader tool.

NinjaTrader's features include:

- **Charts:** Analytical reports and charts that might help you find new trading opportunities.
- **Simulate:** The program aids in experimental tests and simulation to evaluate trading opportunities.
- **Trade:** Both automated and manual trade execution.
- **Build:** Developers are free to provide their own indicators and graphics.
- **Price:** The pricing information for NinjaBroker, which is tailored for both forex and futures, is available on the company's website.

2.4.11 AmiBroker India

This program is an efficient portfolio testing tool for stock analysis.

AmiBroker's technical indicator software offers speedy portfolio backtesting while providing robust and user-friendly charts. It guarantees efficient optimization with customized backtesters, grading, and ranking features. With its batch processor, this program can also automate repetitive activities [21]. Figure 2.9, displays the screen of AmbiBroker India tool.

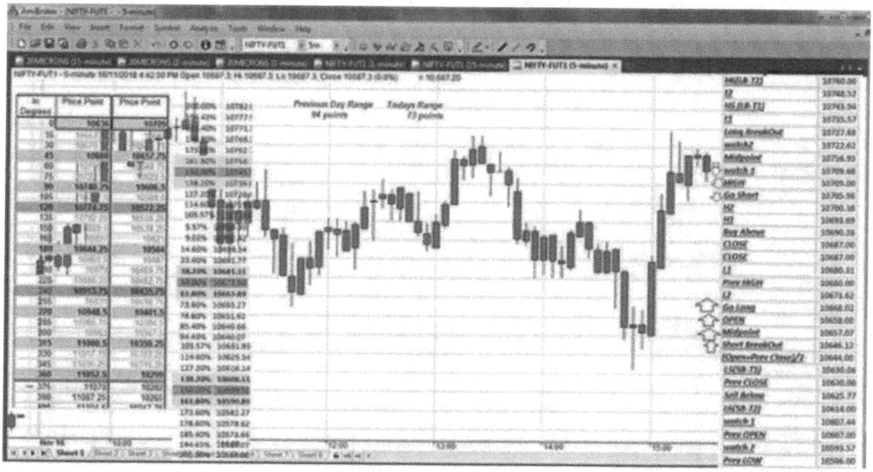

Figure 2.9 AmiBroker India.

AmiBroker India's advantages:

- **Ranking and Scoring:** It offers bar-by-bar ranking to assist customers in finding good trading options.
- **Walking-Forward Testing:** The software evaluates performance to determine the reliability of your system.
- **Simulation with Monte Carlo:** It provides worst-case scenarios to help users prepare for challenging market conditions.
- **Analysis Window:** Everything, including Monte Carlo Simulation investigations and optimizations, is displayed in this window.
- **Screening the Market:** It offers symbolic data in tabular style for multipurpose screening.
- **Pricing:** AmiBroker is offered with two years of service at Rs 37,032.

2.4.12 VectorVest

Perfect for managing stock portfolios and conducting market research for individual investors. Figure 2.10, displays the screen of VectorVest tool.

Use the technical analysis tool VectorVest to create reliable, tested stock recommendation systems and to do stock studies. With the mobile version, you can assess stock details at any time and from any location [22].

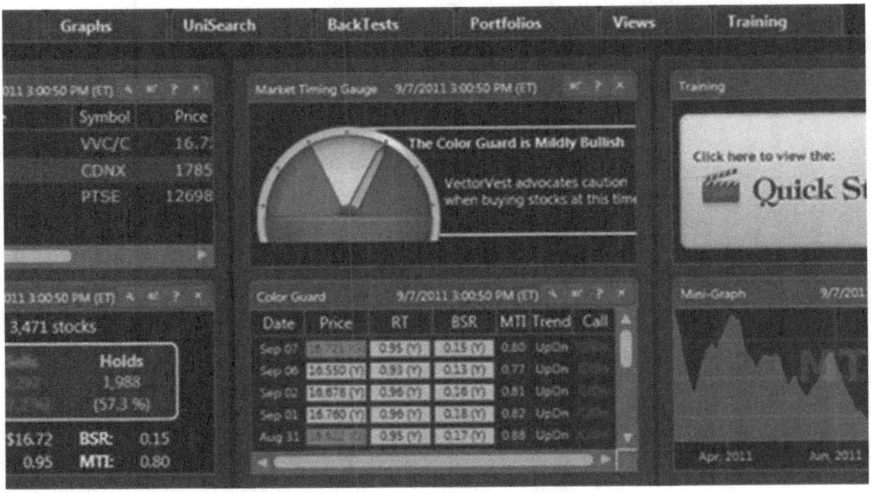

Figure 2.10 VectorVest tool.

The following are some features of VectorVest:
Your trading entry and exit positions will be more precise.

- **Full Investing:** It aids in developing strong investment strategies for trading on the Indian stock market.
- **Compulsory Rankings:** You can quickly find the greatest investment opportunities with forced rankings.
- **Basic Evaluation:** Fundamental analysis combined with market trend analysis guarantees the best outcomes.
- **Pricing:** For the cost of the technical analysis software VectorVest, you can request the price on the official website.

2.4.13 Profit Source Platform

This platform is useful for traders working with short terms to manage entry and exits.

With more than 40 indicators, Gain Source Platform helps stock traders monitor specific stocks and determine the best times to enter and exit the market. The free technical analysis program in India uses quantitative

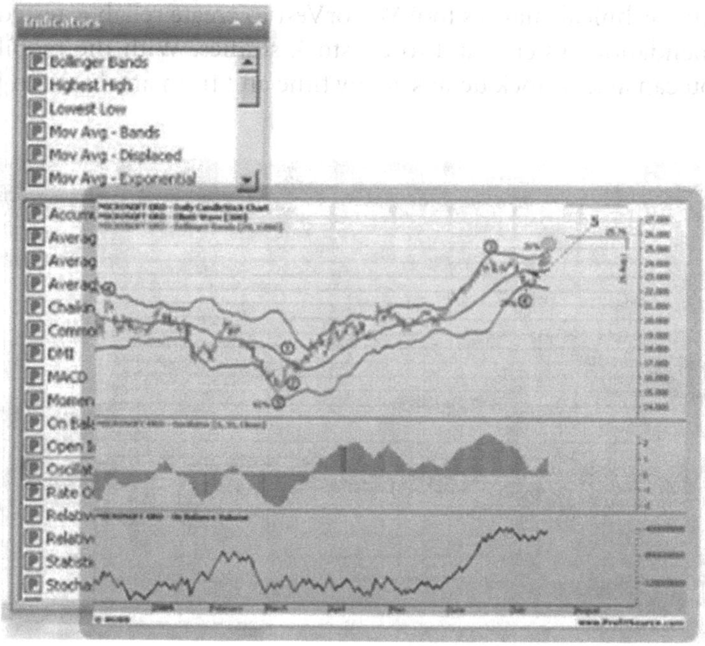

Figure 2.11 Profit Source tool.

indicators to analyze trends, momentum, and market resistance [23]. Figure 2.11, displays the screen of Profit Source tool.

Characteristics of a Profit Source Platform:

- **Elliott Wave Predictions:** It facilitates precise time and cost projection.
- **Tech-Indicators:** Various indicators will be provided to assist you in developing a successful strategy.

Trading Signals for Elliott Waves: You can identify low-risk entry locations.

- **Precalculated Scan:** Your dashboard will begin showing new trading opportunities as soon as you log in.
- **Cost of Profit Source Trading Analysis Software:** You can request the price on the official website.

2.4.14 Algo Trader

It is a useful software for algorithmic trading and quantitative research.

AlgoTrader is a computational trading software used by quantitative hedge funds. This trading software allows for automated trading of cryptocurrencies, including bitcoin. It is also one of the best trading systems in

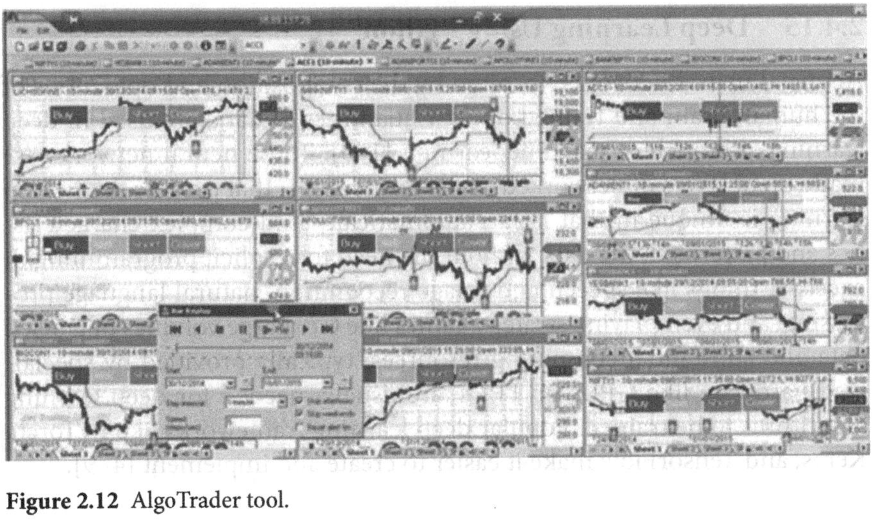

Figure 2.12 AlgoTrader tool.

India for automated statistical trading methods in the derivatives, FX, and equity markets. Figure 2.12, displays the screen of AlgoTrader tool.

The best part is that AlgoTrader makes it simple to automate any type of strategy needed for quantitative trading.

AlgoTrader's main attributes are:

- **Adapters for Market and Broker Data:** The software offers a variety of data and broker adapters. Additional adapters can also be added if needed.
- **Execution and Management of Orders:** AlgoTrader provides adaptable order management methods, making it very simple to execute various order types and algorithms.
- **Instruments and Markets:** This trading program covers multiple markets and instruments, allowing the development and use of various order types and algorithms.
- **Automated Crypto Exchange Trading:** Automated bitcoin trading is supported by AlgoTrader. It has adapters for direct exchange platforms such as Bitfinex and Bitstamp. Additionally, it offers CoinAPI and CoinMarketCap historical data adapters.
- **Reports and User Interface:** Depending on your trading operations, you can customise a variety of administration and reporting options.
- **Pricing:** The software comes with a license that can be renewed annually.

2.4.15 Deep Learning Using Python

Artificial neural networks, inspired by the composition and operations of the human brain and trained on vast quantities of data, are used in deep learning, a branch of machine learning [1–3]. These neural networks are made up of layers of networked nodes, or neurons, that process data. Deep learning is unique in that it can automatically find complex characteristics and patterns in the data without the need for explicit programming. It excels at things like speech and image recognition, natural language processing, and even playing strategy games like Go. Large volumes of labeled data and substantial computing resources, typically provided by specialized hardware like GPUs or TPUs, are usually needed for deep learning algorithms to be trained. Popular deep learning frameworks like PyTorch, Keras, and TensorFlow make it easier to create and implement [4–9].

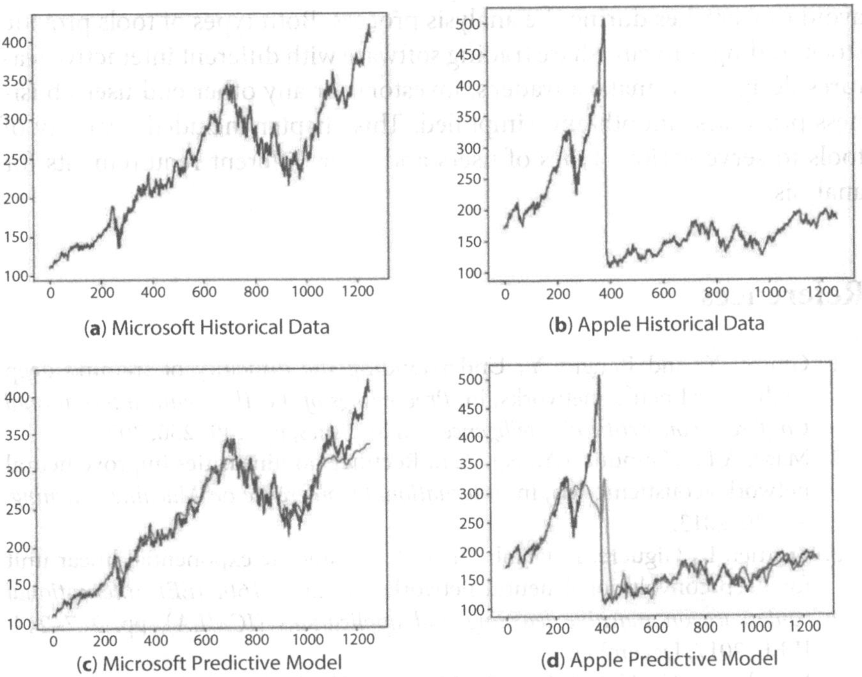

Figure 2.13 Deep learning experimentation for Apple and Microsoft Company historical and deep learning predictive data.

In experimentation, Google Colab is used to avoid compatibility issues of various Python packages. Training and testing data are split over an 80:20 ratio. The 'Selu' activation function is used. Four LSTM layers are employed with 100 epochs, the 'Adadelta' optimizer, and the MSE loss function [10, 11].

Figure 2.13 is an easy interpretation of deep learning experimentation. Figures 2.13a, 2.13c represent Microsoft's historical data and predictive data, where the X-axis contains information on working days and the Y-axis represents stock prices in dollar. Similarly Figures 2.13b, 2.13d represent graphical information for Apple. In Figures 2.13b, 2.13d, the prediction of training data is represented in orange, and the prediction of test data is represented in green.

2.5 Conclusion

Free trading software offers built-in processes to help users make better trading and investing decisions. Licensed tools offer more features and avoid tool crashes during the analysis process. Both types of tools provide stock trading software/share trading software with different interactive features designed to make a trader's, investor's, or any other end user's business processes smooth and simplified. This chapter included a variety of tools to serve various types of users and their different requirements for analysis.

References

1. Glorot, X. and Bengio, Y., Understanding the difficulty of training deep feedforward neural networks, in: *Proceedings of the Thirteenth International Conference on Artificial Intelligence and Statistics*, pp. 249–256, 2021.
2. Maas, A.L., Hannun, A.Y., Ng, A.Y., Rectifier nonlinearities improve neural network acousticmodels, in: *International Conference on Machine Learning*, vol. 30, 2013.
3. Trottier, L., Giguere, P., Chaib-Draa, B., Parametric exponential linear unit for deep convolutional neural networks, in: *2017 16th IEEE international conference on machine learning and applications (ICMLA)*, pp. 207–214, IEEE, 2017, December.
4. Klambauer, G., Unterthiner, T., Mayr, A., Hochreiter, S., Self-normalizing neural networks, arXiv preprint arXiv:1706.02515, 2017.
5. Schmidhuber, J., Deep learning in neural networks: An overview. *Neural Networks*, 61, 85–117, 2015.
6. Dhiman, P., Kukreja, V., Manoharan, P., Kaur, A., Kamruzzaman, M.M., Dhaou, I.B., Iwendi, C., A novel deep learning model for detection of severity level of the disease in citrus fruits. *Electronics*, 11, 3, 495, 2022.
7. Saluja, K., Bansal, A., Vajpaye, A., Gupta, S., Anand, A., Efficient Bag of Deep Visual Words Based features to classify CRC Images for Colorectal Tumor Diagnosis, in: *2022 2nd International Conference on Advance Computing and Innovative Technologies in Engineering (ICACITE)*, Greater Noida, India, pp. 1814–1818, 2022, doi: 10.1109/ICACITE53722.2022.9823727.
8. Sill, J., Monotonic networks, in: *Advances in neural information processing systems*, pp. 661–66, monotonic, 1998.
9. Li, D., Yang, H., Yuan, C.A., Qin, X., Leaf classification utilizing densely connected convolutional networks with a self-gated activation function, in: *Intelligent Computing Methodologies: 14th International Conference, ICIC 2018, Wuhan, China, August 15-18, 2018, Proceedings, Part III 14*, pp. 370–375, Springer International Publishing, 2018.
10. https://archive.ics.uci.edu/ml/datasets/reuters-21578+text+categorization+collection

11. Sharma, O., A New Activation Function for Deep Neural Network, in: *2019 International Conference on Machine Learning, Big Data, Cloud and Parallel Computing (COMITCon)*, IEEE, February 2019.
12. https://www.mastertrust.co.in/product-masterswift
13. https://www.richlivetrade.com/index.html
14. https://www.metatrader4.com/en/trading-platform
15. https://www.motivewave.com
16. https://www.spidersoftwareindia.com
17. https://investarindia.com
18. https://www.esignal.com
19. https://www.sharekhan.com/sharekhan-trade-tiger
20. https://ninjatrader.com
21. https://www.amibroker.com
22. https://www.vectorvest.com
23. www.profitsource.com

3

Challenges and Security Issues in Autonomous Finance

Mukul Gupta[1], Deepa Gupta[1*], Nitin Agrawal[2] and Parth Mukul Gupta[3]

[1]*GL Bajaj Institute of Management, Greater Noida, UP, India*
[2]*Semikron Danfoss, Utica, New York, NY, USA*
[3]*Birla Institute of Technology & Sciences, Pilani, Rajasthan, India*

Abstract
This chapter investigates the mind-boggling security, moral, and functional issues that comprise autonomous finance. The weaknesses of information, the consistent cybersecurity dangers, and the need to safeguard security in a digital financial environment are addressed first. Then, algorithmic bias and fairness are discussed, including dynamic inclinations and the need to maintain reasonableness in all financial activities. The chapter examines the emerging field's significant security, moral, and functional issues. Security and protection are its primary concerns. It emphasizes the need to secure sensitive information in the digital financial system and addresses information security risks. Next, we will discuss algorithmic bias and fairness, including how decisions may be biased and how to level the playing field in financial activities. The article then explores regulatory compliance, including the challenges of understanding and following various legal frameworks and the need for transparency in financially autonomous activities. Operational risks, such as framework glitches and overreliance on technology, are also examined to offer reliable financial services. The chapter additionally addresses ethical issues related to autonomous financial systems, such as balancing trade-offs and being held accountable. The final point emphasizes the importance of consumer trust and how client education and transparency can build it. This paper outlines the security issues with autonomous finance and offers solutions, laying down the foundation for a safer, more egalitarian, and more reliable financial future.

Keywords: Autonomous financing, privacy, data vulnerability, algorithmic bias, operational risks, technology dependence, system failures, consumer trust

**Corresponding author*: dr.deepaguptadg@gmail.com

Deepa Gupta, Mukul Gupta, Rajesh Kumar Dhanaraj, Balamurugan Balusamy and Parth Mukul Gupta (eds.) Computational Intelligence for Autonomous Finance, (43–64) © 2025 Scrivener Publishing LLC

3.1 Introduction

The combination of artificial intelligence, machine learning (ML), and advanced level data analysis in financial services is known as autonomous finance. This new trend has the potential to completely transform how we manage our financial environments. Although this change makes processes more straightforward and faster than ever before, it also introduces numerous issues and security risks that must be carefully studied to devise solutions. This chapter aims to break down these issues and provide a comprehensive overview of the challenges that must be addressed before a fully autonomous financial environment can be established.

At the core of this discussion are the concerns about privacy and security, which are essential for trusting financial transactions. With data becoming increasingly significant, the fact that it can be stolen or misused highlights the importance of having strong protection and security measures. Concerns about fairness and bias in algorithms are amplified by the possibility that using algorithms to make decisions could unintentionally reinforce biases. This means that everyone needs to work together to ensure that financial decisions are fair and equitable.

Another significant area is regulatory compliance. The current legal structures are not keeping up with the rapid changes in autonomous finance, so there is a gap that needs to be filled to ensure transparency and accountability. The stability and reliability of financial services are seriously compromised by operational risks, which are generally caused by system failures and overreliance on technology. This highlights the importance of building systems that can handle failures [1].

Ethical issues, particularly regarding balancing trade-offs and ensuring individuals are held accountable, complicate matters further. Parties must be extremely cautious as they navigate these complex issues [2]. Finally, this chapter emphasizes how significant client trust is for the adoption and success of autonomous finance. It highlight the importance of educating clients and conducting operations transparently to build and maintain this trust.

This chapter utilizes various studies, examples, and theoretical frameworks to develop actionable solutions and strategies for progress. Its objective is not just to identify and understand the numerous issues that exist, but also to recommend ways of solving these issues so autonomous finance can reach its full potential in a safe, fair, and accepted manner.

3.2 A Review of the Literature

Smith and his team have discussed how information is vulnerable in the digital age and how the growing field of autonomous financing has made security and privacy even more crucial [27]. The review shows that hacking risks are particularly high for financial technologies (FinTech), highlighting the importance of robust security measures [4]. Additionally, protecting privacy in digital transactions is becoming increasingly important [23]. They argue that client information should be safeguarded by advanced encryption techniques and privacy-protecting technologies.

Numerous experts have investigated the issue of bias in calculations and its impact on decisions made in autonomous finance. Extensive information is provided [15] on how bias can infiltrate computational processes and cause unfair financial outcomes. Researchers delve deeper into this point and recommend regular audits and the use of bias correction techniques to ensure that financial programs are fair [7, 8].

Another significant issue is understanding how to navigate the complex legal systems surrounding autonomous banking. A balance between technology and regulation [3] is necessary when discussing the complexities of regulatory compliance. Additionally, [34] transparency is crucial in autonomous finance operations, and experts suggest ways to enhance trust and compliance through clear reporting methods.

Wilson and his team examine the practical risks associated with autonomous finance, focusing on system breakdowns and technical dependencies. They emphasize the importance of creating robust systems that can function even when one technology fails. These approach reduces reliance on single technologies [31].

There are many ethical issues that arise when using autonomous banking systems. For example, how do you balance efficiency with ethical concerns? These issues are explored [30] to find the trade-offs between new technologies and conducting business in an honest manner. They call for a framework of accountability to ensure that autonomous systems do not violate any ethical standards.

The importance of client trust cannot be overstated for the success and adoption of autonomous finance. To gain clients' trust, businesses need to educate people about the benefits and functioning of autonomous finance, as well as ensure that systems are safe and fair. They argue that clients should be better informed about these systems and provided with more information on how they work [18].

Some of the most serious issues with the reliability of autonomous finance services involve operational risks, such as system breakdowns and technical dependencies. The study [28] from 2022 explores what happens when a system fails and suggests that to mitigate these risks, we need fall-back systems, thorough testing, and continuous monitoring. It also discusses technology dependence [5], warning of systemic weaknesses and advocating for the development of more robust systems.

In the realm of autonomous banking, there are many complex ethical issues to consider. A 2020 study [2], discusses the ethical issues that self-driving financial systems can cause, focusing on how to make them both efficient and fair while also ensuring that there are clear ways for individuals to be held accountable. To navigate these issues and ensure that autonomous finance operates effectively and ethically, they argue that ethical standards and models are vital.

Research on consumer trust highlights how crucial it is for self-service banking services to be adopted and succeed. To build trust with clients, it is necessary to do more than just ensure that your systems are safe and effective [13]. It is also important to educate people about the technologies behind autonomous finance. To help people understand and trust these systems better, they emphasize the importance of transparency and client involvement.

3.3 Concerns Regarding the Protection of Identity and Privacy in Autonomous Finance

With the utilization of artificial intelligence and machine learning (ML), autonomous finance holds the potential to provide individualized financial services, as well as increased efficiency and transparency [6, 10]. Despite this, we must also address significant concerns around privacy and security as advance the adoption of this transformative technology. Within the scope of this study, we explore three primary concerns: the vulnerability of data, the risks associated with cybersecurity, and the protection of privacy [6, 9].

3.3.1 The Vulnerability of Data

3.3.1.1 The Challenge

Financial systems that operate autonomously are fundamentally dependent on vast volumes of data. To make informed decisions, these systems analyze consumer profiles, purchase history, credit scores, and market trends. However, this data-rich environment presents several critical risks [11, 26].

3.3.1.2 Aspects of Danger

The storage and processing of sensitive information, such as personally identifiable data, financial records, and health details, is a concern for artificial intelligence systems. Data breaches can occur when security measures are inadequate, encryption is insufficient, and access controls are not strictly enforced [16].

Data security can be compromised by internal threats, which include insufficient monitoring and attacks originating from within an organization.

The availability of advance artificial intelligence models, such as GPT-4 or PaLM2, raises the possibility of data exploitation. There is a risk that sensitive information may be exposed by employees experimenting with these models.

3.3.1.3 Various Methods of Risk Reduction

- The utilization of robust encryption techniques is essential for the security of data both while at rest and in transit.
- Access Controls: Limit access to authorized individuals and monitor how data is being used within the system.
- Endeavor Endorsed Arrangements: To prevent privacy concerns, employees should be encouraged to use AI technologies that have been properly vetted [19].

3.3.2 Dangers Posed by Cybersecurity

3.3.2.1 The Challenge

Artificial intelligence systems are vulnerable to adversarial attacks, which include malicious actors manipulating input data to deceive the system. These attacks can potentially disrupt decision-making processes and undermine the credibility of financial security [17, 27].

3.3.2.2 Most Frequent Attacks from the Opponent

- Avoidance Attacks: These attacks are designed to prevent security measures from being detected by creating inputs that avoid detection.
- Model Extraction Attacks: These attacks aim to extract sensitive information from artificial intelligence models [21, 22].

3.3.2.3 *Countermeasures*

- Training artificial intelligence models to be resistant to attacks from adversaries is the focus of robust model training.
- Continuous Monitoring: Consistently assess the system's behavior to identify any anomalies.
- The development of safeguards that can adapt to ever-changing attack strategies is the focus of adaptive defenses.

3.3.3 The Protection of Personal Privacy

3.3.3.1 *The Challenge*

The significance of maintaining client privacy while providing personalized financial services cannot be overstated. There is a requirement for autonomous financial systems to manage sensitive data while preserving individuals' privacy rights [25, 33].

3.3.3.2 *The Dangers to Privacy*

- Organizations may misuse client data for profit, compromising privacy.
- Excessive data collection can result in intrusive profiling, which is a form of unlawful surveillance.
- A lack of transparency is a common issue, as clients often do not insight into how their data is being used.

3.3.3.3 *Preserving Individual Cofense*

- Security by design is an approach that involves incorporating privacy concerns into the design of a system.
- Obtaining Client Consent: Acquiring informed consent prior to collecting and using any data is significant.
- Transparency: Clients should be informed about data practices in a clear and concise way.

To summarize, as the concept of autonomous banking becomes more prevalent in our daily lives, it is crucial to address these issues of privacy and security. Creating a reliable and dependable financial ecosystem requires finding the optimal balance between technology and security.

3.4 Using Algorithms to Make Decisions Can be Biased

3.4.1 Understanding Bias in Algorithms

It is unimaginable to completely eliminate bias from algorithmic systems, even those used in autonomous finance. The following are some potential sources of these biases:

- Bias in the Data: Algorithms learn from historical data, which may have biases inherent in the data itself. If the training data reflects societal biases, the algorithm can continue to reinforce these biases.
- Bias in the Features: The characteristics that algorithms consider (such as age, gender, or ethnicity) can potentially create bias. For example, a credit scoring algorithm that considers gender could inadvertently lead to discrimination against specific groups [14].
- Sampling Bias: The use of incomplete or skewed data samples can result in biased outcomes. This is alluded to as sampling inclination. For instance, if most of the data on credit approvals comes from wealthy areas, the algorithm might favor such areas.
- Model Selection Bias: The choice of a machine learning model and the hyperparameters associated with that model can introduce bias. Certain models naturally handle some aspects better than others.

3.4.2 Repercussions of Bias in the Financial Sector

Outcomes that are serious can be caused by biased algorithms:

- Discrimination: Due to the presence of biased credit scoring programs, some demographics may be unfairly denied credit.
- Market Distortions: Biased trading algorithms can potentially affect stock costs and market stability.
- Reinforcement of Inequality: Using biased lending practices can lead to the perpetuation of economic inequality.

3.5 Ensuring Fairness in Autonomous Finance

3.5.1 Openness and Responsibility for One's Actions

- Financial associations should ensure that their algorithms can be understood by their clients. In some cases, discovery models may be problematic because they make it hard to comprehend the process by which decisions are made.
- The importance of conducting routine audits of algorithms cannot be overstated. Biases can be identified, and corrective actions can be recommended through independent assessments [24].

3.5.2 Measures of Fairness and Compliance Monitoring

- To assess the performance of the model across different groups, fairness measures should be defined. Examples of fairness indicators include differential effect, balanced chances, and segment equality.
- Continuous Monitoring: To detect bias drift, executing continuous monitoring is fundamental. If significant bias is detected, models must undergo retraining.

3.5.3 The Pre-Processing of Data and the Engineering of Features

- Debiasing Data: Eliminate or reduce the presence of biased attributes in the collected training data. Techniques such as reweighting or oversampling can be useful.
- Fair Representations: To ensure fair representations of data, methods such as adversarial training can be employed [19].

3.5.4 Modifications to the Model

- Fairness Constraints: During model training, fairness constraints should be included. For example, penalizing models that exhibit impacts.
- Adjusting Model Outputs: Modify the model outputs in the post-processing step to ensure fairness. Techniques such as re-ranking re-scoring can be used [29, 32].

3.5.5 Considerations of Ethical Implications and Diverse Teams

- Diverse Teams: To ensure that the groups developing these algorithms are varied, it is crucial to promote diversity. Utilizing various perspectives can help in identifying and addressing biases.
- Ethical Frameworks: Establish ethical guidelines for the development of algorithms using ethical frameworks. Consider the societal impacts of financial decisions.
- Algorithmic Bias: Within the domain of autonomous finance, algorithmic bias is a significant issue. By prioritizing fairness, transparency, and continuous monitoring, we can develop financial systems that benefit all individuals without perpetuating bias. We should strive for a future where algorithms empower people and communities rather than marginalize them [2].

3.6 Compliance with Regulations in the Field of Autonomous Finance

3.6.1 Navigating Legal Frameworks

New issues are introduced to regulatory organizations due to autonomous finance, driven by cutting-edge advancements like artificial intelligence (AI) and machine learning (ML) [11]. To ensure compliance with the law, financial institutions must align with current legal frameworks when deploying autonomous systems [3]. Some significant considerations are explained below:

3.6.1.1 Being Able to Adapt to Rapid Change

- To keep up with the fast-changing universe of autonomous finance, administrative organizations need to stay aware of the speed. Because of the likelihood that customary standards do not straightforwardly address computer-based intelligence-driven frameworks, it is important to refresh and alter them.

- To lay out a strong administrative structure, it is fundamental for controllers, industry specialists, and innovation providers to cooperate.

3.6.1.2 *Data Privacy and Security*

- With regards to information protection and security, autonomous finance is emphatically subject to individual information. It is critical to agree with information protection regulations (like the GDPR or the CCPA).
- To safeguard client information and stay away from cybersecurity breaches, financial institutions are expected to implement stringent security measures.

3.6.1.3 *Anti-Money Laundering (AML) and Fraud Detection*

- Autonomous frameworks can possibly further develop hostile-to-illegal tax avoidance (AML) tasks by analyzing exchange designs and identifying dubious ways of behaving.
- It is the obligation of controllers to ensure that these advancements save client security while adhering to tax evasion necessities.

3.6.1.4 *Protection of Consumers*

- Stages for autonomous financing offer direct interaction with clients. Clients should be safeguarded against one-sided results, uncalled-for practices, and disinformation through the execution of guidelines.
- To lay out certainty, it is essential that algorithmic navigation be straightforward.

3.6.1.5 *Operations Across Borders*

- As autonomous finance expands outside geological limits, blending international rules is becoming increasingly significant.

- To overcome issues that are presented by international boundaries, administrative cooperation and standardization are required.

3.6.2 Be Open and Honest

3.6.2.1 Capacity to Explain and Interpret Information

- Autonomous financial systems often have capabilities as dark secret elements, which makes it hard to grasp the decision-making processes that they utilize.
- Controllers ought to ask financial firms to take on straightforward models. These explainable computer-based intelligence procedures can possibly give insight into the dynamic interaction.

3.6.2.2 Fairness and the Elimination of a Bias

- Focusing on fairness is fundamental. Decency measurements, ongoing monitoring, and debiasing approaches ought to be advanced by controllers. It is plausible that one-sided calculations might continue to propagate bias.
- Increased responsibility can be accomplished using transparent reports that unveil predisposition assessments.

3.6.2.3 User Consent and Control

- Clients are expected to be informed about the manners by which their information is utilized and permitted to exercise command over the processing of their information.
- The measures for straightforwardness should stretch out to the collection of information, the training of models, and the arrangement of customized ideas.

Consequently, a complicated balancing act is expected to guarantee administrative consistency in autonomous finance. Controllers are needed to make quick changes, put a high demand on client security, and energize receptiveness [20]. By acting thusly, we will want to utilize the commitment of autonomous finance while at the same time protecting the financial prosperity of individuals and preserving confidence in the system.

3.7 Gaining an Understanding of the Fundamentals of Operational Risk

With regards to the everyday tasks of an organization, operational risks encompasses the various uncertainties and hazards that the organization faces. Then again, functional gamble is restrictive to a specific business or area, rather than methodical gamble, which is brought about by outer factors like monetary occasions, and financial gamble.

1. One of the main parts of functional gamble is the human element: Human blunder is a critical supporter of functional gamble since it is basically reliant upon human activities and choices. Mistakes made by staff members can potentially result in operational breakdowns. The functional gamble landscape is different for every industry. Operational risk, in general, is reduced in industries that involve a minimal human involvement.
2. Factors that add to functional gamble: Functional gamble can be credited to four essential roads, which are as per the following:

    a. People: Blunders, misjudgements, and failures brought about by workers.
    b. Processes: Inefficient or defective internal techniques.
    c. Systems: Disappointments in innovation, programming, or infrastructure.
    d. External Occasions: Unexpected occasions beyond the organization's control.

3. Reducing the Gamble of Functional Exercises
   To properly manage operational risk, consider the following strategies:

    a. The first step is to anticipate hazards, which means identifying potential risks before they become real. Doing proactive risk assessments is fundamental.
    b. The second step is to lead a money saving advantage examination, which involves evaluating the compromises between risk relief initiatives and the effect such endeavors have on corporate tasks.

c. Stay away from unnecessary risks: There are a few perils that might be kept away from. The best way to reduce your exposure is to make informed decisions.
d. Delegation and Key Planning: In request to diminish the gamble of functional disappointment, you ought to guarantee that senior administration is liable for vital planning.

Hence, the concept of operational risk, which is often based on human behavior, is critical in autonomous finance. By gaining an attention to the variables that add to it and putting set up viable gamble the executive's methodology, associations can effectively navigate the intricacies of this consistently changing climate [28].

3.8 Risks Encountered in the Operation of Autonomous Finance

1. Problems with the System (System Failure)

The autonomous banking industry is full of extreme risks due to system failures. These failures can occur at various levels, including:

a) The Errors Caused by Algorithms

Algorithms play a significant role in the decision-making process of autonomous financial systems. If these calculations contain blunders, imperfections, or predispositions that were not intended, they can possibly bring about inaccurate conjectures, financial misfortunes, or breaks of administrative prerequisites.

Incorrect coding, insufficient testing, or unexpected interactions between different parts are expected reasons for algorithmic missteps.

b) Unemployment of the Infrastructure (Infrastructure Downtime)

Technical breakdowns, cyberattacks, or maintenance can cause the infrastructure supporting autonomous finance, which includes servers, databases, cloud services, and communication networks, to experience downtime.

When downtime occurs, it disrupts trading, transaction processing, and communication with clients, ultimately resulting in financial losses and damage to reputation.

c) Concerns Regarding the Integrity of Data

- Autonomous systems rely on specific and reliable data. Corrupted data, incomplete records, or breaks in data security can all compromise compliance.
- The importance of ensuring data integrity through rigorous validation procedures and secure storage cannot be overstated.

2. A Reliance on Technological Advancements (Dependency on Technology)

a) An Excessive Reliance on Artificial Intelligence and Machine Learning Models

- The autonomous financial industry is firmly dependent on those two sorts of models. Despite the way that these models essentially further develop proficiency, they additionally present risks.
- Particularly for the situation of uncommon events, for example, dark swan occasions, an extreme dependence on models that are not exposed to human inspection could bring about blind spots.

b) Risks Associated with Vendors and Third Parties

- Outer sellers are regularly depended upon by financial institutions for the arrangement of innovative arrangements. The strength, security, and consistency of the seller are all in danger because of these conditions.
- It is possible for tasks to be disturbed and basic information to be compromised if a merchant fizzles or penetrates their security.

c) The Absence of Actions Taken by Humans

- Totally automating an interaction might be stacked with risk. Concerning adapting to unanticipated events or startling monetary circumstances, systems that lack the ability of individuals could miss the goal.

- Readiness and chance mitigation are both ensured by selecting a reasonable congruity between human monitoring and computerization.

Thus, safety efforts are fundamental, while managing down to earth takes a chance with independent money. It is expected of financial institutions to prioritize information integrity, make investments in adaptable infrastructure, and strike a balance between technological advancement and human judgment [17, 31].

3.9 Concerns Regarding Ethical Issues in Autonomous Finance

As the cash locale continually assembles mechanized thinking (imitated information), man-made knowledge (ML), and free plans into its undertakings, a crowd of moral concerns arise that challenge the reasonableness and tolerability of these model setting upgrades. This piece makes a square plunge into the most widely recognized moral issues related to free cash and spotlights how these issues can be addressed to establish a monetarily secure and evenhanded climate.

- Issues with Moral Course: Choices that impact people's and establishments' monetary thriving in free money are energetically dependent upon calculations. In any case, these evaluations can unexpectedly help existing propensities or create new sorts of disengagement. For instance, algorithmic inclination can actuate misinformed credit scoring, where limited get-togethers may be ludicrously denied propels or charged higher advancement costs. Insurance and data security are similarly upright issues in light of the fact that free structures accumulate, separate, and store a lot of individual and sensitive information. Individual security and information security face serious risks from the plausible maltreatment of this information, whether with assumption or thoughtlessness.
- Commitment and Transparency: One of the central moral burdens of autonomous cash is the subject of liability. Right when PC-based data-driven structures seek off-track decisions or crash and burn with vengeance, sorting out who is

wary—the educated authorities, the money-related foundations, or the electronic reasoning itself—becomes disappointing. This vulnerability tries to think of parts that cause financial problems, insurance problems, or serious practices. Transparency is also disturbed by the faint idea of various PC-based data algorithms, for the most part called "black box" models. Clients are left with a lack of clarity about how decisions are made, dissolving trust and making it difficult to recognize and address tendencies or bumbles.

- Administrative Consistence and Client Security: The fast advancement of free cash rules existing regulatory plans, leaving openings in client affirmation and consistency. Ethical assessments incorporate guaranteeing that PC-based understanding and recreated insight structures concur with authentic necessities, especially those associating with know your client (KYC) rules, unpleasant to unlawful obligation avoidance (AML), and information security rules. The challenge lies in developing guidelines that are both sufficiently robust to guard against moral lapses and flexible enough to accommodate technological advancements.
- The Study of Moral Decline: Moral evaluations like reasonableness, protection, and consideration should offset capacity in free money structures. To achieve this concordance, deliberate efforts to integrate moral principles into the organization and the application of man-made financial knowledge must be made. It consolidates careful testing for propensities, completing instruments for data insistence, and ensuring that the possible additions of free systems are sufficiently streamed. Furthermore, financial foundations ought to be proactive in showing purchasers the limits, benefits, and risks of free cash, progressing an informed course, and drawing in trust.
- Pushing Ahead: Moral Systems and Multi-Accessory Obligation: To resolve the ethical issues related to free cash, different procedures, including those of regulators, monetary establishments, development designers, and clients, are required. Ethical structures that facilitate the development, implementation, and transfer of monetary-reproduced insight systems are essential. These plans should zero in on transparency, responsibility, sensibility, and client security. Attracting aides through open get-togethers, ethical

examinations, and reliable seeing can help with identifying potential issues and changing practices to satisfy moral guidelines.

3.10 Consumer Trust in Autonomous Finance

The foundation of trust with clients is vital as the robotization of financial services continues to increase. This study presents a total investigation of the significant topic:

3.10.1 Establishing Trust in Financial Systems that are Independent

3.10.1.1 Recognising the Concept of Autonomous Finance

At the point when we discuss autonomous finance, we are referring to financial administrations that are fuelled by calculations and that decide or take action for a shopper. As well as reducing the amount of work that clients need to do, these administrations are intended to work on financial results. Probably the main parts of autonomous finance include the administration of investments, savings, and installments that are robotized.

Client experience (CX) has forever been a main concern for financial help institutions (FSIs), which is why the reason the basic client experience is so significant. Then again, the coronavirus pandemic rushed the requirement for computerized administrations, which has brought client experience to the forefront. FSIs were faced with the double issue of protecting the financial prosperity of their clients while additionally maintaining their own strength.

The Trust Component Trust is the foundation of what makes autonomous finance conceivable. A few pointers are as follows:

It is interesting to note that 55% of Americans accept that calculations are more solid than people with regards to providing the right driving directions.

1. By and by, there is yet an absence of confidence in mechanized investment supervisors, some of the time known as robo-consultants, across all ages and socioeconomics.

With regards to execution, client-driven financial administration institutions (FSIs) outperform their conventional partners. The sending of autonomous finance can possibly cut both an upper hand and a specialty for early adopters.

2. Consistent Integration: Autonomous finance ought to interact easily with the lives and contraptions of clients. Trust might be increased using man-made reasoning, which can ascertain customized esteem assessments [12, 13].

3.10.2 User Education: Filling in the Gaps in Knowledge

3.10.2.1 Challenges in Technology and Expectations

The transition from regular banking administrations to computerized ones is difficult for traditional banks. Neobanks are redefining banking by bringing every one of the administrations together in a single area. Because of the apparent absence of adaptability with respect to conventional banks, numerous clients are switching to fintech options.

Open banking and data-driven approaches are being embraced.

With regards to establishing trust, FSIs are expected to:

- Integrate actually: It is fundamental to streamline office processes from the back to the front. The idea of open banking and biological system coordination is critical.
- Utilize a Data-Driven Approach: The utilization of information is fundamental for trust. Confidence might be increased by transforming an association into a data-driven one.

3.10.2.2 Educating Users

The education of clients is fundamental:

- Transparency: Describe the operation of autonomous finance, with an focus on protecting clients' security and integrity.
- Benefits: Highlight benefits such as personalized experiences, increased efficiency, and improved financial outcomes.

In conclusion, autonomous finance offers a lot of engagement, but efforts should be made to foster confidence. By prioritizing customer centricity, seamless integration, and customer education, financial administrations institutions (FSIs) can confidently navigate this rapidly changing terrain.

References

1. Kumar, A., Gupta, D., Gupta, M., Srivastava, G., India an Emerging Leader after Pandemic: A Strategy for the Development of new India. *Global J. Enterp. Inf. Syst.*, 13, 1, 60–70, 2021, Retrieved from https://www.gjeis.com/index.php/GJEIS/article/view/629.
2. Barnes, S. and Li, T., Ethical considerations in autonomous finance. *J. Financ. Ethics*, 15, 3, 205–220, 2020.
3. Brown, L. and Green, D., Regulatory Compliance in Autonomous Finance: Challenges and Pathways. *Law FinTech Rev.*, 8, 1, 75–89, 2022.
4. Doe, J. *et al.*, Cybersecurity Measures for Digital Finance: A Case Study Approach. *Int. J. Financ. Innov.*, 7, 4, 450–468, 2021.
5. Edwards, A. and Malik, R., Overcoming technology dependency in autonomous finance. *Financ. Technol. Rev.*, 7, 1, 34–49, 2023.
6. European Union Agency for Cybersecurity (ENISA), Cybersecurity Challenges in the Uptake of Artificial Intelligence in Autonomous Driving, 2020, EU Science Hub, https://joint-research-centre.ec.europa.eu/jrc-news-and-updates/cybersecurity-challenges-uptake-artificial-intelligence-autonomous-driving-2021-02-11_en.
7. Financial Stability Board (FSB), Artificial Intelligence and Machine Learning in Financial Services, November 2017, https://www.fsb.org/2017/11/artificial-intelligence-and-machine-learning-in-financial-service/.
8. Garcia, M., Fairness in Financial Algorithms: Frameworks and Solutions. *J. Ethical Finance*, 6, 3, 112–127, 2020.
9. Goodman, B. and Flaxman, S., European Union regulations on algorithmic decision-making and a 'right to explanation'. *AI Mag.*, 38, 3, 50–57 2017.
10. Grant Thornton, Anticipate cybersecurity and privacy risks in AI, https://www.grantthornton.com/insights/articles/advisory/2023/anticipate-cybersecurity-and-privacy-risks-in-ai#:~:text=One%20of%20the%20most%20pressing,individuals%2C%20potentially%20jeopardizing%20their%20privacy.
11. Green, A. and Chen, B., Fairness-aware machine learning in financial services. *Comput. Finance*, 29, 4, 112–127, 2021.
12. Gupta, D., Gupta, M., Rani, S., A Study on Training of Workmen in a Manufacturing Organization—With Reference to Aluminium Foundry, in: *Recent Trends in Industrial and Production Engineering. Lecture Notes in Mechanical Engineering*, A. Dvivedi, A. Sachdeva, R. Sindhwani, R. Sahu (Eds.), Springer, Singapore, 2022, https://doi.org/10.1007/978-981-16-3330-0_19.
13. Jackson, T. and Kumar, D., Building consumer trust in autonomous financial systems. *Int. J. Financ. Innov.*, 3, 2, 89–104, 2021.
14. Kumar, A. *et al.*, Addressing algorithmic bias in autonomous financial decision-making. *J. Financ. Technol. Policy*, 4, 1, 77–93, 2022.
15. Lee, H. and Kim, J., Addressing Algorithmic Bias in Autonomous Financial Decisions. *Financ. Technol. Rev.*, 4, 2, 200–215, 2018.

16. Lee, H. and Kim, J., Cybersecurity risks in financial technology. *Secur. J.*, 33, 2, 231–245, 2020.
17. Lee, K.-F., *AI Superpowers: China, Silicon Valley, and the New World Order*, Houghton Mifflin Harcourt, Publishing Company, USA, 2018.
18. Martin, E. and Thompson, G., Building Consumer Trust in Autonomous Finance. *Consum. Finance Q.*, 15, 4, 398–412, 2020.
19. Mittal, S., Srivastava, P., Gupta, D., Emotional Intelligence: Assessing Its Impact on Financial Productivity in an Organization, in: *Computational and Experimental Methods in Mechanical Engineering. Smart Innovation, Systems and Technologies*, vol. 239, V.V. Rao, A. Kumaraswamy, S. Kalra, A. Saxena, (Eds.), Springer, Singapore, 2022, https://doi.org/10.1007/978-981-16-2857-3_22.
20. Morrison, T. and White, G., Adaptive regulatory approaches for financial technology. *Law Finance Rev.*, 18, 3, 142–158, 2020.
21. Norton Rose Fulbright, *Digital transformation-Key technology, cybersecurity, and privacy risks*, Office of the Privacy Commissioner of Canada: Privacy and Cyber Security, https://www.nortonrosefulbright.com/en-ca/knowledge/publications/4318add0/digital-transformation-key-technology-cybersecurity-and-privacy-risks.
22. Pasquale, F., *The Black Box Society: The Secret Algorithms That Control Money and Information*, Harvard University Press, Cambridge, Massachusetts London, England, 2015.
23. Patel, R. and Kumar, S., Privacy-Preserving Technologies in the Financial Sector. *J. Priv. Financ. Data Prot.*, 3, 1, 30–44, 2019.
24. Patel, R. and Singh, A., Transparency in financial technology: A regulatory perspective. *J. Regul. Econ.*, 59, 1, 67–83, 2021.
25. Rajvanshi, P.R., Singh, T., Gupta, D., Gupta, M., Cybersecurity and Data Privacy in the Insurance Market, in: *Big Data Analytics in the Insurance Market (Emerald Studies in Finance, Insurance, and Risk Management)*, K. Sood, B. Balusamy, S. Grima, P. Marano, (Eds.), pp. 1–20, Emerald Publishing Limited, Leeds, 2022, https://doi.org/10.1108/978-1-80262-637-720221001.
26. Smith, A. and Johnson, B., Data vulnerabilities in the financial sector. *J. Cybersecur. Priv.*, 5, 2, 158–172, 2021.
27. Smith, A. and Jones, B., Data Vulnerability in the Digital Age: Security Risks in FinTech. *J. Cybersecur. Digital Trust*, 5, 2, 123–135, 2020.
28. Thompson, H. and Zhang, L., Mitigating operational risks in autonomous finance. *Oper. Risk Manage.*, 22, 4, 310–325, 2022.
29. Tiwari, S., Sharma, A.P., Gupta, D., Gupta, M., Performance Evaluation of Mutual Funds using Sharpe, Treynor and Jenson Ratios. *Finance India*, 34, 2, 743–752, 2020, Accessed February 19, 2024, https://search.ebscohost.com/login.aspx?direct=true&db=bsh&AN=146922528&site=ehost-live.
30. Turner, A. and Shah, R., Ethical Dilemmas in Autonomous Banking Systems. *Ethics Banking Finance*, 9, 3, 300–315, 2021.

31. Wilson, F. and Davis, L., Operational Risks in Autonomous Finance: A Study on System Failures. *Oper. Risk Manage.*, 11, 2, 158–172, 2019.
32. Zeng, J., Ustun, B., Rudin, C., Interpretable Classification Models for Recidivism Prediction. *J. R. Stat. Soc. Ser. A Stat. Soc.*, 180, 3, 689–722, 2020.
33. Zhao, W. and Chung, H., Privacy-preserving solutions in financial technology. *J. Priv. Confid.*, 11, 1, 15–33, 2019.
34. Zhao, W. *et al.*, Enhancing Transparency in Autonomous Finance. *J. Financ. Transparency*, 2, 4, 234–249, 2020.

4

Involvement of Artificial Intelligence in Emerging Fintech Industry 4.0: A TCCM Framework

Annu* and Ravindra Tripathi

Department of Humanities and Social Sciences, Motilal Nehru National Institute of Technology Allahabad, Prayagraj, India

Abstract

Purpose: This study aims to map the global connectivity and emerging trends related to Fintech and artificial intelligence to determine India's position and obtain answers regarding technology enhancements. Moreover, AI plays an essential role in shaping the Fintech industry's design, as well as manifesting the areas of document publication, authors, papers, and institutional network collaboration.

Methodology: By employing the "Biblioshiny" component of the "R" package, a bibliometric study has been carried out. To gather the data, highly indexed databases were used. The trustworthy indexing of Scopus and the Web of Science serve as data sources. Available adequate articles of high quality indexed journals make reliability to collect data from these resources, that's why these are selected. The data spans from 2014 to 2022, and there are 364 papers.

Findings: The findings show that the rising phase of Fintech began in 2017, with two turning points for its robustness occurring in 2019 and 2021. Despite this, it is still growing. China has dominated both multi-country and single-country Fintech publishing production. Since the beginning of 2017, sources have increased, and various sources are involved in publishing papers in this area. Artificial intelligence is becoming robust in research by its involvement in the Fintech industry and highlights the five ways of artificial intelligence which helps to identify the scenario of Fintech.

Implications: This study significantly impacts the financial technology industry in the technology-driven world.

**Corresponding author*: annu.2021.rhu.10@mnnit.ac.in

Deepa Gupta, Mukul Gupta, Rajesh Kumar Dhanaraj, Balamurugan Balusamy and Parth Mukul Gupta (eds.) Computational Intelligence for Autonomous Finance, (65–80) © 2025 Scrivener Publishing LLC

Originality: The current publication is unique because it uses TCCM framework with bibliometric analysis to determine the research gaps that need to be filled in future studies in this field. It also emphasizes how AI affects the Fintech ecosystem.

***Keywords*:** Fintech, artificial intelligence, web of science, scopus, bibliometric

4.1 Introduction

"Artificial intelligence (AI) is a branch of computer science that focuses on creating computer-based systems that function similarly to humans." Over the years, AI has seen a massive acceleration driven by its breakthrough ingredients, such as high computing power, rapid algorithm evolution, and, most importantly, the vast amount of data generated worldwide [45]. AI enables computers to mimic human abilities, such as coordinated physical tasks (robotics) and decision-making (expert systems). AI aims to make valuable decisions based on stored information. To succeed, AI operations require data extracted from social networks and analytics components. Adopting artificial intelligence (AI) in financial technology (FinTech) can significantly benefit decision-makers. For example, in P2P lending platforms for potential customers, AI has been used to automate rapid credit scoring [1]. It speeds up the process of evaluating applicants' creditworthiness. P2P lending is a fast and efficient method for serving unbanked financial inclusion [42]. Conversely, Social Network Site (SNS) data can enhance credit ratings by providing more insight into each potential consumer.

Inclusion of Artificial Intelligence in Fintech

The advent of disruptive technologies such as blockchain, the Internet of Things (IoT), and Artificial Intelligence (AI) has led to the transformation of conventional financial services commonly referred to as "Fintech" [4, 9, 13]. Financial technology applications have become increasingly prevalent within the financial services sector. The impact of artificial intelligence in the financial technology industry is remarkable [17, 19, 29].

Some cases of AI in Fintech are explained in the section below (Figure 4.1).

1. *Robotic Process Automation*

   The challenges of running routine back-end operations are well-known to any FinTech or banking company. These institutions can fully automate and streamline back-end

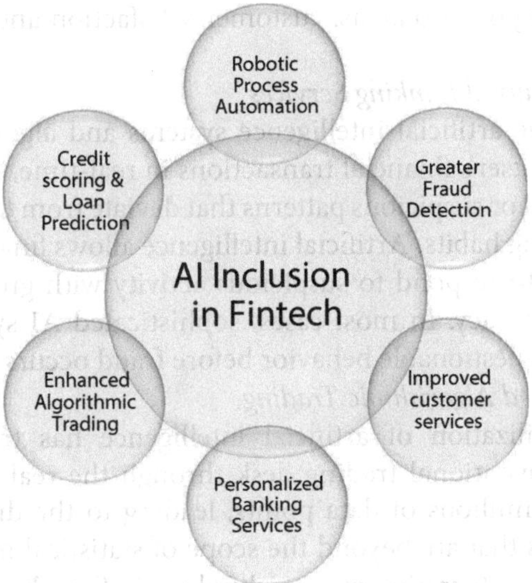

Figure 4.1 AI inclusion in Fintech. Source: Author's illustration.

office processes by using a "smart chatbot." The utilization of RPA software in banking operations can enhance efficiency, speed, and cost-effectiveness, while human agents prioritize the provision of a customer-centric experience.

2. *Greater Fraud Detection*
   Artificial intelligence (AI) systems that are highly effective can facilitate real-time monitoring of financial transactions. By utilizing AI algorithms, anomalies or atypical patterns that diverge from a user's customary spending habits can be identified. Artificial intelligence enables fintech companies to promptly and precisely address potential instances of fraudulent behavior. Advanced artificial intelligence (AI) systems can often identify potentially fraudulent actions prior to their actual occurrence.
3. *Improved Customer Services*
   Artificial intelligence is enhancing customer service in the financial technology sector by means of advanced sentiment analysis. The goal of this strategy is to train chatbots to address previously identified customer service issues by analyzing their interactions with the company. AI-based technology has improved consumer access and communication with fintech. Companies may boost their bottom line by

focusing on two areas: customer satisfaction and employee morale.

4. *Personalized Banking Services*
Effective artificial intelligence systems and algorithms can track a user's financial transactions in real-time, looking for unusual or suspicious patterns that deviate from their typical spending habits. Artificial intelligence allows financial institutions to respond to suspicious activity with greater speed and accuracy. In most cases, sophisticated AI systems can detect questionable behavior before fraud occurs [45, 47].
5. *Enhanced Algorithmic Trading*
The utilization of artificial intelligence has transformed the conventional trading desk through the real-time analysis of millions of data points, leading to the discovery of insights that are beyond the scope of statistical models [31, 37]. The integration of AI technology in fintech has enabled consumers to engage in stock trading through mobile applications that are designed to be user-friendly. Additionally, AI-powered decision-making has been made possible, further enhancing the trading experience.
6. *Credit Scoring & Loan Prediction*
By spotting patterns in historical data, such as customer loan histories, artificial intelligence can assist financial institutions make smarter decisions. Depending on their risk score, clients can be profiled using machine learning algorithms. Credit scoring is therefore regarded as one of the most significant advancements in financial technology [32, 54].

4.1.1 Literature Review

A significant technology in the 2010s, artificial intelligence (AI) is expected to overtake all other technologies in the 2020s [21]. For instance, several businesses have incorporated AI to improve their operations, and a number of multinational companies (such as Facebook, Google, IBM, and Microsoft) have made significant investments in AI to boost productivity [5, 6, 26]. The financial services sector has also significantly benefited from AI applications, particularly when it comes to automating processes [23]. Remarkably, due to the use of AI applications in financial technology (Fintech), the financial services sector has changed [25].

"AI applications are essential for capturing the linear and nonlinear behaviors of financial variables. Mainly, these applications enable us to resolve highly nonlinear issues that conventional models cannot handle." As a result, the banking sector currently extensively uses machine learning (ML) and deep learning techniques. In the meantime, research on ML and deep learning has grown significantly [3, 44, 46, 53]. Authors [22, 27, 38] have attempted to understand the relationship between the financial system and economic development by focusing on India's financial system. This study examines the role of AI applications in various finance-related fields, including bankruptcy prediction, stock price prediction, portfolio management, oil price prediction, anti-money laundering, behavioral finance, and extensive data analysis. According to [53], "there are three major areas of AI and ML research in finance: 1) financial fraud and distress, and valuation; (2) portfolio development and investor behavior; and (3) sentiment inference, forecasting, and planning." After reviewing the literature on the use of AI up to 2009, [3] identified three key areas: 1) credit evaluation, 2) portfolio, 3) financial forecasting and planning, and 4) management. Our research adds to and broadens the work of [3] and [53], including research done up to 2021 in its reviews. Furthermore, we only consider the Scopus and Web of Science journals.

Using a bibliometric approach, we collected the 364 documents published in 2014–2022 from journals indexed in the Web of Science and Scopus databases. Bibliometric analysis is divided into descriptive and network analysis. The study includes co-citation, co-authorship, thematic map, author and institutional collaboration, etc. This study mainly focused on 1) behavioral finance, 2) the involvement of AI in the Fintech industry, and 3) its scope with risk management. As part of the outstanding work on behavioral finance associated with AI and Fintech [5, 10, 24], other notable works include [1, 18, 32] on the impact of AI and Fintech [7, 12] on risk management. The study is divided into sections as follows. *Section 4.2* covers data and methodology, *Section 4.3* presents results and discussion, and *Section 4.4* provides the conclusion.

4.2 Data and Methodology

4.2.1 Data Collection

4.2.1.1 The Source of Data Collection

To accomplish the study's objective, focusing on retention, the conceptual and theoretical framework of artificial intelligence's entrance into the industry of Fintech has been established. With the help of the bibliometric package of Rstudio, the current study analyzes the conceptual aspects of artificial intelligence and the emerging industry Fintech [33, 34, 51–53]. The Scopus and Web of Science databases have been used to collect the data. A minimum contribution of both AI and fintech has been found.

4.2.1.2 Keyword Selection and Refinement Process

The search keywords used "Fintech" and "Artificial Intelligence" in the search box of Scopus and Web of Science, resulting in 328 and 146 papers found, respectively. We finalized 66 documents after refining results from the subject areas, including business, business finance, economics, management, environmental sciences, green sustainable science technology, telecommunications, and social issues from the Web of Science database. Furthermore, by coding in R, 30 duplicate documents were removed, resulting in a final dataset of 364 documents for bibliometric analysis.

The study's data compile various documents elaborated in the various sections. Refer to Figure 4.2, which shows the period of data collection starting in 2014 and ending in 2022. There are 364 comprehensive documents. These documents have been elaborated upon in terms of document types, contents, authors, and author collaboration.

4.3 Results and Discussion

4.3.1 Bibliometric Data Analysis (Descriptive and Network)

The most relevant source, Figure 4.3, indicates which journals are leading in publications related to these emerging areas. The figure shows that high interest has been received in these fields at conferences, and the technical program areas are more engaged.

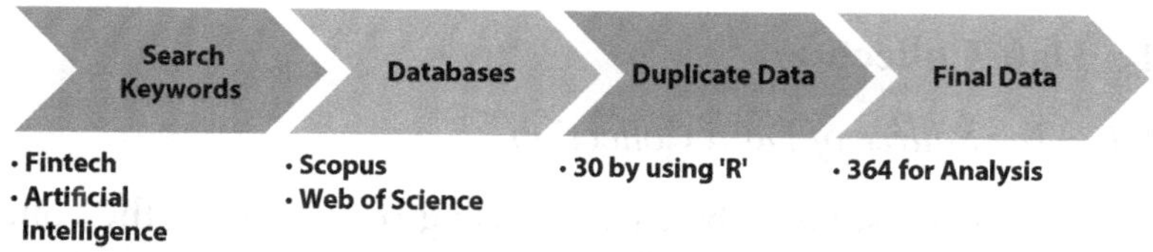

Figure 4.2 Summarization of data. Source: Authors' illustration.

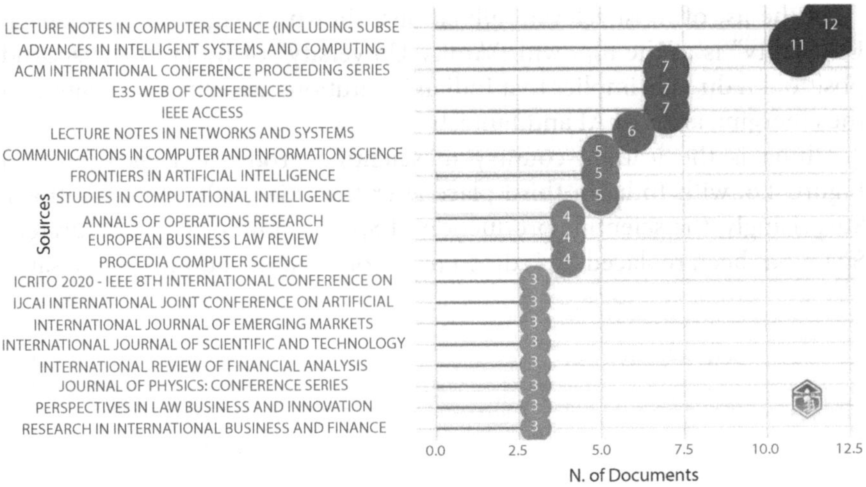

Figure 4.3 Most relevant sources. Source: Biblioshiny output.

In the list of most relevant authors, shown in Figure 4.4, 'Na N' and 'Zhu Z' are at the top. This indicates that their articles are more valuable for studying AI and Fintech and understanding the relationship between these two terms [40, 48]. These authors also strongly associate with clusters, as discussed later in the paper.

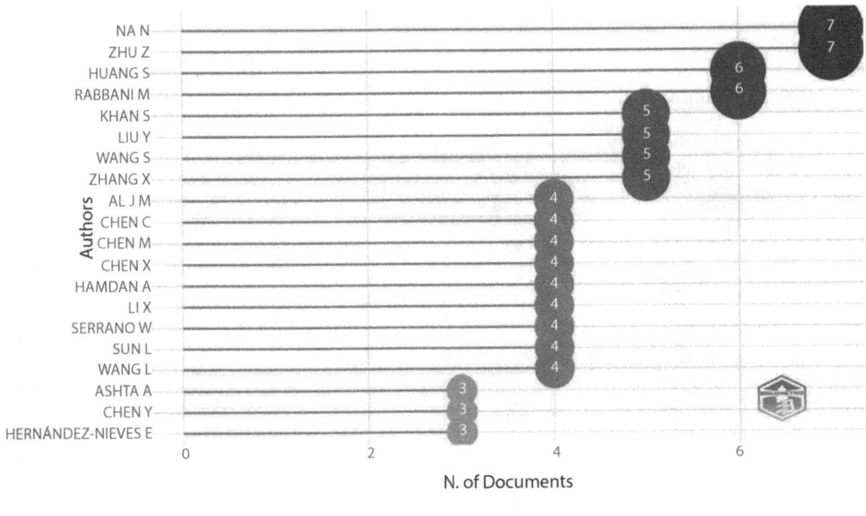

Figure 4.4 Most relevant authors. Source: Biblioshiny output.

In the list of most relevant affiliations, shown in Figure 4.5, "Shenzen University" is at the top, with "Amity University" of India in the second position. It directly implies that Indian institutions are actively engaging in the emerging areas of AI and Fintech.

China is the leading country in scientific production, as shown in Figure 4.6, with India in third place after the USA with 39 publications. Surprisingly, the scientific production of Spain is low, or more accurately, Spain has been replaced by India in terms of scientific output. At the same

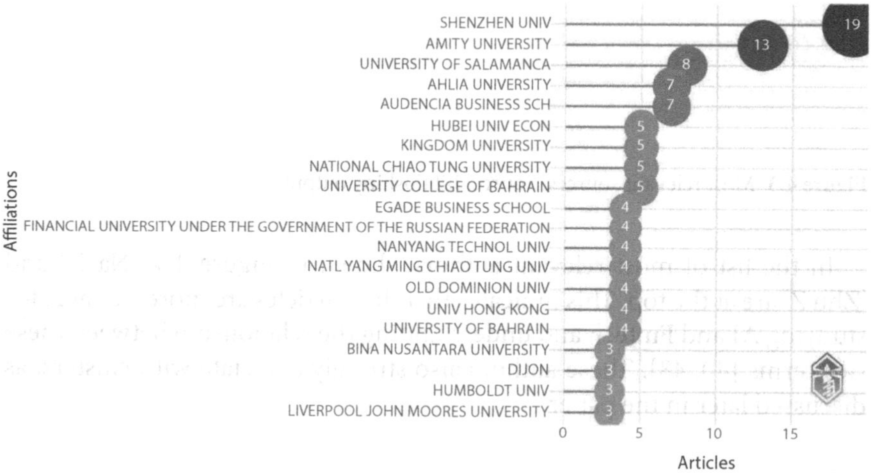

Figure 4.5 Most relevant affiliations. Source: Biblioshiny output.

Country Scientific Production

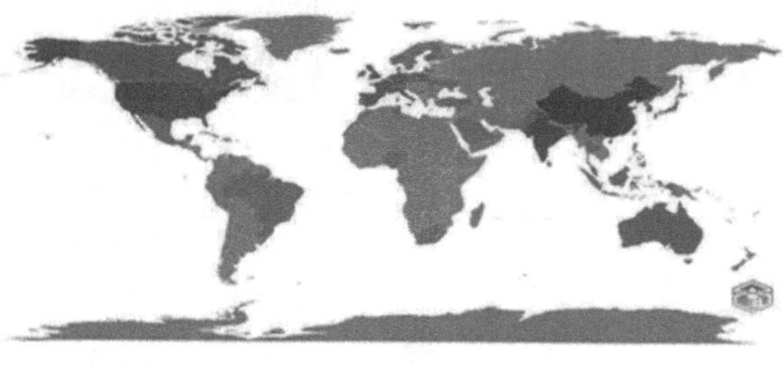

Region	Freq.
CHINA	143
USA	44
INDIA	39
UK	38
MALAYSIA	16
SPAIN	16
GERMANY	15
FRANCE	14
BAHRAIN	11
ITALY	11
SINGAPORE	11
SOUTH KOREA	11
CANADA	9
AUSTRALIA	8
NETHERLANDS	6
INDONESIA	5
POLAND	5
THAILAND	5
FINLAND	4
MEXICO	4

Figure 4.6 Country scientific production. Source: Biblioshiny output.

time, Spain is in the second position on the list of most globally cited countries [35]. Global transition scenarios of finance [18] analyzed China's investment in fossil fuels. [50] distinguished the paper into four views to analyze the impact of the financial and economic crisis on sustainability transitions.

China leads in this area of work. Figure 4.7 indicates the frequency of citations for the most cited countries. India's work has been cited 53 times. However, Spain, the USA, the UK, Finland, and Slovenia are cited more frequently than India.

In the list of most globally cited documents (see Figure 4.8), 'Belanche D 2019. Ind Management data system' has the highest number of citations, with 106 citations, followed by others with their respective citation numbers.

The thematic map (Figure 4.9) section falls under the network analysis division of bibliometric analysis. Nasir *et al.* define the thematic map using four quadrants, each with distinct properties. In the 'Motor theme' quadrant, both density and centrality are high, while the 'Basic theme' exhibits low density and centrality. The 'Che theme' shows high density but low centrality or relevance, whereas the 'Emerging theme' has low density but high relevance in the field. "[14] studied big data in finance, using volume, velocity, and variety as prisms to identify the pros and cons in the fintech industry." The studies of [4, 41] focused on challenges, evidence, and impacts on large-scale firms. The studies of [11, 42] explored the scope

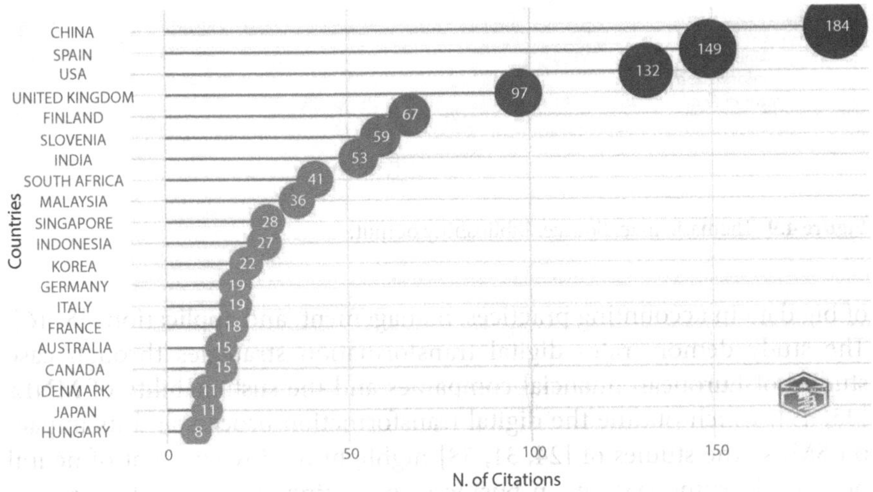

Figure 4.7 Most cited countries. Source: Biblioshiny output.

Figure 4.8 Most global cited documents. Source: Biblioshiny output.

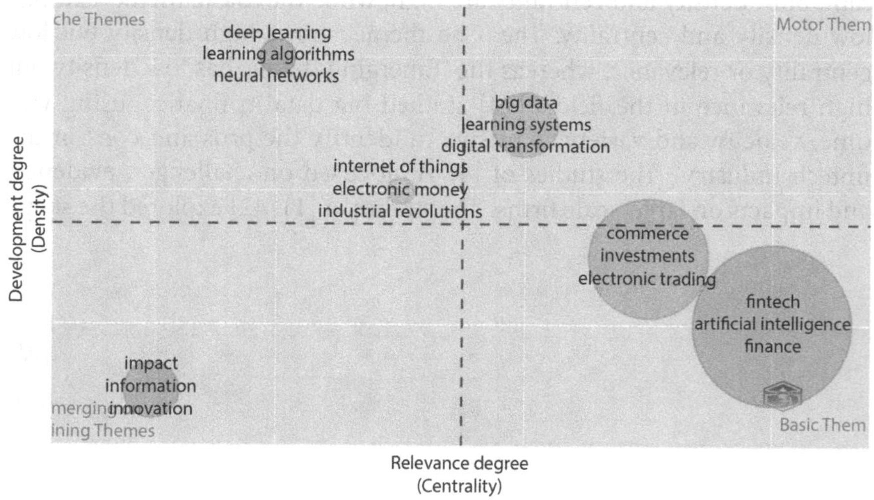

Figure 4.9 Thematic map. Source: Biblioshiny output.

of big data in accounting practices, management, and applications [8, 16]. The study demonstrates digital transformation strategies through case studies of European financial companies and the sustainability of MNEs [43, 49], which outline the digital transformation process and its impact on SMEs. The studies of [24, 31, 38] highlight the involvement of neural network learning systems in business computing and AI applications in e-commerce and finance.

By using a conceptual structure map with multiple corresponding analysis (MCA), Figure 4.10 shows the association of keywords in artificial intelligence and fintech areas through two colors: blue and red. [30] has highlighted financial systems for sustainability. The results are interpreted

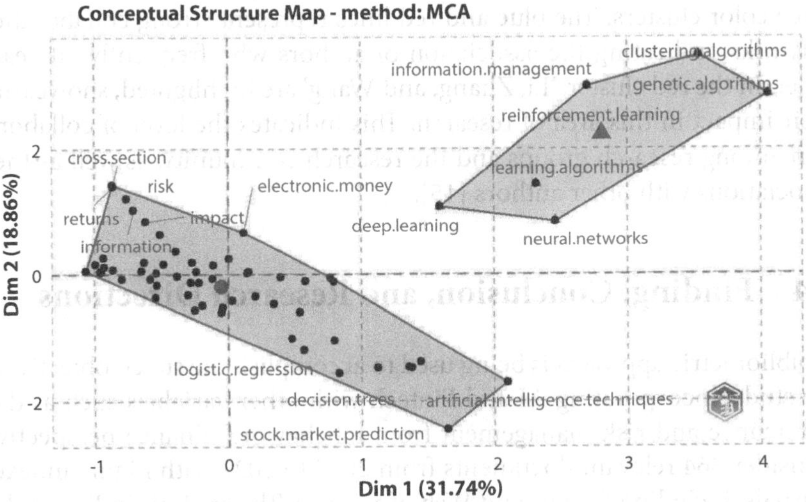

Figure 4.10 Factorial analysis. Source: Biblioshiny output.

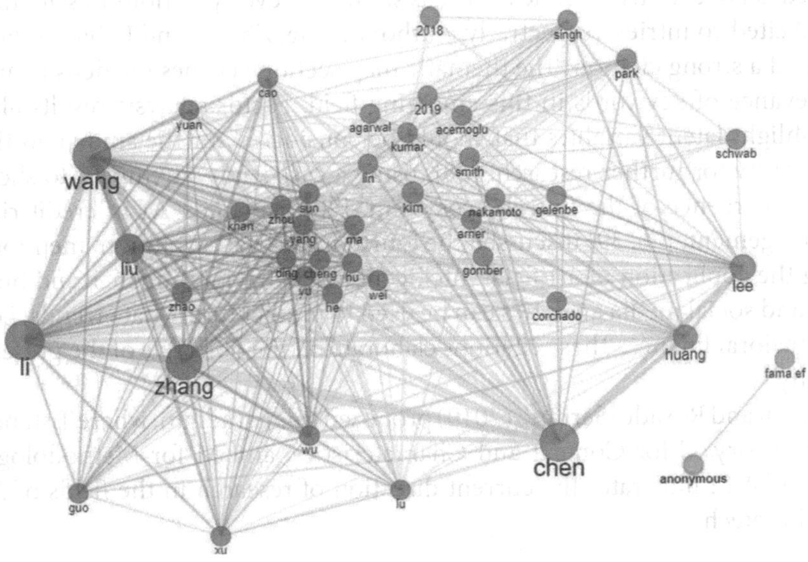

Figure 4.11 Co-citation network (authors). Source: Biblioshiny output.

based on the relative positions of the points and their distribution along the dimensions; words with more similar distributions are closer together on the map [2]. In the red cluster, black dots indicate keywords that are interrelated several times, while in the blue cluster, keywords indicate a need to use these terms with the same relevance in studies.

The co-citation network of authors, shown in Figure 4.11, is divided into three color clusters. The blue and red lines represent strong collaboration networks, indicating the association of authors who frequently cite each other. In the red cluster, 'Li, Zhang, and Wang' are highlighted, showcasing their impact in this area of research. This indicates the level of collaboration among research groups and the research community, as well as their associations with other authors [15].

4.4 Finding, Conclusion, and Research Directions

A bibliometric approach is being used to accomplish the stated objective of the study, incorporating AI and Fintech with other variables such as digital finance and risk management from a behavioral finance perspective. Consider 364 relevant documents from 2014 to 2022 with highly indexed journals, including Scopus and Web of Science. The analysis indicates that the publication trend started in 2017 and has expanded significantly in the past few years. China is leading in scientific production and the most cited list of countries, while India has sixth and seven positions in scientific and cited countries, respectively. Authors Wang, Zhang, and Li have established a strong citation. The thematic map section clarifies the density and relevance of keywords in this emerging field. Factor analysis results also highlight latent variables that should be considered for the study and the necessity for further research. [28], using a case study, attempted to show the emergence of the fintech ecosystem. [20] explained AI in credit risk management. [36, 39] discussed the fourth industrial revolution, mentioning the application of artificial intelligence to behavioral finance and how AI and social media analytics can be used to predict future data trends, i.e., behavioral finance. These citations elaborate on the objective of the present study.

Paul and Rosado-Serrano (2019) proposed this paradigm, where T stands for Theory, C for Context and Characteristics, and M for Methodology. Figure 4.12 illustrates the current direction of research in the fields of AI and Fintech.

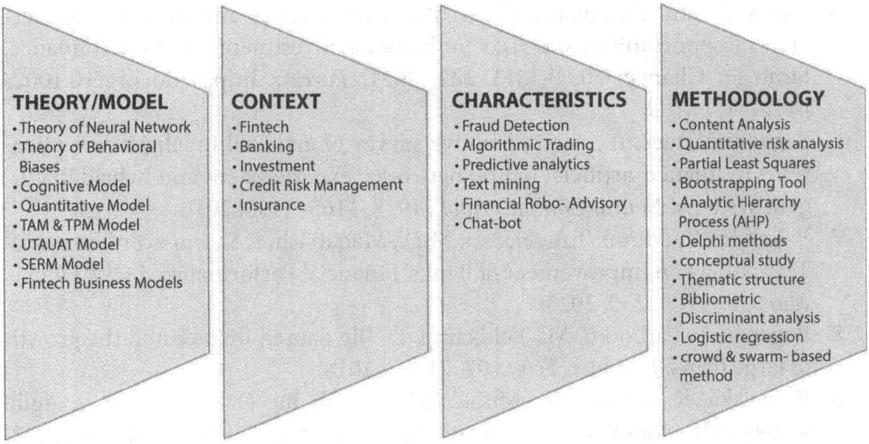

Figure 4.12 TCCM framework. Source: Author's Illustration.

4.5 Summary

The utilization of Artificial Intelligence has become increasingly prevalent in the fintech sector, where it plays a significant role in various areas such as fraud detection, risk management, and augmented customer services. Numerous scholars are conducting research with the aim of enhancing global comprehension. The findings indicate that China holds the greatest influence among all countries. The presence of diverse models and theories for implementation has added an intriguing dimension to the field of research on motivation.

References

1. Ahmed, Z., Ahmad, M., Rjoub, H., Kalugina, O. A., Hussain, N., Economic growth, renewable energy consumption, and ecological footprint: Exploring the role of environmental regulations and democracy in sustainable development. *Sustain. Dev.*, 30, 4, 595–605, 2021, Portico, https://doi.org/10.1002/sd.2251.
2. Anshari, M. *et al.*, Digital marketplace and FinTech to support agriculture sustainability. *Energy Procedia*, 156, 234–238, 2019.
3. Alshater, M.M., Polat, O., El Khoury, R., Yoon, S.-M., Dynamic connectedness among regional FinTech indices in times of turbulences. *Appl. Econ. Lett.*, 1–6, 2022, https://doi.org/10.1080/13504851.2022.2141443.
4. Aria, M. and Cuccurullo, C., bibliometrix: An R-tool for comprehensive science mapping analysis. *J. Informetr.*, 11, 4, 959–975, 2017.

5. Ashta, A. and Herrmann, H., Artificial intelligence and fintech: An overview of opportunities and risks for banking, investments, and microfinance. Strategic Change, 30, 3, 211–222, 2021, *Portico,* https://doi.org/10.1002/jsc.2404.
6. Bahrammirzaee, A., A comparative survey of artificial intelligence applications in finance: artificial neural networks, expert system and hybrid intelligent systems. *Neural Comput. Appl.*, 19, 8, 1165–1195, 2010.
7. Baker, H., Kaddumi, T.A., Nassar, M.D., Muqattash, R.S., Impact of Financial Technology on Improvement of Banks' Financial Performance. *J. Risk Financ. Manage.*, 16, 4, 230, 2023.
8. Begenau, J., Farboodi, M., Veldkamp, L., Big data in finance and the growth of large firms. *J. Monet. Econ.*, 97, 71–87, 2018.
9. Biesialska, K., Franch, X., Muntés-Mulero, V., Big Data analytics in Agile software development: A systematic mapping study. *Inf. Softw. Technol.*, 132, 106448, 2021.
10. Brika, S. K. M, A Bibliometric Analysis of Fintech Trends and Digital Finance. *Front. Environ. Sci.*, 9, 2022, https://doi.org/10.3389/fenvs.2021.796495.
11. Bussmann, N. *et al.*, Explainable AI in fintech risk management. *Front. Artif. Intell.*, 3, 26, 2020.
12. Chanias, S., Myers, M.D., Hess, T., Digital transformation strategy making in pre-digital organizations: The case of a financial services provider. *J. Strateg. Inf. Syst.*, 28, 1, 17–33, 2019.
13. Chartier, E. *et al.*, Behavioral finance: the impact of artificial intelligence and social media analytics. *SSRN Electron. J.*, 2021.
14. Cobo, M.J. *et al.*, Science mapping software tools: Review, analysis, and cooperative study among tools. *J. Am. Soc. Inf. Sci. Technol.*, 62, 7, 1382–1402, 2011.
15. Cockroft, S. and Russel, M., Big Data Opportunities for Accounting and Finance Practice and Research: Big Data in Accounting and Finance. *Aust. Account. Rev.*, 28, 3, 323–333, 2018.
16. Daud, S.N.M., Khalid, A., Azman-Saini, W.N.W., FinTech and financial sta-bility: Threat or opportunity? *Finance Res. Lett.*, 47, 102667, 2022.
17. Doumpos, M., Zopounidis, C., Gounopoulos, D., Platanakis, E., Zhang, W., Operational research and artificial intelligence methods in banking. *Eur. J. Oper. Res.*, 306, 1, 1–16, 2023, https://doi.org/10.1016/j.ejor.2022.04.027.
18. Fang, B. and Zhang, P., Chapter 11: Big data in finance, in: *Big Data Concepts, Theories, and Applications*, 2016.
19. Fatima, S., Kapooor, V., Ansari, A., Relation between Fintech Trends and Digital Finance: A Bibliometric Analysis. *The Adoption of Fintech*, 277–293, 2024, https://doi.org/10.4324/9781032644165-18.
20. Geels, F.W., The impact of the financial–economic crisis on sustainability transitions: Financial investment, governance and public discourse. *Environ. Innov. Soc. Transit.*, 6, 67–95, 2013.

21. George, G. and Schillebeeckx, S.J.D., Digital transformation, sustainability, and purpose in the multinational enterprise. *J. World Bus.*, 57, 3, 101326, 2022.
22. Gosens, J. and Jotzo, F., China's post-COVID-19 stimulus: no green new deal in sight. *Environ. Innov. Soc. Transit.*, 36, 250–254, 2020.
23. Goodell, J.W., Kumar, S., Lim, W.M., Pattnaik, D Artificial intelligence and machine learning in finance: Identifying foundations, themes, and research clusters from bibliometric analysis. *J. Behav. Exp. Finance*, 32, 100577, 2021.
24. Gupta, A. *et al.*, Comprehensive review of text-mining applications in finance. *Financ. Innov.*, 6, 1–25, 2020.
25. Hassan, M.K., Zulfikar, Z., Rabbani, M. R.,Atif, Mohd., Fintech Trends: Industry 4.0, Islamic Fintech, and Its Digital Transformation. *FinTech in Islamic Financial Institutions*, 113–130, 2022, https://doi.org/10.1007/978-3-031-14941-2_6.
26. Joo, B.A. and Durri, K., Comprehensive review of literature on behavioural finance. *Indian J. Commer. Manage. Stud.*, 6, 2, 11–19, 2015.
27. Königstorfer, F. and Thalmann, S., Applications of Artificial Intelligence in commercial banks–A research agenda for behavioral finance. *J. Behav. Exp. Finance*, 27, 100352, 2020.
28. Li, Y. *et al.*, On neural networks and learning systems for business computing. *Neurocomputing*, 275, 1150–1159, 2018.
29. Mamoshina, P. *et al.*, Converging blockchain and next-generation artificial intelligence technologies to decentralize and accelerate biomedical research and healthcare. *Oncotarget*, 9, 5, 5665, 2018.
30. Mhlanga, D., Industry 4.0 in finance: the impact of artificial intelligence (ai) on digital financial inclusion. *Int. J. Financ. Stud.*, 8, 3, 45, 2020.
31. Hadji Misheva, B., Hirsa, A., Osterrieder, J., Kulkarni, O., Fung Lin, S., Explainable AI in Credit Risk Management. *SSRN Electron. J.*, 2021, https://doi.org/10.2139/ssrn.3795322
32. Mushtaq, G., An Analysis of Indian Financial System and Its Effect over Indian Economy. *Indian J. Commer. Manage. Stud.*, 2, 6, 62–67, 2011.
33. Muthukannan, P. *et al.*, The emergence of a fintech ecosystem: A case study of the Vizag Fintech Valley in India. *Inf. Manage.*, 57, 8, 103385, 2020.
34. Mulyani, M.A. *et al.*, Smartphone adoption in mobile learning scenario. *2019 International Conference on Information Management and Technology (ICIMTech)*, vol. 1, IEEE, 2019.
35. Naidoo, C.P., Relating financial systems to sustainability transitions: Challenges, demands and design features. *Environ. Innov. Soc. Transit.*, 36, 270–290, 2020.
36. Pallathadka, H. *et al.*, Applications of artificial intelligence in business management, e-commerce and finance. *Mater. Today Proc.*, 2021.
37. Patel, R., Migliavacca, M., Oriani, M., Blockchain in Banking and Finance: A bibliometric review. *Res. Int. Bus. Finance*, 62, 101718, 2022.

38. Pattnaik, D., Kumar, S., Burton, B., Thirty years of the Australian accounting review: A bibliometric analysis. *Aust. Account. Rev.*, 31, 2, 150–164, 2021.
39. Pattnaik, D., Kumar, S., Vashishtha, A., Research on trade credit–a systematic review and bibliometric analysis. *Qual. Res. Financ. Mark.*, 12, 4, 367–390, 2020.
40. Polzin, F., Sanders, M., Serebriakova, A., Finance in global transition scenarios: Mapping investments by technology into finance needs by source. *Energy Econ.*, 99, 105281, 2021.
41. Vijayakumar Bharathi S., Pramod, D.m Raman, R., Intention to use Artificial Intelligence services in Financial Investment Decisions. *2022 International Conference on Decision Aid Sciences and Applications (DASA), IEEE*, 2022.
42. Sarkar, A. and Goswami, S., Leverage and Financing Decision–An Empirical Analysis. *Indian J. Commer. Manage. Stud.*, 2, 6, 107–113, 2011.
43. Singh, S. *et al.*, Convergence of blockchain and artificial intelligence in IoT network for the sustainable smart city. *Sustain. Cities Soc.*, 63, 102364, 2020.
44. Singh, G., Garg, V., Tiwari, P., Application of Artificial Intelligence on Behavioral Finance, in: *Recent Advances in Intelligent Information Systems and Applied Mathematics, Springer International Publishing*, 2020.
45. Subrahmanyam, A., Big data in finance: Evidence and challenges. *Borsa Istanbul Rev.*, 19, 4, 283–287, 2019.
46. Sun, Y., Shi, Y., Zhang, Z., Finance big data: management, analysis, and applications. *Int. J. Electron. Commer.*, 23, 1, 9–11, 2019.
47. Tan, T. and Phan, T.Q., Social media-driven credit scoring: The predictive value of social structures. *SSRN Electron. J.*, 2018, https://doi.org/10.2139/ssrn.3217885.
48. Ulas, D., Digital transformation process and SMEs. *Procedia Comput. Sci.*, 158, 662–671, 2019.
49. Walczak, S. and Cerpa, N., Heuristic principles for the design of artificial neural networks. *Inf. Software Technol.*, 41, 2, 107–117, 1999.
50. Wong, B.K. and Selvi, Y., Neural network applications in finance: A review and analysis of literature (1990–1996). *Inf. Manage.*, 34, 3, 129–139, 1998, https://doi.org/10.1016/s0378-7206(98)00050-0.
51. Wu, K., Fu, Y., Kong, D., Does the digital transformation of enterprises affect stock price crash risk? *Finance Res. Lett.*, 48, 102888, 2022.
52. Zhang, X.P.S. and Kedmey, D., A budding romance: Finance and AI. *IEEE Multimed.*, 25, 4, 79–83, 2018.
53. Zhu, Z., Sun, L., Yung, K., Fundamental strength strategy: The role of investor sentiment versus limits to arbitrage. *Int. Rev. Financ. Anal.*, 71, 101452, 2020.
54. Zhu, Z. *et al.*, Oil price shocks and stock market anomalies. *Financ. Manage.*, 51, 2, 573–612, 2022.

5

Robotic Process Automation in the Financial Sector

Neha Sonik[1]*, Deepa Gupta[2] and Parul Gupta[3]

[1]*BBK DAV College for Women, Amritsar, Punjab, India*
[2]*GL Bajaj Institute of Management, Greater Noida, UP, India*
[3]*Utica National Insurance Group, New Hartford, New York, USA*

Abstract
This chapter gives readers a broad overview of robotic process automation's potential applications in finance. The market for robotic process automation in the financial industry was estimated to be worth $340.95 million in 2020 and is projected to expand by 30% from 2021 to 2030, reaching $4,883.41 million. This chapter is written with experienced robotic process automation users and all technology enthusiasts in mind. The aim of RPA is to assist users in performing repetitive tasks in the banking industry automatically. In this chapter, we will discuss thoroughly RPA-based banking robots, covering how they can help with operations such as clicking and accessing various programs, sending emails, verifying transactions, and transferring data from one banking system to another. A detailed discussion will be provided on the influence of RPA adoption by banks.

Keywords: Automation, finance, robots, banking, reports

5.1 Introduction

Let us grasp the present situation before we begin with robotic process automation for financial services. In this ever-changing climate, the corporate environment is also constantly altering. The banking sector is under intense pressure to reduce expenses, improve client services, and maintain its market edge. In today's world, consumers demand rapid services, great

**Corresponding author*: Nehasonik2012@gmail.com

Deepa Gupta, Mukul Gupta, Rajesh Kumar Dhanaraj, Balamurugan Balusamy and Parth Mukul Gupta (eds.) Computational Intelligence for Autonomous Finance, (81–100) © 2025 Scrivener Publishing LLC

customization, and better value. Financial institutions can only accomplish their goals by keeping overall costs low and leveraging robotic process automation facilities. This involves bots that simulate daily, repetitive actions followingspecific business rules and are amenable to automation. To meet these demands, a considerable number of financial institutions have adopted robotic process automation.

The primary reason for adopting robotic process automation is the security it provides. Technical developments lead to quick and dependable services, contributing to exponential growth in recent years. To remain competitive, banking companies have had to find and rely on means that provide a great user experience, particularly with virtual banking. According to Gartner, the pandemic has sparked corporate measures to adjust to employee and consumer needs, making digital solutions the future of financial services [12]. Account opening, the KYC procedure, customer care, and many other time-consuming, repetitive activities can all be automated in the banking sector with the help of RPA. With the usage of RPA, banking companies ensure that their overall costs decrease, and processes are carried out on time, further streamlining efficiency. Studies predict that RPA in the banking industry will reach $1.12 billion by 2025. Additionally, the banking sector can automate complex decision-making processes like fraud detection and anti-money laundering by using AI technologies in conjunction with RPA [5].

5.1.1 Robotic Process Automation in Banking

Computerized accounting, also called accounting process automation, is primarily defined by tools like Blue Prism and Uipath, which reduce human labor—an crucial requirement to cut labor costs and handle finance department activities. Accounting robots are tools that can reduce the time and effort needed to move routine data between various systems and perform other activities, rather than being restricted to one function. Sometimes, accounting is considered an alternative to human work, but it is more like a bionic arm that directly helps speed up the processing of work with the assistance of finance professionals.

5.1.2 What is Finance Automation?

Financial automation employs technology to carry out financial operations, requiring less manual labor and leading to more affordable and effective financial procedures. Automating these processes gives staff members more time for complex tasks. This economic transformation aims to digitize as many professions as feasible while maintaining a high degree of quality and speed. It involves setting up several tasks (called workflows) and utilizing technology to initiate predefined processes. As a subset of process automation under the umbrella of machine learning, it is gaining popularity across all industries [9].

Robotic process automation (RPA) is still on the rise, gaining popularity and automating laborious tasks. The RPA market is now worth billions of dollars, indicating that financial automation is no longer a pipe dream but a fully realized reality [9].

RPA in finance helps save significant time and effort, which are undoubtedly the most valuable resources. Everyone from the C-suite to sales needs complete data in an organized and insightful manner, such as diagrams and visual presentations, to help them make timely decisions.

Additionally, crowded BFS industries need help to remain vigilant and competitive in the changing financial automation market. By automating many manual activities using RPA, such software can help reduce significant errors, and improve operational effectiveness by cutting costs, increasing accuracy, and adhering to regulatory requirements [4].

5.2 How are Financial Institutions Making Use of Robotics and Automation?

Financial institutions and insurance organizations are the most notable users of its automated procedures. The prime goal of national and cooperative banks is to improve client satisfaction to compete with virtual banking operations. Keeping their goal in mind, they have chosen to automate their processes to increase efficiency and optimize resources. Banks and other financial institutions may use automation for two significant purposes: installing end-user device software bots and creating an AI workforce [7].

In the financial sector, RPA is a crucial instrument for meeting sector demands and improving efficiency by cutting costs through the services-through-software paradigm. To capture the emerging potential in their sector, financial institutions should adopt a strategic approach. RPA in the financial services industry focuses on mundane administrative tasks, such as copying data from emails into the system. Financial services operations at the presentation layer include data scraping connected with many straightforward tasks that occupy a significant portion of the day [13]. Several US banks and insurance institutions have already adopted information technology techniques, automating around 800 tasks. According to recent research, the finance industry will be valued at $2.9 billion by 2023, a significant rise from $250 million in 2016. This indicates that the industry will continue to develop exponentially [7].

5.2.1 Importance of Banking in Robotic Process Automation

Employees at banks must deal with a lot of consumer data, and wherever data is in written form or manual procedures have been followed to keep such data, it is prone to mistakes on a vast scale. Banking activities are especially susceptible to errors when large amounts of data are manually processed. Furthermore, a single mistake in a technical financial procedure can result in theft, fraud, and money laundering. Simple consumer data validation from two systems can be completed in seconds with the help of bots, compare to minutes by people. Automating these tasks using bots can reduce processing expenses by 30% to 70% [5].

5.3 Major Use Cases of Robotic Process Automation in Banking and Finance

In the BFSI sector, RPA may be used to free up labor for more critical projects. These procedures include, among others:

Consumer Assistance
Daily, the bank deals with numerous inquiries about everything from account information to processing various applications related to account balances. Banks find it challenging to deal with every query quickly. Such rule-based procedures can be automated with the help of robotic process automation to answer every question instantly and reduce the turnaround time from minutes and hours to seconds, freeing personnel for more critical tasks. Artificial intelligence enables RPA to answer questions that require judgment. Chatbot automation uses NLP to allow bots to comprehend the natural language used in client chat and reply according to the system setup [5]. The RPA solution helps the bank automate repetitive activities to respond to real-time customer inquiries efficiently and drastically cut response time.

Banking is the economic hub and is heavily regulated, subject to several compliance requirements. According to 73% of respondents in a 2016 Accenture poll, RPA may be a crucial facilitator of compliance. RPA boosts productivity with round-the-clock accessibility and the highest accuracy level, enhancing the compliance process's effectiveness [6].

Accounts Payable

The procedure for paying bills is straightforward yet tedious in the banking industry. To complete the payment, vendor information needs to be extracted, verified, and processed. Since this does not require intellect, it is the ideal application for RPA [5].

Handling accounts payable manually takes time since staff members must digitize vendor invoices, check all the information, and process the payment. RPA can replace this work in accounting, which has been augmented using OCR. OCR can extract invoice information and send it to machines for payment processing and approval. The system will inform bank workers of any mistakes [1]. This issue can be resolved by adopting OCR technology and RPA. Optical character recognition helps read vendor data from a digital copy presented in physical form and gives the RPA system information. RPA processes the payment after validating the data against the data stored in the system. It has a remarkable ability to alert the executive to any existing errors so they can be resolved [5].

Credit Card Processing

Validating consumer information and approving credit card applications can take weeks if the traditional procedure is followed. In the past, waiting times for credit card applications could last for weeks, making customers unhappy and even leading them to abandon their requests. Long waiting times made consumers unhappy and cost banks money. However, RPA may allow banks to provide credit cards more quickly [6].

In only a few hours, RPA software can compile all client documents, perform extensive criminal record and credit checks, and reach decisions based on previously established standards. RPA has significantly improved the payment card processing process, simplifying life for consumers and banking staff. RPA can interact with multiple systems simultaneously to verify information, such as required documents, criminal record checks, and credit checks, and make decisions on whether to approve or reject an application according to predefined rules. Using a rule-based approach, RPA makes quick decisions on whether to grant or deny the application [5].

Mortgage Loan RPA

Processing a mortgage loan typically takes approximately 50 to 53 days in the United States. Approval involves multiple inspections, including credit checks, repayment histories, job verification, and assessment. A small mistake can cause delays. RPA can expedite the process and eliminate bottlenecks, reducing the processing time from days to minutes by following a specific set of rules and checks.

The House report claims that banks take up to 60 days to process applications related to home dealing. Loan officers must complete numerous procedures, such as checking their credit, verifying current job status, and performing various checks and inspections. Additionally, even a minor mistake by the employee or the applicant can significantly slow down the process. Robotic process automation in the financial industry can reduce the time it takes to handle loans by 80%, providing substantial relief for both banks and customers. Radius Financial Group used RPA to expedite mortgage processing. Before RPA, processing 30 loans would overburden lenders, but now they comfortably handle up to 50 loans with the help of robotic assistants. This setup reduced loan processing costs by 70%. Even during the COVID period, Radius prospered due to intelligent robotic automation. Compared to the Mortgage Bankers Association average, the company's income from loan origination increased by 30%, and its net income was nearly 50% higher than the banking industry average [1].

Many steps in the mortgage lending process can be easily automated with robotic process automation. These steps includes initiating the loan, processing all documents, making financial comparisons, and performing quality control. As a result, loans are authorized more quickly, increasing client satisfaction. Another significant advantage is that RPA in mortgage lending relieves staff from manual tasks, allowing them to concentrate on more valuable activities, thereby increasing productivity [2].

Account Creation

Previously, the account opening procedure was lengthy and time-consuming. However, RPA simplifies and speeds up the process. Robotic process automation improves data quality by systematically removing transcription mistakes between the core banking system and new account requests. Global banks are deploying robots to extract data from input forms feed it into various host apps during the account creation process. RPA reduces labor-intensive and error-prone manual entries, significantly decreasing turnaround time TAT [2].

Detecting Fraud

Financial institutions in the US and Canada spent $31.5 billion on anti-money laundering legal expenses in 2019. Further studies show that highly trained analysts have been hired to gather crime data. Both activities have become automated, enabling fraud prevention experts to concentrate on their primary duties [1].

The primary issue that banks face related to digital technologies is fraud. It is difficult for banks to keep track of every transaction made to commit fraud. On the other hand, RPA monitors the transactions in real-time and alerts users to transaction patterns indicating fraud. By imposing certain restrictions on account processing, fraud can be stopped with the help of RPA [5]. The emergence of modern digital technologies has been time-saving, but it has also increased the number of financial scams. As a result, it has become difficult for banks to review each transaction to detect fraud in real-time [6]. Robotic process automation uses the if–then strategy to identify suspected fraud and flag it for speedy resolution by the department. By using the "if–then" strategy to identify possible fraud, robotic process automation can aid anti-money laundering investigations [1].

Reconciliation of Daily Sales (DSR)

The customer conducts a sizable volume of cash and credit card transactions daily across multiple locations. The management team needs to track these activities to provide real-time financial performance information. POS files from various locations are manually reviewed to generate journal entries. Subsequently, all cash, credit card, and Amex transactions are reconciled against the bank statement to clear the transactions. If any irregularities are discovered, a detailed investigation of the transactions is conducted. The main challenge with this method is its time-consuming nature, especially as transaction volumes increase across sites. The more transactions there are, the longer reconciliation takes. Handling a large volume of transactions also increases the likelihood of errors. Introducing new technology that automates repetitive tasks can address these challenges. It allows bots to extract sales amounts, compare them with the bank statement for each transaction type, and alert users to any discrepancies [7].

Customer Onboarding

A solid relationship with the consumer begins with this. The customer onboarding process can take quite a long time because various papers need to be checked manually. By using optical character recognition technology to extract the data, RPA makes the whole process very simple. The information the customer provides in the form can then be compared with the data in the system. RPA can automate onboarding activities such as KYC or ID verification. After onboarding, if a client emails the support staff with a question, the bots may read the email and forward it to the appropriate department, whether it is for a loan application, account questions, credit card requests, loan processing, or anything else. Refinitiv conducted a poll, showing that the typical onboarding period is 30 days. More than online forms are required if one wishes to automate the procedure. Online forms are still being verified, and the data is still being mapped to another spreadsheet by a person. Using tools like Doc AI, the data from documents is instantly retrieved and sent to the CRM system by the bot. Release the staff from many back-office tasks so they can forge genuine connections with consumers [10].

After the automated matching, if there are no significant variances, the information is loaded into the client management interface. In addition to reducing human errors, RPA automation in client onboarding also helps personnel save a significant amount of time and effort [2].

Know Your Customer

KYC is a procedure that all customers must go through with their banks. Approximately 500 to over 1,000 FTEs are used in this step to perform the essential client checks. According to Thomson Reuters, banks spend more than $384 million annually on compliance with the KYC procedure. Banks can finish the procedure more precisely with less staff and error [5] and without worrying about FTEs. Robotic process automation in banking will reduce mistakes that would otherwise require unpleasant client encounters to address the issues. RPA will thereby quicken the onboarding of new customers and improve the customer experience [1].

Bank Reconciliation (BRS)

Bank reconciliation is the process of comparing cash account balances shown in the financial reports of the firm with the relevant information shown in the bank statement. A bank reconciliation statement aims to identify the variances between financial reports and bank account statements and make corrections in the accounting records if required. To ensure that the company's cash records are correct, BRS must be done periodically for all bank accounts. Otherwise, cash levels might be far lower than anticipated, resulting in rejected checks. On Oracle, the bills are cleared. The BRS method first identifies the common and uncommon assessments in files downloaded from Oracle and bank statements to remove the standard checks in both the Oracle file and the bank statement. The BRS procedure also involves reconciling cash and credit card transactions with the Oracle file and the bank statement. RPA enables the business to quickly save money while adjusting the workload of back-office workers so that saved time can be used to focus on rewarding projects. Banking institutions can even create applications to reconcile automated journal entries, make complex data comparisons, and archive long-term data using RPA technologies [6].

Accounting General Ledger

Banks must maintain a general ledger containing information regarding the financial statements covering revenue, assets, liabilities, and expenditure. The company's stakeholders can view these records, as they are open to the public. Given the amount of specific information in the report, mistakes and errors in such data can have a disastrous impact on the reputation of the banks.

Since these systems cannot interact, banks need to update the data from multiple older systems, check it, and ensure that the general ledger is free of errors before developing the reports. Errors are inevitable with this volume of data from so many different systems. In such a situation, RPA comes to the rescue by combining historical and present data to develop the reports cooperatively. As a result, less time and effort are required to manage the data. Even when the data is not in a similar format, RPA is independent of technology and can combine the data from several legacy systems to present it in the required format. This cuts down on labor-intensive data handling [5].

Automated Reporting

Numerous reporting events, such as monthly closures, reconciliations, and report management, can be automated with the help of financial RPA. Financial institutions must abide by compliance regulations to create reports highlighting performance and challenges and send such notifications to the board of directors to make significant decisions. Such reports contain a considerable amount of data, making them time-consuming. Robotics in finance can rapidly compile data from numerous sources, present it clearly and structured, and provide error-free reports. Societe Generale Bank Brazil simplified a workflow that required six hours of workers' time by integrating RPA for report production into their procedures.

Before collecting the necessary data and submitting the SAR, RPA technology with natural language generation skills can read through lengthy compliance paperwork. The RPA software can be trained for the best results using compliance officers' comments on the sections of each document that most effectively suit every component of the report. This reduces operational costs and expedites the time needed to complete the task [2]. Along with helping employees create reports, RPA in banking can help compliance officers process suspicious activity reports (SAR). Instead of reviewing lengthy paperwork by hand, officers use software that can process natural language. Such a system can gather the needed data and fill out the SAR form [1].

Banks must create reports and provide them to their stakeholders to demonstrate their performance, just like all other publicly traded corporations. The bank must make good decisions, given the report's significance. RPA systems can write reports by automatically populating the given report format, allowing them to do so in the shortest amount of time and with the fewest mistakes [5].

Process for Closing Accounts

The volume of data submitted by users requesting account closure is tremendous. One factor is the bank's failure to comply with the requirements when submitting the necessary documents [2]. Robotic process automation helps banks effortlessly track submitted information by sending automated messages, reminders, and notifications about submitting necessary documents. With the large client base, banks receive account closure requests every month. Robotic process automation makes tracking such accounts simple by providing automatic alerts and scheduling calls for required document submissions. RPA can also help banks close accounts in exceptional instances, such as when customers fail to provide KYC paperwork.

Underwriter Support

The process of determining the risk associated with financial transactions such as bond offerings, bank loans, and insurance policies is known as underwriting. Processing data manually is a laborious and time-consuming operation, requiring a great deal of human effort and efficiency to gather data from various systems, analyze it, and enter it into the system. RPA can automate the underwriting process more effectively. Automated underwriting procedures in banking allow loan-related decisions to be made based on algorithms rather than relying on human judgment. RPA in underwriting mitigates biases in decision-making and reduces the possibility of manual errors and incorrect perceptions of loan risks [5].

Cash Collection and Deposits

Another area that banks and financial organizations frequently need to improve is cash collection and deposits. It is inefficient to gather data from many points of sale and appropriately migrate them to various branches. RPA in banking can handle all records from multiple sources and combine them into a centralized system for easy access and sharing, eliminating the need for people to manage the data records. Additionally, transactions are kept secure, there is no chance of stolen money, and fraud is reported immediately.

Account Opening Procedure

From application and underwriting through money disbursal, account creation takes a lot of time. Banking service desk employees must navigate several stages of the loan origination process, including pre-qualification documents, application processing, underwriting, credit decisions, quality checks, and loan financing initiation. RPA implementation eliminates the need for manual data gathering, reduces errors throughout the process, speeds up loan processing, and ensures compliance with all regulations [5].

5.4 Minding Gaps in Financial Process Automation

Even businesses that have effectively implemented automation may still encounter implementation flaws. When firms address these gaps, which represent missed opportunities, their teams can identify even more exciting advancements.

Automating entire operational cycles, such as procure-to-pay, record-to-report, and order-to-cash, is one of the most common scenarios for digital procedure overhauls in companies today. Automation gaps often occur when specific tasks need to be performed across multiple computer systems. A typical example is manually retyping data from one application to another. Other instances include using cumbersome spreadsheets for data management and manually updating financial data in ledgers. Intelligent deployment of RPA can help fill these gaps [3].

Let us explore a few typical scenarios where further RPA integration could be ideal for accounting and finance.

Automating Supplier Onboarding in Procure to Pay: Clerks often manually handle the onboarding of new suppliers to acquire necessary commodities. Setting up a robot to conduct supplier screening, manage tax data, retrieve credit reports, and more can streamline this process effortlessly.

Portal Requests: Many firms use digital portals for supplier management, but these platforms are often kept separate from core business processes in software silos. Why have workers manually copy and paste information back into the primary software? Use RPA to integrate the portals and establish more efficient workflows.

Comparing Costs: Companies may purchase specific items only when the best prices are available. Use a robot to track price fluctuations across providers and identify the best deals at predetermined intervals [3].

Business Intelligence: Once suppliers are chosen, they often need to adhere to specific requirements. Manually evaluating these credentials can be time-consuming prone to delays. Instead, set up a robot to generate regular reports and streamline this process.

Gaps in Quote-to-Cash Automation

Comparisons of Supplier Prices: Providing clients with accurate estimates is crucial for their satisfaction, but obtaining correct prices can be challenging. Installing a robot to collect this data can save firms from time-sensitive procedures [3].

Order Exception Processing: Robots can automatically conduct price checks for orders with price-hold restrictions.

Reconciliations of Deliveries: To prevent recurring errors, it is essential to cross-check submitted orders with received shipments. Robotic software can compare purchase orders (POs) against shipment receipts and highlight discrepancies [3].

Record-to-Report Automation Gaps

Financial Closure Assistance: Closing sub-ledgers, generating financial reports, and submitting required filings to regulators often involve time-consuming tasks, including data transfers between computer systems and Excel. RPA can streamline this process.

Obtaining Data for Accounting Closure: Each division or department within a corporation maintains separate transaction logs, making reconciliation and consolidation challenging. Deploying a robot with the ERP system can manage this [3].

Data Management: Managing all the financial and performance data a company generates can be daunting. Robots alleviate the workload on staff while providing the C-suite with necessary decision-making information.

Closing these gaps effectively requires more than just recognizing them. Investing in advanced technologies that provide a framework for bridging automation gaps is crucial. Organizations can leverage Kofax RPA to implement intelligent, faster automation effectively. Kofax RPA offers a direct path to reducing error rate, increasing productivity per employee, and achieving measurable benefits when combined with other process improvements like automating account payments. This RPA platform provides comprehensive solutions with both low- and no-code options [3].

5.5 The Key Benefits of Finance Automation

Finance and accounts payable automation offer an excellent opportunity for complete digital transformation in any company.

Boost Operational Effectiveness

One of its most significant benefits is the time savings that financial automation can provide. It creates a leaner supply chain with tighter controls. Digitization reduces time spent on manual tasks such as data entry, bookkeeping, and routine workflows. This allows for more effective time management and greater focus on business growth. Teams can think strategically and transform raw data into actionable insights [9].

Reduce Errors

Human errors in data entry can have significant financial implications, especially if errors are only discovered after entries are already incorrect. The same applies to instances where AP overlooks a bill or leaves it unattended on someone's desk for approval. Such costly mistakes are minimized with digitalized operations. Robots ensure meticulous attention to payment details. Established workflows ensure tasks are consistently completed according to protocol, even when personnel are away from the office [9].

Ensure Uniformity

When multiple people are involved in a business task, it tends to be completed differently each time. Despite existing standards, individuals have their own ways of accomplishing tasks. Finance automation ensures consistency at every step of the process. Computers perform tasks exactly the same way every time, minimizing time-consuming variations due to different strategies and perspectives. Standard procedures ensure consistent delivery of shared services across all departments, tasks, teams, and clients [3].

Team Empowerment

The company's finance team should be more than just a group of data crunchers. By eliminating tedious tasks, every employee can add value. Finance talent extends far beyond manual data entry. Automation enables teams to think strategically and derive valuable insights from raw data due. Financial industry executives can now:

- Identify and challenge business strategies.
- Offer practical solutions.
- Build business relationships.
- Continuously monitor reporting, accounting, and controllership.

With more time available, teams can focus on strategic initiatives and career advancement within the organization. This fosters a content and productive financial staff [9].

Extract Insights

Financial automation guarantees more accurate reporting and provides in-depth, valuable insights. Eliminating manual data entry typically results in more accurate information. Today's intelligent financial solutions integrate various applications and consolidate data into a single location. This simplifies data sourcing and allows more time for analyzing information rather than collecting it. Transforming comprehensive information into revolutionary action plans may require the expertise of an accounting professional. The time saved by financial automation enables personnel to utilize data more strategically [9].

Challenges

The Influence of AI and Automation

While certain accounting operations are mechanized, most accounting duties, such as collecting receipts and translating invoices into financial statements, are now automated with advancements in artificial intelligence and virtual technology. Automated systems in accounting and finance can save up to 25,000 hours labor hours, significantly boosting productivity. While this is beneficial for banks and companies, it also poses risk to the jobs of accountants. Automation often undermines employee morale, as it is commonly misunderstood. The concern that "robots are taking our jobs" is legitimate. Employee communications should focus on emphasizing higher-level work to alleviate fears of job loss.

Reporting

Poor implementation of RPA in financial processes can result in inaccurate reports, comments, and reputational damage. To prevent these issues, it is crucial for a company to ensure that automation is properly set up from the onset [9].

Operations

Improperly planned automation systems can slow down operations and increase processing errors. Inadequate system management or monitoring will lead to operational deficiencies. Successful automation implementation requires careful change management, strong internal controls, ongoing monitoring, and robust bots. With proper planning, RPA can have a positive impact [9].

Need for Online Accounting Services

Since the onset of the pandemic, many businesses have transitioned to offering virtual accounting services. These accounting firms now face the challenge of effectively conducting client meetings remotely, as many companies have shifted to remote or hybrid work arrangements. Meanwhile, traditional firms that have yet to modernize and digitize their practices are at a disadvantage compared to online accounting service providers.

Competition

There is intense competition in the finance industry, with customers preferring personalized one-on-one sessions and demanding more user-friendly digital solutions. Organizations that implement these initiatives effectively stand to gain significant market share. Customer loyalty and brand identity have become less critical if their needs are met. Existing customers are likely to continue patronizing establishments that meet these expectations.

Arrangement of Big Data

Big data presents both opportunities and challenges for companies in the financial services sector. With an increasing volume of data generated from diverse sources, the complexities of big data continues to grow. Traditional information structures struggle to handle the vast and varied nature of this data, which includes both organized and unstructured information [11].

5.6 A List of Accounting and Financial Services Companies That are Using RPA

International insurer Zurich has streamlined up to 40% of its commercial underwriting process through its application. This enhancement has enabled them to focus on high-value tasks and allocate more time to complex policies. Zurich reported achieving a 50% cost reduction through its pilot program, prompting broader deployment and earning recognition for its achievements.

The installation has significantly benefited a large multinational insurer with global operations across various industries. Previously, the insurer had to manually check 26 websites and conduct repeated searches multiple times each month to verify claims payments. Since implementation, this previously 4-day process now takes only 2 h, saving thousands of FTE hours annually and reducing errors.

OCBC has reduced the time it takes to re-price home loans from 45 min to just 1 min using automation. Additionally, the bot verifies customer eligibility, suggests loan re-pricing options, and can create a recommendation email for clients. Japanese financial organization Sumitomo Mitsui saved 400,000 labor hours by automating its operations.

Trade Finance: Blue Prism provides banks with access to a digital workforce that conducts matching and validation before delivering finished products to the institution's document management systems [8].
Trade Settlement: BNY Mellon uses RPA to autonomously settle trades and validate proper allocation, a task that was previously carried out manually and was time-consuming.
Reporting: EnableSoft's user-friendly Foxtrot software allows banks to automate labor-intensive reporting processes. Employees who can perform these tasks manually can train Foxtrot using drag-and-drop tools [8].
Reconciliation of Credit Cards: Evention's RPA technology handles credit card reconciliation, combining data from multiple systems to verify the accuracy of inputs from credit card processors, general ledgers, and point-of-sale systems regarding revenue.
Fraud Detection and Prevention: Paypal, the industry leader in online auctions, uses RPA, AI, and machine learning to identify suspicious behavior and distinguish between genuine and false alarms, enhancing fraud detection and prevention.
Regulatory Compliance: UiPath features a central log that saves and tracks robot operations, making information easily accessible for audits and regularly updated for regulatory changes [8]. RPA minimizes monotonous compliance tasks, freeing human workers for tasks requiring reasoning and judgment.
Customer Service: USAA uses artificial intelligence and virtual assistants to improve customer service, offering a more authentic experience for its customers. The company refers to this ability to understand behavior and preferences as "digital empathy."
Financial Planning: Pegasystems (Pega) combines robotic technology with artificial intelligence to automate and customize interactions in wealth management. This approach aims to develop a more intelligent, successful, and forward-thinking business strategy.
Mortgage Processing: CSI's Intelligent AI Process Automation software provides real estate professionals with instant document access, automated data entry, and round-the-clock processing. This innovation increases office productivity, reduces personnel expenses, and improves data quality [8].

5.7 Steps to Deploy RPA in Banking and Finance

Ensuring that the accounting procedure is worthwhile involves several steps:

(1) List Existing Procedures.
Determine automation priorities. Choose which tasks to automate first, considering factors such as:

- Repetitive and regular tasks performed by employees.
- Tasks requiring minimal human contact or personal interaction.
- Tasks that do not require extensive thought or creativity.

List all tasks that fit these criteria and prioritize them. Avoid trying to automate all processes simultaneously.

For instance, if the team takes too long to send reminders for past-due tasks, focus on automating notifications to eliminate the need for manual work.

(2) Reviewing the Current Setup.
Consider the systems currently in place at the company. Automation depends on modern technology and cooperative software. Recently, specialized platforms for automation have appeared on the market to link all systems before automating. Zapier, Kissflow, and Integrify are three systems that will connect existing programs and allow them to "talk" to one another.

(3) Choose a Stakeholder.
Even if an automated process will operate independently, it is wise to designate a person or group to manage workflows and optimize processes. Have a "point person" supervise the procedure to ensure everything is going as planned and rectify any mistakes as they arise [9].

(4) Establish Workflows.
Setting up workflows is essential during the automation process since they will guide the technology's future direction. Each workflow should include:

> **Trigger:** The initial event that starts the automation. For example, a document that needs approval, an overdue payment, or a received invoice. This might trigger an SMS, send a reminder email, etc.

Result: The trigger's primary objective. For example, the client pays their bill by clicking the link in the email reminder. This process is straightforward. In some automated workflows, there may be numerous triggers and resulting actions. It depends on the intentions and the objective one hope to achieve.

(5) Examine the Workflows.
Once everything is set up, test the processes to ensure they function correctly. When the finance staff moves away from the robots to concentrate on other important jobs, this will provide them with additional peace of mind. Identifying precise and practical procedures is often the first step in implementing the RPA solution in banking. Banks and financial organizations must narrow down the techniques used by evaluating them according to their total impact. Here, we have defined the critical phases for implementing RPA successfully.

(6) Complete Assessment.
To identify the appropriate processes for RPA deployment, it is essential to undertake a comprehensive examination and exhaustive analysis. Make a list of the significant operational issues that RPA can target and fix, then evaluate the impact and viability of each subject [2].

(7) Construct a Business (Use) Case.
Calculate the cost savings and efficiency improvements that the installation of RPA will bring to the firm in the next stage. Make a quick comparison of the advantages of RPA based on many parameters, including time, efficiency, resource usage, and effort. Set attainable and practical goals for cost reductions and ROI (return on investment) to minimize disappointments brought on by unrealistic expectations [2].

(8) Prepare a Thorough Execution Plan.
Choose appropriate operational model and personnel to manage the execution based on the unique organizational demands. At this point, selecting the best partner for a full-stack RPA deployment is vital, including planning, execution, and support. Remember that not all RPA suppliers can satisfy an organization's particular needs. Selecting the right RPA technology and execution partner can significantly influence the project's outcomes [2].

5.8 Conclusion

RPA has a promising future in banking and finance. Since its debut in the commercial sector, robotic process automation has come a long way. Today, it is a crucial component of a larger automation plan. Several banks and financial institutions are already using RPA in their operations since it is quicker and simpler to execute than large-scale transformations because it serves as an impulsive and point-based solution. By automating tedious, repetitive, and time-consuming operations, RPA services have the potential to fundamentally alter the banking industry. Automating such routine processes would improve productivity, significantly lower mistake rate, and achieve remarkable turnaround times.

Nevertheless, partnering with an experienced with RPA tools and technologies provider is crucial throughout the deployment process. This not only provides significant advantages to banks and other financial organizations, but also guides them when and how to transition from RPA to other cutting-edge tools like artificial intelligence (AI), cognitive process automation (CPA), and beyond. Configured and deployed correctly, RPA and similar technologies can result in substantial time and cost savings for companies. As the digital landscape grows more complex, more sophisticated tools and an integrated approach are necessary. Without this, organizations may resort to fragmented and unsuccessful solutions. An integrated strategy, grounded in intelligent automation principles, not only leverages RPA where beneficial but also incorporates other essential technologies like AI, machine learning, OCR, and more.

References

1. Alkhaldi, N., RPA in Finance and Banking: Use Cases and Expert Advice on Implementation, ITRex, *How to implement RPA in finance and banking*, 1, 1–11, Sept. 4, 2022, itrexgroup.com/blog/rpa-in-finance-banking-use-cases-implementation-expert-advice/, Accessed 17 May 2023.
2. Ariwala, P., 8 Benefits of Implementing RPA in Banking and Finance, Maruti Techlabs, 1, 4–8, Oct. 4, 2019, marutitech.com/rpa-in-banking-and-finance/, Accessed 17 May 2023.
3. Aslani, O., RPA in Accounting and Finance: 20 Innovative Use Cases. *RPA in Accounting and Finance*, 4, 7–8, June 15, 2020, Www.kofax.com, www.kofax.com/learn/blog/12-innovative-use-cases-rpa-finance-accounting, Accessed 25 May 2023.

4. Infosys, How RPA Helps Finance Industry | Infosys BPM. *Robotic Process Automation*, 1, 2–4, 2022, Www.infosysbpm.comwww.infosysbpm.com/blogs/finance-accounting/the-strategic-role-of-rpa-in-finance.html#:~:text=RPA%20can%20keep%20accounts%20receivables, Accessed 25 May 2023.
5. Jameson, Robotic Process Automation (RPA) in Banking Industry, AutomationEdge, 2, 5–7, Jan. 4, 2023, automationedge.com/blogs/robotic-process-automation-rpa-in-banking-industry/#:~:text=RPA%20can%20talk%20to%20multiple, Accessed 17 May 2023.
6. Janeja, H., 10 Benefits of Implementing RPA in Banking-Data Semantics, 1, 8–10, Sept. 28, 2021, DataSemantics.com data semantics.co/10-important-banking-processes-to-automate-with-rpa-in-2021/, Accessed 25 May 2023.
7. Kaur, J., Robotic Process Automation (RPA) for Financial Services, 2, 14–16, May 9AD. www.xenonstack.com www.xenonstack.com/blog/rpa-for-financial-services, Accessed 17 May 2023.
8. Thomas, M., 11 Robotics Applications in Banking and Finance, Built In, 1, 4-5, Apr. 1, 2019, builtin.com/robotics/robo-banking-robotics-applications-banking-and-finance, Accessed 25 May 2023.
9. Tipalti, *Guide to Finance Automation in 2023*, Tipalti, California, USA, July 18, 2022, Tipalti.com, tipalti.com/finance-automation-guide/#:~:text=Financial%20automation%20is%20the%20process, Accessed 25 May 2023.
10. Vuram, ▹ RPA in Banking Industry : How It Works, the Impacts & Use Cases. *Vuram*, 1, 7–8, 2022, www.vuram.com/blog/whats-the-impact-of-robotic-process-automation-in-banking/, Accessed 25 May 2023.
11. Rajvanshi, P.R., Singh, T., Gupta, D., Gupta, M., Cybersecurity and Data Privacy in the Insurance Market, in: *Big Data Analytics in the Insurance Market (Emerald Studies in Finance, Insurance, and Risk Management)*, K. Sood, B. Balusamy, S. Grima, P. Marano (Eds.), pp. 1–20, Emerald Publishing Limited, Bingley, 2022, https://doi.org/10.1108/978-1-80262-637-720221001.
12. Kumar, A., Gupta, D., Gupta, M., Srivastava, G., India an Emerging Leader after Pandemic: A Strategy for the Development of new India. *Global J. Enterp. Inf. Syst.*, 13, 1, 60–70, 2021, Retrieved from https://www.gjeis.com/index.php/GJEIS/article/view/629.
13. Singh, S., Gupta, D., Gupta, M., Optimized Task Allocation Technique using Mathematical Fuzzy Logic in heterogeneous Distributed Computational System. *2022 International Conference on Computational Intelligence and Sustainable Engineering Solutions (CISES)*, Greater Noida, India, pp. 37–45, 2022, doi: 10.1109/CISES54857.2022.9844410.

6

Integration of Fintech with Data Science (DS) and Artificial Intelligence (AI): A Challenging Footstep

Ankur Goel[1]*, Monisha Awasthi[2], Anamika Rana[3] and Sushma Malik[4]

[1]*Meerut Institute of Technology, Meerut, India*
[2]*Uttaranchal School of Computing Sciences, Uttaranchal University, Dehradun, India*
[3]*Maharaja Surajmal Institute, New Delhi, India*
[4]*Institute of Innovation in Technology & Management, New Delhi, India*

Abstract

Financial Technology or simply a 'Fintech,' is a buzzword today within financial institutions and the overall financial industry. Traditional financial services have significantly changed due to innovation and technology. Today, technology appears to be a crucial factor in the expansion of the digital economy. With the growth of the market and advancements in technology, Indian financial service providers have also actively embraced technology over time to improve client reach, service delivery, and operational efficiency. However, financial technology usage is still lagging below its potential and facing numerous challenges. The aim of this study is to obtain an understanding of 'Fintech,' its various applications in financial industry, the integration of data science and AI with Fintech, and to explore the use cases of data science in Fintech. This study is based entirely on conceptual and narrative search of literature through peer-reviewed journals, articles, and other literature. It discovered that Fintech is still in a nascent stage in the Indian financial market. Although the integration of DS and AI is making it more accessible and acceptable, numerous challenges remain for overall implementation. This study is highly significant from a future perspective, as 'Fintech' is poised to be one of the most leveraging, disruptive, and revolutionizing technologies in the coming era.

Keywords: Artificial intelligence (AI), block chain, data science (DS), Fintech, financial institution, banking

**Corresponding author*: mrankurgoel@gmail.com

Deepa Gupta, Mukul Gupta, Rajesh Kumar Dhanaraj, Balamurugan Balusamy and Parth Mukul Gupta (eds.) Computational Intelligence for Autonomous Finance, (101–122) © 2025 Scrivener Publishing LLC

6.1 Introduction

Fintech (Financial Technology) is "disruptive," "revolutionary," and equipped with "digital weapons" that will "tear down" walls and conventional financial institutions. Fintech, according to [4], is the application of technology to the financial sector that results in new products, services, technologies, and business models. It has the potential to affect monetary stability, the stability of the financial sector, and the effectiveness, smoothness, safety, and dependability of the payment system. Fintech has the potential to undermine stability and endanger conventional institutions. In other contexts, Fintech refers to technologically produced innovations in financial services or products [6]. Changing consumer expectations are a result of technical improvements, extensive global acceptance of mobile and internet, and their widespread use. Financial services are experiencing significant changes due to the proliferation of businesses and startups using Fintech-related products [28]. Since the Fintech sector is still developing, new goods and services are continually being created [2]. The phrase "Fintech" has been coined to describe the financial industry's digitalization. Fintech is a tool utilized in the financial sector that is primarily internet-based. It encompasses all financial products and services previously provided by the financial industry, but it is not limited to any particular industries, such as the banking sector, or specific business theories, such as peer-to-peer (P2P) financing [2]. This technology needs more study and deep investigation to understand it thoroughly in all aspects. It requires more fundamental and literature-based review to explore the deep roots of Fintech to make it overall fruitful. The objectives of this study are to obtain an understanding of 'Fintech' with its historical background, its various applications in the financial industry, the integration of data science and AI with Fintech, and to explore the use cases of data science in Fintech. This study is based entirely on conceptual and narrative search of literature through peer-reviewed journals, articles, and other literature.

6.2 Historical Background of Fintech

Figure 6.1 shows the historical development of Fintech 1.0 to Fintech 4.0.

6.2.1 Fintech 1.0

The first wave of Fintech occurred between 1866 and 1967, marking the beginning of the connection between money and technology. Early

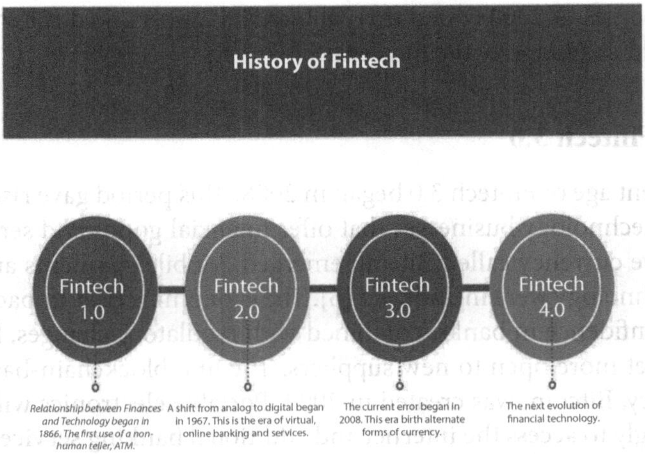

Figure 6.1 History of Fintech [3].

innovations like the telegraph, railroads, and steamboats made it possible to conduct business internationally. The infrastructure needed to support globalized financial services was being built. The first transatlantic cable was completed in 1866, and Fedwire was established in the USA in 1918. Although straightforward by modern standards, the ability to conduct financial transactions over long distances was revolutionary at the time, as transportation and infrastructure were developing rapidly [5].

6.2.2 Fintech 2.0

The period covered under Fintech 2.0 is 1967 to 2008, during which technology transitioned from analog to digital. Virtual and online banking started to provide a higher level of convenience. Real-time trading data viewing and electronic securities trading were developed during this time. The block chain model was crucially developed by a team of programmers [3]. In 1967, Barclays installed first ATM, transforming the financial system to digital. Both NASDAQ and SWIFT, which allowed for a substantial number of inter-border payments, were developed during this period. The development of bank mainframe computers also occurred during this time, continuing throughout the 1980s. Consumer process changed as online banking grew throughout the 1980s. The rise of the internet changed how people viewed financial institutions. Beginning in the 1990s, connected consumers began to manage their money in various ways, marking the transition to digital banking [5]. The economy appeared to be performing well, and the "end of boom and bust" was declared. However, the world financial crisis of 2008 ended this Fintech era and sparked the innovation that would characterize the next era.

6.2.3 Fintech 3.0

The present age of Fintech 3.0 began in 2008. This period gave rise to start-ups and technology businesses that offer financial goods and services. An alternative currency called Bitcoin emerged. Mobile payments and blockchain technology were introduced [6]. The economic crisis' impact on consumer confidence in banks, combined with regulatory changes, has made the market more open to new suppliers. The first blockchain-based cryptocurrency, Bitcoin, was created in 2009. Portable electronics will be used increasingly to access the internet and additional banking services as more people use smartphones. Customers' and investors' insatiable hunger for novel, cutting-edge products and services has ushered in the start-up age. The distinguishing characteristic of Fintech 3.0 has been the move away from the conventional banks of Fintech 2.0. Even well-known companies are starting to operate and present themselves in a startup-like manner. New technology has made it easier to create electronic banking services utilizing Open Banking, which gives outside companies access to financial data [7]. The development of "neo-banks"—digital banks that have emerged with an emphasis on enhancing the client experience—has been significant.

6.2.4 Fintech 4.0

Fintech 4.0 has emerged to change bankers' behavior and improve internet accessibility in the developing world. The countries that use fintech the most, China and India, are the furthest along in this development. Because they are not constrained by the physical banking infrastructure of the West, these countries have been able to adopt innovative concepts more quickly than their Western counterparts. Fintech 4.0 acknowledges global achievements in digital banking and signals a departure from the Western-dominated financial system [6].

6.3 Advantages of Fintech

It is obvious that the Fintech industry is always evolving. The aforementioned types are expected to grow or even change entirely in the upcoming years. For the time being, various Fintech types can be grouped according to the services they provide [11]. In a variety of ways, financial technology (Fintech) is changing the financial sector and how it operates. Some applications are:

6.3.1 Block Chain and Crypto Currency

Due to the presence of smart contracts, proof-of-work, peer-to-peer transactions, blockchain-powered trading platforms, decentralized ledgers, and immutable records, Fintech and blockchain are ideal examples of how Fintech is influencing the speed of services [11]. Thanks to blockchain technology, financial transactions may now be monitored more covertly, securely, and transparently throughout their entire lifecycle. The decentralized and distributed nature of cryptocurrencies, enabled by blockchain technology, enhances their popularity and users' trust in them [12]. The development of blockchain technology is still in its infancy, and new directions are being investigated through ongoing research. Many different platforms use blockchain technology, including Ethereum, Bitcoin, Chain, Bloq, and Wirex.

6.3.2 Insurance (InsurTech)

The development of high-value insurance products by the insurance sector is a response to the expansion of digital financial ecosystems and the desire to improve the client experience. Insurance companies are combining smartphone apps, drones, IoT, AI, Big Data, ML, and other technologies to better serve their customers and other users of their services. Insurtech, which offers advantages such online marketplaces, simpler and more specialized techniques, personalized profiting, and many more, is rapidly changing how customers view insurance products. The insurance industry has been able to grow and quickly develop thanks to the deployment of technical expertise in areas where traditional methods of production would seem tedious [12].

6.3.3 Regulatory (RegTech)

In 2015, the Financial Conduct Authority described RegTech as "a subset of FinTech that focuses on technology that may support the delivery of regulatory obligations more efficiently and effectively than existing capabilities." RegTech refers to the application of cutting-edge technology to enhance compliance and adopt straightforward, secure, and economical laws. New legal frameworks are required to keep up with the developments in a world where finance is increasingly dominated by various technologies. RegTech is generally used to promote and advance visible regulatory processes, automating the complete compliance system. Regulation reporting, risk management, transaction tracking, and adherence are just a few situations where Regtech is being used to provide regulatory solutions [13].

6.3.4 Lending (LendTech)

This domain uses technical expertise to provide clients with financial solutions through more rapid and accurate systems. Artificial intelligence and machine learning approaches are used by intelligent systems that verify and authenticate identify credentials to generate error-free outcomes [1]. When technology is employed in loan processing, it can quickly predict income projections, analyze credit history, calculate the value of collateral, and anticipate changes.

6.3.5 Payments (PayTech)

FinTech is revolutionizing the payments domain through the creation and fusion of digital applications and various networks. Customers are being provided with wearable technologies and smart devices to increase digital connectivity and safeguard user identity. Asset management and digital transactions are made secure and simple by payment technology (PayTech). PayTech is used by a number of payment platforms, including PayPal and GPay [2].

6.3.6 Mobile Payments

Mobile payments and wallets are used almost everywhere for all types of monetary transactions. Without widely available mobile payment options, the majority of transactions would be challenging to commence and complete due to the restrictions imposed by conventional methods [8]. Customers all throughout the world utilize digital wallets like Apple Pay and Google Wallet. While being safe and easy to use, these systems enhance the overall consumer experience [9].

6.3.7 Trading (TradeTech)

Trade technology (TradeTech), in its most basic definition, is the use of IT to decrease the costs of global trade, enhance trade financing, and increase visibility in trading procedures for both businesses and consumers. Global cooperation is required for it to reach its full support and benefits.

TradeTech uses IT platforms for SCM (Supply Chain Management) of finance and asset logistics to support and facilitate global trade [9].

6.3.8 Robo-Advising and Stock-Trading Apps

Apps for stock trading and robot-advising use technology to create and provide customers with diversified investment portfolios, eliminating the need for an investing expert or consultant. Robo-advisors was created for beginning investors to help with risk control and expert investment management. Stock trading programs make buying and selling stock assets simpler and more effective than using conventional methods. Any online broker with the necessary capabilities uses these stock trading programs to trade investments and assets. An example of an investment and stock trading app in the US is Finch Money [10].

6.3.9 Personal Finance (WealthTech)

This area of FinTech, known as WealthTech, focuses on enhancing wealth management and retail investing services by utilizing technology to supplement and deliver operations in a more effective and automated manner. These online processes are applied to generate new ones, improve existing ones, and make them accessible to new investor groups. A personal finance app for Egypt is called Monie [11]. WealthTech streamlines the investing process, making it easier for investors to manage their investment portfolios. By using the latest investment techniques and retirement technologies, WealthTech is being introduced into the financial sector [14].

6.3.10 International Money Transfers

Integrating technology into payment gateways has eliminated onstacles to enable cross-border money transactions. Traditional payment methods are less efficient and effective in this Fintech space because newer, more efficient payment methods are now available, streamlining, securing, accelerating, and simplifying the entire process for customers and companies [11].

6.3.11 Equity Financing

Selling stock is one way to raise money or capital. The money obtained is then used to expand existing businesses or launch new ones. By using technology, crowdfunding can reach a broader group of potential investors

[12]. Prizes are offered to participants on crowdsourcing websites like Kickstarter, Pebble, and many more [12].

6.3.12 Accounting

Automation and transparency in accounting are being improved through technological breakthroughs such as ML, AI, IoT, digital tax platforms, and others. With the advent of software packages, technology has improved data access and analysis in this sector of finance. With the advancement of Fintech, less time is required by accountants to manage invoices, predict cash inflow, and meet other accounting requirements [12].

6.3.13 Banking for Consumers (BankTech)

Several financial organizations are using digital technology to deliver services in a more simplified and effective way. BankTech is the application of digital setups to offer customers banking services and goods. Compared to traditional banking techniques, BankTech provides various benefits, including a better user experience, cheaper costs, and fewer errors [15].

6.4 Role of Data Science and AI

Data scientists combine arithmetic and statistics, advanced programming, advanced analytics, AI, and ML with specialized expertise to find latent actionable insights in a company's data. According to experts, data science is a multidisciplinary field that uses scientific methods, processes,

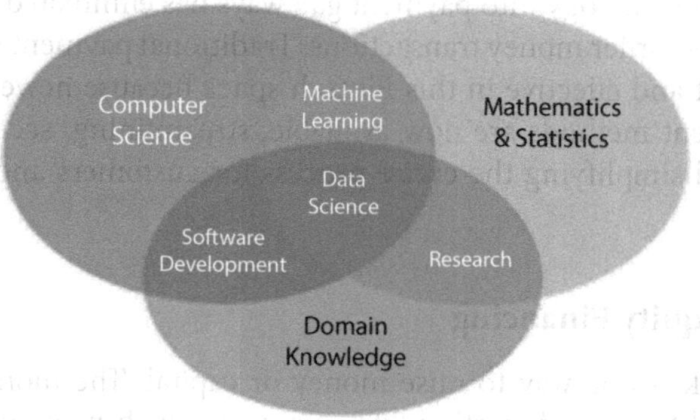

Figure 6.2 Data science structure [15].

algorithms, and systems to extract knowledge from data. Artificial intelligence is the concept and development of computer systems capable of performing activities that typically require human intelligence. As a subfield of data science, AI is widely used to replicate human cognitive functions [17]. Real-world applications of AI include chatbots, automated recommendations, voice assistants, language translation, image recognition, and more.

Companies can achieve the unimaginable with the aid of data science and artificial intelligence. Figure 6.2 indicates the complete structure of data science embedded with other fields.

The study of massive amounts of structured and unstructured data using modern analytical methods is known as data science. The amount of data gathered in 2021 increased by 37% compared to 2020, totaling 74 trillion gigabytes. Figure 6.3 demonstrates the 'Volume of Data' available & expected at internet related to 'Data Science' from 2019 to 2025.

Both the quantity and diversity of data being collected have increased, making it challenging for humans to analyze and organize this information. Data science can help with this. Companies can employ data science to obtain thorough data analysis, projections, and insights that can be applied in all aspects of their operations. Figure 6.4 shows the integration of data science with other relevant disciplines.

Companies can more quickly understand information and identify connections between seemingly unrelated items thanks to this set of tools. Organizations collect a significant amount of data from the Fintech industry. Due to the rapid advancement and development of modern technology, the Fintech sector is combining an increasing number of financial statements and accounts, such as balance sheets, cash flow statement, fund flow statements, and income statements, for analysis [16]. With the help of this information, financial institutions can develop well-thought-out plans and gain a deeper understanding of their clients. Big Data is built on three values, often referred to as the three Vs:

- **Volume:** Unique techniques and technology are required to gather such vast amounts of data because conventional technologies cannot handle it.
- **Velocity:** Data must be analyzed in real-time to obtain the most recent information.
- **Variety:** A wide range of data forms, including tweets, audio, and video, must be handled.

These advantages require the processing of data using unique methods, and data science aims to accomplish this [18]. The results become more

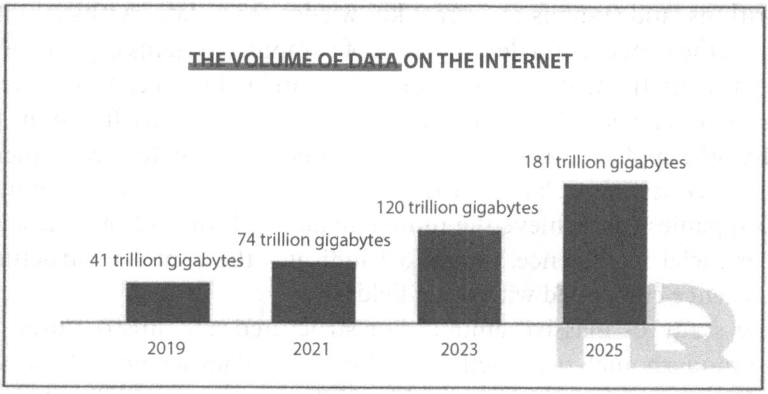

Figure 6.3 Quantum of data at internet [4].

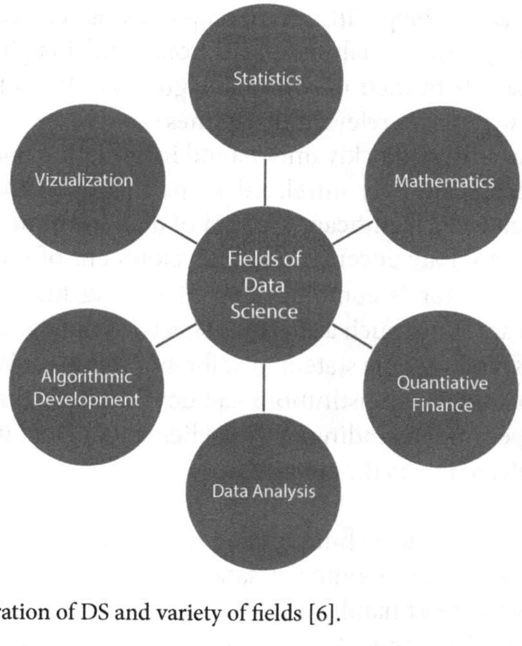

Figure 6.4 Integration of DS and variety of fields [6].

thorough and relevant as more data is analyzed by the algorithms. This explains why data science is so popular in the Fintech sector, where vast amounts of data are collected. Financial institutions can use data science to make informed decisions and provide a customized customer experience.

6.5 Data Science and AI (DSAI) Making Smart Fintech

DSAI is restructuring and redefining the concepts, goals, contents, and tasks of EcoFin and Fintech. Essentially, it changes how contemporary economic and financial firms function, conduct business, communicate with, and collaborate with their stakeholders, including customers, markets, and regulators. In addition to enhancing the overall performance, cost-effectiveness, consumer satisfaction, risk coverage, regulation, and safety of current economic systems, data science and AI also develop novel, more intelligent, safer, and more dynamic products and services that constitute the new sector of smart Fintech [19]. These products and services are becoming increasingly common in the financial sector as they impact and benefit customers while also helping banks operate more efficiently [32].

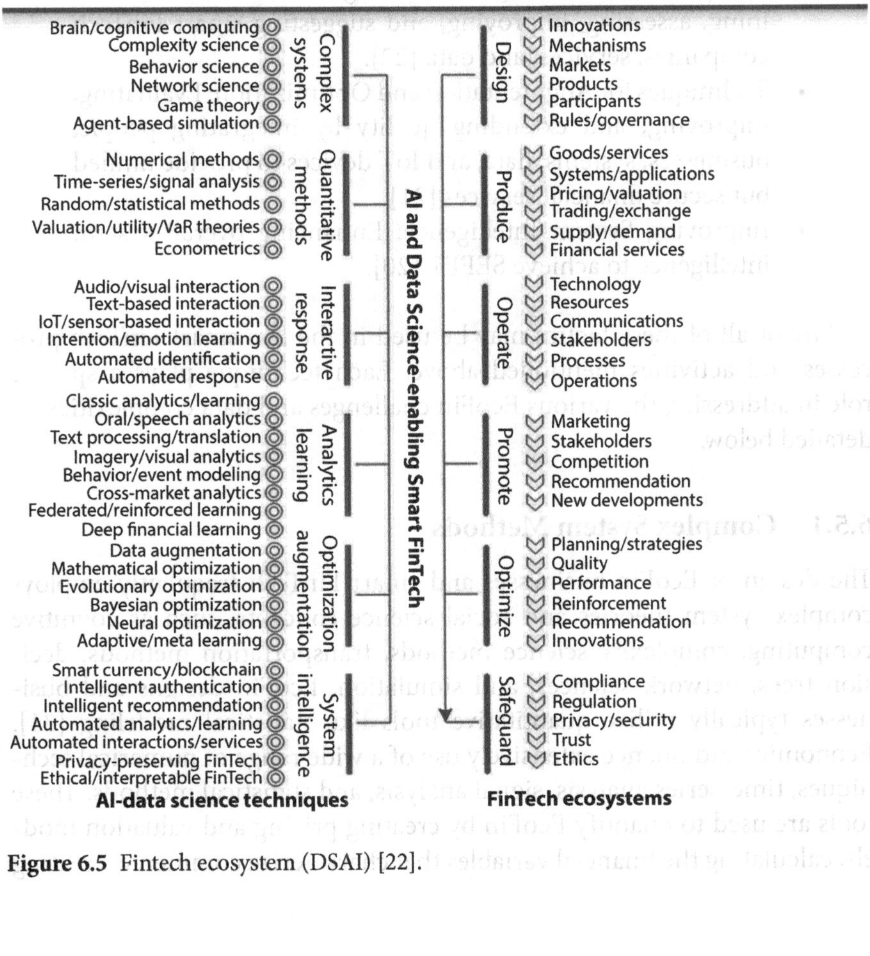

Figure 6.5 Fintech ecosystem (DSAI) [22].

The smart FinTech goals and EcoFin enterprises listed above necessitate the use of a wide range of DSAI approaches [6, 11, 15, 16]. The methodologies enabling intelligent FinTech can be categorized in various ways. For instance, Figure 6.5 divides the methodologies into the following categories: (a) mathematical and statistical modeling; (b) complex system methods; (c) classic analysis and learning methods; (d) computational intelligence methods; (e) recent DSAI methods; and (g) hybrid methods [22].

Here, we broaden the aforementioned focus and quickly go over a variety of intelligent domains necessary for smart EcoFin and FinTech (SEFFT).

- Intelligent Interactions and Responses: Intelligent man-machine combinations, successful discussions with stakeholders, and personalized responses [20].
- Quantitative Techniques: Techniques for evaluating EcoFin enterprises and designs.
- Analytics and Learning Methodologies: Methods for examining, assessing, improving, and suggesting smart FinTech companies, services, and data [22].
- Techniques for Augmentation and Optimization: Evaluating, improving, and extending quality by integrating people, businesses, systems, data, and IoT devices to provide unified but secure financial services [21].
- Improving System Intelligence: Enhancing overall system intelligence to achieve SEFFT [20].

Any or all of these tactics may be used in the five smart FinTech processes and activities mentioned above. Each technique plays a specific role in addressing the various EcoFin challenges and data complexities, as detailed below.

6.5.1 Complex System Methods

The design of EcoFin businesses and smart FinTech frequently employs complex system theories and social science concepts, such as cognitive computing, complexity science methods, transportation methods, decision trees, network sciences, and simulation. EcoFin designs and businesses typically utilize quantitative tools like statistical modeling [31]. Economics and finance extensively use of a wide range of numerical techniques, time-series analysis, signal analysis, and statistical methods. These tools are used to quantify EcoFin by creating pricing and valuation models, calculating the financial variables that characterize commerce, creating matrices for evaluating quality and performance, determining and adjusting supply and demand, examining theories and mechanisms, and predicting issues such as uncertainty in businesses.

6.5.2 Automatic Contact Recognition and Response Synthesis

These are two additional examples of autonomous, open-domain, context-aware, multi-turn, multi-level, multilingual, and knowledge-based discourse, interactions, and communications, including:

- Autonomously deciphering spoken, visual, video, retrieval, or text-based interactions or queries to identify interacting objects.
- Understanding the intent of a relationship.
- Analyzing feelings and emotions.
- Developing and suggesting follow-up interactions and activities for automated responses [24].
- Tracing the context and feedback of previous dialogues, etc.

6.5.3 Analytics, Teaching, and Learning Strategies

EcoFin and FinTech are increasingly relying on both conventional and cutting-edge analytics and learning methodologies to become smarter, more effective, adaptive, and evolving [25]. Methods such as pattern analysis, representation, tree models, and factor models are interconnected by:

- Forecasting market shifts, for instance, by integrating data from multiple sources, heterogeneous information, financial events, and sentiments from social media [6].
- Developing algorithmic based trading solutions, such as forecasting security price movements or analyzing financial event-based price movements from stock news [21].
- Detecting illegal or unethical activities, such as identifying market manipulation from unusual investor behaviors [8].
- Modeling volatility spillover, investment herding, cross-market investment strategies, and risk management [28, 29].
- Modeling the implications of exogenous events on financial markets, such as the impact of cybersecurity issues [22].

6.5.4 Deep Financial Modeling

It encompasses three subcategories: deep cross-market, section, and factor modeling, along with deep distributed financial modeling, focusing on key issues categorized under deep prediction [9]. These tasks utilize deep learning models such as basic deep neural networks and their more recent advancements. Examples include adversarial learning, autoencoders, image nets, attention networks, memory networks, etc. In the financial realm by DSAI, recurrent neural networks are employed for multivariate time-series forecasting, temporal and sequential modeling of financial variables, and predicting price or index trend [21, 22, 26].

Deep reinforcement learning techniques, such as deep Q-networks, are utilized for stock forecasting, optimal portfolio management, and developing high-frequency trading algorithms for algorithmic trading [24, 27, 30]. Deep neural networks encompass various types including deep transfer learning models, recurrent neural networks, regression networks, and graph neural networks. Recent advances in deep learning have significantly influenced the community of DSAI-driven finance and Fintech. Deep learning is also applied to detect risky and unlawful activities such as insider trading, financial reporting discrepancies, and accounting fraud in financial statements and services [12].

6.5.5 Techniques for Augmentation and Optimization

Augmentation and optimization approaches [29] are instrumental in managing business and data complexity in Ecofin businesses. They enhance the objectives, mechanisms, capacity, and strategies of Fintech design, as well as improve the capability, quality, and overall performance of Fintech. Ecofin and Fintech face challenges such as transactional, picture, audio, visual, textual, and quality-related issues such as noises, inconsistencies, heterogeneity, and hidden feature [23]. Data augmentation techniques, including adding random noise, adversarial training, masking, generative adversarial networks, and neural transformation, improve data quality and better achieve Fintech goals. Examples include enhancing contrast, translating, optimizing pricing and valuation, managing investment value at risk, transaction costs, portfolio management, and cross-market investment and risk management. Optimization is increasingly crucial for creating robust and effective Fintech [11, 21].

6.5.6 Smart EcoFin Companies and Services

Improving system intelligence is crucial for Fintech intelligence, which relies not only on the methods listed above but also on additional system intelligence. Here, we give a succinct summary of the techniques used to boost system intelligence in the financial technology industry [15, 23, 25]. These techniques include intelligent (re-)identification and authentication, automated analytics and learning, personalized interactions and services, intelligent recommendation, smart block chain, and ethical and interpretable Fintech.

6.5.7 Automated Analytics and Learning

This is based on automatically restored and processed EcoFin data and business, offering tie-ups opportunities (such as alerts, reactions, and ideas), enhancing EcoFin services which include:

- Intelligent Recommendation: Customizing EcoFin products and services (including stocks, portfolios, financial plans, and promotions) for specific clients by consideration their needs, spending patterns, changing circumstances, feedback, and other variables [17].
- Automated, Tailored, Context-Aware Dialogues: Using visual, spoken, image, text, or multi-modal interactions with customers, accounting for their needs, wants, situations, intentions, and context [16].
- Micro-Service Architectures: Protecting privacy by building local services from complex, large-scale enterprise-wide infrastructural components and object-oriented microservices for efficient computing [18].
- Ethical and Understandable Fintech: Ensuring EcoFin businesses and services are safety-protected, accountable, visible, unbiased, and interpretable, in their designs, products, pricing, quality, accessibility, recommendations, and risk management [18].

6.5.8 Whole-of-Business and Privacy-Preserving Federated Fintech

As the world is becoming more networked and globalized, all facets of the economy are becoming more interconnected and interdependent, including design, technical, manufacturing and trading, supply chains, cross-border and multinational e-commerce, customer services, and financial services. EcoFin enterprises commonly utilize a wide range of various, large-scale, dispersed, and privacy-sensitive products, services, platforms, applications, markets, organizations, application domains, client communities, locations, and data sources [23]. An example is a smart residential neighborhood or chain of properties where intelligent buildings connect services for housing, strata, utilities, parking, community, commerce, and healthcare. These diverse businesses require FinTech-focused solutions.

6.6 Use Cases of Data Science in Fintech

6.6.1 Fraud Prevention

Every financial business fears the worst—fraudsters stealing both money and company information. Therefore, they are defending information with every anti-fraud weapon at their disposal. For instance, companies can employ Regtech, or regulatory technology, to enhance security measures. This includes blockchain technology for securing specific transactions, ML for communication checking and client recognition, single-risk platforms for fraud prevention, and intelligence applications for anti-money laundering (AML) [29]. Figure 6.6 shows that how the 'Data Science' protects companies from fraud prevention [29].

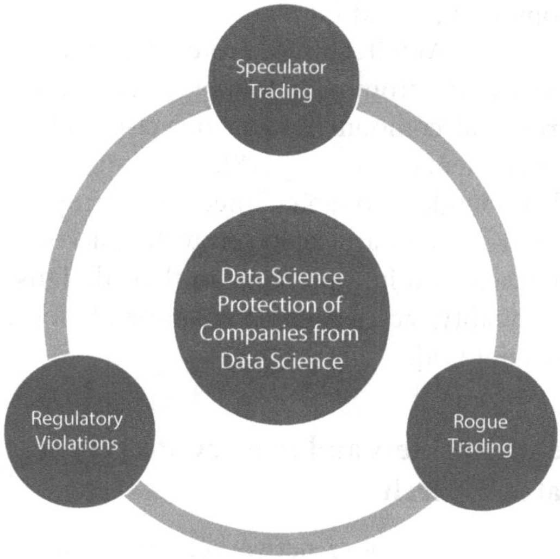

Figure 6.6 Risk analysis and prevention of fraud.

Additionally, ML algorithms can evaluate the most recent user experience and compare them to all prior actions. As a result, businesses can respond proactively to unusual behavior [29].

6.6.2 Risk Analysis

Deep risk analysis provided by DS aids in risk management by incorporating new risk detection system features. Organizations can prepare for potential issues by modeling specific hazards in a virtual environment. For instance, risk analysis determine whether a potential borrower is likely to repay a loan. Companies can better understand risk prerequisites and manage them across the organization using risk simulation. Additionally, since developing a risk assessment plan is an essential step in the auditing process, the application of DS, can enhance audit procedures. Figure 6.7 indicates the ways that how 'Data Science' overall helps.

6.6.3 Customer Behavior Analysis

Natural Language Processing (NLP), text analysis, and data mining are used in data science to analyze substantial amounts of behavioral data. Financial companies can use customer behavior analysis to increase cross-selling by providing customers with additional products or services they might find interesting; evaluate and boost client lifetime value; reduce losses by eliminating low-value clients; segment clients; and increase the brand's trustworthiness. Data science offers the opportunity to conduct real-time and predictive financial analyses, enabling the creation of customer behavior models. Figure 6.8 shows the applications and benefits of 'Data Science' in customer behavior.

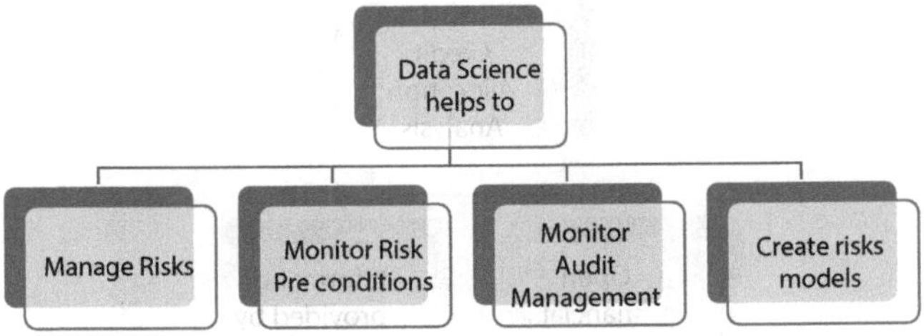

Figure 6.7 Risk analysis and DS [29].

Figure 6.8 Application of DS in consumer behavior [30].

6.6.4 Credit Allocation

In this instance, Fintech data science examines client-provided open financial data, banking databases, and credit histories. Additionally, certain banks are permitted to share certain financial data, providing an opportunity to learn more about customers. This helps banks automate the process of calculating each client's credit score, eliminating the need for manual labor. Moreover, machine learning can forecast loan repayment likelihood by comparing user behavior to credit score models [29]. Figure 6.9 shows the exact analysis of credit allocations by the banks through 'Data Science'.

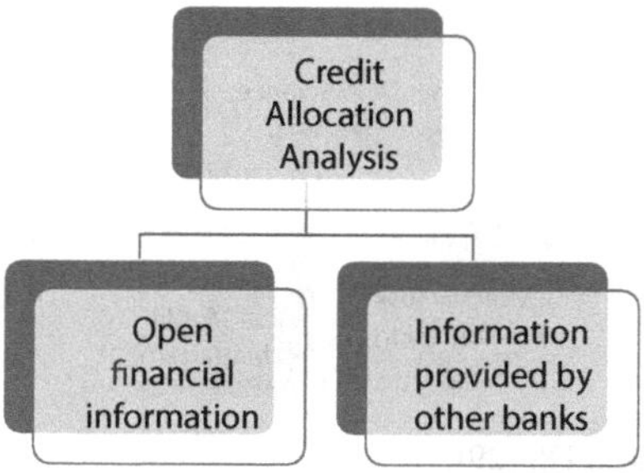

Figure 6.9 Analysis of credit allocation by banks [30].

6.6.5 Predictive Analytics

Predictive analytics forecast future patterns by extrapolating from the most recent data. By predicting stock market movements and price, customers can use Fintech data science to make wise investments or develop financial plans [31].

6.6.6 Product Development

Developing methods for product improvement is another use of data science. It helps businesses modernize their goods, understand the shortcomings of their current offerings, and adapt to shifting market expectations. Thanks to data science, financial companies can offer new offerings to customers at the most opportune time for maximum market response [23].

6.6.7 Algorithmic Trading (AT)

AT involves using a set of commands to address trade-related problems while considering factors such as price, volume, and timing. Algorithmic trading seeks out even the most improbable prospects for profitable trading, using mathematical calculations, models, and human control. This combination enables businesses to decide whether trading on a specific market at a specific moment is profitable. The ability to move quickly and respond to the results of decisions is a major advantage of using specialized Fintech data science applications [27].

6.6.8 Personalized Marketing

Financial organizations can offer customized marketing and products for each user category through deep analysis of projections and consumer choices. Tailored campaigns are more effective at reaching the target audience, retaining customers, and improving user experience. Additionally, personalization raises conversion rates and returns on investment, enhancing an organization's financial performance. Personalized marketing campaigns boost revenue by increasing conversion rate and returns on investment [26].

6.7 Conclusion

This descriptive study concluded that 'Fintech' is the most demanding and revolutionary technology in the current digitalized scenario. The financial and banking industry, when integrated with 'Data Science and Artificial Intelligence' becomes more enhanced and compatible with consumers, investors, stockbrokers, and all other stakeholders associated with the industry. However, 'Fintech' encounters several severe challenges on a routine basis, including:

- Data security and government regulation compliance
- Lack of tech and mobile expertise
- Issue of integration of AI and Big Data
- Exact implementation of blockchain
- User engagement and experience problems
- Unavailability of powerful marketing strategies for acquiring clients
- Service personalization challenges.

However, organizers and end-users on 'Fintech' always strive to strike a balance between applying new technologies and adhering to established parameters and protocols to completely disrupt the financial sector. Traditional banking faces challenging in adopting new trends and technologies, yet it is believed that mobile technologies will increasingly be employed in the financial industry as they enhance people's lives and make banking more convenient and transparent overall.

References

1. Alameda, T., DATA, AI AND FINANCIAL INCLUSION: THE FUTURE OF GLOBAL BANKING. *Responsible Finance Forum, Responsible Finance Forum BBVA 2020*, 2020, Available online: https://responsiblefinanceforum.org/data-ai-financial-inclusion-future-global-banking/ (accessed on 12 July 2023).
2. *Mainstream Science on Intelligence:An Editorial with 52 Researchers*, pp. 13–23, Wall Street Journal, USA, 1994.
3. Beck, T., Demirgüç-Kunt, A., Honohan, P., Access to financial services: Measurement, impact, and policies. *World Bank Res. Obs.*, 24, 119–45, 2009.
4. Bourreau, M. and Valletti, T., Enabling Digital Financial Inclusion through Improvements in Competition and Interoperability: What Works and What Doesn't?, *CDG Policy Paper*, 1–35, 2015, Available online: http://www.cgdev.org/publication/enabling-digital-financial-inclusion-through-improvements-competition- (accessed on 12 July 2023).
5. Burns, S., M-Pesa and the "Market-Led" Approach to Financial Inclusion. *Econ. Aff.*, 38, 406–21, 2018.

6. Chatterjee, P. and Sarangi, S., The Economics of Microfinance. *South. Econ. J.*, 23, 1, 73–259, 2006.
7. Colom, R., Karama, S., Jung, R.E., Haier, R.J., Human intelligence and brain networks. *Dialogues Clin. Neurosci.*, 12, 489–501, 2010, Available online: https://www.ncbi.nlm.nih.gov/pmc/articles/pmc3181994/ (accessed on 14 July 2020).
8. Dawei, L., Anzi, H., Gen, L., Big Data Technology: Application and Cases, in: *Handbook of Blockchain, Digital Finance, and Inclusion*, pp. 65–82, Elsevier Inc., Amsterdam, 2018.
9. Demirguc-Kunt, A., Klapper, L., Ansar, S., Jagati, A., Making It Easier to Apply for a Bank Account A Study of the Indian Market, pp. 1–30, Policy research Working paper Series 8205, World Bank Group, 2017, Available online: https://elibrary.worldbank.org/doi/abs/10.1596/1813-9450-8205 (accessed on 12 July 2023).
10. Frank, M.R., 8The Evolution of AI Research and the Study of Its Social Implications, *MDPI J.*, 143–155, 2019, MIT MEDIA LAB 2019, Available online: https://medium.com/mit-media-lab/the-evolution-of-ai-research-and-the-study-of-its-social-implications-4a9598b3d7db (accessed on 25 June 2020).
11. Gomber, P., Koch, J.-A., Siering, M., Digital Finance and FinTech: Current research and future research directions. *J. Bus. Econ.*, 87, 537–80, 2017.
12. Gottfredson, L.S., Why g matters: The complexity of everyday life. *Intelligence*, 24, 79–132, 1997.
13. Harkut, D.G. and Kasat, K., Introductory Chapter: Artificial Intelligence—Challenges and Applications, in: *Artificial Intelligence—Scope and Limitations*, IntechOpen, London, 2019.
14. *Handbook of Blockchain, Digital Finance, and Inclusion*, pp. 405–29, Elsevier Inc., Amsterdam, 2017.
15. Ingenta Connect, The Digitalisation of Payments in South-East Asia. *J. Digital Banking*, 4, 76–84, 2019, ingentaconnect.com. Available online: https://www.ingentaconnect.com/content/hsp/jdb001/2019/00000004/00000001/art00008 (accessed on 12 July 2023).
16. Kaya, D. and Pronobis, P., The benefits of structured data across the information supply chain: Initial evidence on XBRL adoption and loan contracting of private firms. *J. Account. Public Policy*, 35, 417–36, 2016.
17. Levin, R.B., Waltz, P., LaCount, H., Betting Blockchain Will Change Everything-SEC and CFTC Regulation of Blockchain Technology, in: *Handbook of Blockchain, Digital Finance, and Inclusion*, pp. 187–212, Elsevier Inc., Amsterdam, 2018.
18. Lopes, J. and Pereira, J.L., Blockchain technologies: Opportunities in healthcare, in: *Advances in Intelligent Systems and Computing*, pp. 435–42, Springer, Cham, 2019b.
19. Osah, O. and Kyobe, M., Predicting user continuance intention towards M-pesa in Kenya. *Afr. J. Econ. Manage. Stud.*, 8, 36–50, 2017.

20. Ozili, P.K., Impact of digital finance on financial inclusion and stability. *Borsa Istanb. Rev.*, 18, 329–40, 2018.
21. Park, C.-Y. and Mercado, R., Financial Inclusion, Poverty, and Income Inequality in Developing Asia. *SSRN Electron. J.*, 426, 12–16, 2015.
22. Park, C.-Y. and Mercado, R., Financial inclusion, poverty, and income inequality. *Singapore Econ. Rev.*, 63, 185–206, 2018.
23. Paul, S., Use of Blockchain and Aritificial Intelligence to Promote Financial Inclusion in India, Smita Miglani Indian Council for Research on International Economic Relations, *Special Theme for Inclusiveness and Equality, Tech Monitor*, 11–16, 2019, Available online: https://economictimes (accessed on 28 July 2023).
24. Peric, K., Digital financial inclusion. *J. Paym. Strategy Syst.*, 9, 212–14, 2015.
25. Rathi, V., India amidst digital banking and financial inclusion—A review. *Int. J. Manage. Soc. Sci.*, 6, 24–28, 2016, Available online: http://journals.foundationspeak.com/index.php/ijmss/article/view/340 (accessed on 25 July 2023).
26. Salampasis, D. and Mention, A.-L., FinTech: Harnessing Innovation for Financial Inclusion, in: *Handbook of Blockchain, Digital Finance, and Inclusion*, pp. 451–61, Academic Press, Cambridge, 2018.
27. *Handbook of Blockchain Digital Finance, and Inclusion*, pp. 361–85, Elsevier Inc., Amsterdam, 2017.
28. Van Hove, L. and Dubus, A., M-PESA and financial inclusion in Kenya: Of paying comes saving? *Sustainability*, 11, 568, 2019.
29. Visser, W. and Prahalad, C.K., The Fortune at the Bottom of the Pyramid, in: *The Top 50 Sustainability Books*, pp. 200–203, 2013, Available online: https://www.csrwire.com/pdf/Prahalad-excerpt-001-022.pdf (accessed on 5 May 2020).
30. Wang, X. and He, G., Digital financial inclusion and farmers' vulnerability to poverty: Evidence from rural China. *Sustainability*, 12, 1668, 2020.
31. Yang, L. and Zhang, Y., Digital Financial Inclusion and Sustainable Growth of Small and Micro Enterprises—Evidence Based on China's New Third Board Market Listed Companies. *Sustainability*, 12, 3733, 2020.
32. Yuan, Y., Hu, Y., Gao, P., Farmers' Choice and Informal Credit Markets in China, *China Agric. Econ. Rev.*, 4, 2, 1-15, 2011, Available online: https://ageconsearch.umn.edu/record/103887/ (accessed on 2 July 2023).

7

Evaluation of Fintech: The Techno-Functional Application in Digital Banking

Priyanka Verma[1]*, Rajesh Kumar Dhanaraj[2], Deepa Gupta[3] and Mukul Gupta[3]

[1]*College of Business Administration, University of Fujairah, Fujairah, United Arab Emirates*

[2]*Symbiosis International (Deemed University), Pune, Maharashtra, India*

[3]*GL Bajaj Institute of Management, Greater Noida, India*

Abstract

In the case of modern technological evaluation, Fintech is one of the most effective approaches that can be used. Financial services, along with innovation, are major applications that enhance the working process in the business process area. In financial services, the impact of technology is crucial for measuring security and ensuring successful implementation of the working process. The banking sector also benefits from maintaining a suitable working process. Zero barriers and higher work efficiency are major applications that enhance overall financial operations in the business process area. Risk management and automated services are crucial parts that create significant changes in business operations. The advanced security and structure of the work also measure the value of the application in the business process area.

***Keywords*:** Fintech, digital banking, financial services, technological innovation, risk management, automated services, security, business process optimization

7.1 Introduction

The banking industry has transformed rapidly in this era of digitalization and has taken active role on digital media platforms. A mixture of physical and online presence has created a hybrid model, expanding opportunities

**Corresponding author*: Pv12kumar@gmail.com

Deepa Gupta, Mukul Gupta, Rajesh Kumar Dhanaraj, Balamurugan Balusamy and Parth Mukul Gupta (eds.) Computational Intelligence for Autonomous Finance, (123–142) © 2025 Scrivener Publishing LLC

for fintech companies to emerge and make industrial practices more efficient. The shape of digital banking has also transformed users' practices globally. Digitized tools such as robotics, artificial intelligence (AI), the Internet of Things (IoT), augmented reality (AR), blockchain technology, and others have had a significant impact on every segment of the banking industry. This impact is forcing business experts to rethink the heavy dependency on fintech technologies, not only to make operations easier and more time-saving but also to serve customers with a higher degree of efficiency.

This chapter aims to analyze and critically discuss the drastic evolution in the banking industry due to the integration of techno-functional applications, commonly known as fintech. The study focuses on evaluating various related directions to this topic to create a clear and valuable understanding.

7.2 Overview of Fintech

Fintech refers to the combination of finance and technology, providing the world with a new approach that any organization can use to offer financial support and assistance from anywhere in the globe. The feature of automated delivery of financial services has helped the Fintech industry emerge in companies, business practices, and consumer forums, ensuring better management systems [2]. Since the mid-21st century, Fintech has been involved in the back-end systems of well-established institutions with advanced tech infrastructure. The use of software and algorithms has made financial services easily accessible via mobile phones, tablets, and computers. Fintech now emphasized customer-centric operations even more [3]. Techno-functional applications are increasingly used in various sectors, from education practices to retail banking, investment management, and fundraising.

Development in cryptocurrencies, such as Bitcoin, have experienced-significant growth due to the Fintech model, which is shifting towards digital operations and transforming traditional banking practices with its multi-trillion-dollar market capitalization. Fintech applications include investment apps, peer-to-peer (P2P) lending apps, crypto apps, payments apps, robo-advisors, more, all of which are connected to banking operations [1]. From the invention of digital money to double-entry bookkeeping, industrial innovation has transformed people conduct business. To provide modern tech-banking solutions, Fintech start-ups are gradually rising. Data collected by Statista in 2022 revealed that the growth of industrial investment has been fluctuating, but after 2017 it received a significant boost, reaching $148.6 billion dollars with continuous growth the following year [1]. However, during the COVID-19 period, there was a notable drop,

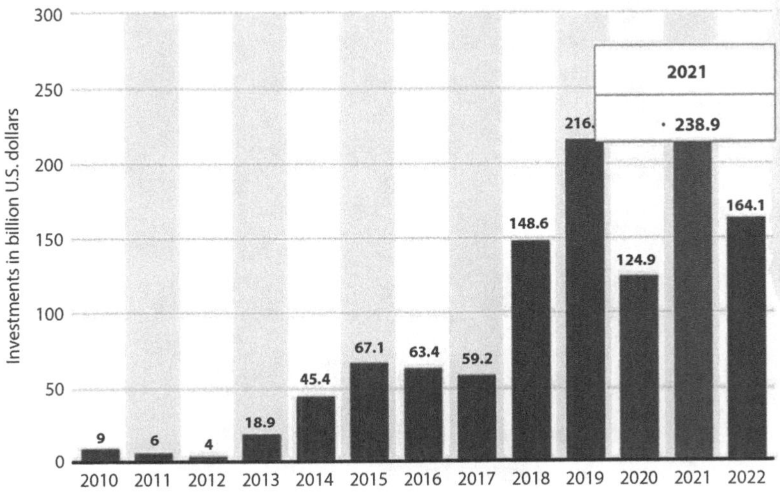

Figure 7.1 Investment of Fintech companies (2010 to 2022).

with investments estimated at $124.9 billion dollars [1]. The growth of the Fintech market is allowing the global business platform to access financial products at lower costs compared to traditional players. Consequently, corporate financial services have seen notable changes through automated financial service improvements. Figure 7.1 above highlights the investment of Fintech companies (2010 to 2022).

7.2.1 Details of the Working Algorithm

From individuals to large-scale companies, AI is increasingly applicable in Fintech, enhancing asset management and financial transaction procedures. Managing clients' debt portfolios is a priority matter for the banking industry, and Fintech, with its AI capabilities, can help track recurring expenditures and predict economic trends at both national and global levels [4]. Predicting client investment strategies through smart programming based on financial data is beneficial for identifying fraudulent activities. In this context, a four-step approach to wealth management—optimization of quantitative portfolio management, risk management, identification of timelines, and changing variables for better ROI—utilizes machine learning algorithms to solve complexities [5]. To achieve an optimal portfolio for clients and meet their expectations for Fintech-oriented banking services, understanding the risk-return concept for both short- and long-term investments is crucial, using the best-coded algorithms. Figure 7.2 below illustrates the C++ code for client portfolio management based on basic inquiry and expectation.

```
#include<iostream>
#include<conio.h>
#include<cmath>
#include<string>
#include<iomanip>

using namespace std;

int main()
{
    string s;
    float y;
    float r;
    cout << "Input any value you want to
store in the string: ";
    cin >> s;
    cout << "Input any two float values:
";
    cin >> y >> r;

    // You can add additional logic here
based on what the original code was
supposed to do

    return 0;
}
```

Figure 7.2 C++ code for client portfolio management based on basic inquiry and expectation.

Converting input into valuable output is the prime goal of Fintech algorithms, typically achieved through "*processing logic (= algorithms)*". The process logic components can be categorized into five different types:

1. *Calculation of Specific Values*: Using mathematical formulas to generate precise outputs (e.g., reimbursement schedules for future payable interest amounts or credit, rates of return on investments, payback periods). This requires accurate input information.
2. *Data Lookups*: Extracting output data in processed or raw forms such as aggregated, filtered, or sorted data [5]. For example, generating the total transaction amount based on the number of customers and grouping them by country simplifies the data retrieval process.

3. *Expert Systems*: Creating decision trees in the form of flowcharts or workflows using "If–Then–Else" clauses or similar condition logics. This hekps determine the correct path for business logic by integrating algorithms to evaluate various conditions.
4. *Optimization of Problems*: Focusing on finding the best possible solution, though it is often challenging due to constraints related to financial resources, time, and portfolio balances [5]. Processing power limitations can hinder the accuracy of results in resource scheduling, investment constraints, model portfolios, and other areas.
5. *System Identification (SI) and Machine Learning (ML)*: Addressing problems that are difficult to define with standard algorithm rules. In the digital banking sector, where corruption and fraud are significant concerns, SI and ML algorithms help detect fraud by estimating numerous parameters, creating coefficient matrices, and matching best test data [4].

Apart from these, *Monte Carlo Tree Search (MCTS)* is another AI driven algorithm for probability analysis in Fintech, evaluating different optimal options to provide correct actions. The selection of the most appropriate business algorithm or logic from these options must include *flexibility* to adapt the algorithms' behavior. Additionally, the algorithms' behavior must be compared to *operational complexities* to validate expectations [7]. *Knowledge* of driving the logic with its higher ability and *implementation complexity* should also be considered to assess the code correctly.

The Fintech model holds significant importance in guiding investors to avoid risks and adhere to financial regulations. The investing mindset in banking finance is particularly influenced by stock market positioning, where the Fintech index demonstrates greater ability to predict the nonlinear and nonstationary of stocks [6]. The volatility characteristic of this model complicates the prediction process using traditional time series methods. Therefore, various algorithms, such as the "genetic algorithm" (GA), "support vector regression" (SVR), "deep neural network" (DNN), and "random frog" (RF), are currently employed in financial activities for better predictions. By initializing hyperparameters through the combination of "*RF-GA-DNN prediction algorithm*," true values can be calculated by positioning three segments—Section 2.1, Section 2.2, and Section 2.3 as found in the figure below.

7.2.2 Relationship Between FINTECH and Modern Financial Application in Digital Banking

In 2008, during the global financial crisis, the banking industry emerged as a healthier and reliable option to climb the financial ladder. Based on these industrial practices, the global financial asset reached $154,211 in 2022, a 3.79% increase compared to 2021 [8]. Major banks such as Bank of America, JPMorgan Chase, Wells Fargo, and others are focusing on attracting new customers and retaining existing ones by introducing neo-banking schemes with new convenient features. These disruptive banking technologies have transformed banking practices and provided a new direction, represented as Fintech. Fintech combines various digital applications with modern banking business needs [9]. Customers' experiences are improving over the passing time with the adoption of advanced technologies, indicating that Fintech has a deeper relationship with the modern digital world, driving evolution in banking financial practices. Figure 7.3 illustrates the RF-GA-DNN algorithm workflow.

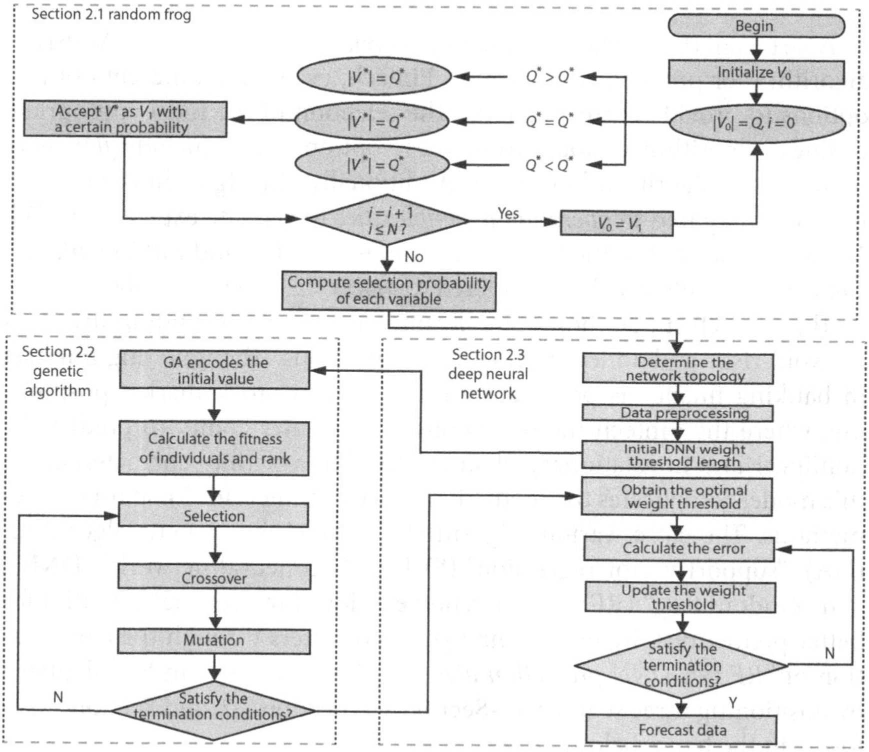

Figure 7.3 RF-GA-DNN algorithm workflow.

From developing to developed countries, all are engaged in this revolutionary transformation of the banking industry, where the role of technologies cannot be ignored. Recent studies of the Indian banking industry have revealed an intention to surpass highly developed countries (United Kingdom, USA, Singapore, Germany, and others) in terms of rapid sector growth [10]. Between 2015 and 2018, approximately 1,500 fintech-based startups were launched in India, raising expectations for evolving Fintech in core practices for a better ecosystem. With multi-currency digital payments becoming the norm, peer-to-peer lending has gained popularity among banking users [11]. In just a few minutes, users can claim insurance and easily assess the banking applications. Figure 7.4 given below presents the framework combining Fintech and innovation for improvising digital financial inclusion.

Financial turmoil has increased the need for a better financial landscape by new innovations and technologies. The necessity for digital technologies has grown rapidly, with Fintech referring to economic companies that provide financial services by combining various technologies [12]. A contradiction arises by stating that Fintech and digital banking are two different concepts, yet their dependency on digital platforms and technologies has merged them into a single entity. Fintech offers a trustworthy and transparent business model to the banking and other industries, while digital

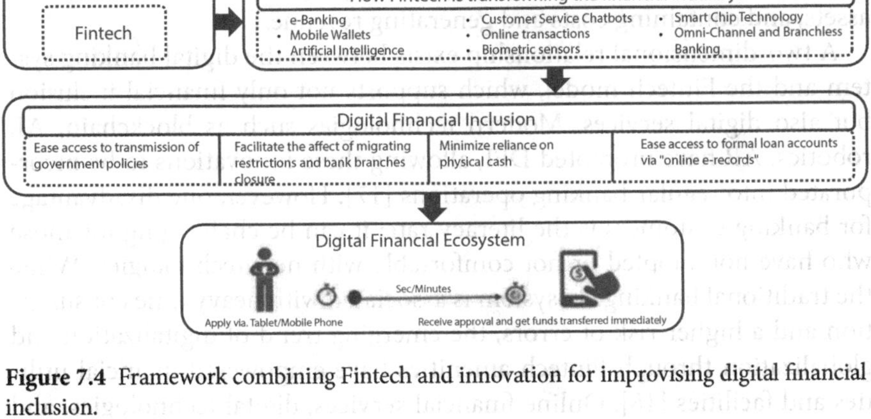

Figure 7.4 Framework combining Fintech and innovation for improvising digital financial inclusion.

banking uses modern digital channels to expedite interactions between banks and customers [13]. The assimilation of innovative technologies in Fintech is supported by digitized services through mobile banking and smart devices, enhancing the capabilities of the global economic system for every individual end-user.

To achieve the general purpose of making countries cashless, ATM machines were introduced in the 1960s, along with debit and credit cards. The triggered financial innovation, transforming financial and trading systems with efficient modifications [14]. Focusing on this innovation, Fintech emerged, making the digital banking process both affordable and essential for payments, deposits, transfers, loan and other services. This digital era with financial service inclusion has shifted the focus from formal banking channel to mobile banking (m-banking). Various financial entities such as telecom services, distributary channels, insurance providers, Fintech companies, policymakers, and banks have collaborated in the financial inclusion process, collectively saving approximately $4.2 trillion through a mobilized automated or digital finance system [15]. This has strengthened "*digital financial inclusion*" (DFI), allowing the population to avoid unofficial banking methods and other conventional operations.

Fintech and digital banking processes both leverage the Cloud, helping organizations manage and store data for longer periods and beyond space limitations. The shift from traditional to digital has created new business frontiers, making it easier for Board members, C-suite executives, and Chief Information Officers to recognize capital market opportunities [16]. Banks and Fintech organizations now have access to advanced software via the internet. An array of "innovative products-as-a-service" has been integrated into digital banking processes, especially in operation models, which is closely improving customer insight, delivering market-relevant products more efficiently and quickly, helping organizations monetize data assets, and containing costs and generating revenue.

A two-dimensional relationship exists between the digital banking system and the Fintech model, which supports not only financial inclusion but also digital services. Modern technologies such as blockchain, AI, robotics, AR have promoted DFI, allowing these innovations to be incorporated into regular banking operations [17]. However, one disadvantage for banking customers is the literacy rate; it can be challenging for those who have not adopted or not comfortable with new technologies. While the traditional banking ecosystem is associated with heavy time consumption and a higher risk of errors, the emerging trend of digitalization and globalization through Fintech amenities have empowered financial utilities and facilities [18]. Online financial services, digital technologies, and virtual modes have created an unbanked facility that Fintech has significantly contributed to, promoting financial inclusion.

7.2.3 Advantages of the Application

The acceleration of digital banking processes began with the use of cardless cash withdrawals, "tap and pay," paperless customer onboarding, and submitting "know-your-customer" (KYC) information through mobile devices, considering these as technology-first tools. Consequently, the opportunities to leverage technologies with better capabilities have driven fundamental changes in the financial value chain [19]. A more agile and versatile experience that users have obtained from the digital banking industry is reflected through five pioneering Fintech innovations in the Figure 7.5:

1. ***Capabilities of Advanced Self-Services***: In traditional physical banking, customers had to wait long queues to complete banking formalities, seek assistance from bankers, and fill out forms [20]. Fintech banking services have allowed customers to manage their banking operations digitally with the help of AI. Customers can now open new bank accounts, transfer money, check balances online, and buy insurance. These self-services have not only saved time and established better financial habits but also given customers control over their financial positions, enabling them to compare various schemes and choose the best alternatives for themselves and their families [20]. In these busy lifestyles, 93% banking

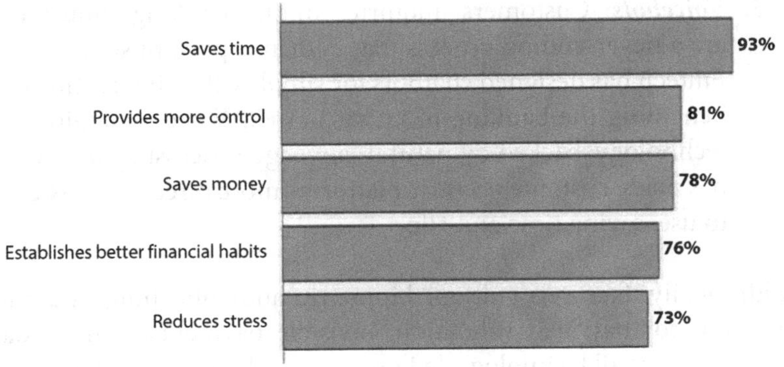

Figure 7.5 Advantages of using Fintech by banking users.

users report satisfaction with Fintech banking services for saving time and making the process more convenient.

2. ***Making Instant Payments***: During the COVID-19 pandemic, the world recognized the importance of online buying, which requires instant payments to complete transactions. The concept of "point of sale" (POS) terminals rapidly integrated into banking processes during this period, with demonetization and mobile internet playing crucial roles in global acceptance. Several countries, such as India, have initiated incentive programs for users who adopt digital banking through Fintech, aiming to make the country cashless.
3. ***Neobanking Mode***: Numerous digital financial apps and websites, licensed by different banks offer customers a wide range of banking and financial services without physical branches [21]. This neobanking mode allows customers to easily access instant loans, savings accounts, lending products, mutual funds, and fixed deposits through digital means.
4. ***Application Programming Interface (API) and IMPS (Immediate Payment Service)***: A worldwide transformation has been noted in terms of banking customers' demands, prompting countries to consider providing API and IMPS facilities. These innovations simplify the banking process by allowing banking products and services to integrate with third parties. API serves as a bridge between banks and third parties, ensuring safe real-time leverage [22]. From the customer's perspective, it is now possible to apply for loans based on credit scores and bank balances independently. This has made the banking process faster and requires comparatively less effort from end-users.
5. ***Voicebots***: Customers' inquiries in the banking industry are a never-ending process that demands prompt solutions. Fintech has designed chatbots for simplify B2C interactions, benefiting the banking industry as well. Voice recognition technology, backed by natural language processing and AI, has made customer-centric platforms more direct and easier to use, saving time and effort.

Additionally, face recognition, biometric authentication, and thumb impressions for payment validation, invisible payments, and validation chip for cards are all technology-led processes enhancing the banking process. A study conducted by McKinsey estimates that Fintech, through AI, can generate approximately $1 trillion in additional value in a single fiscal year for the banking industry. To resist encroachment, financial institutions such as banks must adopt an AI-driven mindset, facilitating faster expansion of technologies across branches [20]. To drive financial outputs, machine-based identification or an automatic factor discovery is needed in the form of AI semantic representation, which can generate excellent and easily understandable computing graphs. Traditional banking services struggle to identify complex financial networks and patterns, whereas Fintech aids in the integration of far-reaching disparate data sources.

The agility of digital-native companies has increased over time, as the banking industry eagerly collaborates extensively with non-bank partners. This collaboration brings a new value proposition to the financial journey, integrating data sets and technology platforms. Fintech innovations are advantageous for accessing digital wallets, non-fungible tokens (NFT), decentralized finance (DeFi), and digital assets by establishing a chain of different protocols [20]. Distributed Ledger Technology (DLT) in this value chain explores the worth of blockchain within the tech-banking industry, facilitating real-time transaction settlements, support services for digital assets, and zero-knowledge proof for authenticating the financial ecosystem.

7.2.4 Barriers in the Implementation Process

Discussing the issues with implementing Fintech in the banking sector, several aspects highlight the challenges involved. The barriers and issues can create significant diversities in the business process, reducing the success level of the approach in the market.

The Regulatory Environment: This is a major aspect that needs to be managed to maximize success. Implementing rules and regulations is crucial in the banking industry to maintain business ethics and stability. Often, Fintech does not adhere to the same standards, creating significant issues during implementation. Generating better leads can offer major advantages for the business, enhancing performance in the process area [23]. Critical protection of customers is a key responsibility that might improve business process evaluation and performance. However, Fintech's automated verification and storage procedures can be challenging for businesses, potentially reducing the success level of Fintech applications in the financial industries.

Funding: Proper funding is crucial for maximizing the efficiency of Fintech implementations. Adequate funding can help generate better leads and improve the organizational performance. Evaluating the structure of funding can enhance working capabilities, leading to successful performance in the banking sector. Conversely, a lack of funding can hinder the implementation process and negatively impact performance. In digital banking, the high cost of structure and infrastructure can pose significant challenges for business units [24]. Insufficient funding can prevent the establishment of the necessary infrastructure for successful implementation. Entrepreneurs must secure proper funding for creating value, and venture capital can be a helpful option for development, maximizing working performance. Fintech requires substantial funding to engage organizations effectively, which will help build a robust working structure and infrastructure.

***Technology*:** Technological development is crucial for application development in Fintech. An improper infrastructure can disrupt the working flow within an organization. Properly deriving processes can enable superior business development and infrastructure in the market [25]. Fintech requires advanced technology for security systems, which can present challenges for organizations. Establishing a proper data management infrastructure is essential. Ensuring system compatibility acts as a major catalyst in application development. Digital banking also involves the use of digital signatures, and their effective implementation can improve performance measures. Properly valuing the work involves strategic actions [26]. However, maintaining development in banking processes can lead to issues such as hacking or data leakage, which may be problematic for users. Ethical considerations can also be compromised by an improper infrastructure in automated banking application.

***Competition*:** Competition is another issue in the implementation of Fintech that creates significant differences. Many brands are performing in the same field with similar products, making market competition hectic for proper implementation and evaluation. In B2B scenarios, maintaining better business progress is crucial for achieving success. Higher competition can drive progress by pushing companies to evaluate their success levels and improve. Strategic implementation is essential for enhancing organizational effectiveness [27]. Many customers are not aware of modern technology, which can create significant differences in implementation. Therefore, a value-based approach is needed to improve business performance. In digital banking, it is essential to create a proper and user-friendly infrastructure that fosters superior business approaches and processes. Developers must adopt a strategic direction for successful implementation. Compared to other applications, Fintech can be cost-effective, maximizing organizational performance. Thus, a proper strategy is necessary for successful implementation.

7.2.5 Details of the Security System Present in the Application

The security system is one of the most important parts of financial applications, enhancing customer value and trust. Providing proper security measures, such as KYC, is crucial for maintaining privacy within the application. General data protection is another critical aspect, ensuring a smooth and secure working process [28]. The Act on the Protection of Personal Information is included in Fintech, making the working process effective with this development segment. Focusing on overall progress and derivation, process management is essential. Fintech applications involve customer knowledge, including personal information verification, which makes the entire working process authentic and improves operational effectiveness [29]. Additionally, structuring the work to enhance efficiency maximizes the application's capability.

GDPR: These rules protect privacy in FinTech applications that process the data of European Union residents. GDPR is not limited to European companies—if you plan to work with EU residents and businesses, you must comply with this regulation.
PSD2: The revised Payment Services Directive regulates the operation of electronic payment services in the EU to help banking services protect their technology. As noted in the Deloitte Legal 2018 study, PSD2 and GDPR often overlap and lack legal clarity. Therefore, consulting experts on this matter may be necessary.
eIDAS: Electronic Identification and Trust Services is another EU regulation on cross-border electronic transactions. It aims to create a single legal framework for secure transactions between FinTech organizations, businesses, government agencies and end users.
FCA: The Financial Conduct Authority oversees financial services in the UK, focusing on safe consumer protection and market integrity. Additionally, local FinTech service providers must register with the Finnish Competition Authority.
GPG13: The Good Practice Guidance affects suppliers and subcontractors involved in the UK government system. This compliance guide is part of the official security policy, focusing on cyber security, event logging, and intrusion detection systems. Vendors of financial technologies that process personal data of Japanese residents are subject to the Personal Data Protection Act. This regulation, like the GDPR, is extraterritorial, meaning it applies to companies operating in other countries.
The Personal Data Protection Act: This act regulates the security measures for private data of private and government agencies in South Korea. Unlike

the other FinTech compliance documents, violations of PIPA can result in financial penalties and criminal liability.

***PCI DSS*:** The Payment Card Industry Information Security Standard applies to entities that collect process and use credit card information. For example, MasterCard and Visa require providers to comply with this standard. There are four levels of PCI DSS; the more transactions you handle each year, the more requirements you must meet.

ISO/IEC 27001: This set of FinTech information security standards contains policies and frameworks that help organizations worldwide build and maintain secure information management systems. Its practices include cryptography, access control, clear display, and information security. However, the full range of standards required depends on the size and location of your business. The security system also helps customers take proper actions and evaluate activities. It also increases the sustainability of application development on the server side.

7.3 Theoretical Overview

Moving towards the theoretical overview and application, different factors can be included that makes the process effective in the business area. The Technology Acceptance Model is one of the most effective applications that enhances the working process and development of services, perceiving better business evaluation. According to the model, innovation and development are crucial for implementing the working process in the performance area. Adopting new technology will also be helpful for the brand and customers in maintaining a proper workflow [30]. In the case of digital banking, the usefulness of the application needs to be demonstrated properly to make the structure successful. Stating the proper workflow will include several aspects that are crucial for maintaining the value of the work and process in the performance area. A superior working structure, along with better stability, can enhance the stability and sustainability of working efficiency. Therefore, the theoretical model will include a superior working infrastructure and security measures to improve performance.

The perceived usefulness of the product and innovative approach needs to be demonstrated properly to maximize performance in the business process. Understanding the details will also include a better approach to work and value in the application. Attitude and behavioral approach are another part that will improve the performance measures. Additionally, creating the structure will maintain a proper working structure in the performance area [31]. Understanding the behavioral intentions of customers will help the marketing team to know the details successfully. These intentions will also provide a superior approach to work effectively in the market segment. It has also been seen that technology-savvy customers will be interested in this application and development. Therefore, a proper marketing approach will create a better business strategy in the specific market area. Experiencing a superior service will also recommend needed changes and development in the particular working area [32]. Construct validity and reliability were assessed by testing the contingency of self-reported use of IS in organizational contexts with the two proposed factors. The developed scales showed excellent psychometric properties. The model was further validated by confirming significant relationships between perceived usefulness, perceived ease of use, purpose, and usage behavior.

Perceived ease of use is another factor that needs to be managed to expand product distribution at a higher level. A user-friendly approach and design of the application are helpful for all types of customers in the market. Ease of use also includes better interfacing and distribution of features to the customers, which will enhance customer orientation toward the brand. In the financial area, it is essential to develop a better infrastructure for the customers to ensure proper business evaluation. Fintech is focused on achieving significant goals and objectives for customers to enhance their experience [33]. In this case, the developers need to use different and innovative solutions to increase customer satisfaction. This factor in the business development process will contribute significantly to the success level of the implementation. Therefore, the overall process and evaluation of the strategic derivation will lead to a superior approach in the process area. Adopting a proper interface design structure will help customers in digital banking improve their user experience.

7.4 Measurement of the Success Factor of Fintech in Digital Banking

In modern technical development and innovation, Fintech is one of the most successful implementations in the banking sector. The superior success level of the application is attributed to its numerous features and environmental approaches, which create substantial value.

The cross-sectional skill set in Fintech is essential for competing effectively in any working approach, making the process successful in the progress area. It has also been observed that this approach can enhance performance significantly. The combination of highly sought-after resources makes the application a leader in its field [34]. The extensive range of the features in the application contributes to its success in its specific area of application. Talent management in the software further enhances the working structure and process management. Integrating financial and computer science under a single framework is crucial for leading the overall process effectively. Proper resources and useful tools in the software make the application distinctive [35]. High-value domains and enhanced processes have helped the platform achieve a superior market position among rivals in the financial market.

The user ecosystem is another crucial factor that helps software maintain a strong market position. Proper management of the distribution channel and vendoring is essential for improving the positioning and evaluation of the process in a specific area. Developing a robust infrastructure for the application ecosystem will enhance working efficiency. Specific knowledge in the application and strategic evaluation will act as positive catalysts in development. The business approach and distribution channel are also well-positioned in the financial market [36]. Fintech holds a strong position in its market segment by adopting a better approach to work. Funding and jurisdictions are key success factors that enhance the overall process and improve working efficiency. Sourcing talent and optimizing the working process are major components that contribute to the brand's superior outcomes. In digital banking, ensuring a well-designed interface and security system is essential for improved performance. Effectively creating the structure will also generate a better working environment, ultimately enhancing business value.

Market positioning and structure are also key success factors for the brand in its particular market. In the financial market, many companies maintain stable positions. In this environment, Fintech drives significant changes and progress, enhancing the business process structure. Targeting product distribution to underserved markets can help business performers capture a larger customer segment [37]. Sales and popularity of the product will increase through effective marketing actions. Fintech has the potential to achieve this, improving working efficiency and progress. New offerings should be compelling to increase customer interest. Fintech offers superior security and a user-friendly interface, enhancing the overall process. Online service and customer support are crucial in digital banking for maintaining high customer satisfaction. This, in turn, increases the success level of application distribution in the target market.

Financial services is a highly regulated industry, and although regulators aim to create a more innovation-friendly business environment by following the principles of proportionality and technological neutrality, FinTechs are also heavily regulated to maintain a stable working structure [38]. With the unification of financial sector regulations, especially rapid in Europe, opportunities for regulatory arbitrage are gradually disappearing. From a regulatory perspective, the financial sector is becoming more equal globally. Implementing policies and rules in the working area ensure better ethical consideration in the market.

7.5 Summary

Concluding the evaluation and impact of Fintech in this digital banking era has become clearer after this critical discussion. The financial sector is one of the most successful business markets with a significant market position. Monte Carlo Tree Search (MCTS) is an AI-based algorithm considered probabilistic in Fintech, analysing various optimal options to determine the right actions. The choice of the most appropriate business algorithm or logic among all the paths must include flexibility and the ability to change the behavior of the algorithms. Additionally, the behavior of the algorithms must be compared with the complexity of the operation to define its expected validation. Knowledge of logic control, with its higher capability and implementation complexity, should also be considered to properly evaluate the code.

Discussing the issues in this area, several factors can be included that significantly impact the implementation. Regulatory acts and security measures are among the most important aspects that organizations must maintain. These measures increase the stability of the working process and manage the business structure. Providing proper infrastructure is also essential for ensuring the success of the process and achieving superior market positioning. To maximize product distribution and capture better customer segment, technology acceptance models can be adopted by the business sector.

References

1. Statista, Total value of investments into fintech companies worldwide from 2010 to 2022, 2022, Available at:https://www.statista.com/statistics/719385/investments-into-fintech-companies-globally/ [Accessed on: 15th February, 2023].

2. Berg, T., Fuster, A., Puri, M., Fintech lending. *Annu. Rev. Financ. Econ.*, 14, 187–207, 2022.
3. Bollaert, H., Lopez-de-Silanes, F., Schwienbacher, A., Fintech and access to finance. *J. Corp. Financ.*, 68, 101941, 2021.
4. FINTECHNA, Algorithms in the Financial Services industry - The right choice for the right problem, 2021, Available at: https://www.fintechna.com/articles/algorithms-in-the-financial-services-industry-the-right-choice-for-the-right-problem/ [Accessed on: 15th February, 2023].
5. towardsdatascience.com, How can AI facilitate fintech algorithms to manage your finances?, 2020, Available at: https://towardsdatascience.com/can-ai-facilitate-fintech-algorithm-to-manage-your-finances-2c11a1afec74 [Accessed on: 15th February, 2023].
6. hindawi, Machine Learning in Mobile Computing: Methods and Applications, 2021, Available at: https://www.hindawi.com/journals/wcmc/2021/3950981/ [Accessed on: 15th February, 2023].
7. Świechowski, M., Godlewski, K., Sawicki, B., Mańdziuk, J., Monte Carlo tree search: A review of recent modifications and applications. *Artif. Intell. Rev.*, 56, 1–66, 2022.
8. insiderintelligence.com, The digital trends disrupting the banking industry in 2023, 2023. Available at: https://www.insiderintelligence.com/insights/banking-industry-trends/ [Accessed on: 15th February, 2023].
9. Jensen, J.H., A graph-based genetic algorithm and generative model/Monte Carlo tree search for the exploration of chemical space. *Chem. Sci.*, 10, 12, 3567–3572, 2019.
10. Goldstein, I., Jiang, W., Karolyi, G.A., To FinTech and beyond. *Rev. Financ. Stud.*, 32, 5, 1647–1661, 2019.
11. Tao, R., Su, C.W., Naqvi, B., Rizvi, S.K.A., Can Fintech development pave the way for a transition towards low-carbon economy: A global perspective. *Technol. Forecast. Soc. Change*, 174, 121278, 2022.
12. Hassan, M.K., Zulfikar, Z., Rabbani, M.R., Atif, M., Fintech Trends: Industry 4.0, Islamic Fintech, and Its Digital Transformation, in: *FinTech in Islamic Financial Institutions: Scope, Challenges, and Implications in Islamic Finance*, pp. 113–130, Springer International Publishing, Cham, 2022.
13. Gunawan, C. and Somantri, B., Financial inclusion in MSME: the role of technology adoption and digital economy, in: *FORUM EKONOMI*, vol. 25, pp. 7–14, February 2023.
14. Zachariadis, M., How "Open" Is the Future of Banking? Data Sharing and Open Data Frameworks in Financial Services, in: *The Technological Revolution in Financial Services. How Banks, FinTechs, and Customers Win Together*, pp. 129–157, 2020.
15. Ferrata, L., Digital financial inclusion–an engine for "leaving no one behind". *Public Sect. Econ.*, 43, 4, 445–458, 2019.

16. Senyo, P.K., Gozman, D., Karanasios, S., Dacre, N., Baba, M., Moving away from trading on the margins: Economic empowerment of informal businesses through FinTech. *Inf. Syst. J.*, 33, 1, 154–184, 2023.
17. Larsson, B. and Rolandsson, B., *The digital transformation of financial services and labour relations in theFinTech sector: Summary report*, FinTech Trade unions.com, 2022.
18. Sabourin, V. and Aka-Brou, M.C., Blockchain Technology and New Business Models for Banks in the Financial Services Industry, in: *Influence of FinTech on Management Transformation*, pp. 1–38, 2021.
19. mckinsey.com, Seven technologies shaping the future of fintech, 2021, Available at: https://www.mckinsey.com/cn/our-insights/our-insights/seven-technologies-shaping-the-future-of-fintech [Accessed on: 15th February, 2023].
20. forbes.com, 5 Ways Fintech Is Transforming Banking In India, 2021, Available at: https://www.forbes.com/advisor/in/banking/5-ways-fintech-is-transforming-banking-in-india/ [Accessed on: 15th February, 2023].
21. Shabu, K. and Ramankutty, V., Neobanking in India: Opportunities and Challenges from Customer Perspective, in: *Proceedings of the International Conference on Innovative Computing & Communication (ICICC)*, 2022. Available at SSRN: https://ssrn.com/abstract=4037656.
22. Sharma, H. and Aggarwal, S., *Study on Digital Banking Financial Services in India: Trends, Opportunities & Challenges*, EasyChair, 2023.
23. Pizzi, S., Corbo, L., Caputo, A., Fintech and SMEs sustainable business models: Reflections and considerations for a circular economy. *J. Cleaner Prod.*, 281, 125217, 2021.
24. Babu, X. and Motiwalla, L., *Secured Serverless Microservices Architecture for Digital Process Innovation: A FinTech Case Study*, 2021.
25. Alijoyo, F.A., Bonita, I., Sirait, K.B., The risk management maturity assessment: the case of Indonesian fintech firm, in: *Proceedings of the 4th International Conference on Research in Management and Economics*, pp. 1324, 2021.
26. Siddik, A.B., Yong, L., Rahman, M.N., The role of Fintech in circular economy practices to improve sustainability performance: a two-staged SEM-ANN approach. *Environ. Sci. Pollut. Res.*, 30, 107465–107486, 2023.
27. Shala, A. and Perri, R., Regulatory barriers for fintech companies in Central and Eastern Europe. *East. J. Eur. Stud.*, 13, 2, 292–316, 2022.
28. Lim, S.H., Kim, D.J., Hur, Y., Park, K., An empirical study of the impacts of perceived security and knowledge on continuous intention to use mobile fintech payment services. *Int. J. Hum.-Comput. Interact.*, 35, 10, 886–898, 2019.
29. Nangin, M.A., Barus, I.R.G., Wahyoedi, S., The effects of perceived ease of use, security, and promotion on trust and its implications on fintech adoption. *J. Consum. Sci.*, 5, 2, 124–138, 2020.

30. Kemp, A., Palmer, E., Strelan, P., A taxonomy of factors affecting attitudes towards educational technologies for use with technology acceptance models. *Br. J. Educ. Technol.*, 50, 5, 2394–2413, 2019.
31. Rafique, H., Almagrabi, A.O., Shamim, A., Anwar, F., Bashir, A.K., Investigating the acceptance of mobile library applications with an extended technology acceptance model (TAM). *Comput. Educ.*, 145, 103732, 2020.
32. Yuen, K.F., Cai, L., Qi, G., Wang, X., Factors influencing autonomous vehicle adoption: An application of the technology acceptance model and innovation diffusion theory. *Technol. Anal. Strategic Manage.*, 33, 5, 505–519, 2021.
33. Ammenwerth, E., Technology acceptance models in health informatics: TAM and UTAUT. *Stud. Health Technol. Inform.*, 263, 64–71, 2019.
34. Karmańska, A., Critical success factors for FinTech, in: *The Digitalization of Financial Markets*, pp. 101–122, 2021.
35. Ryu, H.S. and Ko, K.S., Sustainable development of Fintech: Focused on uncertainty and perceived quality issues. *Sustainability*, 12, 18, 7669, 2020.
36. Goswami, S., Sharma, R.B., Chouhan, V., Impact of financial technology (Fintech) on financial inclusion (FI) in Rural India. *Univers. J. Account. Finance*, 10, 2, 483–497, 2022.
37. Roh, T., Yang, Y.S., Xiao, S., Park, B.I., What makes consumers trust and adopt fintech? An empirical investigation in China. *Electron. Commer. Res.*, 24, 1, 3–35, 2024.
38. Wagdi, O. and Hasaneen, A., Obstacles and success factors for entrepreneurship: a comparative analysis between Egypt and Nigeria. *Entrep. Sustain. Iss.*, 7, 2, 962–976, 2019.

8

Real-Time Data Visualization and Autonomous Finance: Uses of Emerging Technologies

Govind Singh[1]*, Lokesh Verma[2] and Anshika Baliyan[1]

[1]Quantum University, Roorkee, Uttarakhand, India
[2]Faculty of Management Studies, Shri Ram Group of Colleges, Muzaffarnagar, Uttar Pradesh, India

Abstract
In a globalized where technologies are continuously evolving, these new techniques significant impact business and finance. In this chapter, we will discuss some of the important emerging technologies that are influencing the fields of entrepreneurship, application development, finance, and business. We will begin by introducing the evolution of business, finance, entrepreneurship, and applications, highlighting how these fields evolve continuously. We will then explore the adoption of emerging technologies by industries, focusing on changes in technologies with particular reference to developing and developing countries Moving forward, we will discuss emerging technologies in both current and future business contexts. Some of the technologies we will cover include embedded business intelligence, augmented visual presentation, augmented analytics, and cloud management.

In addition to these technological advancements, we will explore the increasing automation in the finance industry, including blockchain, cloud banking, robotic process automation, and the Internet of Things. This chapter will provide comprehensive information to help you understand what, why, where, when, and how these technologies are transforming the current business and financial environment. Like the two sides of a coin, these new technologies can be very beneficial to businesses and their finances but also carry certain risks that pose serious threats to our daily lives and businesses. Therefore, we will also discuss the potential dangers associated with these technologies. Finally, we will conclude the chapter with safety advice and recommendations for managing these technologies.

**Corresponding author*: govindsingh282@gmail.com

Deepa Gupta, Mukul Gupta, Rajesh Kumar Dhanaraj, Balamurugan Balusamy and Parth Mukul Gupta (eds.) Computational Intelligence for Autonomous Finance, (143–166) © 2025 Scrivener Publishing LLC

***Keywords*:** Autonomous finance, automation, digitalization, emerging technologies, technical advancement

8.1 Introduction

The constant research, improvement, and implementation of technology have changed how business and financial activities are conducted. Today, corporate houses do not rely on traditional methods and technologies. Fast-evolving technologies have revolutionized how companies operate and interact with their customers. There is no doubt that automation is crucial to the success of the modern enterprises. Whether it is idea validation, finding a name for a business, branding, or managing operations, advanced technologies enable efficient and effective solutions. These technologies include generative artificial intelligence, embedded business intelligence, amplified visual presentation, augmented analytics, cloud team management, and artificial intelligence.

Financial service firms have adopted new technologies to enhance consumer interaction, improved efficiency, and elevate customer experience. Innovations in information technology have driven the digitalization and transformation of financial services through advanced customer experience management. Blockchain, for instance, provides a secure and transparent environment for transactions. Key technologies in finance include cloud banking, robotic process automation, blockchain, IoT, and autonomous finance [1].

The industry has a long history, beginning in the 1800s, and has undergone three industrial revolutions. Today, we are entering the fourth industrial revolution. The revolution features the automation of supply chain monitoring and analysis through smart technologies. Driven by Industrial IoT and self-organizing systems using algorithms based on digital devices, this transformation integrates with back-end systems like enterprise resource planning to enhance everything from manufacturing to supply chain management, followed by monitoring and control. To understand innovative technologies, we first need to understand the underlying business and financial processes.

8.1.1 Industry 4.0

Technology is the key to revolutionizing the distribution and manufacturing of global business. This can only be achieved through a comprehensive set of system of business, operation, and management processes.

Efficient resource utilization is directly related to managing assets, improving labor productivity, optimizing inventory, enhancing quality, matching supply with demand, offering services and after-sales support, reducing time to market, and staying abreast of technology and market trends. Numerous tools and techniques are used to enhance the mechanical devices of Industry 4.0, which form the foundation of the global business environment [1].

Figure 8.1 shows value drivers, resources, and processes can increase production by 3–5% through smart energy usage, intelligent lots, and real-time yield optimization. The societal marketplace concept has significantly impacted services and after sales offerings through forecasting, remote protection, and guided self-service, reducing maintenance costs by 10–40%. Customer discretion, parallel engineering, and rapid experimentation have significantly reduced the time to market for value drivers in technology by 20–50%. Under asset utilization, a 30–50% reduction in machine time is observed through concepts such as routing flexibility, machine flexibility, remote monitoring and administration, digital performance management, and programming of knowledge work. Accuracy in forecasting to match supply and demand has increased by 85%, driven by data-driven decision-making, demand prediction, and design-to-value principles. Statistical quality control, multivariable predictive control, and cloud-based digital quality management have reduced quality costs by 10–20% and stock costs by 20–50%. Technological advancements like 3-D printing *in situ* and real-time supply chain optimization have led to a 45–55% increase in productivity among technical professions. This is achieved through the cyberization of knowledge work, machine collaboration, remote surveillance and control, digital performance management, and automation of knowledge work.

8.1.2 Business Process

Business process is a set of activities with a specific organizational purpose aimed at achieving a consistent outcome. BMP operates systematically to control cost and outsource processes to achieve desired goals. Visibility and mapping are crucial in defining business processes. Business processes refer to the systematic execution of important tasks by individuals in the organization, connecting with organizational goals, whether they involve a product or a service. Many interconnected processes are involved in daily operations.

For an organization to produce the desired output, its functioning must be executed correctly. The business process is directly related to the output of the organization, so clear goals and objectives are essential. These goals must be supported by different processes, such as the management process, the organizational process and the supporting process.

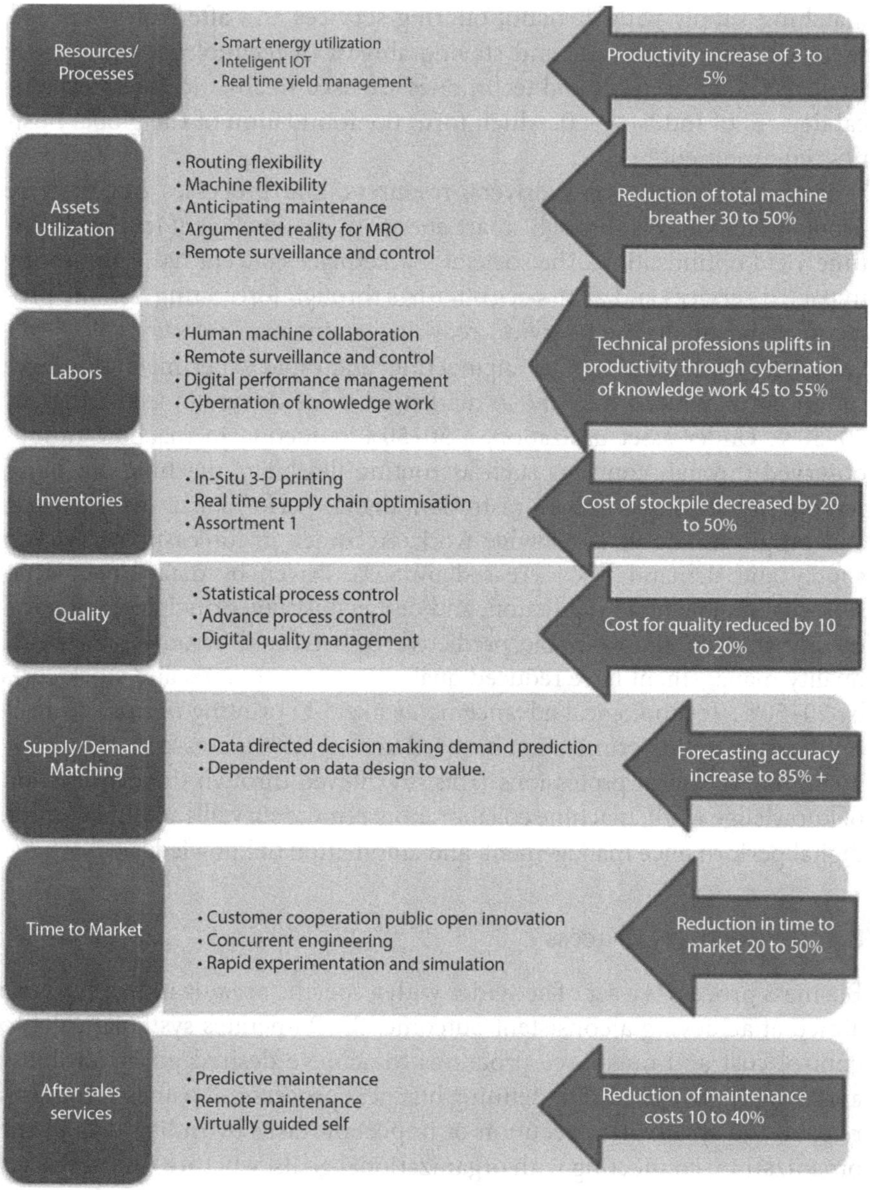

Figure 8.1 Industry 4.0 bar value drivers.

8.1.2.1 Management Process

The management process includes all functions necessary for the long-term stability of the organization, such as planning, organization, leadership, and control. These are the routine activities that the organization performs.

8.1.2.2 Operating Process

The operating process is a group of activities which must be performed with a high level of excellence to maintain the company's competitive edge in the market by providing value-added services in both business operations and results. This includes activities such as selling, marketing, customer support, and operations.

8.1.2.3 Support Process

The primary objective of support processes is to ensure the proper functioning of operational activities and to support the operating process. These processes add value to internal activities. BPM is crucial for the proper functioning of the business. In simple terms, BPM is concerned with the productivity of the organization. Technological advances are enhancing BPM by increasing transparency, customer focus, and knowledge work. Artificial Intelligence is helping companies validate their ideas faster than before. Technologies such as cloud team management automate processes, improve security, support governance and compliance, monitor performance, and manage costs. These are examples of the technologies we will discuss.

8.1.3 Finance

Finance is one of the most critical aspects of any commercial enterprise. It involves the management of money, encompassing various activities such as forecasting, saving, borrowing, and investing. Since finance is the foundation of every business, it is almost impossible to succeed without strong financial management. Finance is used to buy assets, goods, raw materials, and anything else that will give momentum to a business. Therefore, finance and funds are the most important parts of any organization. If business finances are mismanaged, ot can lead to significant losses. Thus, mastering business finance is a top priority and its importance should never be underestimated. A business cannot function properly unless it has enough money to operate. Business finance is used for a variety of crucial purposes such as strategic planning, financial management, and promotion.

The pandemic has prompted business leaders to transition gradually to digital platforms, favoring online services over traditional ones, and making these activities more precise, easy to execute, and cost-effective. This shift has led financial firms to quickly adopt new technologies, incorporate cutting-edge advancements into their offerings, and continuously improve customer service. Technology continues to drive progress in the finance sector, with many new technologies redefining the financial world. Data security is a major concern in the modern digital world, especially in the finance sector due to the increasing number of data breaches on Meta and other platforms. Advancements in cybersecurity and blockchain are essential for ensuring the transparency and security of users' data. Cloud-based banking architecture makes banking more convenient and accurate, providing an ideal solution for seamless global payments, P2P (peer-to-peer) transfers and contactless payments. Neo-Banking is a new revolution in banking, making banking easier and more accessible for everyone. This is due to the lower cost of banking infrastructure, as most banking activities are conducted online, with physical branches playing a minor role.

8.2 Thriving in the Tech Age: How Businesses Adapt to Emerging Technologies

The pace of technological progress and automation is surging at an unprecedented rate, transforming both society and the business world. Just a decade ago, the landscape looked vastly different:

- The Internet of Things (IoT) did not connect everyday devices, making information at our fingertips a futuristic dream.
- Voice-activated searches were unheard of, and traditional methods dominated information retrieval.
- Remote work lacked the seamless, centralized platforms seen today, hindering collaboration and flexibility.
- Social media marketing tools like Instagram and short-form video platforms were non-existent.

To stay ahead of the curve, businesses must embrace innovation and adapt to evolving technologies. It is not just about adopting the latest trends; it is about harnessing their full potential to optimize efficiency across all areas of operation. The key to success lies in understanding that every company approaches innovation differently. Some may wholeheartedly embrace a new technology, while others might view it as unnecessary. This diversity allows each organization to tailor its approach and leverage technology in a way that best suits its specific needs and goals [2].

8.2.1 Boosting Efficiency and Innovation: The Critical Role of Adapting to New Technologies

The importance of adapting to new technologies cannot be overstated. Keeping up-to-date with automation and technical innovation is essential for the success of any business. Adopting the right technologies can increase flexibility, streamline operations, and help organization adapt to a constantly changing marketplace. Environmental companies, in particular, must constantly adapt to the ever-evolving technological world. The main benefits of adapting to technologies include:

- **Enhanced Productivity and Efficiency:** New technologies automate tasks and streamline processes, enabling you to achieve more with less [3].
- **Gaining a Competitive Advantage:** Staying ahead of the curve with innovative tools allows you to stand out from the competition and offer superior value to your customers [3].
- **Empowering Remote Work:** Modern technologies remove geographical barriers and facilitate seamless collaboration, regardless of location.
- **Building Robust and Scalable Workflows:** Integrating new technologies creates a stronger foundation for your business, enabling it to adapt and grow with ease.
- **Positioning for Long-Term Success:** Embracing innovation equips your business with the tools and capabilities needed to thrive in an ever-evolving landscape.

8.2.2 Navigating the Digital Age: The Current State of Technological Adoption

The future holds exciting possibilities with the continuous emergence of innovative technologies like the Metaverse and Augmented Reality. These advancements, alongside numerous others, are transforming various industries and reshaping our world. To navigate this evolving landscape, understanding how different companies approach technological adoption is crucial. By analyzing comparative data through graphs and other visualizations, we can gain valuable insights into how individual organizations integrate new technologies based on various factors.

8.2.3 The Driving Force: Why Businesses Embrace New Technologies

Companies invest in new technologies for a variety of strategic reasons:

- **Staying Ahead of the Curve:** Embracing new technologies allows businesses to leverage the latest advancements, maintain a competitive edge, and future-proof their operations.
- **Enhancing Efficiency and Productivity:** Modern technologies often automate tasks, streamline workflows, and optimize processes, leading to significant time and resource savings.
- **Meeting Evolving Customer Needs:** As customer expectations and market demands shift, businesses need to adapt by adopting technologies that enhance user experience and offer innovative solutions.
- **Supporting Business Growth:** Scaling operations effectively often necessitates integrating new technologies that can facilitate expansion and accommodate growing demands.
- **Addressing End-User Requirements:** Staying responsive to the needs and preferences of employees and customers is essential. New technologies can empower workforces and fulfill user expectations more effectively.
- **Unlocking New Capabilities:** Utilizing cutting-edge features and functionalities allows businesses to explore new possibilities, improve existing services, and drive innovation.

8.2.4 Top Seven Emerging Technologies Businesses are Embracing

- **Artificial Intelligence (AI):** Revolutionizing decision-making, automation, and data analysis.
- **Internet of Things (IoT):** Connecting devices and collecting valuable data to improve efficiency and insights.
- **Robotic Process Automation (RPA):** Automating repetitive tasks to free up human resources for higher-level work.

- **Cloud Native Development:** Building and deploying applications designed for the cloud environment, promoting scalability and agility.
- **API Brokerage:** Managing and securing Application Programming Interfaces (APIs) to facilitate communication and data exchange between different systems.
- **Blockchain:** Providing a secure and transparent way to record transactions and build trust in decentralized systems.
- **Serverless Computing:** Eliminating the need to manage servers, allowing businesses to focus on developing and deploying applications faster.

8.3 The Future of Work and Innovation: Emerging Technologies Transforming Businesses

8.3.1 Actionable Insights at Your Fingertips: The Power of Embedded BI

In the age of digitization, every company has become a data company. The ability to store, analyze, and use data effectively can set industry leaders apart from the competition. Businesses seek actionable insights from their data, and this is where Business Intelligence (BI) comes in. BI encompasses the technical and procedural infrastructure used for collecting, storing, and analyzing data generated from business activities. It involves a broad spectrum of activities, including data mining, process analysis, benchmarking, and descriptive analytics. By collecting data and presenting it in reports, BI empowers management to make informed decisions. Traditionally, BI functioned as a standalone application, requiring users to switch between their main business application and separate BI tools for data analysis. This approach hampered work efficiency and user adoption. However, the introduction of Embedded Business Intelligence (EBI) has revolutionized this paradigm.

Embedded Business Intelligence (EBI) empowers users with data insights directly within their everyday business applications. This innovative approach integrates self-serve BI tools, interactive reporting, and data visualizations, leading to a seamless and enhanced user experience. EBI extends its reach beyond office walls, allowing mobile access for dispersed workforces. With real-time data at their fingertips, teams can collaborate effectively on projects, regardless of location.

Unlike traditional BI with its limited data scope, EBI offers significant customization. Users can integrate data from diverse sources, ensuring they have a holistic view and can fulfill their specific needs. Business users are increasingly leveraging BI tools to make data-driven decisions. EBI further empowers them by integrating seamlessly with their existing workflows. By automating specific tasks based on pre-defined parameters, EBI streamlines operations and enhances efficiency and accuracy [4].

8.3.1.1 *Application of Embedded BI*

Embedded BI holds immense potential to empower businesses in various ways, and the Human Resources (HR) department offers a prime example.

HR manages critical functions like hiring, training, and event planning, demanding multifaceted solutions. Embedded BI can provide unique value by integrating modern employee records with data on turnover costs. This empowers HR to:

- ➢ Develop and implement well-timed, well-planned, and well-executed strategies and improvement programs to build a reliable workforce with deep expertise and control.
- ➢ Align all business activities and departmental objectives with corporate goals through strategic alignment.
- ➢ Analyze the effectiveness of recruiting strategies compared to employee attributes, skill sets, and factors affecting voluntary resignation. This data-driven approach optimizes recruitment and retention efforts.
- ➢ Measure and compare employee performance to identify areas, roles, or individuals requiring improvement.

8.3.1.2 *Embedded BI in Supply Chain Management and Logistic*

Currently, logistics and supply chain management companies use GPS to monitor vessels or vehicles during the transportation of stocks. Embedded analytics combines the location-based statistics with other relevant data to enhance the operational performance. By adding embedded BI capabilities, the management company can:

- ➢ Understand and leverage the customer's profitability
- ➢ Improve customer service
- ➢ Increase capacity planning, allocation, and visibility of the supply chain

- Analyze drivers' and carriers' performance fairly and efficiently.

8.3.1.3 *Embedded BI in Sales and Services*

Equipped with embedded analytics, staff can gain real-time insights into customer purchase history and product usage. This empowers them to identify cross-selling and up-selling opportunities, tailor recommendations to individual customer needs and maximize the potential for successful deals.

8.3.2 Augmented Analytics

As we have discussed the significance of data in the modern economy, the sheer volume of data can be overwhelming for human to analyze and interpret. This is where Augmented Analytics plays a crucial role. Augmented Analytics is a branch of data analysis which "augments" data using a combination of technologies such as Artificial Intelligence (AI), Machine Learning (ML), and Natural Language Processing (NLP). Machine Learning automates complex processes such as data preparation, data analysis, and generating meaningful insights. NLP simplifies user interaction with data, allowing users to ask questions in their natural language and receive accurate answers. Businesses that use augmented analytics derive tremendous value from it. This technology enables them to obtain valuable data much quicker without needing expertise in handling big data. It helps business users get relevant data more easily by asking the right questions and immediately finding insights related to their business.

8.3.2.1 *Importance of Augmented Analytics Prospecting the Opportunity of Big Data*

Companies can make important decisions such as when to produce, from whom to source, how to market, and much more after analyzing a set of data. However, in today's data-driven world, it is difficult for companies to interpret data without any bias. If an immediate response is needed, it becomes impossible. Artificial intelligence and machine learning are essential for finding insights from large datasets. This is where augmented analytics comes in, combining data analysis with artificial intelligence to analyze vast amounts of data effectively.

8.3.2.1.1 Minimizing the Dependency on Data Scientist

The data analytics process involves time-consuming and complex tasks that typically require a data scientist. The cost of hiring these data scientists is high due to the global shortage of data professionals.

While augmented analytics cannot replace specialists, it can significantly streamline their workflows. By automating tasks like data collection, preparation, cleaning, and analysis, augmented analytics frees up valuable time for data scientists. This allows them to focus on higher-level tasks such as interpreting results and generating strategic insights, ultimately enhancing their value within the organization.

8.3.2.1.2 Empowering Everyone: Making Data Analysis Accessible for All

One of the key advantages of augmented analytics is that even non-professionals can use it effectively. Since augmented analytics automates complex analytics processes and allows users to find data by simply asking a few questions, professionals without prior experience in data science can benefit from advanced analytics. ML guides the user by suggesting what questions to ask, and the answers to these questions come in the form of graphs, charts, and maps. This means users do not have to prepare these visualizations themselves and can explore the data with ease.

8.3.2.1.3 Natural Language Interaction

In augmented analytics, natural language processing allows users to type questions in plain language to query the data instead of using data query code. The system provides a guided experience by first translating the user's text into a query and then making suggestions to fill in the gaps, ensuring it understands the intent and context of the user's question. This enables users to gain a detailed understanding of their data without needing a thorough knowledge of data models. Additionally, the system generates textual descriptions of insights from the data, which also explain visual data. This helps users understand the insights without requiring deep knowledge of interpreting visualizations.

8.3.2.2 Benefits and Uses of Augmented Analytics in Business

Some of the advantages of augmented analytics include agility, accuracy, efficiency, and confidence. Business use cases for augmented analytics include finance, accounts receivable, sales and marketing, manufacturing, and human resources.

8.3.2.3 *Use of Analytics in Business*

8.3.2.3.1 Finance

With the help of advanced analytics, a financial analyst can easily predict and control costs across different business segments.

8.3.2.3.2 Accounts Receivable

ML can be used by financial managers to forecast future cash flows, predict timely payments, and develop appropriate recovery strategies.

8.3.2.3.3 Sales and Marketing

Sales and marketing teams will benefit from increased customer leads and the ability to quickly identify cross-selling and up-selling opportunities.

8.3.2.3.4 Manufacturing

With augmented analytics, manufacturers can predict future product demand and strategize spending across different departments.

8.3.2.3.5 Human Resource

HR managers can forecast employee performance, analyze their performance, and take corrective actions.

8.3.3 Cloud Computing

Cloud management is the process of controlling and maintaining the public, private, hybrid, or multi-cloud environments. It involves a set of processes, policies, policies, and technologies used to manage cloud computing technologies that operate in the cloud. Cloud management is highly efficient and effective for IT firms to gain full control over an expandable and dynamic cloud environment. It combines different technologies to provide a consistent and cohesive strategic process [5].

Cloud management coordinates the delivery and management of cloud computing infrastructure, applications, data, and access control. Enterprise software and tools are increasingly being deployed to the cloud to reduce the upfront investment compared to installing on-site infrastructure. With cloud management, administrators can monitor a wide range of cloud activities, including application deployment and utilization, lifecycle management of resources, data integration, and risk management.

8.3.3.1 How Cloud Management Works

Usually, companies install cloud management systems in their dedicated cloud infrastructure. Once installed, the management system monitors and records performance and activity, which is then displayed on a web-based dashboard for user performance. System administrators can use the cloud management platform as a single point of control to resolve potential issues.

8.3.3.2 Benefits of Cloud Management

Here are some general benefits of cloud management.

8.3.3.2.1 Overwhelming Automation

Managing different applications is a repetitive and complex task, especially in a large and intricate cloud environment. Cloud management enables software resource management, automation of power control, continuous integration, and management reduction.

8.3.3.2.2 Capacity Management

Acquiring intangible virtual infrastructure is much easier than acquiring tangible assets. However, this ease of acquisition can lead to the risk of over-provisioning or underutilizing these technologies.

Accurate reporting and detailed analysis of cloud management help organizations anticipate and plan their needs, improving resource acquisition, utilization, and placement.

8.3.3.2.3 Compliance and Management

Moving to a cloud-based infrastructure relinquishes control over certain physical assets and applications, but the enterprise must still monitor access rights to maintain compliance. Cloud management ensures that users configure settings according to regulatory requirements by providing timely notifications.

8.3.3.2.4 Control and Registration

Cloud management allows for the recording and monitoring of every transaction in the company. This helps monitor and understand activities in business environments. It can be used to collect, analyze, and correlate logs, which aids in identifying errors, automating risk management, and optimizing performance.

8.3.3.2.5 Performance and Cost Reporting

Cloud computing costs can easily exceed an organization's budget if not closely controlled. Cloud management equips managers with tools for cost control, forecasting, and reporting, enabling them to visualize accurate data on resource usage by type and timing. This leads to efficient allocation of resources, better understanding of cash flow, and elimination of unnecessary costs.

8.3.3.2.6 Security

The combination of machine learning capabilities and cloud management tools empowers organizations with robust threat intelligence and detection. This powerful synergy also streamlines security monitoring processes, enhancing overall security posture.

8.3.4 Artificial Intelligence

Artificial Intelligence (AI) is the imitation of human rational functions, particularly by electronic devices. It is controlled by systems and overseen specialists in speech recognition, natural language processing (NLP), and electronic devices with an AI-specific vision [6].

8.3.4.1 Learning Processes

In the learning processes of artificial intelligence, writing computer programs involves information collection and the development of structures that convert this information into valid information. The standards or structures, also known as algorithms, convey explicit instructions to computer hardware to perform specific functions.

8.3.4.2 Reasoning Process

In reasoning branch of AI, software design focuses on determining the optimal algorithm for achieving a certain goal.

8.3.4.3 Self-Correction Process

In self-correction, AI programming continuously involves algorithms to ensure they provide the most accurate results.

8.3.5 Current Scenario of Artificial Intelligence in Businesses

Organizations utilize AI in various ways, with most applications focusing on supporting growth and innovation. AI and machine learning are being used creatively by companies to enhance corporate performance. AI offers the following business benefits:

- Enhancing efficiency through process automation
- Improving services through accelerated processes
- Utilizing consumer insights for decision making
- Discovering new product and service opportunities.

8.3.6 Application of Artificial Intelligence in Businesses

Some of the most frequent uses of AI include needs machine learning, cybersecurity, customer relationship management, internet searches, and personal assistants.

8.3.6.1 Machine Learning

Machine learning is widely used in systems that collect massive amounts of data. For example, smart energy management systems gather data from sensors linked to various assets. Machine learning algorithms contextualize these data before presenting it to decision-makers, enabling them to better understand energy use and maintenance needs [7].

8.3.6.2 Cybersecurity

Artificial intelligence is a valuable ally in identifying vulnerabilities in computer network defenses. AI systems may identify cyber-attacks and other cyber threats by recognizing patterns in data intake. When a threat is identified, AI can analyze user data to determine the source and help prevent future threats. The constant vigilance and consistency of AI provide an additional layer of security, significantly benefiting the management if user infrastructure [7].

8.3.6.3 Customer Relationship Management

Artificial intelligence is also transforming Customer Relationship Management (CRM) systems. Platforms like Zoho and Salesforce typically require human input to remain accurate and up-to-date. When artificial intelligence (AI) is integrated into these platforms, a standard CRM system evolves into an auto-updating, self-correcting system that manages user connections efficiently.

8.3.6.4 *Internet and Data Research*

AI enhances internet research and data analysis by identifying patterns in users' search habits to deliver more relevant information. As AI technology advances and users engage with their devices more frequently, they will experience a more personalized experience. This will significantly impact small businesses by simplifying the process of targeting highly specific niche markets.

8.4 Major Emerging Technologies in Finance

8.4.1 Robotics Process Automation (RPA)

One of the terms most frequently used in the modern world is "automation." In addition to being commonly used, automation is a fundamental component of almost every industry today. The use of automation technologies has accelerated development to entirely new levels. One significant addition to the rapidly expanding automation sector is robotic process automation (RPA). RPA is a type of business process automation technology that uses digital workers with artificial intelligence (AI) or robots with specialized software. It involves software with machine learning (ML) and artificial intelligence (AI) capabilities to handle repetitive, high-volume tasks previously performed by humans. These tasks include conducting interviews, performing computations, maintaining documents, and making connections. When users hear the term automation, they might picture a robot working independently of humans to complete tasks. While this is partly true, there are some misconceptions, such as the following:

- RPA is not a physical robot and is not humanoid.
- Humans cannot be fully replaced by RPA bots.
- RPA bots cannot mimic human intellectual functions because they lack the ability to reason logically or make decisions.

Features of RPA include:

- rich analytical speed
- scriptless automation
- security
- creation of bots
- debugging.

RPA's advantages include:

- higher customer satisfaction
- faster processing
- better quality and scalability
- lower costs and operational risk
- increased consistency and accuracy.

Types of RPA

- **Unattended and Autonomous RPA:** Ideal for reducing labor-intensive tasks like background data processing. These do not need any human interference and integrate computer vision, cognitive automation, AI, machine learning, and other technologies.
- **Attended RPA:** Frees up resources for higher-value tasks within the organization by recording and replaying manual, repetitive front-office tasks in real time, and mimicking mouse clicks made by users on their desktop or in their browser.
- **Hybrid RPA:** A combination of attended and unattended RPA. These bots handle both front- and back-office work for the company.

Use of RPA:

- Banking and finance
- Human resource
- Marketing and sales
- Insurance agencies
- Customer relation management
- IT integration process.

8.4.2 Blockchain

Blockchain first appeared in 2008 by Satoshi Nakamoto. Blockchain can be described as the collection of records called blocks, linked with each other, strongly resistant to alteration, and protected using cryptographic hashes as unique IDs. Blockchain is a decentralized data ledger that is securely exchanged, allowing a restricted number of people to share data. Blockchain provides remarkable advancements in decentralization, security, unaltered data and transparency, making it the ideal tool for upcoming applications. There are numerous benefits of using Blockchain Technology, such as transparency, lower transaction cost, faster transaction, and more.

8.4.2.1 Types of Blockchain

There are four types of Blockchain:

- ➢ Consortium Blockchain
- ➢ Hybrid Blockchain
- ➢ Private Blockchain
- ➢ Public Blockchain

8.4.2.1.1 Consortium Blockchain

Another name for consortium blockchain is federated blockchain. It resembles a hybrid blockchain system and is more secure to public blockchains. Research, banking, payments, and food tracking companies like Swiggy and Zomato, use it. ICICI Bank, Axis Bank, and other banks are also utilizing blockchain technology.

8.4.2.1.2 Hybrid Blockchain

Organizations that desire the best of both private and public blockchains sometimes employ a hybrid blockchain. This type of blockchain includes the characteristics of both private and public blockchain systems, allowing businesses to create a private permission-based system that is secure and cost effective. It is used by real people.

8.4.2.1.3 Private Blockchain

A private blockchain operates with a restricted context, often as a closed network managed by single entity. These networks are typically smaller and run on small network within a firm. Private blockchains are faster, with higher transactions per second (TPS), and are used for managing supply chain management, asset ownership, internal voting, etc.

8.4.2.1.4 Public Blockchain

A public blockchain is completely open to everyone, allowing anybody to join the system. Every authorized member has a copy of the digital ledger, ensuring complete openness and transparency of data. It is decentralized and secured, meaning data cannot be altered or manipulated once it is recorded on the blockchain. Public blockchains are also known as permissionless blockchains. They are trusted and secure, suitable for applications like voting and fundraising.

8.4.3 Autonomous Finance

Autonomous technology refers to technology capable of operating under various conditions without human intervention. Similar to human learning and development, artificial intelligence continuously absorbs information to improve decision-making. One prominent example of autonomous technology is artificial intelligence (AI), which can operate independently and make decisions without human input. Examples include chatbots, drones, humanoid robots, functional robots, and self-driving cars. In corporate finance, staying current with artificial intelligence advancements is crucial as it transforms industries. Autonomous accounting and finance features can revolutionize tasks such as annual report creation, book closing, and debt collection. Autonomous finance involves performing routine financial operations with minimal human intervention. Technologies such as artificial intelligence (AI), natural language processing (NLP), robotic process automation (RPA), cloud computing, and advanced analytics form the foundation of autonomous finance.

Companies can benefit from autonomous finance in several ways, including:

- ➢ **Time savings:** Labor-intensive operations like payment aggregation and reconciliation time-consuming. Automating these tasks can save employee significant time and effort.
- ➢ **Decreased human error:** Manually handling financial and accounting tasks often results in errors. Finance automation tools can minimize these mistakes..
- ➢ **Improved consistency:** Automating financial processes based on industry-specific best practices ensures standardization, reducing inconsistencies in data collection and information sharing.
- ➢ **Data security:** Storing sensitive financial data in spreadsheets can lead to data misplacement and breaches. An ideal

automation solution restricts data access to only authorized users, enhancing security.

- **Intelligent analytics:** Autonomous finance solutions provide robust analytics and reporting capabilities, offering greater insights into an organization's finance functions. This improves decision-making and risk assessment.
- **Scalability**: Automation solutions enable companies to scale without needing additional employees, reducing overhead and increasing working capital.
- **Optimized resource utilization:** Boost employee productivity by allowing finance leaders to focus on high-impact tasks and tackle critical business challenges.

8.4.4 Internet of Things (IoT)

The Internet of Things describes the network of physical objects—"things"—that are embedded with sensors, software, and other technologies for the purpose of connecting and exchanging data with other devices and systems over the internet. Internet of Things application use machine learning algorithms to analyze massive amounts of data in the cloud. These algorithms can identify equipment irregularities and send alerts to users. Cloud-based IoT applications in business can help users rapidly enhance existing processes for supply chains, customer service, human resources, and financial services, without the need to recreate complete business processes. One example is the use of IoT to increase efficiency and safety in connected logistics for fleet management. Companies can use IoT fleet monitoring to direct trucks in real time, improving efficiency [8].

The Internet of Things has been influencing the financial sector in various ways:

- IoT enables financial organizations to provide better services to their customers by analyzing critical data to understand their needs and suggest customized products.
- Banks and financial institutions utilize IoT to reduce risks, block hacked accounts, and analyze suspicious user data.
- Banking transactions have become more convenient with advanced contactless payment services.
- IoT provides real-time data that banks can use to update customers about offers that best suit their needs and speed up decision-making [9].

Internet of Things applications in the financial services sector:

1. IoT can enhance fraud detection and data security.
2. Customizing the customer experience can be facilitated by IoT.
3. With IoT technology, banks can remotely monitor and better manage their clients' needs.
4. Businesses can gain from the real-time data visibility provided by IoT-powered systems.
5. IoT has the potential to revolutionize traditional banking by enabling users to access their funds from anywhere at any time. Advanced technology in wearables and IoT integration offers convenient payment functionality.
6. IoT ensures that a branch's resources are utilized to their fullest potential to boost productivity and reduce overhead.
7. It increases customer trust and benefits security.

Advances in technology have led to improvements in the operations of banking and financial services organizations. These include the adoption of open banking, faster payments, and more responsive mobile services. The Internet of Things encompasses, among other things:

- Contactless payments
- Smart contracts
- Smart ATMs.

8.5 Risk Associated with Emerging Technologies

Organizations face new challenges due to the rapid changes in the corporate environment. Businesses must contend with a range of unexpected events, such as a global pandemic, changing stakeholder expectations, unstable economic conditions, and stricter regulations. Many businesses are turning to emerging technologies to stay competitive [10].

However, the advantages of emerging technologies must be carefully weighed against their drawbacks. ISACA's "The Pulse: Emerging Technology 2021" study found that emerging technologies can disrupt incumbents by solving current challenges and problems. When implementing new technologies, businesses need to consider both the advantages and disadvantages simultaneously.

In the ISACA survey, participants were asked about the risks involved in using the technology to gain a better understanding of how people perceive it. Only 9% of respondents thought AI posed a high risk, compared to the 30% and 33% who assessed the risks as low or medium, respectively. To ascertain the actual risk to the organization, businesses must consider the sophistication and maturity of AI-enabled business processes [11].

8.6 Conclusion

Businesses may find that new technologies do not meet their expectations. To mitigate this risk, a clear vision backed by attainable goals must be developed. Extensive research is necessary to determine the requirements for new projects that will significantly impact the business as part of the due diligence process. The adoption of new technologies should be heavily influenced by IT governance. The governance process should include representation from IT departments such as application development, infrastructure, and security. This will facilitate communication with different departments within the company, streamline project execution, and help determine any additional requirements. Senior leadership should be monitored and given regular status updates during the project and after launch to ascertain whether ROI was realized or miscalculated.

Changing regulations pose risks that could impede the success of emerging technologies. Privacy laws related to the collection of consumer data may hinder businesses' ability to effectively utilize certain emerging technologies, as these laws can disrupt the production of existing goods and services. Additionally, new regulations concerning algorithmic bias in customer-facing technologies are on the horizon. To adapt, models must incorporate agile development processes and ongoing regulatory monitoring to stay compliant with new and evolving regulations.

Lastly, an algorithmic error could result from a technological problem, compromising data security and degrading its quality. These risks can be minimized by implementing effective change management protocols. Peer reviews for coding and model changes should be conducted, and version controls should appropriately log changes to models and source code repositories. Additionally, these processes efficiently create and run test cases. During the planning and construction stages, it is crucial to pay attention to the data set to identify any potential biases and ethical dilemmas. While emerging technologies can provide competitive advantages, they also come with risks. By collaborating with internal audit or enterprise risk management, process owners can proactively identify risks. Discussing risks and controls early on will make it easier to find any unresolved problems, implement process improvements, and ensure that emerging technologies are successfully incorporated into the business.

References

1. Madu, U.A., Assessment of the Adoption Rate of Technologies among Fadama III Farmers in Adamawa State, Nigeria. *Asian J. Agric. Rural Dev.*, 3, 9, 657–666, 2013.
2. The Indian Express, US follows India on disclosure of CEO-staff pay ratio at companies, 2013, https://indianexpress.com/article/business/companies/us-follows-india-on-disclosure-of-ceostaff-pay-ratio-at-companies/.
3. The eSoft Editorial Team, AI in Streamlining Workplace Operations and Maximizing Efficiency, web link -https://esoftskills.com/ai-in-streamlining-workplace-operations-and-maximizing-efficiency/.
4. Campagne, C.S., Roche, P., Müller, F., Burkhard, B., Ten years of ecosystem services matrix: Review of a (r)evolution. *One Ecosyst.*, 5, e51103, 2020, doi: 10.3897/oneeco.5.e51103.
5. Certificación como ARQUITECTO DE NUBE CERTIFIED TRAINING, Cloud Architecture, Web Link- https://1library.co/document/zg6enwnq-certificacion-como-arquitecto-de-nube-certified-training-cloud-architect-cloud-architecture-cloud-architect.html#google_vignette.
6. *Study On The Impact Of Artificial Intelligence On The Infringement And Enforcement Of Copyright And Designs, Impact of Technology Deep Dive Report I*, European Union Intellectual Property Office, Alicante, Spain, 2022.
7. AXIOM Groupe, How Artificial Intelligence Will Transform Businesses, 2024, https://www.vertexplus.com/blog/artificial-intelligence-business-transforming-business#:~:text=By%20augmenting%20human%20decision%2Dmaking,and%20fostering%20a%20competitive%20advantage.
8. Marszałek, P. and Ratajczak-Mrozek, M., Introduction: Digitalization as a Driver of the Contemporary Economy, in: *Digitalization and Firm Performance*, M. Ratajczak-Mrozek, and P. Marszałek (Eds.), Palgrave Macmillan, Cham, 2022, https://doi.org/10.1007/978-3-030-83360-2_1.
9. Hu, Y., A game-based virtual machine pricing mechanism in federated clouds. *Int. J. Intell. Syst. Technol. Appl.*, 18, 6, 606–622, 2019, https://doi.org/10.1504/IJISTA.2019.102668.
10. Academic Journals, Online learning during the COVID-19 pandemic from the perspectives of English as foreign language students. *Educ. Res. Rev.*, 16, 7, 279–288, July 2021, doi-https://doi.org/10.5897/ERR2021.4169.
11. Ondemand International, International Business Environment: Economic Environment & Benefits Discussed, Web Link- https://ondemandint.com/resources/international-business-environment/.

9

AI and ML Modeling and Autonomous Finance in Microfinance: An Overview

D. N. Rao[1]* and Maheswaran Mahalingam[2]

[1]*Faculty of Management Science, SRMS College of Engineering & Technology, Bareilly, Uttar Pradesh, India*
[2]*Financial Analytics, IQturf Consulting Solutions, Mumbai, India*

Abstract

Microfinance gained international recognition when Muhammad Yunus and the Grameen Bank were awarded the Nobel Peace Prize in 1996. Since then, Microfinance has undergone significant transformations in coverage, asset management, and financial prudence. This chapter explores the next evolution in Microfinance through the adoption of Autonomous Finance, which integrates Artificial Intelligence (AI), Hyper Automation, and Data Management to redefine customer expectations and enhance operational efficiency.

The objective of this chapter is to analyse how Autonomous Finance can drive the future of Microfinance. Gartner's 2022 report emphasizes the shift towards finance operations increasingly driven by AI and other technologies, aiming to reduce human intervention. Autonomous Finance, with a market size estimated at USD 15 billion in 2022 and projected to grow at a CAGR of 17% from 2022 to 2030, offers extensive applications across banks, financial institutions, and healthcare. For Microfinance Institutions (MFIs), Autonomous Finance can streamline the entire customer lifecycle, from group finance marketing and lending to collection and delinquency management. This transition is essential to overcome the scalability limitations posed by traditional ground-level account management.

Forrester defines Autonomous Finance as "algorithm-driven services that make financial decisions and take actions on a customer's behalf". This study reviews existing practices and technological advancements, focusing on AI and Machine Learning (ML) in microfinance. Autonomous technologies can enhance customer enrolment efficiency, create robust credit risk frameworks, and use predictive analytics for delinquency management. These advancements automate

**Corresponding author*: raodn77@gmail.com

Deepa Gupta, Mukul Gupta, Rajesh Kumar Dhanaraj, Balamurugan Balusamy and Parth Mukul Gupta (eds.) Computational Intelligence for Autonomous Finance, (167–198) © 2025 Scrivener Publishing LLC

labour-intensive processes, increasing the speed and reach of financial services to underserved populations, thus enhancing financial inclusiveness.

Key suggestions foresee that Autonomous Finance can transform microfinance by reducing inefficiencies and expanding service delivery. AI and ML optimize financial decision-making, improve data governance, and ensure regulatory compliance. Autonomous Finance enhances MFIs' scalability, enabling them to serve a larger customer base more effectively and efficiently.

The chapter concludes that the adoption of Autonomous Finance is vital for MFIs to sustain growth and meet increasing demands in a post-pandemic world. It recommends a phased implementation strategy, focusing on the integration of AI-driven solutions and continuous monitoring of technological advancements. This approach will help MFIs maintain a competitive edge and achieve broader financial inclusion.

***Keywords*:** Autonomous finance, microfinance, artificial intelligence (AI), machine learning (ML), predictive analytics, robotic process automation (RPA), financial inclusiveness, credit risk framework

9.1 Understanding Autonomous Finance and Microfinance

9.1.1 Context

Microfinance was brought to the limelight when the Nobel Committee awarded the Peace Prize to Muhammad Yunus and Grameen Bank in 1996 [1]. Since the early 2000s, microfinance has witnessed value transformation through improved coverage, asset management, and overall financial prudence. With evolving disruptive technologies, microfinance is rapidly gearing up to embrace advanced analytics and financial governance to maintain its scale and speed.

To sustain the pace of growth, it needs uninterrupted technology to avoid future slowdowns like those experienced during COVID-19. Hence, it is paramount to adopt an alternative modus operandi to supplement existing analytics utilizing Autonomous Finance. The next wave of microfinance is being powered by Autonomous Finance, reinventing customer expectations with AI, hyper-automation, and data management.

9.1.1.1 Application Areas

Gartner, in its report on Top Priorities for Finance Leaders in 2022 [2], identified that CFOs are *"laying critical groundwork for an autonomous future—one in which finance operations are increasingly driven by artificial intelligence and other technologies, reducing the need for human intervention.*"

In the overall context, including microfinance, Autonomous Finance is applicable across banks, financial institutions, and healthcare, with its market size estimated at US$ 15 billion in 2022 and growing at a CAGR of 17% for 2022–2030 [3]. The area of Autonomous Finance is to be achieved across business processes, functions, and workflows through automation, leveraging self-learning software, and deploying AI and ML-embedded robotics.

By overlaying this framework of Autonomous Finance, the application areas across the customer lifecycle of the microfinance journey are identified. The journey cycle includes group finance marketing, group lending, collection, delinquency, sales prospects, and renewal. Most of the existing processes are driven by on-the-ground accounts management executives conducting due diligence, thereby limiting the scale of operations.

9.1.1.2 Scope

Forrester defines Autonomous Finance as '*Algorithm-driven services that make financial decisions and take actions on a customer's behalf*' [4].

The ongoing process of identifying target groups for microfinance is bottom-up and requires ground-level engagement. The operations team implements interactive, inclusive practices to identify groups, nurture them with financial inclusiveness, and acclimate them to financial acceptance through revenue-oriented engagement and funding. Developing an engaging target group is time-consuming and labor-intensive, limiting scale and speed. Deploying an appropriate Autonomous Finance framework can address the growing need for financial inclusiveness by bringing more target groups under the broader microfinance umbrella.

As personalization paves the way for focusing on targeted customers in retail finance and marketing, creating analytically driven clusters and embedding autonomous triggers in financial approvals can improve time to finance and help the target groups achieve faster time to market. A few areas where Autonomous Finance can enhance microfinance are outlined below:

i. Autonomous Enrollment: Leveraging technology to enroll people/groups for access without field workers reaching out individually to start the process.
ii. Credit Risk Framework: Providing an appropriate credit risk framework for timely and accurate approval.

Currently, Non-Performing Assets (NPA) as a percentage of loans outstanding varies between 2% and 19% across various Indian states [5]. Globally, the portfolio at risk for 30 days [6] is 6%. The NPA and portfolio risks mentioned here are indicative, as NPA is estimated for 90 days.

iii. Predictive Analytics: Establishing analytical triggers with early warning signals powered by predictive analytics for proactive delinquency management.

9.1.1.3 *Significance*

The scars of COVID-19 and the need for remote working have created a new paradigm in customer engagement. While Fintech has improved the financial accessibility of retail finance, microfinance is still finding ways to adopt disruptive technologies. Autonomous Finance is an appropriate method to bring the much-needed paradigm shift in microfinance. By leveraging robotized process flows and embedding AI and ML in analytical intelligence, the next wave of financial inclusiveness for the masses can be best assured through Autonomous Finance.

9.2 Readiness of MFIs for Autonomous Finance Transformation

9.2.1 Autonomous Finance and Microfinance—A Prelude

Autonomous Finance is gaining ground in the era of ChatGPT and the AI-driven digital world. The process of decision-making and financial process is being transformed under Autonomous Finance. Traditional finance processes, dominated by human intervention, are widely seen in budgeting, savings, investing, and debt management. By deploying AI and ML-driven process automation, human interactions are minimized, providing persona-based financial solutions.

Powered by Robotic Process Automation (RPA) and predictive analytics, Autonomous Finance enables financial data integration, automated financial reporting, automated financial planning and budgeting, and cash flow optimization. This helps organizations automate their accounts payable and receivable processes while integrating with external financial services. The overall positive impact of Autonomous Finance is likely to be seen in better risk management and compliance, enabling intelligent financial decision support.

The technology driving Autonomous Finance is visibly adopted in other Fintech-enabled institutions. However, in the case of Microfinance Institutions (MFI), adoption bottlenecks are evident during the customer acquisition phase.

MFIs focus on a group lending model targeting priority sectors such as women, self-help groups, and allied segments important for community development. Customer acquisition is driven by a deliberate and comprehensive strategy that considers financial requirements, social effects, and the local environment. In such circumstances, MFIs still adopt a hands-on approach by making field visits, socializing with targeted segments, educating potential beneficiaries, and creating an environment that encourages participation.

9.2.2 Diverged Microfinance Global Market

As microfinance gains ground globally as an inclusive finance gateway, the approach to identifying targeted segments varies from region to region. The scale and diversity of each region have evolved multiple practices to address the customer journey in the microfinance life cycle.

The World Bank estimates that there are now over 7,000 MFIs, serving some 16 million poor people in developing countries [7]. The global microfinance market is expected to reach a value of $394.8 billion by 2027 [8].

MFIs provided services to 139.9 million borrowers in 2018, up from just 98 million in 2009. With 85.6 million borrowers in 2018—a higher number than in any other region—South Asia is a leading force in the world of microfinance, with significant contributions from India, Bangladesh, and Vietnam. In 2018, African MFIs served 6.3 million borrowers, despite facing challenges such as a low-quality portfolio (13.6% of their portfolio was at risk of becoming overdue after 30 days in 2017) and high costs per borrower [9].

A variety of innovative financial instruments aided by technology is pioneered by the Multilateral Investment Fund (MIF). MIF, a member of the Inter-American Development Bank (IDB) Group, is the main donor of grants to help Latin America and the Caribbean's (LAC) micro- and small businesses become more competitive [10]. These LAC regions encompass 600 MFIs that have lent $12 billion benefitting more than 10 million underprivileged clients.

9.2.3 Autonomous Finance as a Turning Point

Autonomous Finance is ushering in a digital transformation in finance. Existing Fintech players have already institutionalized key components of lending, yet there are still inefficiencies in customer acquisition, real-time updates, risk mitigation, and targeted reach. It is estimated that a $5 billion company could save more than $8 million a year through autonomous finance [11]. With a $395 billion market, autonomous finance can save up to $632 million.

9.2.3.1 Key Components of Autonomous Finance

The success of improving the operational efficiency of microfinance lies in deploying its key components. MFIs powered by Fintech are successful in automating the KYC process, disbursing loans, and ensuring timely follow-up for repayments. However, the automation of MFIs has been primarily focused on customer transactions. To achieve greater success, organizational efficiency can be enhanced by integrating the key components of autonomous finance.

1) Data Aggregation 2) Financial Planning and Goal Setting 3) Automated Budgeting and Expense Tracking 4) Intelligent Savings and Investments 5) Automated Bill Payments	6) Credit Management and Optimization 7) Intelligent Alerts and Notifications 8) Security and Privacy Measures 9) Machine Learning and AI Algorithms 10) Integration and Open API

The applicability of the above-listed key components of autonomous finance for MFIs depends on the size of the MFI and their specific financial requirements. These components are designed to use technology to automate and optimize financial operations, improve decision-making, and increase operational efficiency within business entities.

9.2.3.2 Technology Drivers of Autonomous Finance

With the emergence of digital technology, autonomous finance is set to bring significant changes to the field of microfinance. This includes the application of modern technology to automate and optimize financial operations and decision-making. These impactful technologies enable systems to operate autonomously and make financial decisions with little or no human intervention. Here are a few significant technologies that support autonomous finance.

Customer-centric technologies include chatbots, virtual assistants, biometrics, natural language generation (NLG), and authentication technologies. These technologies can improve customer experience and facilitate borrowers' swift and appropriate access to finance. MFI process improvement technologies include robotic process automation, blockchain, cloud computing, cybersecurity, and data privacy. Deploying such process-driven technologies is bound to improve the implementation of autonomous finance and could reduce operational expenses.

Other drivers, such as artificial intelligence (AI), big data analytics, and the Internet of Things (IoT), create a synergy between customers and operations to accelerate the implementation of the autonomous finance agenda of MFIs. While these technologies contribute to the advancement of autonomous finance, their adoption and implementation may vary depending on the core focus each MFI and the regulatory settings of each country.

9.3 Solution Drivers in the Life Cycle Journey of an MFI Customer

AI and ML algorithms behind the analytical scoring engines support MFIs across multiple phases of each customer touchpoint. A microfinance customer's life cycle journey typically includes several stages, from initial contact with the MFIs until the loan or financial service fulfilment is completed.

9.3.1 The Life Cycle Journey of an MFI Customer

To understand the various analytical intervention tools, it is essential to create a broad outline of the different phases of the process. The following Figure 9.1 shows the various activities involved in the journey, right from creating awareness to renewal.

Note: Figure 9.1 illustrates the life cycle journey of an MFI customer, highlighting stages from awareness to renewal & growth, essential for understanding the customer journey in microfinance.

MFI services extend beyond just loan disbursement. Typical additional services include financial literacy training, community development

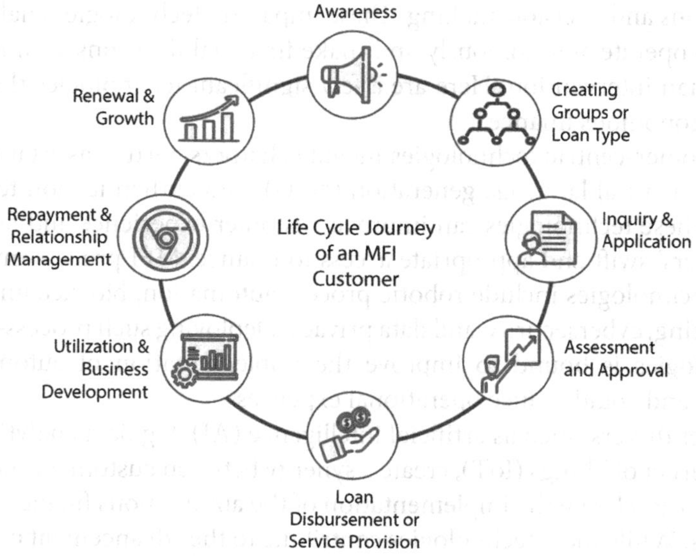

Figure 9.1 Life cycle journey of an MFI customer. Source: Authors.

workshops, and knowledge about other financial products like insurance and savings. Key phases of the life cycle journey are outlined below:

1. Awareness: Making the Self-Help Group (SHG), Joint Liability Group (JLG), or community members aware of the MFI's presence and services is best achieved through word-of-mouth and community outreach programs.
2. Creating Groups or Loan Type: MFI personnel create a cluster or engage with SHGs or JLGs to brief them about the product and create a customized financial plan.
3. Inquiry and Application: Based on the suggested product, the group or consumer opts for the suggested plan and initiates the application procedure with relevant credentials.
4. Assessment and Approval: A field visit by MFI personnel is conducted to review credit checks and the plan for utilization, followed by approval.
5. Loan Disbursement or Service Provision: The loan amount is credited to the customer's account by wire transfer, UPI transfer, or by issuing a debit card, as per the product needs.
6. Utilization and Business Development: Besides facilitating appropriate utilization of funds, the MFIs provide additional

assistance through counseling and training for efficient use of the funds.
7. Repayment and Relationship Management: Monthly repayments are collected according to the fund utilization and repayment schedule.
8. Renewal and Growth: Timely and consistent repayments improve the credit history, opening up better financial opportunities for the next level of growth.

9.3.2 Solution Drivers Across the Phases of the Life Cycle Journey

To help MFIs build a seamless autonomous finance platform, all phases of the life cycles need to be integrated for day-to-day business transactions. FinTechs supporting MFIs offer custom-built predictive models to provide foresight, enabling MFIs to anticipate future developments.

With professional customization of autonomous finance, a ready-to-use analytical framework is likely to emerge, helping MFIs harness analytics with a shorter turnaround time.

Note: Figure 9.2 depicts the life cycle journey of an MFI customer with integrated analytical drivers, emphasizing technological innovations and data-driven strategies in microfinance customer management.

Across each of the phases and technology drivers, inbuilt scoring engines and machine learning algorithms are likely to help MFIs look beyond the hindsight of their internal database. Autonomous finance would also help seamlessly integrate business decisions across branches and enterprise levels of MFIs. In addition to the multiple solutions driving autonomous finance in microfinance, the following solutions distinctively impact the reach of MFIs.

Note: Figure 9.3 outlines key technological tools such as AI, big data, biometrics, and blockchain, highlighting their applications in enhancing security, automation, and personalized financial services.

1. Chatbots, Virtual Assistants: Natural Language Generation (NLG), and voice recognition and speech synthesis powered by ChatGPT or Google Bard are powerful conversational AI chatbots. Due to their support for multiple languages and dialogues, these tools, available on mobile phones, are likely to create more awareness about microfinance solutions.

2. Socio-Economic Multivariate Clusters: Identifying look-alike socio-economic clusters helps in creating allied SHGs or JLGs, minimizing time to market and reaching the unreached.
3. Onboarding Needs: eKYC, biometrics, and authentication technologies enable swift verification, moving beyond document verification and video KYC. Biometrics-embedded verification tools help eliminate fraud and scams.
4. UPI, Mobile Banking, and Instant Transfers: These technologies power digital-first banking practices. Instant payments, electronic wallets, payments banks, e-RUPI, and M-Pesa have improved financial inclusiveness and provide rich transaction data.
5. Alternate Scoring: For thin-file customers without a bureau score, alternate scoring is used for real-time underwriting. Mobile recharge practices, UPI transfer practices, and utility payments are used for risk profiling of individuals.
6. Integrated Payments: Tracking fund utilization across inventory and equipment to expand operations can be assessed in real-time based on point-of-sale (POS) transactions. This triggers fund utilization parameters and avoids unwanted fund utilization.
7. Auto Repayment of Loans and Predictive Delinquency: Deployed at the customer level, delinquency algorithms

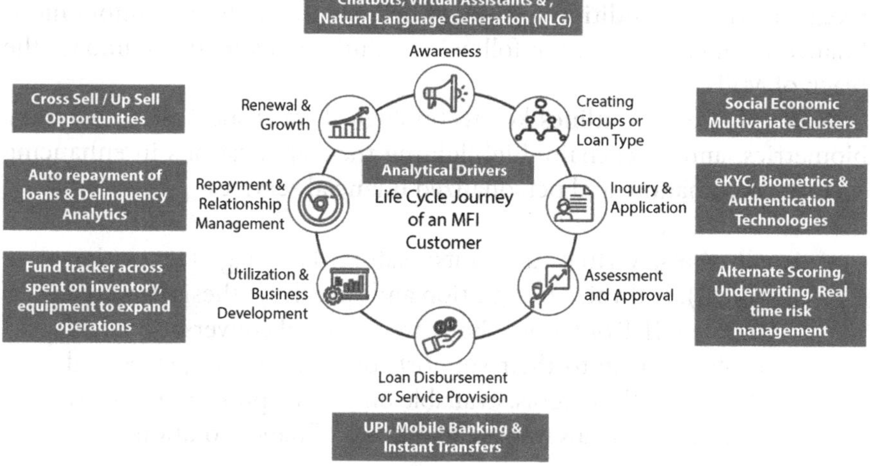

Figure 9.2 Life cycle journey and analytical drivers. Source: Authors.

for early prediction provide heads-up to likely delinquent customers.

8. Cross-Sell or Upsell Opportunities: Based on existing loan transactions and behavioral analytics, MFIs can identify the next level of financial needs, helping to retain customers with new financial products and reducing acquisition cost.

9.3.3 The Impact of Autonomous Finance in the Journey Cycle

MFIs are already deploying automation to improve borrower engagement, benefiting customer access. However, the technology stacks and process automation at the backend have yet to reach their maximum potential. To ensure minimal human intervention, the following key technologies are pivotal for the successful deployment of autonomous finance in MFIs.

The impact of AI and ML-enabled autonomous finance in microfinance can enhance data privacy and provide transparency to the overall framework. Algorithm-driven decision-making also improves data governance practices in MFIs, as more and more small banks begin providing microfinance.

9.4 Readiness of MFIs for Autonomous Finance Operations

There are multiple ERPs, CRMs, and data lakes as part of the enterprise-level operational framework. Similarly, the presence of RPAs, OCRs, big data solutions, and AI and ML models in various functions is quite visible. Yet, the buzz about autonomous finance is growing louder.

The key transformation highlighted under autonomous finance is the minimization of human intervention to accelerate the decision-making process. While autonomous finance is primarily focused on the finance team, its impact on allied business-facing functions is tremendous. Traditional ERPs are manually triggered by uploading relevant documents or entering relevant information. The deployment of OCR and RPA has facilitated considerable automations.

The different stages of autonomous finance maturity are briefly summarized below.

Stage 1: In this stage, several automations are assisted by technologies such as ERP and OCR but still require human review.

Artificial Intelligence (AI)	✓ Identify patterns ✓ Make predictions or recommendations
Big Data Analytics	✓ Aggregate and analyse large data volume ✓ Identify trends and detect anomalies
Biometrics &Authentication Technologies	✓ Behavioral analytics for the identity of users ✓ Ensure security and prevent fraud
Blockchain	✓ Decentralized and secure ledger ✓ Autonomous execution and verification
Chatbots and Virtual Assistants	✓ Personalized financial advice ✓ Round-the-clock assistance
Cloud Computing	✓ Personalized financial advice ✓ Round-the-clock assistance
Cybersecurity and Data Privacy	✓ Robust cybersecurity measures ✓ Ai-based security to prevent breaches
Internet of Things (IoT)	✓ Sensors and wearable devices ✓ Automate processes on real-time data
Natural Language Generation (NLG)	✓ Automatic investment summaries ✓ Personalized advice for customers
Robotic Process Automation (RPA)	✓ Rule-based financial tasks ✓ Reconciliation and report generation

Source: Authors

Figure 9.3 Tech solutions and outcomes.

Stage 2: This stage represents the next level of automation, where human intervention is required only for flagged items. However, in autonomous finance, the margin between automation and human flagging is eliminated with AI and ML algorithms, empowering systems to make business decisions.

Stage 3: The ideal scenario where business decisions are fully automated, making the entire function autonomous.

All three stages of autonomous finance penetration are illustrated below, with varying percentages of automation. This is only indicative, and the actual penetration and coverage of functions across various stages may vary from MFI to MFI.

Note: Figure 9.4 illustrates the stages of automation in financial processes, from manual entry (ERP) to fully autonomous workflows, highlighting increasing levels of technological integration and efficiency.

Many MFIs are still in Stage 1, while a few Fintech-enabled MFIs have reached Stage 2. In almost all MFIs, validation, human intervention, and review are still provided by human intelligence. Stage 1 and Stage 2 MFIs face challenges of implementing technology-enabled business models, which restricts their efficiency and exposes them to higher risk.

Gartner named autonomous finance as "Touchless" and conducted a survey on its readiness. The Gartner Finance Survey shows that "55% of functions are aiming for a touchless close by 2025" [12]. The survey listed the following top four financial close targets that CFO respondents hope to attain by 2025.

Note: Figure 9.5 presents survey results on the readiness of autonomous finance, with key metrics including faster real-time processing, cost reduction, error-free operations, and targets for 2025.

The Gartner survey outcome shows that the finance department in top corporations have made significant investments in general ledger technology, financial close solutions, and automated workflow. However, to achieve a touchless close, there is a need to progress beyond basic automation towards autonomous finance. Following this general trend, MFIs are likely to exhibit the same vigor in reaching autonomous finance as leading corporations.

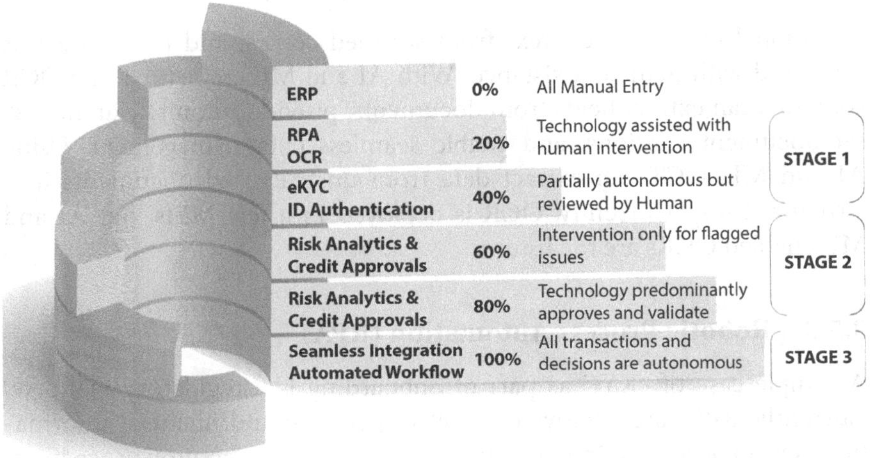

Figure 9.4 Stages of autonomous finance maturity. Source: Authors.

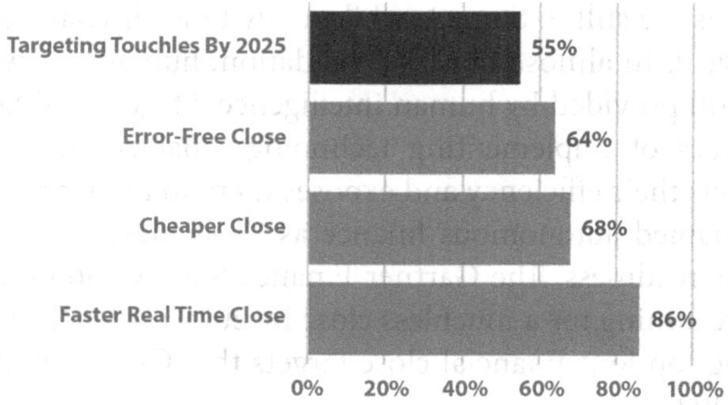

Figure 9.5 Survey on readiness of autonomous finance. Source: Gartner.

9.5 Technology and AI and ML Enablers of Autonomous Finance for MFIs

9.5.1 Technology Enabled Autonomous Finance for MFIs

As part of autonomous finance, the mere deployment of robotics and automation cannot fulfil the needs of MFIs. The automation process and robotics tools need inbuilt intelligence, enabled by data science and analytics supported by AI, ML, and deep learning. The following tools with embedded intelligence could accelerate the process of autonomous finance.

9.5.2 Optical Character Recognition (OCR)

Traditional OCR extracts text from scanned copies, and its accuracy is improved with manual assistance. With AI and ML embedded, the OCR solutions can extract fields from documents, provide automatic archiving, set document relations, and enable seamless data management. Using AI and ML, OCT can extract data from unstructured documents in a structured way. Currently, OCR is deployed in a few MFIs, but AI and ML-enabled OCRs are the future.

9.5.3 Robotic Process Automation (RPA)

A sample case of eKYC as part of onboarding is a regulatory mandate. Currently, RPAs are deployed to collect personal and financial information, set up accounts, implementing data archiving, monitor procedures, and verify information through authorized governmental organizations.

In this process, no intelligence is deployed. Beyond traditional mandatory process completion, the power of AI and ML can foster image forensics by matching submitted photos, videos taken, and back-end government record authentication of credentials. Besides eliminating fraud in identity changes, ML and deep learning also classify images for archiving and authentication.

9.5.4 Big Data Driven Automated Approvals

Credit risk is partially governed by risk models in many MFIs, which are backed by external credit bureaus. While a few Fintech-powered financial institutions have their alternate credit scoring models powered by AI and ML algorithms, it is not yet widely practiced in financing SHGs and JPGs for group finance by MFIs.

MFI customers are emerging as the hub of granular transaction data with socio-economic attributes. The emerging scoring system is likely to include value systems, attitudes, and related integrity responses as part of psychometric evaluations. Besides transactional history, these psychometric attributes, combined with AI and ML scoring models, can open up alternate credit risk models backed by big data.

Other related AI and ML enablers are summarized below.

1) Automated Loan Underwriting 2) Credit Scoring and Risk Assessment 3) Customer Relationship Management (CRM) 4) Fraud Detection and Prevention	5) Loan Portfolio Management 6) Personalized Financial Advice 7) Predictive Analytics for Financial Planning

As narrated above, OCR, RPA, and big data are only indicative tools of autonomous finance. There are other essential business needs in finance including autonomous receivables, autonomous treasury, and autonomous accounting, which require a rich blend of intelligent technologies. While MFIs currently leverage these tools or solutions in silos within their organizations, they need to move beyond deploying similar tools, gadgets, and technologies by adding intelligence.

9.6 Critical Business Needs of Autonomous Finance

9.6.1 Autonomous Receivables

The processes that deploy automation and artificial intelligence technology to optimize a company's accounts are termed autonomous accounts receivable. This differs from loans given to customers, as it is purely part of an accounts management system that covers invoices and payments, as well as outstanding accounts and reconciliation. A few indicative applications and usages of autonomous finance in account receivables are summarized below.

Note: Figure 9.6 highlights use cases of receivables in autonomous finance, detailing deployment areas like payment tracking, cash flow forecasting, and risk assessment for enhanced efficiency and customer experience.

9.6.2 Autonomous Treasury

Deploying cutting-edge technology to improve treasury management's efficiency helps address cash management, financial planning, and automating the entire workflow.

Note: Figure 9.7 illustrates treasury use cases in autonomous finance, focusing on areas like cash management, risk management, fraud detection, and workflow automation through API, RPA, and chatbots.

9.6.3 Autonomous Accounting

Despite the use of automation and Enterprise Resource Planning (ERP) tools, human supervision and expertise are still necessary. However, by deploying RPAs, NLP, and AI and ML technologies can minimize supervisory roles, ensuring accuracy in various accounting procedures.

Note: Figure 9.8 details accounting use cases in autonomous finance, highlighting areas like data entry, financial reporting, and compliance enhanced by AI and machine learning for improved accuracy and efficiency.

The Touchless Model, or Autonomous Finance, enhances current technology by adding intelligence to deliver decisions for managing MFIs.

9.7 AI and ML Analytical Models for MFIs

To understand how deploying various analytical models can accelerate autonomous finance for MFIs, it is essential to have a brief overview of indicative analytical models.

Receivables Use Cases	Areas of Deployment
Calculating the likelihood that a client will pay an invoice on time	✓ Invoice Generation ✓ Payment Tracking ✓ Collection Optimization ✓ Cash Flow Forecasting ✓ Risk Assessment ✓ Efficiency and Cost Savings ✓ Improved Customer Experience
Forecasting future cash flow and working capital levels	
Flagging high probable dispute cases and providing a preventive solution	
Source: Authors	

Figure 9.6 Use cases of receivables.

Treasury Use Cases	**Areas of Deployment**
Deploy API and RPA to extract customer data from various ERP packages.	✓ Cash Management ✓ Risk Management ✓ Fraud Detection ✓ Payments and Transactions: ✓ Investment Management: ✓ Compliance and Regulation ✓ Data Analytics and Reporting ✓ Workflow Automation
Chatbots with RPA assistance can free up account teams on client inquiries about payments	
Once invoices are due, RPA Bots can be configured to pay vendors automatically.	
Source: Authors	

Figure 9.7 Use cases of treasury.

Accounting Use Cases	**Areas of Deployment**
Implementing Generative AI models can automate personalized financial reports and visualizations	✓ Data Entry and Transaction Processing ✓ General Ledger and Bookkeeping ✓ Bank Reconciliation ✓ Financial Reporting ✓ Compliance and Regulation ✓ Audit and Internal Controls ✓ Expense Management ✓ Scalability and Efficiency
Accounting teams will be able to close the books faster and more accurately with AI ML-powered automation detecting errors and omissions.	
Source: Authors	

Figure 9.8 Use cases of accounting.

The finance industry is one of the pioneers in leveraging analytical models, with scores provided by Compuscan, Baihang Credit, Experian, Equifax, FICO, Korea Credit Bureau (KCB), Pudao Credit, TransUnion, and XDS (to name a few) used for credit approvals.

These bureaus, on behalf of banks, construct records of all personal credit transactions and prepare credit scores based on statistically significant behavioral attributes such as:

1) Debt repayment history	4) Tenure of Bank Accounts
2) Amounts Outstanding	5) Usage of Credit
3) Frequency of Loan Application	6) Honoring Debt Obligation

A three-digit figure, ranging from 0 to 999, represents the credit score. The range spread and indicative remarks are shown in the following Figure 9.9. Note: Figure 9.9 shows a credit score range indicator, categorizing scores from 300 to 900 into Poor, Fair, Good, and Excellent, providing a quick reference for creditworthiness assessment.

There are minimum credit score requirements that differ from country to country and bank to bank when evaluating a loan application. Whether or not someone is approved for a loan is heavily influenced by their credit score.

For a credit score to be available, the individual needs to have a rich credit transaction history. However, in most cases of MFI customers, due to their socio-economic background, their credit transactions are not substantial enough to provide credit scores. Customers lacking a credit transaction history are called Thin Filed Customers.

Traditionally, quantitative predictive modeling is deployed to build multiple models/algorithms to train the data as per business needs. Indicative models include Logistic Regression, Logistic Regression with Ridge Regularization, Linear Discriminant Analysis, K-Nearest Neighbor, Decision Trees, Support Vector Machines, and XGBoost. Financial Institutions traditionally leverage Logistics Regression for building credit scores.

9.7.1 Logistic Regression

Customers with a higher delinquency rate can be defined as BAD, and customers with zero delinquency can be termed as GOOD. If converted into binary, a BAD customer can be represented as one (1) and a GOOD customer as zero (0). This can be reversed depending on the objective of the models.

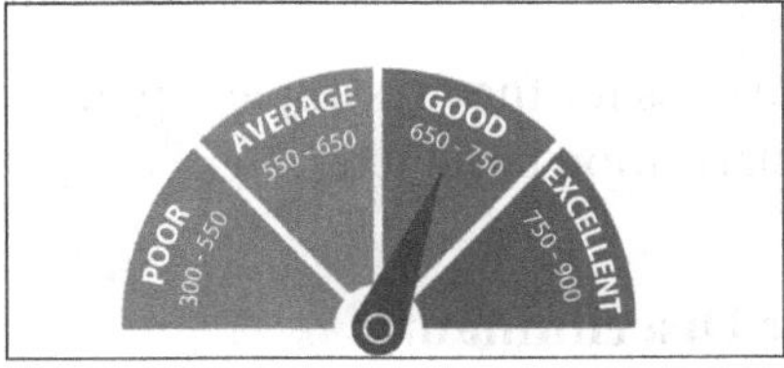

781 to 900. Excellent

650 to 750. Good

550 to 650. Fair

300 to 550. Poor

(Only indicative)

Source: Authors

Figure 9.9 Credit score range and remarks. Source: Authors.

The probability of a binary outcome between zero and one can be predicted using the statistical modeling technique known as logistic regression, by using one or more independent variables. Concerning its independent variables (behavioral attributes mentioned earlier), logistic regression seeks to estimate the likelihood that a particular observation belongs to the positive class (1).

The logistic regression model uses a logistic function, also referred to as the sigmoid function, to translate the linear combination of the independent variables into a probability value between 0 and 1.

The logistic regression model can be represented mathematically as:

$$P(Y = 1|X) = 1/(1 + e \wedge (-\beta 0 - \beta 1X1 - \beta 2X2 - \ldots - \beta nXn))$$

In the above equation, the probability of the dependant carriable is 1 concerning independent variables such as X1, X2, ..., Xn.

The coefficients of the model are β0, β1, β2, ..., βn

9.7.2 Logistic Regression with Ridge Regularization

This is a modification of logistic regression that includes a regularization term to prevent overfitting and improve the model's applicability. L2 regularization is a subclass called ridge regularization.

To handle large coefficient values, ridge logistic regression adds a term to the likelihood function.

The intended use of ridge logistic regression is as follows:

$$J(\beta) = -[\Sigma(y\_i * \log(p\_i) + (1 - y\_i) * \log(1 - p\_i) +] + \lambda * \Sigma(c\_j^2)$$

The objective function = J(β),

*j*th coefficient of the model = β_j,

observed result for the ith sample = y_i,
projected probability of the positive class for the ith sample = p_i,
degree of frequentization = λ (regularization parameter).

9.7.3 An Examination of Linear Discriminants

Some uses for discriminant analysis: [13]

1. Determine the most suitable statistical technique for classifying individuals into distinct groups.
2. Maintain maximum differentiation between the groups.
3. Remove factors that have little impact on group differences.

In the study by [13], LDA was used to predict the expected status of consumer credit clients at KCB—Kisumu Branch. The estimated function achieved over 75% accuracy in predicting financial health and was significant at the 1% level. The study suggested that demographic, socio-economic, and loan-related characteristics could determine the projected group membership of borrowers at KCB—Kisumu Branch.

9.7.4 K-Nearest Neighbor

The popular supervised machine learning technique K-Nearest Neighbor (KNN) is utilized for both classification and regression tasks. KNN is a straightforward yet powerful method capable of handling regression problems, as well as binary and multi-class classification issues. It is often used as a foundational technique and can yield effective results, particularly when the underlying data exhibits a distinct decision boundary or when the dataset is modest in size.

In an MFI environment, Thin File customers are common, and field organizers often spend time creating groups based on socio-functional attributes. This process can be expedited by deploying KNN classification to group individuals with similar characteristics, facilitating a quicker go-to-market approach.

9.7.5 Decision Trees

"Decision Trees generate a structure like a tree by classifying instances using a recursive partitioning algorithm" [14]. Branching shows the test results, represented by internal nodes for each attribute, with each leaf node corresponding to a class label [15].

In microfinance, especially for credit scoring and risk assessment, decision trees can be a useful tool for analysis and forecasting. Decision trees can be deployed across MFIs for credit scoring, risk assessment, loan product recommendation, portfolio analysis, and fraud detection.

However, decision tree models are prone to overfitting and require structured tabular data. Alternate ensemble techniques like random forests or gradient boosting can be deployed to address such issues. Similarly, other methods such as gradient boosting, support vector machines (SVM), or neural networks, may be more appropriate for addressing complex nonlinear connections. The Classification and Regression Tree (CART) algorithm is one of the popular algorithms for decision trees.

9.7.6 Support Vector Machines

In microfinance, Support Vector Machines (SVM) can be leveraged for tasks such as classification (classifying income groups and loan types of borrowers who are likely to have similar credit risk groups), regression, and anomaly detection.

An emerging area of SVM is in OCR as part of Autonomous Finance, in improving the accuracy of text and image recognition. In many cases, handwritten text is prevalent in rural and underprivileged sections, necessitating appropriate OCR to accurately convert text. When scanning handwritten documents, pixel intensity is used as the feature vector.

OCR errors, such as misreading "l" as "I," are a common mistake. Such errors could be minimized using the SVM algorithm. Fonseca [16] investigated utilizing SVM to automatically choose the right replacement for typos in OCR text. In one of their trials, they achieved an accuracy of 96.72%, a precision of 91.58%, and a recall of 58.63%.

It is crucial to remember that for SVMs to perform at their best, considerable attention must be given to the selection of hyperparameters, such as the kernel function and regularization parameter.

9.7.7 XGBoost

Credit scoring is traditionally built for individuals. In microfinance, since the lending is done for groups, the traditional technique needs to be recalibrated to suit group lending needs. A pioneering effort [17] to build a credit default prediction model for microfinance group lending using machine learning techniques explored the use of XGBoost and allied ML models.

Extreme Gradient Boosting (XGBoost) is a machine learning technique that combines the output of several weaker, simpler models (decision trees) to accurately estimate a target variable (GOOD or BAD).

9.8 Overall Deployment and Suitability

The deployment of the above indicative models (Logistic Regression, Logistic Regression with Ridge Regularization, Linear Discriminant Analysis, K-Nearest Neighbor, Decision Trees, Support Vector Machines, and XGBoost) can be leveraged for a single objective, such as credit scoring. In such cases, the outcome of various models can be compared for higher accuracy.

9.9 Roadmap for Autonomous Finance in MFIs

9.9.1 Transformation Operations for MFI

Implementing Autonomous Finance is an enterprise-wide project and is not just limited to the finance department. Hence, a detailed transformation roadmap for Autonomous Finance deployment is critical for the success of MFIs. A total of 14 milestones are identified as part of the roadmap, divided into the following three key stages of operations. Figure 9.10 shows the analytical models performance comparison results.

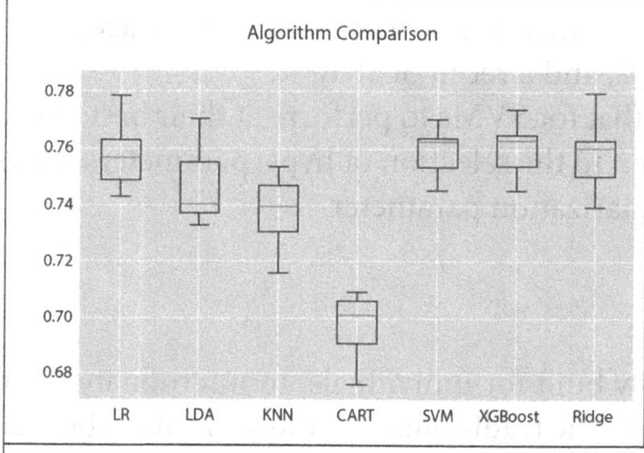

LR	Logistic Regression
LDA	Linear Discriminant Analysis
KNN	K-Nearest Neighbours
CART	Classification And Regression Tree
SVM	Support Vector Machines
XGBoost	Extreme Gradient Boosting
RIDGE	Ridge Regression

Note: Comparison is done for the same set of data for the same desired objective. The above comparison is not to be considered as an outcome of the different use cases mentioned in the above examples.

Source: Authors

Figure 9.10 Comparison of the performance of analytical models.

Stage-1: Operation Moonwalk
The first stage is to set the guiding objectives that provide measurable goals and direction to the complete roadmap. It encompasses prioritizing financial goals enabling digitization towards implementing Autonomous Finance.
Stage 2: Operation Sunshine
Operation Moonwalk sets the phase for transformation with clear-cut KRIs and milestones. The next stage is to create the needed budget, people, processes, and technology to kick-start the process. This stage, called Operation Sunshine, ensures milestone-based progress to achieve successful results that align with the earmarked KRIs.
Stage 3: Operation Bloomsdale
Operation Bloomsdale assists in raising the bar and enhancing the acceleration phase as the project progresses. To reap the benefits of implementing Autonomous Finance, it is essential to scale and monitor the emerging technologies and continue their adoption.

A summary of all three stages and key tasks is provided below for a holistic view of the roadmap.

Note: Figure 9.11 outlines the stages of a roadmap for autonomous finance, detailing key operations: Moonwalk, Sun Shine, and Bloomsdale, each focusing on governance, digitization, and emerging technologies.

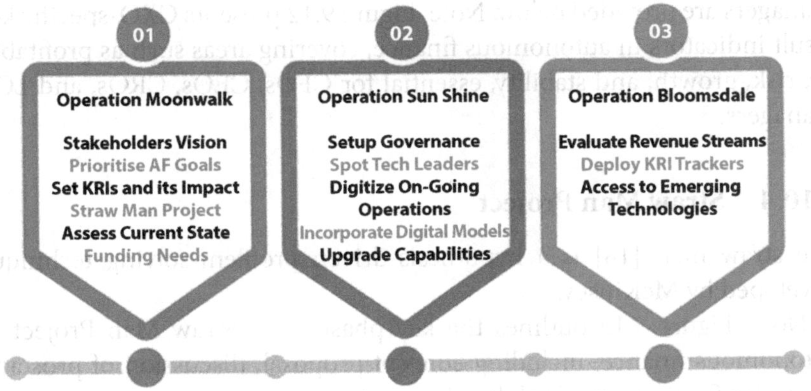

Figure 9.11 Stages of roadmap. Source: Authors.

9.10 Stage-1: Operation Moonwalk

9.10.1 Stakeholders Vision

Besides the CFO, buy-in from all CXOs is critical. Key teams within MFIs include the Finance Team, Operation Team, Risk Team, Sales Team, and Backend Support Team. Since the technology permeates each process, its success will have a broad and visible impact. For instance, introducing Intelligent OCR is likely to reduce the time required for onboarding.

9.10.2 Prioritize Autonomous Finance Goals

Technologies such as RPA, OCR Ai, eKYC, analytics-driven models, IoT, and biometric authentication are part of autonomous finance accelerators. Benefits like increased process efficiency, improved accuracy, and cost savings need to be quantified, and the project management team must clearly define these outcomes. Based on a cost–benefit analysis, the leadership team should prioritize the deployment of these technologies.

9.10.3 Set KRIs and Its Impact

It is imperative to set key result indicators (KRIs) for each stakeholder to measure and review the outcome of the deployment of Autonomous Finance. Indicative KRIs for each CXO and Line of Business (LOB) Managers are provided below. Note: Figure 9.12 presents CXO-specific key result indicators in autonomous finance, covering areas such as profitability, risk, growth, and stability, essential for CFOs, CEOs, CROs, and LOB managers.

9.10.4 Straw Man Project

The straw man [18] is a hypothesis-driven problem-solving technique developed by McKinsey.

Note: Figure 9.13 outlines the key phases of a Straw Man Project in autonomous finance, including concept proposal, discussion of pros and cons, clarification, and final decision-making.

The idea is to produce a rough version of multiple procedures, steps, and a streamlined evaluation model. This serves as a preliminary to creating an implementation proposal.

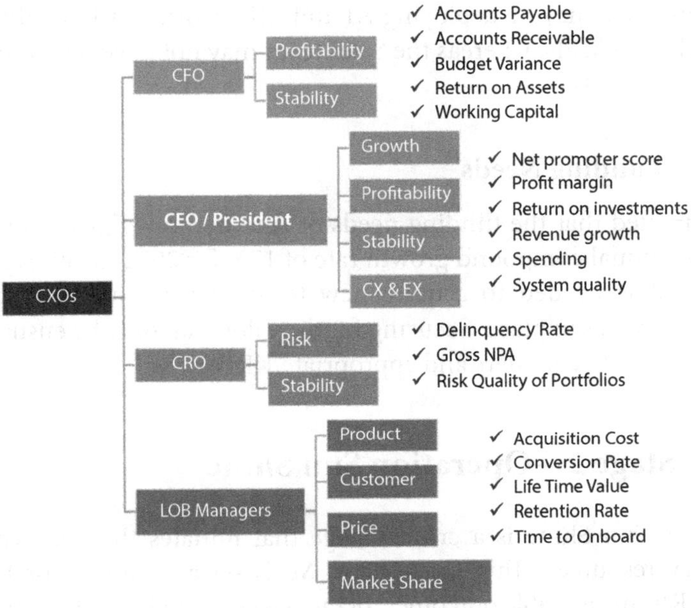

Figure 9.12 CXO specific key result indicators. Source: Authors.

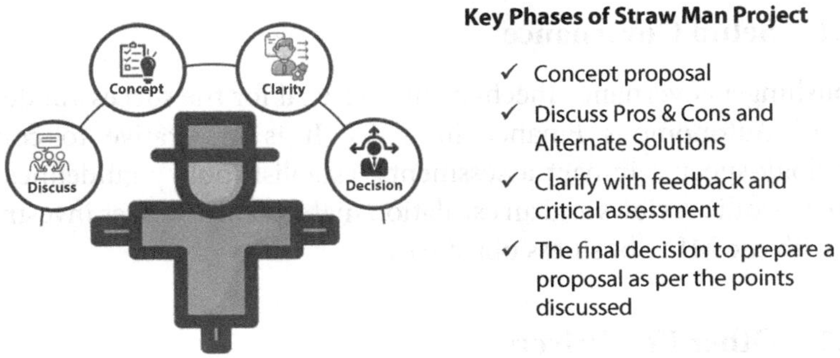

Figure 9.13 McKinsey's straw man modules. Source: Authors and McKinsey.

9.10.5 Assess Current State

In the earlier part of this chapter, various stages between One to Three are described under the title "*Readiness of MFIs for Autonomous Finance Operations.*" With due diligence, the demarcation of various stages of each business function needs to be assessed and prioritized. Some LOBs may already be in an advanced stage, such as the Risk Function, for example.

Risk Functions may be deploying AI and ML algorithms in credit underwriting by the MFIs, whereas the Sales team may not have operationalized analytical models.

9.10.6 Funding Needs

It is estimated that the funding needs of Autonomous Finance are growing at an annual compound growth rate of 17% for 2022–2030. Significant investment is needed to acquire new technologies, and resources and deploy processes in place. Securing funding flow can only be ensured with the buy-in of stakeholders and appropriate KRIs.

9.11 Stage 2—Operation Sun Shine

Operation Sun Shine is a critical stage that initiates the deployment of necessary resources. This phase helps MFIs set a roadmap for business goals, KRIs, measurable outcomes, plans, and required investments. As the impact of Autonomous Finance spreads across the enterprise, digital transformation is essential to enhance customer experience (CX) and employee experience (EX).

9.11.1 Setup Governance

Establishing a governance mechanism is crucial for the successful deployment of Autonomous Finance in MFIs. It is imperative to conduct technology-specific impact assessments, establish policy guidelines, and ensure periodic reviews and an escalation matrix. This ensures investments align with the MFI's business objectives.

9.11.2 Other Key Drivers

People, processes, technology, and content are essential parts of implementing Autonomous Finance transformation. The traditional roles of Chief Information Officer (CIO) or Chief Digital Officer (CDO) may not be sufficient. Instead, a Chief Strategic Innovation Officer (CSIO) is needed. This role focuses on recruiting tech leaders, digitizing ongoing operations, incorporating digital models, and upgrading the capabilities to add momentum to the transformation. To implement this transformation, collaboration with various technology vendors and Transformation SMEs with MFI knowledge is essential. Additionally, a strong, full-time Project

Management Office (PMO) and periodical reviews are necessary for a successful Autonomous Finance transformation.

9.12 Stage 3 Operation Bloomsdale

MFIs usually start realizing the benefits of shorter onboarding time, reduced delinquency, improved report accuracy, and better customer experiences. To keep pace with the dynamics of technological evolution, MFIs need to swiftly adopt new technologies and minimal human intervention. Operation Bloomsdale helps monitor progress, take corrective measures, and adapt to emerging business paradigms. As ROI begins to reflect, evaluating revenue streams and cost overheads will likely result in better profits. This revenue growth and improved margins can impact the KRIs Trackers raising the bar for the next level of business transformation.

9.13 Improvement Opportunities of Autonomous Finance for MFIs

9.13.1 Precautions in Adopting Autonomous Finance by MFIs

More and more automation with less human intervention characterized the evolving trend facilitated by the adoption of Autonomous Finance. Automated Chartered Accountants handle financial planning and analysis (FP&A), while AI and ML embedded systems acquire customers and approve loans within MFIs.

However, in this environment of reduced human intervention, the need for human touch remains paramount. The essence of this new form of Autonomous Finance can be enhanced with smarter human intelligence. For instance, in detecting fraud, where specific patterns emerge, AI and ML systems can be trained using historical data for future occurrences. Yet, the predictive capability for innovative future fraud incidents remains untested without human intelligence. Despite these challenges, RPAs and Intelligent OCRs play a crucial role in minimizing operational ineffectiveness in MFIs.

9.13.2 Data Privacy

As part of Autonomous Finance, a new professional role emerging in MFIs is the establishment of dedicated privacy practice. Currently, data privacy is governed by country-specific laws, but not all MFIs have dedicated privacy practices in place. As customer experience evolves, privacy user experience is expected to significantly impact future customer touchpoints.

9.13.3 AI and ML Governance

While building models, few countries have guidelines prohibiting the use of racial, gender, age, and other personal data. However, in countries where MFIs are prevalent, specific regulations on such variables are not uniformly enforced. According to a Gartner survey [19], 40% of organizations reported an AI privacy breach. There is a constant risk of introducing biased data into training models, which could influence recommendation engines and result in unsustainable products.

9.13.4 More Machine vs Less Human

The initial focal point in the transition to Autonomous Finance is the potential job displacement, particularly roles overseeing data accuracy in capture processes. Replacing human resources must be complemented by reskilling and reorienting them for new responsibilities. Alongside technological substitution of people and processes, the clarity of content and intent must be established.

Another concern arises from scenarios where AI agents could outperform human intervention due to corrupted codes. Similar to Isaac Asimov's "Three Laws of Robotics," guidelines to regulate AI agents are crucially needed.

9.13.5 Ethical Considerations

Human intervention to override RPAs and AI and ML-derived decision support systems would be necessary to counter technology-derived decisions. Human judgment remains pivotal in crucial areas such as Portfolio Management, Investment Decisions, Credit Approvals, and prioritizing automation modules. Maintaining judgment and empathy in responding to customer and employee feedback will remain essential, subject to regulatory oversight. The call for nationwide and region-specific AI policies, beyond standard privacy laws, is gaining momentum.

9.13.6 Regulatory Compliance

Banks, NBFCs, and MFIs are subject to regulation by country-specific regional banks and their respective finance ministries. The adoption of Autonomous Finance ensured regulatory compliance to a greater extent than ever before. The full spectrum of Fintech solutions, including eKYC, mobile finance, approvals, and digital banking is managed with improved compliance measures. Autonomous Finance further enhances financial inclusion for underbanked and marginalized communities.

9.13.7 Surveillance and Discrimination

Algorithmic decisions in recommending products, cross-selling, upselling, and adjusting credit levels are among the benefits of Autonomous Finance. However, enhanced access to personal data and financial approvals through integrated data management could increase surveillance and potential discrimination. If AI algorithms are configured to minimize delinquency, there is a risk they could inadvertently incorporate racial or regional data, leading to heightened surveillance of specific demographic groups and potential racial discrimination in credit approvals.

9.14 Embracing Future AI Agents and Robotics of Autonomous Finance

AI agents and robots attending to MFI as part of Autonomous Finance are already in an evolutionary phase. While back-office operations will continue to be aggressively autonomous, fieldwork and front-office activities will maintain their current *modus operandi*. Field workers are likely to use RPAs and chatbots increasingly to raise awareness about financial inclusion.

With augmented intelligence, field workers could form new Self-Help Groups and offer innovative financial products. Onboarding can be expedited using biometric solutions to swiftly authenticate users and sanction credit limits. With more integrated data and historical transactions, retaining groups and reallocating individuals to more suitable groups can enhance risk management and operational efficiency.

Autonomous Finance, with AI agents and intelligent solutions, has the potential to revolutionize the way MFIs manage fund disbursement, collection, and retention. Early adoption of Autonomous Finance by MFIs can provide a competitive edge, improve financial inclusiveness, and boost social prosperity.

References

1. Jolis, A., J The Nobel Peace Prize 2006, The Nobel Foundation, p. 1A, 2006. https://www.nobelprize.org/prizes/peace/2006/yunus/facts/.
2. Gartner Stamford, Conn., Gartner Identifies Top Five Trends in Privacy Through 2024, 2022, https://www.gartner.com/en/newsroom/press-releases/2022-05-31-gartner-identifies-top-five-trends-in-privacy-through-2024.
3. Midha, P., Future of Finance: Autonomous Banking, BFSI Economic Times, 2023, https://bfsi.economictimes.indiatimes.com/news/banking/future-of-finance-autonomous-banking/99153012.
4. Wannemacher, P., Principal Analyst, Berdak, O., VP, Research Director, Introducing Autonomous Finance: Forrester's New Research on Algorithm-Based Financial Services. https://www.forrester.com/blogs/introducing-autonomous-finance-forresters-new-research-on-algorithm-based-financial-services/#:~:text=Forrester's%20current%20working%20definition%20of,action%20on%20a%20customer's%20behalf.
5. NABARD, Status of Microfinance In India 2021-22, https://www.nabard.org/auth/writereaddata/tender/2707225843somfi-2021-22-final-english.pdf.
6. Convergences, Global microfinance figures. https://www.convergences.org/en/119115/.
7. Srinivas, H., *MICRO-FACTS: Data Snapshots on Microfinance*, GDRC Research Output. Global Development Research Center, Kobe, Japan, 2023, https://www.gdrc.org/icm/data/d-snapshot.html.
8. Globe Newswire, Global Microfinance Market, p. 1A, 2021. Yahoo Finance, https://finance.yahoo.com/news/global-microfinance-market-reach-us-101400648.html?fr=sycsrp_catchall.
9. Convergences, Microfinance Barometer, 2019, https://www.convergences.org/wp-content/uploads/2019/09/Microfinance-Barometer-2019_web-1.pdf.
10. Improving Lives, Microfinance in Latin America and the Caribbean, (p. 1A), Inter American Development Bank, 2015. https://www.iadb. org/en/topics/microfinance/microfinance-latin-america-and-caribbean.
11. AppZen, How Ready are you for Autonomous Finance Operations?, (p. 1A), Harvard Business School Publishing, 2021. https://hbr.org/sponsored/2021/08/how-ready-are-you-for-autonomous-finance-operations.
12. Gartner, These Are the Top CFO Priorities for 2022, (p. 1A), 2022. https://www.gartner.com/en/articles/these-are-the-top-cfo-priorities-for-2022.

13. Bakker, D. and Esekon, J., *Discriminant Analysis in Loan Granting-A Case Study of KCB Kisumu*, Lap Lambert Academic Publishing, 2013. https://www.researchgate.net/profile/Daniel-Bakker-4/publication/343472275_Discriminant_Analysis_In_Loan_Granting_-_A_Case_Study_of_KCB_Kisumu/links/5f2c7860458515b7290acaeb/Discriminant-Analysis-In-Loan-Granting-A-Case-Study-of-KCB-Kisumu.pdf?_tp=eyJjb250ZXh0Ijp7ImZpcnN0UGFnZSI6InB1YmxpY2F0aW9uIiwicGFnZSI6InB1YmxpY2F0aW9uIn19.
14. Baesens, B., Roesch, D., Scheule, H., *Credit Risk Analytics: Measurement Techniques, Applications, and Examples in SAS*, John Wiley & Sons, Hoboken, 2016, https://doi.org/10.1002/9781119449560.
15. Marqués, A.I., García, V., Sánchez, J.S., Exploring the Behaviour of Base Classifiers in Credit Scoring Ensembles. *Expert Syst. Appl.*, 39, 10244–10250, 2012, https://doi.org/10.1016/j.eswa.2012.02.092.
16. Fonseca Cacho, J.R. and Taghva, K., OCR Post Processing Using Support Vector Machines, in: *Intelligent Computing, Proceedings of the 2020 Computing Conference*, vol. 2, pp. 694–713, 2020, https://www.researchgate.net/publication/342681828_OCR_Post_Processing_Using_Support_Vector_Machines.
17. Pradnyana, K.D. and Rahadi, R.A., Loan Default Prediction in Microfinance Group Lending with Machine Learning. *Int. J. Bus. Technol. Manage.*, 4, 4, 83–95, e-ISSN: 2682-7646, 2022, https://myjms.mohe.gov.my/index.php/ijbtm/article/view/20641.
18. Sridharan, M.A., Straw Man Proposal, p. 1A, Think Insights, 2019. https://thinkinsights.net/consulting/strawman-proposal/.
19. Gartner, Touchless. https://www.gartner.com/en/newsroom/press-releases/2022-09-22-gartner-finance-survey-shows-55-percent-of-functions-aiming-for-a-touchless-close-by-2022.

10

Application of Machine Learning Models in the Field of Autonomous Finance

Umesh Gupta[1]*, Shriyash Saxena[1], Sachin Kumar Yadav[2] and Aditya Bhardwaj[1]

[1]SCSET, Bennett University, Greater Noida, Uttar Pradesh, India
[2]Dept. of CEA, GLA Mathura, Uttar Pradesh, India

Abstract
Using Artificial Intelligence (AI) in Autonomous Finance (AF) helps reduce error and biases caused by humans. By automating duties and functions previously performed manually, such as data entry, analysis, and decision-making, AI enhances the efficiency of financial institutions. This automation reduces costs, improves efficiency, and ensures more accurate and consistent decisions. AI algorithms help identify fraudulent activities, making financial institutions more secure and better at managing risks. By scrutinizing vast data sets and detecting iterations, repetitions and anomalies, AI can identify and prevent fraudulent transactions in real-time. Additionally, AI algorithms provide personalized services and products according tailored to individuals' distinctive financial preferences and priorities. By analyzing data and making future predictions, AI recommends personalized investment options, insurance products, and other financial services.

Keywords: Markov decision process, neural network, reinforcement learning, sentiment analysis, autonomous finance, deep learning

10.1 Overview

Machine learning (ML) and AI are among the latest technologies people aspire to work in. Terms like data mining and statistical learning have a lot in common and are used vaguely, with definitions and

**Corresponding author*: er.umeshgupta@gmail.com

Deepa Gupta, Mukul Gupta, Rajesh Kumar Dhanaraj, Balamurugan Balusamy and Parth Mukul Gupta (eds.) Computational Intelligence for Autonomous Finance, (199–220) © 2025 Scrivener Publishing LLC

associated characteristics/applications mixed or interchanged for convenience [1, 2, 33]. Although these technological fields are frequently highlighted in articles and newsletters as hot topics in industrial and societal contexts, clear distinctions between these fields are often neglected or underemphasized in the rush to publish content in popular culture. These fields have enormous potential applications in daily life and have transformed how people interact with technology [3, 38]. ML, a subset of AI, has always been a field of interest for computer scientists and engineers. ML focuses on developing algorithms and statistical models that enable computers to learn, recognize patterns, make predictions from the data they are fed, and improve their performance on tasks over time [4–6].

Broadly, ML can be classified into three main types: supervised learning, unsupervised learning, and reinforcement learning. In supervised learning, the algorithm is trained on already classified or tagged data, where the correct answers or outputs are known beforehand, allowing it to predict these outputs for new, unseen inputs. Unsupervised learning deals with untagged or unclassified data and aims to find patterns or repetitions without predefined tags or classifications [7–10]. Reinforcement learning (RL) involves an agent learning via trial and error, receiving feedback in the form of rewards or punishments [3, 36, 37]. ML has become essential for many applications, such as image and speech recognition, recommender systems, and autonomous vehicles. One such application area is Natural Language Processing, which involves using computational methods to analyze and generate natural languages and their pronunciations. ML algorithms also analyze and predict from extensive datasets in healthcare, finance, and social sciences. As ML advances, there is a growing need for a common understanding of key concepts, terminology, and best practices [11, 12]. This requires collaboration among researchers, practitioners, and policymakers to ensure that ML is developed and deployed responsibly and trustworthily [35–37]. ML has the potential to revolutionize many industries and improve lives in countless ways, with one notable application being Autonomous Finance [13, 14].

Autonomous Finance is an emerging field that uses AI and ML to automate financial processes and make data-driven decisions. With the power of AI can analyze large amounts of data, identify patterns, and make informed decisions in real time [15]. AI is a critical technology in AF, enabling financial institutions to automate processes, reduce risk, and provide personalized services to customers. AF refers to an economic system that uses AI/ML technologies to automate financial processes and decision-making. Deep learning (DL), a subset of ML, has emerged as a crucial technology in AF [16–19]. DL algorithms use neural networks to analyze vast expanses of data, learn from patterns, and make predictions or make decisions. Neural networks are ML models inspired by the human brain and consists of interconnected nodes or "neurons" that process and transmit data. Deep learning helps extract complex features and patterns from raw data using neural networks with multiple layers [3, 6].

DL has enormous applications in AF, helping to increase efficiency, accuracy, and cost-effectiveness. For example, DL algorithms can automate investment decisions, risk management, fraud detection, and credit scoring. They can identify specific repetitions, iterations, and trends in financial data that are not immediately perceivable to human analysts [32–34]. In areas like credit scoring, neural network models can be trained on historical data to identify patterns in borrower behavior and predict the likelihood of default [20–22]. Similarly, in asset management, DL algorithms analyze the market, enabling informed investment decisions. However, applying deep learning in AF presents challenges, including the need for high-quality data, interpretability of results, and potential biases in the algorithms. It is essential to ensure deep learning models are developed and operate transparently and ethically, with appropriate oversight [23, 24]. Using DL in autonomous finance has the potential to revolutionize the financial industry, improving efficiency, accuracy, and risk management, while enhancing accessibility to financial services and overall customer experience.

10.2 Introduction

There are topics to be discussed as we explore the avenues of applied DL models in autonomous finance. We start our journey step-by-step, beginning the basic idea of the application of AI in finance. We will then cover financial machine learning, move ahead with the detailed passage of AF, and finally discuss autonomous financial operations. We will also explore various concepts of DL models and neural networks. Ultimately, we will examine the domains of AI and ML algorithms/training models that could be applied in various areas of autonomous finance [10, 14–18].

Let us start with the essential aspect of what AI can contribute to existing financial systems. Artificial intelligence has helped companies boost productivity and cut operational costs by 70%. AI-developed software plays a role in the banking sectors by assisting assessing potential borrowers by analyzing numerous factors, thus making the process faster and more cost-effective. AI is vital in trading, as it quickly analyze massive amounts of data and make accurate predictions by examining extensive historical data

[6, 23–26]. It also helps analyze an investor's long- and short-term goals, providing recommendations on the most robust portfolios. AI-powered fraud detection tools can analyze clients' behavior, purchasing habits, and locations to detect suspicious activities [27]. Personalized financial advice and chatbots help reduce call center loads, and products like customer recommendations, AIML. and fraud detection (which are part of machine learning), Robo advice (where natural language processing is applied), and algorithmic trading (obtained by analyzing large amounts of data over time) all benefit from AI. AI has helped set new security standards by enabling systems like speech recognition and facial recognition in banks, which are more effective than traditional security measures like passwords and captchas [27–29].

After thoroughly discussing AI usage in finance, let us dig deep into AI itself and understand its foundations, the mathematical concepts involved, and what ML and DL are. In ML, humans create algorithms that explore data, learn from it and derive from it. DL is radically different. It is based upon artificial neural networks, which imitate the functioning of the human brain. DL machines do not require programmers' interference; they are self-sufficient. Concepts like artificial neural networks have enabled computers to process data like the human brain [30–32]. These networks form the base of deep learning models and use interconnected neurons or nodes distributed in layered structures, starting from the input layer to the middle layers and, finally, the output layer. Each layer's node connects to the nodes of other layers through channels [26–28]. Each of these channels is assigned a numerical value called weight. The inputs of the neural network are multiplied by weights, and their sum then enters the neurons of the middle layer, where a numerical value called bias is added to the weighted sum. This value is then put into the activation function, a non-linear function that decides whether that neuron can contribute to the next layer. In the output layer, the neuron contains the probability of its predictions [28–31]. The neuron with the highest value determines the final output. Additionally, the learning process of neural networks, which includes the methods of forward and backward propagation, makes deep learning so powerful in making predictions and analyzing data autonomously without programmers' interference [32–35].

There are various deep learning models based on deep learning algorithms like autoencoders, restricted Boltzmann machine, deep belief models, multilayer perceptron, generative adversarial networks, and others that have been applied in fields like defense, healthcare, statistics, and finances. These models specifically needs to be discussed in detail. But before that, let us understand the difference between autonomous and automated systems [22–25]. Nowadays, many of us have digitized smartwatches that are automated in nature, meaning they can measure our heartbeats, predict our health, and suggest appropriate medical steps. In contrast, autonomous systems would automatically call an ambulance after analyzing the person's readings, assessing the risk, and deciding what needs to be done. They would tell the person to get in, as there might be a risk of a cardiac issue [26]. The same concept applies to autonomous finance. Instead of automating one or two parameters or tools for collecting, analyzing, and predicting data, the goal is to make the entire system autonomous. This system would predict stock markets trends, plan the list of goods and services in demand for sellers in upcoming quarters, and perform sentiment analysis of people by analyzing data from social media. To make systems efficient and capable to this extent, the applications of DL models in AF cannot be ignored [28–30, 33].

Autonomous finance comprises three significant technologies: blockchain, artificial intelligence, and hyper-automation. These three tech pillars have been game changers in the financial industry, paving the way for a transformative impact on our economic ecosystems worldwide. Among all corporate functions, finance is the one most likely to become autonomous due to the constant flow of data, codes, and rules through organizations in this digital era [25–27]. With persistent inflation and slowing growth, it is crucial for companies to be more predictive in optimizing their inventories, supply chain pricing, and maintaining an efficient relationship with global supply chains. Autonomous finance refers to being more predictive and prescriptive, making decisions based on the analysis of a constant flow of data rather than merely applying a particular technology to some systems to make them more efficient and less time-consuming. Statistics suggest that in the future, there will be a massive reduction in the cost of corporate finances. This shift will prompt CFOs in autonomous finance to rethink core finance operations, integrate organizations, and reconsider how work is done. A discussion on terms related to ML models used specifically for financial automation is essential [12–18].

10.3 Reinforcement Learning

RL has a solid mathematical structure in which agents interact directly with their surroundings. It is considered a robust autonomous learning model where the agent's efficiency is enhanced through trial and error to optimize cumulative rewards. The advantage of RL is that it does not require labeled data to achieve this optimization. Policy and value function approximations are crucial in activating autonomous learning strategy. RL uses both gradient-based and gradient-free approaches to create a stochastic process for discrete and continuous state-action situations [13–15]. For example, consider an economic problem where RL imposes significant market constraints to allow for more optimal strategies in areas like market analysis and forecast.

10.3.1 Demerits of Reinforcement Learning Techniques

Despite its successful results, RL lacks scalability, and its incapability to manage high-dimensional problems makes the use of DL combined with RL (DRL) necessary to solve such problems efficiently. The DRL technique incorporates deep learning with dynamic function approximation, leveraging the learning capabilities of deep neural networks (DNN) to handle complex non-linear patterns in economic data, thus proving valuable for financial applications. Let us discuss the terms of RL [16, 17].

10.3.2 Markov Decision Process (MDP)

Usual ratification of successive decision-making occurs when actions impact not only direct rewards but also subsequent decision-making. In these scenarios, immediate rewards are influenced by activities and subsequent states as well as the future rewards associated with those states. This process involves delays in rewards and the need to trade off delayed rewards with immediate ones [1, 16–19]. MDPs are used to achieve a structured approach to learning from interactions to pursue an objective. They interact with the external environment, also known as the agent's surroundings as shown in Figure 10.1. The interaction between agents and the environment is a continuous process where agents select actions and the environment responds

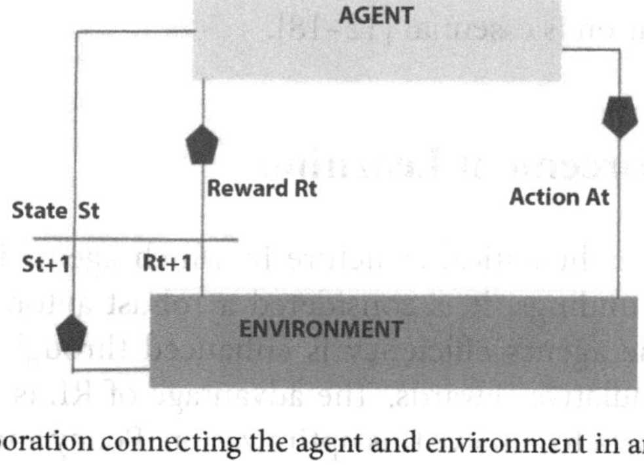

Figure 10.1 Collaboration connecting the agent and environment in an MDP.

by presenting new states to the agent. MDPs are composed of states, actions, interstate transitions, and reward functions [2, 8–10].

• States and Actions

A state, by definition, can be characterized as a unique representation of all relevant aspects in a modeled problem. It is better to imagine it as the finite set {} where the size of the state space is N, i.e., |S| = N. (in tic-tac-toe for a 3 × 3 board, a state could be a tuple of nine elements, each corresponding to a separate section of the panel. Each cell could be blank or occupied by one of the players, containing either X, Y, or null (or any other three symbols) [1–4]. We have confined ourselves into a discrete state set S, where each state represents a distinct symbol with a sense of legality assigned to all states s ∈ S.

Actions are employed to control the state of the system. The set of actions available in some state ∈ S is denoted as A(s), in which A(s) ⊆ A. The set of actions A is represented by the finite set {, . . .,}, where the size of the action space is K, i.e., |A| = K. Although not every action cannot be executed in each state, we will assume that A(s) = A for every s ∈ S.

10.3.2.1 Transition Function

When an action from set A is applied in a state from S, it transitions from a state s to a new state within S based on the probability distributions over a set of possible transitions [4–8]. The transition function is defined as

$$T : S * A * S \text{ tending to } [0,1] \tag{10.1}$$

The equation denotes the probability of ending in state s′ after taking action in state s represented as T (s, a, s′). It is formulated such that for every action a, and for every state s and s′:

$$\text{T (s,a, s')} \geq 0 \text{ and T (s,a, s')} \leq 1 \tag{10.2}$$

Moreover, for every state s and action a,

$$\Sigma_{s' \epsilon S} T(s,a,s') = 1 \tag{10.3}$$

Here, T defines a proper probability distribution function over the possible next states. To determine the order in which actions occur, we use a discrete global clock t belonging to {0,1,2,3……}, so the state and action at time t are represented accordingly [1]. The system in control is considered

Markovian, meaning the result of a particular action depends only on the current state and not on previous actions and states visited.

$$P(s_{t+1}|s_t,a_t,s_{t+1},a_{t-1},\ldots) = P(s_{t+1}|s_t,a_t,) = T(s_t,a_t,s_{t+1},) \quad (10.4)$$

• *Reward Function Plus Markov Decision Process:* Reward functions determine how the MDP system needs to be controlled. The agent manages the system's control by selecting actions that lead to rewards over time. In classical optimization problems, the goal is to maximize or minimize cost functions under certain conditions. In RL, the agent's goal is formalized with the help of special signals (rewards) [2–5, 35–37] that pass through the environment towards the agent. This can be mathematically described as

$$R : S * A * S \rightarrow IR \quad (10.5)$$

where R stands for reward.

Considering the basic idea of these functions, let us move to MDP, which can be represented as a tuple (S, A, T, R), where S is a state of a finite set, A is an action of a finite set, T is the transition probability function. T: S × A × S ! [0, 1], and R is the reward function, R: S × A × S à R.

Further clarification can be achieved by examining a movable pawn being moved to a specific location on a grid. Accordingly, in Figures 10.2 and 10.3, one can make the following judgments considering State, Actions, Transition Probabilities, and Rewards.

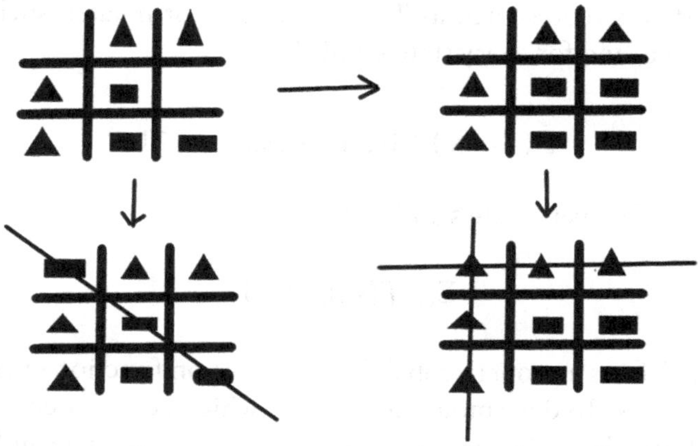

Figure 10.2 At a point of state during tic-tac-toe gameplay, actions possible.

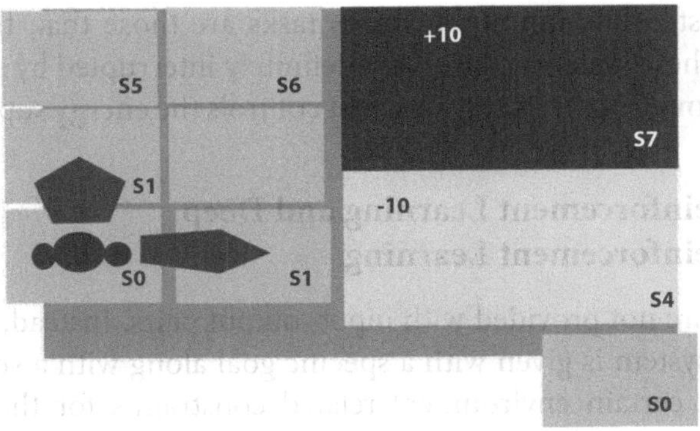

Figure 10.3 Showing a movable pawn piece on a chessboard.

$$\text{States S} = \{\text{s0, s1, s2, ...s7}\}$$

Action s = {up, down, right, left}, dependent of the current state S

$$\text{Transition probabilities} = \{T_{s0,s3}^{up} = 0.9; T_{s0,s1}^{right}\} = 0.1; \ldots.. \quad (10.6)$$

$$\text{Rewards} = \{R_{s6,s3}^{right} = +10; R_{s2,s4}^{up} \ \textit{otherwise}, R = 0\} = -10; \quad (10.7)$$

Start in S_0

Game over when reaching S_7

There are several systems in which an MDP can be modeled, such as episodic or continuing tasks. Episodic tasks involve episodes of specific lengths, with the ultimate goal of bringing agents to a final goal state. The differentiation between fixed and indefinite horizon tasks is important to note. Episodes can still have arbitrary lengths, as seen in games like tic-tac-toe and chess as shown in Figures 10.2 and 10.3.

Another example is a robot learning how to walk. Initially, the rate of falls will be higher, resulting in shorter episodes. However, as the learning process progresses, the robot will eventually achieve the ability to walk or run indefinitely.

The system's opening state is initialized at each episode using the initial state allocation.

$$\text{I:S} \rightarrow [0,1] \quad (10.8)$$

In contrast, while infinite horizons tasks are those that, theoretically, never end. These systems continue indefinitely interrupted by an intervention. An example of this is software that controls the energy supply to a city.

10.3.3 Reinforcement Learning and Deep Reinforcement Learning

RL systems are not provided with input–output pairs. Instead, the current state of the system is given with a specific goal along with a set of actions allowed and certain environment-related constraints for the outcomes. An agent is expected to optimize maximum reward by interacting with the environment through trial and error. These models are applicable in closed-world environments like gaming and have shown their relevance in multi-agent systems such as electronic marketing segments.

Q(s,a) or V(s) are the functions used by popular RL algorithms to estimate the total discounted rewards. These functions are tabular mappings of discrete inputs to outputs, which are limited when dealing with several continuous or many states. Neural networks can estimate the number of states [3, 22–24]. Functional approximation is a method that eliminates the need to store several state and value pairs in the table, allowing the agent to generalize state values it has not previously encountered. This method uses partial information to apply similar state values, also known as reference.

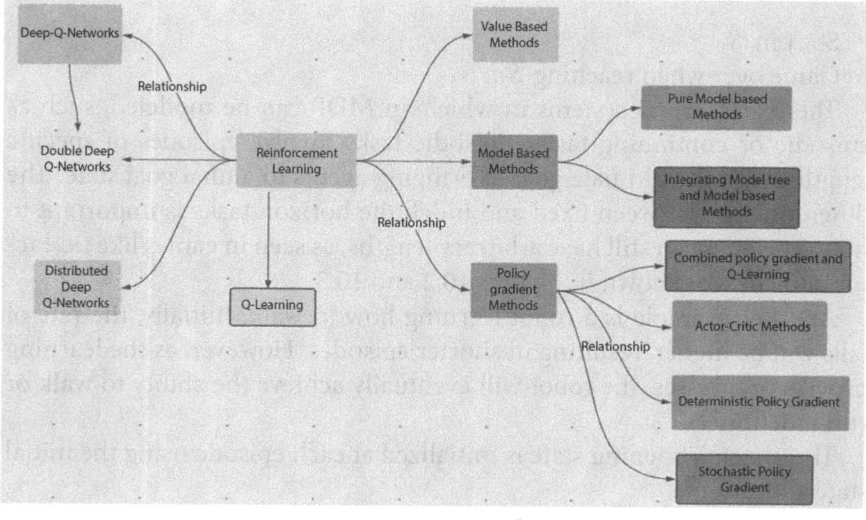

Figure 10.4 The figure shows a conceptual flow of varied fields from the RL branch of AI.

RL dynamically learns using trial and error methods to maximize rewards as shown in Figure 10.4. In contrast, deep reinforcement learning applies its existing knowledge to new datasets.

10.3.3.1 Deep Reinforcement Learning

As the subject suggests, this involves associating DL methods with RL techniques. One of the most viable areas of application is self-driving cars. When incorporating DL, the policy is often represented as $\pi(a|s)$ or through various learned functions as a neural network [3, 27, 37, 38]. This approach supports the development of specialized algorithms that perform well in these settings.

10.4 Neural Network Basics

As stated earlier, we need a detailed understanding of the functioning of neural networks and their mathematical foundations. They are non-linear functions generally represented by neurons with several layers connected to operators, filters, pooling, and gates. These networks map the input variable Rn to the output variable Rm, where n,m belongs to z+.

Figure 10.5 explains the basic architecture of a perceptron, where a particular instance for training is of the form (X,y), with X = [x1,......] consisting of feature variables d and y being a value in {−1,1}, representing the value in observation of the second class. The detected value is used to set the training data in parts, keeping in mind our objective to forecast the class variables [28–30] for those sets of circumstances for which we do not have an observation. When the input layer containing the d nodes transmits d features X = [ω1 ....] to the output node, the input layers do not perform any computation. The linear function is calculated at the output node, and the result is used to forecast the dependent variable y. The prediction y is calculated as follows:

$$\text{Y cap} = \text{sign}\ \{W.X\} = \text{sign}\ \{dj = 1\ \omega\ j\ \chi\ j\} \tag{10.9}$$

The following are the three network architectures that are the most common:

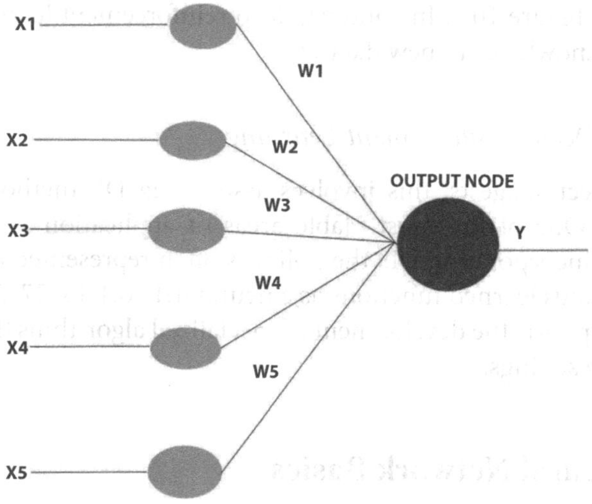

Figure 10.5 The figure above shows how a neural network is structured.

10.4.1 Fully Connected Neural Network (FNN)

The most straightforward neural architecture among all types of neural networks is a fully connected neural network, where each neuron is connected to every neuron in the previous layer. To describe this setup, the neural network consists of several layers L є Z+, each with a specific width or number of neurons (the *i*th layer has ni є Z+ for i = 1,2….,I).

Thus, for a given input variable input z є Rn, the functionality of FNN in a mathematical format can be denoted by:

$$F(z; W, b) = W(z; W, b) = WI \bullet a(vvt - 1 ...a(VVIZ + bl)... + bl - 1) + bl. \tag{10.10}$$

where (W,b) represents all the parameters in the neural network, with W = (W1,W2,W3.....WI) and b = (b1,b2,b3.....bI).

In the literature of neural networks, the WI's are denoted as weight matrices, while the bI's represent bias vectors, and sigma refers to an activation function. Activation functions can be represented by various choices such as

- ReLU with sigma(*u*) = max(*u; 0*),
- Leaky ReLU with sigma(*u*) = a1 max(*u; 0*) – a2 max(–u, 0)

where a1; a2 >0, along with certain smooth functions like sigma(.) = tanh(.).

10.4.2 Convolutional Neural Network (CNN)

CNNs are a variety of feed-forward neural networks that are extremely useful in the field of image processing. These neural networks also find application in the financial domain; CNNs have delivered successful results in price prediction problems, where input images contain conceptions of trading volumes and price dynamics. CNNs are made up of two main fundamental blocks: pooling layers and convolutional layers. Convolutional layers comprise input data, a feature map, and a filter. CNNs help detect local patterns in images, which explains their utility in image processing. Pooling layers are used for dimensionality reduction and improving computational efficacy as shown in Figure 10.6.

Typically, a CNN can be demonstrated in the form of equations like:

$$F(z;H,W,b) = W \bullet \text{sigma}(z * H) + b \tag{10.11}$$

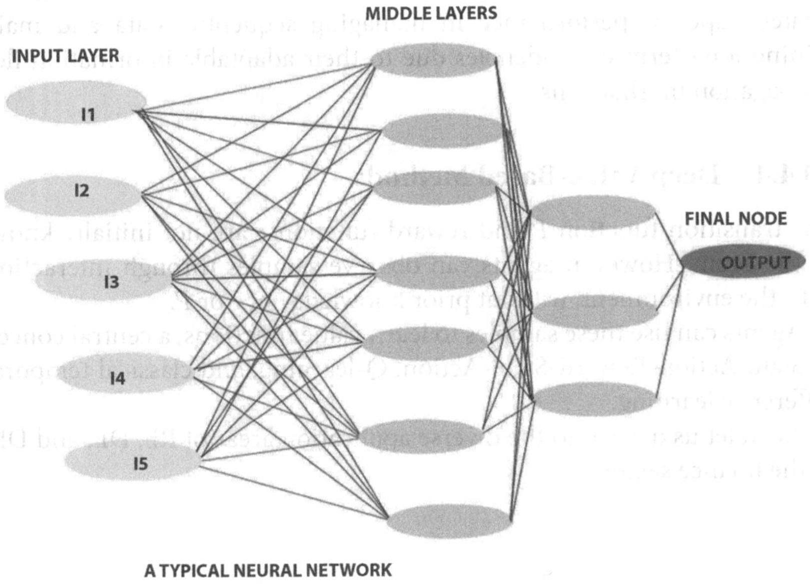

Figure 10.6 Figure shows the complexity of a typical neural network.

10.4.3 Recurrent Neural Networks (RNN)

RNNs are a subset of neural networks used to process sequential data, ranging from text and speech to economic time series data. In RNNs, the connectivity between the units form a directed cycle, unlike in feed-forward neural networks. RNNs have internal memory to process sequences of inputs, making them suitable for tasks like sequential data processing.

The input for an RNN is a sequence of data Z1,Z2……Z_t.

The internal state (ht) of RNN models is represented with a recursive relation.

$$ht = F(ht - 1, Zt; \theta)$$

where F is a neural network with parameters θ (for example, θ = (W, b)).

Henceforth, the output is formulated by:

$$s\text{^}t = G\ (ht - 1, Zt; 0)$$

where G is another neural network with parameter (θ). The vanilla RNN has two variations: Gated Recurrent Units (GRUs) and Long Short-Term Memory (LSTM). Unlike vanilla RNNs, LSTMs, and GRUs have demonstrated superior performance in managing sequential data and maintaining long-term dependencies due to their adaptable information flow propagation mechanisms.

10.4.4 Deep Value-Based Methods

The transition function *P* and reward function *r* are not initially known to the agent. However, agents can observe samples through interactions with the environment, without prior knowledge of *r* or *P*.

Agents can use these samples to learn value functions, a central concept in State-Action-Reward-State-Action, Q-learning, and classical temporal-difference learning.

Next, let us delve into the diverse application areas of RL, DL, and DRL in the finance sector.

10.5 Management of Information for Credit Risk

These learning algorithms are applied in risk assessment for firms, individuals, products, and banks. PL research has primarily focused on areas such as credit rating, bankruptcy prediction, bond rating, loan/insurance underwriting, consumer credit determination, corporate credit rating, and mortgage choice detection. Risk assessment has always emphasized credit scoring and bank distress classification, while some studies also cover crisis forecasting and detecting high-risk transactions.

10.5.1 Management of Information for Fraud Detection

Fraud cases can take many forms, such as credit card scams, tax evasion, money laundering, and insurance claim fraud. These finance areas are complex, and research in AI/ML disciplines under anomaly detection treats them as classification problems.

10.5.2 Portfolio Optimization Driven by Big Data

In portfolio optimization problems, a trader is expected to select the best assets to maximize certain objective functions, considering the probability of returns along with specific risk measures. Investment in such diversified portfolios allows traders to achieve a higher return per unit of risk, compared to investing all in one asset based solely on its performance.

10.5.3 Management of Information for Assets and Derivative Market

Valuation of assets and accurate pricing are fundamental research areas in finance. AI/ML models have evolved for real estate, banks, derivative products, and corporations. RL algorithms and associated models are expected to aid researchers and valuation experts on pricing assets. Effective deep feedforward neural network (DFNN) models have been used in sentiment analysis for stock price prediction. Developing RL models could benefit areas such as option pricing, financial engineering with futures, options, and forward contracts, and hedging strategy development. These areas have garnered attention from researchers, showing interest in RL models to provide solutions in these challenging and complex fields.

10.5.4 Algorithmic Trading

Algorithmic trading uses algorithms in finance to make buy–sell decisions based on predefined rules, complex functions, and mathematical models. The increasing popularity of online trading platforms has made algorithmic trading a hugely successful application in recent years. Many algorithm trading applications now incorporate price prediction and modeling for real-time market systems. Coupling several algorithmic trading systems with price prediction has been done for market timing. The study of microstructure-based trade indicators of the market has been used to input RNNs along with Graves' LSTM to perform predictive pricing of algorithmic stock trading. Technical indicators have been used as input in wavelet transforms and LSTM in autoencoders for forecasting stock prices. A CNN, along with an LSTM model, was implemented, with the CNN used for selecting stocks and the LSTM for predicting prices. Fuzzy deep direct reinforcement learning (FDDR) has been used in trading signal generation and stock price generation.

10.5.5 Big Data Analysis with the Usage of Text Mining

The rising reach of social media and other factors such as more accessible access to information and real-time streaming have helped enhance financial models. With time, various works has focused on sentiment analysis, examining source materials and applying natural language processing techniques to understand social media users' attitudes towards the subject. Typically, sources need to be classified into positive or negative segments, along with data mining being used for sentiment analysis. DL techniques are employed to determine the expectation of investors regarding stock prices and predict market trends based on their messages. In data mining, feature selection after identification is one of the most challenging tasks, especially in sectors like big data, which is why DL techniques are employed.

Several DL algorithms are used to draw complex data at high levels of abstraction, where high-level features with more abstraction are viewed as low-level features with lower levels of abstraction. DL can distinguish variations in data sources, such as objects, shapes, lights, and other associated materials. Hierarchical learning, a concept inspired by the primary sensory areas of the human brain's neocortex, can also be implemented using DL.

10.5.6 Essence of Convolutional Neural Network

CNNs are a diverse type of DL model popularly used in image analysis, and they can be used to understand the internal structure of data through convolutional layers. CNNs are gaining attention for their ability to comprehend the internal structure of text documents, aiding in tagging, sentence modeling, and entity search. DL algorithms effectively learn data representation techniques, making them particularly useful for big data analysis. In big data analytics, DL excels at extracting non-linear, complex features, which are then used as input for linear models. This capability simplifies the general discriminative tasks associated with big data analytics. For instance, when performing a search using big data, DL can draw out high levels of complex abstractions from massive unsupervised data sets. This makes DL desirable, as demonstrated by products like Google's DNN, which can extract high-level features from unlabeled data, showcasing the ability of learning models to derive high-level features from unsupervised data.

10.6 Sentiment Analysis with Data Mining Approach

10.6.1 Case Study of Wang [2]

Wang employed a blend of supervised learning methodologies to ascertain the sentiment of messages within the stock Twitter collection. In the second step, preprocessing techniques were applied to the dataset to remove stop words, stock symbols, and company names [2]. Subsequently, various data mining algorithms, including naïve Bayes, support vector machine, and decision trees, were employed to make predictions based on the dataset. After running tenfold cross-validation, a 76.2% accuracy was obtained using a support vector machine model. Additionally, unigrams were also used as features, but since n-grams can lead to data sparsity, infrequent unigrams that occurred less than 300 times in the messages were removed. This step was necessary because using lower-order n-grams can otherwise cause a decrease in performance. Using lower-order n-grams can lead to the loss of the order of words in a sentence, which is crucial for increasing the accuracy of the analysis.

After completing the aforementioned steps, DL nonlinear feature extraction is used to improve the results of data mining and classification modeling. The sigmoid function is often used in logistic regressions to classify input values. However, it exhibits comparable functionality to DL without including hidden layers. Logistic regression is frequently employed in the concluding layers of DL models. This implies that DL algorithms tend to work as multi-feature learning steps, while logistic regression is used for its speed and simplicity, making it suitable for large datasets.

10.7 Conclusion

The performance of DL and neural networks has been commendable and is a promising approach in several areas, especially natural language processing. It also has a high potential to address data analysis and learning problems related to big data. With DL algorithms and hidden layers transforming their input, one can enhance the shallow learning process of data mining. Hierarchical learning in DL helps find the semantics of words and their associated relations, making it a valuable method for sentiment analysis.

References

1. Calvo-Pardo, H.F., Mancini, T., Olmo, J., Neural Network Models for Empirical Finance. *J. Risk Financ. Manage.*, 13, 11, 265, 2020, https://doi.org/10.3390/jrfm13110265.
2. Wang, G., Wang, T., Wang, B., Sambasivan, D., Zhang, Z., Zheng, H., Zhao, B.Y., Crowds on wall street: Extracting value from collaborative investing platforms, in: *Proceedings of the 18th ACM Conference on Computer Supported Cooperative Work & Social Computing*, pp. 17–30, February 2015.
3. Sohangir, S., Wang, D., Pomeranets, A., Khoshgoftaar, T.M., Big Data: Deep Learning for financial sentiment analysis. *J. Big Data*, 5, 1, 1–25, 2018.
4. Pistor, K., The rise of autonomous financial power, in: *Capital Claims: Power and Global Finance*, 2022.
5. Yusuf, A., Qureshi, S., Shah, S.F., Mathematical analysis for an autonomous financial dynamical system via classical and modern fractional operators. *Chaos, Solitons Fractals*, 132, 109552, 2020.
6. Guarino, A., Grilli, L., Santoro, D., Messina, F., Zaccagnino, R., To learn or not to learn? Evaluating autonomous, adaptive, automated traders in cryptocurrencies financial bubbles. *Neural Comput. Appl.*, 34, 23, 20715–20756, 2022.

7. Roseline, J.F., Naidu, G.B.S.R., Pandi, V.S., alias Rajasree, S.A., Mageswari, N., Autonomous credit card fraud detection using machine learning approach☆. *Comput. Electr. Eng.*, 102, 108132, 2022.
8. Robinson, R., Digital twin modeling in virtual enterprises and autonomous manufacturing systems: deep learning and neural network algorithms, immersive visualization tools, and cognitive data fusion techniques. *Econ. Manage. Financ. Mark.*, 17, 2, 52–66, 2022.
9. Tao, G., Sun, W., Han, T., Fang, C., Zhang, X., RULER: discriminative and iterative adversarial training for deep neural network fairness, in: *Proceedings of the 30th ACM Joint European Software Engineering Conference and Symposium on the Foundations of Software Engineering*, pp. 1173–1184, November 2022.
10. Islam, A., Amin, R., Sharan, M.H., Ushno, J.A., Islam, K.M.T., Hossen, D., Alam, M.S., Designing an autonomous framework to detect and classify the fabric defects using wavelet transform and neural network, in: *AIP Conference Proceedings*, vol. 2788, AIP Publishing, July 2023.
11. Gogas, P. and Papadimitriou, T., Machine learning in economics and finance. *Comput. Econ.*, 57, 1–4, 2021.
12. Boute, R.N., Gijsbrechts, J., Van Mieghem, J.A., Digital lean operations: Smart automation and artificial intelligence in financial services, in: *Innovative Technology at the Interface of Finance and Operations: Volume I*, pp. 175–188, 2022.
13. Gallagher, M., Pitropakis, N., Chrysoulas, C., Papadopoulos, P., Mylonas, A., Katsikas, S., Investigating machine learning attacks on financial time series models. *Comput. Secur.*, 123, 102933, 2022.
14. Cao, L., Yang, Q., Yu, P.S., Data science and AI in FinTech: An overview. *Int. J. Data. Sci. Anal.*, 12, 81–99, 2021.
15. Hazarika, B.B., Gupta, D., Gupta, U., Intuitionistic Fuzzy Kernel Random Vector Functional Link Classifier, in: *Machine Intelligence Techniques for Data Analysis and Signal Processing: Proceedings of the 4th International Conference MISP 2022*, vol. 1, pp. 881–889, Springer Nature Singapore, Singapore, May 2023.
16. Zizi, Y., Oudgou, M., El Moudden, A., Determinants and predictors of some financial failure: A logistic regression approach. *Risks*, 8, 4, 107, 2020.
17. Adams, J. and Hagras, H., A type-2 fuzzy logic approach to explainable AI for regulatory compliance, fair customer outcomes and market stability in the global financial sector, in: *2020 IEEE international conference on fuzzy systems (FUZZ-IEEE)*, IEEE, pp. 1–8, July 2020.
18. Haney, B. and Chaudhury, A., Algorand Autonomous, in: *Brian Haney and Archie Chaudhury, Algorand Autonomous*, 2021.
19. Cavalcante, R.C. and Oliveira, A.L., An autonomous trader agent for the stock market based on online sequential extreme learning machine ensemble, in: *2014 International Joint Conference on Neural Networks (IJCNN)*, IEEE, pp. 1424–1431, July 2014.

20. Coats, P.K. and Fant, L.F., Recognizing financial distress patterns using a neural network tool. *Financ. Manage.*, 22, 3, 142–155, 1993.
21. Gupta, D., Gupta, U., Sarma, H.J., Functional iterative approach for Universum-based primal twin bounded support vector machine to EEG classification (FUPTBSVM). *Multimed. Tools Appl.*, 83, 8, 1–33, 2023.
22. Gupta, U., Gupta, D., Agarwal, U., Analysis of randomization-based approaches for autism spectrum disorder, in: *Pattern Recognition and Data Analysis with Applications*, pp. 701–713, Springer Nature Singapore, Singapore, 2022.
23. Hájek, P., Municipal credit rating modelling by neural networks. *Decis. Support Syst.*, 51, 1, 108–118, 2011.
24. Boyacioglu, M.A., Kara, Y., Baykan, O.K., Predicting bank financial failures using neural networks, support vector machines and multivariate statistical methods: A comparative analysis in the sample of savings deposit insurance fund (SDIF) transferred banks in Turkey. *Expert Syst. Appl.*, 36, 2, 3355–3366, 2009.
25. Nikolaidis, S. and Refanidis, I., Consolidating incentivization in distributed neural network training via decentralized autonomous organization. *Neural Comput. Appl.*, 34, 22, 19599–19613, 2022.
26. Njegovanović, A., Digital financial decision with a view of neuroplasticity/neurofinancy/neural networks. *Financial Markets, Institutions and Risks (FMIR)*, 2, 4, 82–91, 2018. http://doi.org/10.21272/fmir.2(4).82-91.2018.
27. Chatigny, P., Patenaude, J.M., Wang, S., Spatiotemporal adaptive neural network for long-term forecasting of financial time series. *Int. J. Approx. Reason.*, 132, 70–85, 2021.
28. Beltratti, A., Margarita, S., Terna, P., *Neural networks for economic and financial modelling*, International Thomson Computer Press, London, UK, 1996.
29. Hafezi, R., Shahrabi, J., Hadavandi, E., A bat-neural network multi-agent system (BNNMAS) for stock price prediction: Case study of DAX stock price. *Appl. Soft Comput.*, 29, 196–210, 2015.
30. Gupta, U. and Meher, P., Statistical analysis of target tracking algorithms in thermal imagery, in: *Cognitive Informatics and Soft Computing: Proceeding of CISC 2019*, Springer Singapore, pp. 635–646, 2020.
31. Gupta, U. and Gupta, D., Bipolar fuzzy based least squares twin bounded support vector machine. *Fuzzy Sets Syst.*, 449, 120–161, 2022.
32. Magazzino, C., Mele, M., Santeramo, F.G., Using an artificial neural networks experiment to assess the links among financial development and growth in agriculture. *Sustainability*, 13, 5, 2828, 2021.
33. Singh, V., Chen, S.S., Singhania, M., Nanavati, B., Gupta, A., How are reinforcement learning and deep learning algorithms used for big data-based decision making in financial industries–A review and research agenda. *Int. J. Inf. Manage. Data Insights*, 2, 2, 100094, 2022.
34. Van Otterlo, M., The logic of adaptive behaviour. In Knowledge representation, IOS Press, US, 2009.

35. Hambly, B., Xu, R., Yang, H., Recent advances in reinforcement learning in finance. *Math. Finance*, 33, 3, 437–503, 2023.
36. Nashed, S.B., Svegliato, J., Blodgett, S.L., Fairness and Sequential Decision Making: Limits, Lessons, and Opportunities, arXiv preprint arXiv:2301.05753, Cornell University, arxiv.org, Computer Science, Computers and Society, New York, 2023.
37. Azarpanah, A., Bielby, J., Ingram, K., Mousavi, E., Nye, H., Rockwell, G., Yoldas, T., On the Ethics of Artificial Intelligence, in: *CSDH-SCHN 2020*, May 2020.
38. Ledziński, L. and Grześk, G., Artificial Intelligence Technologies in Cardiology. *J. Cardiovasc. Dev. Dis.*, 10, 5, 202, 2023.

11

Machine Learning Algorithm in Indian Stock Market for Revising and Refining the Equity Valuation Models

Nitha K. P.[1], Suraj E. S.[2]* and Ranjith Karat[3]

[1]*Sree KeralaVarma College, Computer Science Department, Kerala, Thrissur, India*
[2]*MBA Department, KCT Business School, Coimbatore, Tamil Nadu, India*
[3]*SME, Kerala University of Fisheries and Ocean Studies (KUFOS), Kochi, Kerala, India*

Abstract
Predicting stock prices using machine learning approaches has become an attractive topic for researchers. Traditional statistical methods are increasingly seen as inadequate for analyzing large volumes of data effectively. Machine learning methods excel in uncovering hidden patterns and forecasting future trends and behaviors in the stock market. This study focuses on supervised machine learning algorithms applied to classify stock market data in India. The study aims to enhance existing equity valuation models to improve prediction accuracy. These model results will assist in making informed decisions on whether to buy, sell, or hold stocks in the Indian stock market

Keywords: Machine learning, classification, supervised machine learning

11.1 Introduction

The stock market involves several purchasers and sellers. Many studies have been conducted to forecast stock prices using both traditional and modern methods. This study was conducted to understand the advantages of the machine learning approach in stock price prediction after revising the equity models. Predicting the stock market is a difficult task that consists

**Corresponding author*: surajandsuraj@yahoo.com

Deepa Gupta, Mukul Gupta, Rajesh Kumar Dhanaraj, Balamurugan Balusamy and Parth Mukul Gupta (eds.) Computational Intelligence for Autonomous Finance, (221–242) © 2025 Scrivener Publishing LLC

of several factors, including economics, accounting, and market sentiment. Machine learning is used in many sectors to determine the pulses of the stock market. One of the most popular applications of machine learning is stock-market prediction. Machine learning algorithms are either supervised or unsupervised. In supervised learning, the characterized input data are trained and the algorithm is realistic. Classification and regression are supervised learning methods. It provides an advanced and precise environment. Unsupervised learning uses unlabeled data but has a less controlled environment. It analyzes patterns, correlations, and clusters. The readings also shield various unsupervised machine learning algorithms and the statistical methods used in stock price forecasting. The study has been exposed to creating a portfolio of stocks that capitalize on profit with minimum risk.

11.1.1 Multiple Regression Machine Learning Algorithm

The multiple regression is used in statistics to understand the association between a dependent variable and more than one independent variables. In machine learning it is used to predict a dependent variable with more than two independent variables. The main applications of the multiple regression machine learning algorithm are

- Assessing the effectiveness of independent variables on prediction,
- Predicting the impact of changes in the model on the results.

11.1.2 Classification

Classification, a field in statistics, involves the process of assigning an observation to the appropriate category or class. In machine learning, classifiers are trained with the appropriate features that represents each class. This trained model then predicts an unlabeled observation x into a predicted label y. The model's performance is evaluated using measures such as accuracy, precision, recall, and F1-score. In this study, the Random Forest classifier is used for the classification of the stocks into one of four class labels. The advantage of Random forest classifiers is that it reduces overfitting. This study primarily focuses on revising and refining existing equity valuation models using a machine learning approach for Sensex stock price prediction.

11.2 Objectives of the Study

1. To understand the machine learning algorithm approach for stock price prediction in the Indian stock market.
2. To study, revise, and refine the selected equity valuation model using multiple regression models.
3. To improve stock price prediction for Sensex stocks using the revised and refined model with a machine learning approach.

11.3 Methodology

Secondary data, including the yearly annual reports and the websites of BSE (www.bseindia.com), NSE (www.nseindia.com), Centre for Monitoring Indian Economy (CMIE) Prowess, Confederation of Indian Industries (CII) library, and the annual report library services like Ebsco Services, is considered. Table 11.1 shows the list of Sensex stocks selected for the study.

Table 11.1 List of Sensex stocks.

Sl. no.	Name of the stock
1	BharathiAirtel
2	Coal India
3	HCL Tech
4	HDFC
5	Axis bank
6	Asian Paints
7	Bajaj Auto
8	Bajaj Finance
9	HDFC Bank
10	Hero Motors
11	Hindustan

(Continued)

Table 11.1 List of Sensex stocks. (*Continued*)

Sl. no.	Name of the stock
12	ICICI Bank
13	IndusInd Bank
14	ITC
15	Kotak Bank
16	Larsen & Toubro (L&T)
17	Maruti
18	Mahindra & Mahindra (M&M)
19	National Thermal Power Corporation Ltd (NTPC)
20	Oil and Natural Gas Corporation Limited (ONGC)
21	Power Grid
22	Reliance
23	State Bank of India
24	Sun Pharma
25	Tata DVR
26	Tata Motors
27	Tata Steel
28	Tata Consultancy Services (TCS)
29	Vedanta
30	Yes Bank

11.3.1 Softwares Used

R Software 4.0.2 has been used to evaluate and analyze the data. To refine the best three equity valuation models and build an integrated model using machine learning or sentiment indicators, R python, is used in this study.

11.4 Review of Literature

Patel and his team [1, 2] conducted an analysis using machine learning mechanism for stock price forecasting. This study aimed to improve the predictive performance of the stock market and verify the targeted value of the forecast by comparing different machine learning mechanisms. Machine learning has been applied to different sectorial indices to determine whether to invest in a particular company at a given time. [3] utilized Hybrid Clustering-GWO-NARX neural organization strategy in predicting stock prices and found that the K-means clustering algorithm was effective in identifying the most promising clusters. This strategy can be used for predicting stock market prices by applying the NARX neural network algorithm. The performance of the forecast through experimentation was compared and evaluated to assist investors in making investment decisions. The study focused on developing a hybrid model for stock prediction and assessing the forecast performance in other financial markets.

The data from [5] examined stock price prediction using support vector relapse for daily and up-to-the-moment prices. This AI technique, called Support Vector Regression (SVR), was used to predict stock prices for large and small capitalization companies in three different markets. Prediction errors of the model were projected and compared with the random walk model proposed by the efficient market hypothesis. The results demonstrated that SVR has predictive power, especially when the model is updated periodically. The improved prediction accuracy was particularly evident during periods of low volatility. [7] utilized novel approaches to Sentiment Analysis for Stock Prediction. A supervised learning model can predict stock movement direction by combining technical information and sentiment from news sources. This study in India focused on predicting stock price direction using different techniques, including SVMs and neural networks, by adopting an AI approach.

Augby [6] and Das [4] used Sentiment Analysis dependent on informal communities for stock value expectations in securities exchanges. This examination zeroed in via online media, such as "Twitter and Facebook," for financial exchange expectation purposes. This investigation showed that the web-based media impact can be utilized for transient value forecasting, and wistful examination can be considered as a helpful factor in the expectation of stock costs. Atkins [8] used monetary news to predict financial exchange unpredictability. It was discovered that unpredictability developments are more surprising than resource value developments when utilizing monetary news as an AI input. In addition, expectation results depend only on the data obtained from the news source.

Naik and Lakshman [9] contemplated the beneficial exchange rules for financial exchange ventures. They utilized man-made brainpower methods to the inclined bearing of the cost for BSE file (India Concrete Stock Value File (ICSPI)) prospects with a few specialized markers for corporate share warning reasons. Then, at that point, they mined the exchange rules to decide the contention among the yields of the main stage by utilizing the developed learning strategy. Nyman and Rickard [10] contemplated the monetary determinants that appraise the qualities of yield, swelling, work, spending, and so on, which are valuable to direct activity. He considered audits on large information, which gives numerous possibly energizing opportunities to find information through whimsical ways.

Lima [11] analyzed the relationship between news stories and stock varieties, which can be improved using different markers. This examination gathered news stories from three unique spots and the stock past from the New York Stock Exchange to continue the information mining order calculations. Articles in papers and magazines were named based on their feeling, the immediate connection to a particular organization, and the geographic market impact. This investigation can recognize the examples between the pointers through the proposed model to anticipate stock value varieties with an accuracy of 100%. [12] suggested profound realization which will be valuable for time-driven stock price development forecasts, by suggesting a new neural tensor organization. Additionally, this examination utilizes a profound convolutional neural organization to display the consolidated influence of long-haul occasions and momentary times on stock value progress. It was observed that a profound convolutional neural organization can capture the more extended term impact of information occasions than a standard feed-forward neural organization.

Among his fellow workers, Wanzala [15, 16] conducted an exact investigation of traditional microstructure-based liquidity measures to examine the market strength proxies by LR3, LR4, and VR. All the explicitly, the examination was coordinated to deciding if the market strength was an indicator of the monetary development contingent interaction model (CPM). This model can be used for examination because it provides space for both the immediate and aberrant impacts of market versatility on monetary development. Kaushik [14] discovered that stock market prediction is an important issue for financial market investors. The comparative performance of efficiency techniques is useful for predicting stock prices in the market efficiently. This research will also be useful in implementing an economic growth model for stock price prediction in the future. Kanade [17] used the historical data examination expectation model to work with online media, an enormous information logical capacity investigation, and AI to occasionally foresee the pattern of financial exchanges. The future execution and unpredictability of the business sectors in the framework are influenced by political and monetary news and the impact of web-based media. The calculation utilized for the supposition examination utilizes a summative evaluation of the assumptions in a specific tweet or news story, which improves for accuracy of the forecast.

Liu [18] utilized enormous information investigation to build a calculation stage for stock determination and exchanging methodologies. It receives world-class molecular swarm improvement (EPSO) to explain ideal exchanging openings and consolidates becoming a progressive self-arranging map (GHSOM) and EPSO in its stock determination technique. This investigation shows that stock examples, such as star development stocks, and loads of ineffectively working organizations, stocks supported by steady or rising working productivity, and stocks supported by falling working benefits can be grouped for choosing protected, quality stocks by financial backers in securities exchange. Liu [13], Bach [19], and Kavitha [21] examined the large information innovations, data put away in different wellsprings of semi-organized and unstructured information. This examination zeroed in on the scholarly center of the field; strategies utilized in the monetary area for text mining, in the time of the Internet, large information, and online media. Wells of information are frequently utilized for text mining in the monetary area, and for which purposes. Finally, it was discovered that profundity investigation for text mining in money ought to be directed, zeroing in addition to the interior records as the space of the investigation.

Kavitha [20] focused on the huge information examination, particularly prescient investigation, which will impact the monetary market with its arising advances in stock trade. This examination investigated the fluctuating procedures utilized for dissecting unstructured data such as stock trade audits and chronicled measurement of monetary data and shows that SVM calculation is essentially utilized for wistful grouping because of its solid and exact outcomes compared with AI calculations. Yablonsky [22] provided an inside-and-out examination of the advanced stages utilizing IBM Watson Analytics as a guide to foster prescient models for stock cost determination. This examination correlates with traditional scientific econometric stages and models with present-day insightful stage models. It was tracked down that prescient models for stocks depend on the ideas of IBM Watson Analytics, which have shown results that are better than any other model.

Er. Hari [24] considered the presentation of Support Vector Regression Kernels (direct, polynomial, and RBF) to determine the prescient force. Distinctive execution pointers, such as the moving average technique, correlation of loan costs, and stock explicit news slant examinations, are broken down and assessed. Approval is performed by taking diverse time spans of stock conduct and looking at the real and anticipated stock costs. The venture choice is based on the speculation methodology created to permit the least dangerous venture for financial backers.

In his work, Umer Ghani [25] utilized machine learning algorithm focused on Linear Regression (LR) and Time Series Forecasting, using MS Excel as primary tool for graphical representation of prediction results. After obtaining data from Yahoo Finance for selected stocks, linear regression effectively predicted stock market trends for the following month and estimated accuracy accordingly. Bibasadia [23] evaluated and reviewed a more plausible technique to predict stock movements with higher accuracy. This study examines the use of the prediction system in the real world and issues related with the accuracy of overall values. The paper presents an AI model to anticipate the longevity of stocks in a competitive market.

Researchers [27] studied the recorded information on stock costs of recorded firms dependent on the reason to apply AI calculations, for example, Linear Regression progressed profound learning procedures like Long-Term Short Memory and applying specialized apparatuses to apply the Modern Portfolio Theory on the lookout. This methodology would be a strange assistance for representatives and monetary sponsors to place cash in the securities exchange meanwhile they depend on a marvelous scope of reported information.

Bhorkar [26] assessed the papers and found that AI calculation can be used for making financial exchange forecast, and the programming language used for prediction is Python. The studies utilized dataset from either Yahoo Finance or Google Finance for prediction. The dataset includes information about the stock, such as High, Low, Open, Close, Volume, etc. Support Vector Machine (SVM) and Artificial Neural Network (ANN) are commonly used for stock prediction. Calculated Regression and Random Forecast are used and provide good results in studies.

11.5 Machine Learning for Equity Valuation Models

In this study, three equity valuation models have been selected for the purpose of the study: the P/E Model, the P/B Model, and CAPM. These three models have been revised and refined using machine learning approach.

Linear regression is a simple algorithm primary developed in the field of statistics. It is a method used to determine the relationship between a response variable and one or more predictor variables. A linear association occurs between the input (independent) variables and a single (continuous, dependent) output variable. Therefore, the output variable, is considered to be a linear combination of the input variables.

Two key types of linear regression exist:

1. Simple linear regression: This occurs when there is only one independent variable.

   It is used to model the relationship between a single input and output variable. For example, if the repo rate explains the market price, the regression is expressed as:

$$\text{market price} = \beta 0 + \beta 1 * \text{repo rate} + \varepsilon.$$

2. Multiple linear regression: This is used when there are multiple independent variables.

   Multiple linear regression takes a step further by including more than one independent variable. For instance, if additional variables like DPR and EPS affect the market price, the calculation becomes:

$$\text{market price} = \beta 0 + \beta 1 * \text{repo rate} + \beta 2 * \text{DPR} + \beta 3 * \text{EPS} + \varepsilon.$$

There are mainly three areas where regression-based machine learning algorithms [2] can be useful.

- Measuring the relationships between variables: Correlation categorizes the strength and direction of the link between two variables. These relationships are measured using multiple regression.
- Forecasting: Regression ability to calculate the link can used to solve prediction problems.
- Predicting: Estimating some variables of interest for a future period is another area where multiple regressions perform well. Prediction is similar to forecasting, but the estimates are made for a longer period of time compared to the precise date estimates made in forecasting.

Multiple linear regression works by adjusting the constraint values to minimize the cost, which is the degree of error between the predicted value and the values of the training set. The general equation of multiple linear regression is expressed as:

$$Y = b_0 + b_1x_1 + b_2x_2 + b_3x_3 + \ldots + b_nx_n$$

- Y represents the dependent variable
- b_0 represents the axis intercept
- n signifies the number of variables in the dataset
- x_1 through x_n are independent variables in the dataset.
- $b_{1,}$ $b_{2\ldots\ldots}$ b_n are coefficient parameters.

The equation represents a hyperplane. A line of best fit for data in three or more dimensions is called a hyperplane. The goal of the regressor will always be to create an equation of a hyperplane that best represents the training data. The regressor tries out several different equations to see which equation best fits the data.

A scoring metric known as the cost function controls how well a hyperplane represents a training set. The cost function characterizes the degree of error between the hyperplane's predictions and those of the training set. Various formulas can compute the cost. The one that the regression model uses is called the mean squared error (MSE). This cost function determines how well a hyperplane represents the data. The regression model can adjust the parameter values to find the best fit hyperplane that describes the data using the gradient descent function.

The gradient descent function assists the machine learning models in improving their limitations so that optimal standards for the coefficient of the hyperplanes can be recognized. The algorithms use gradient descent to find a parameter value that yields the lowest error. The models can then use these values for future forecasts with new sets of data. In this study, multivariate gradient descent is used as we are dealing with a multilinear regression model.

After performing gradient descent, the model will determine the coefficients b_0, b_1, $b_2 \ldots b_n$ and confirm the constraint values, thus creating the equation for the optimal hyperplane. Finally, inputting actual values into this improved hyperplane equation will provide the projected value of the model.

The empirical study of the three equity valuation models used in the study had errors. So, to revise and refine the model, the multiple linear regression machine learning algorithm is used. The various stages involved in creating the machine learning model are:

1. Data Preprocessing
2. Creating Training and Testing Datasets
3. Creating and Training the Linear Regressor
4. Testing the Linear Regressor

Data Preprocessing: All the variables discarded in the data set were numerical. Detecting and eliminating inaccurate records from the dataset, as well as identifying unfinished, unreliable, inaccurate, and non-relevant portions of the data was performed to clean the data. The inconsistencies identified or disregarded may have been caused by user entry errors during storage.

Figure 11.1 shows the modified steps involved in the multiple linear regression machine learning model. The independent variables and one for the dependent variable, which is specific to the next step of the model.

Creating the Model: The multiple linear regression is used to model revised P/E, P/B, and CAPM. The independent variables are selected within a range to create the model for the predictor or dependent variables. For example, market price is the dependent variable, the independent variables for the regressor are:

For P/E, the independent variables are EPS, EPS Growth, DPR, repo, ROE

For P/B, the independent variables are BVPS, repo, EPS, EPS Growth, DPR, ROE

For CAPM, the independent variables are R_f, R_m, beta.

Figure 11.1 Steps used in the multiple linear regression machine learning model.

Preparing the Training and Test Data: The entire dataset is divided into two sets: the training set and test set. The 80:20 ratio is chosen, with 80% of the data allocated to the training set and the remaining 20% to the test set.
Training the Linear Regressor: A linear regression model assigns a coefficient to each input variable, determining its importance. The values of the input variables are then multiplied by their corresponding coefficients, and the bias (intercept) term is added to the sum. This results in the predicted value.
Testing the Linear Regressor: To test the regressor, use the model to predict the test data. RMSE, MSE, and R-squared are commonly used metrics to assess the effectiveness of a model.

11.6 Architecture of Refined Equity Models

This section covers the architecture of the revised equity valuation models for predicting the prices of Sensex stocks in the Indian stock market.

11.6.1 Architecture of Refined Price to Earnings Model (P/E) Using Multiple Regression Machine Learning Approach

Figure 11.2 shows the architecture of the refined P/E model, which consists of four input variables: repo rate, EPS growth rate, DPR, and EPS. Market price is the output variable in the model.

11.6.2 Architecture of Refined Price to Book Value Model Using Multiple Regression Machine Learning Approach

Figure 11.3 shows the architecture of the refined P/B model consisting of five input features: repo, EPSg, DPR, ROE, and BVPS as input variables in the model, and IV as the output variable.

11.6.3 Architecture of Refined Capital Asset Pricing Model Using Multiple Regression Machine Learning Approach

Figure 11.4 shows the architecture of the refined CAPM which consists of three input features: repo, Rf, and Rm in the input layer, and IV as the output variable.

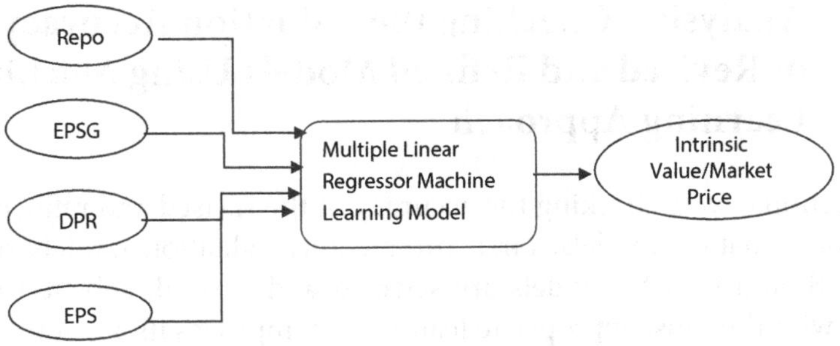

Figure 11.2 Architecture of refined P/E model using multiple regression machine learning.

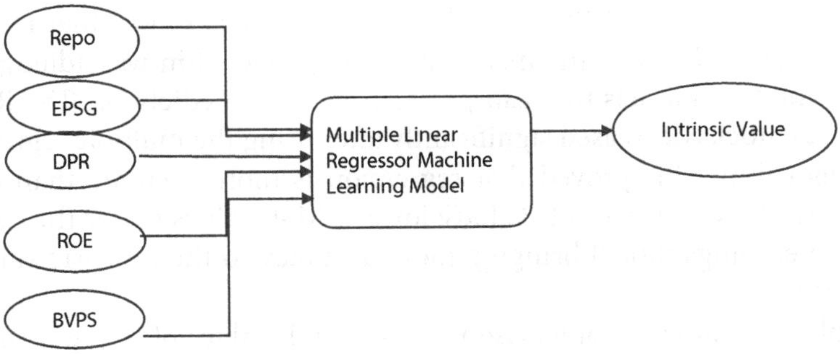

Figure 11.3 Architecture of refined P/B model using multiple regression machine learning approach.

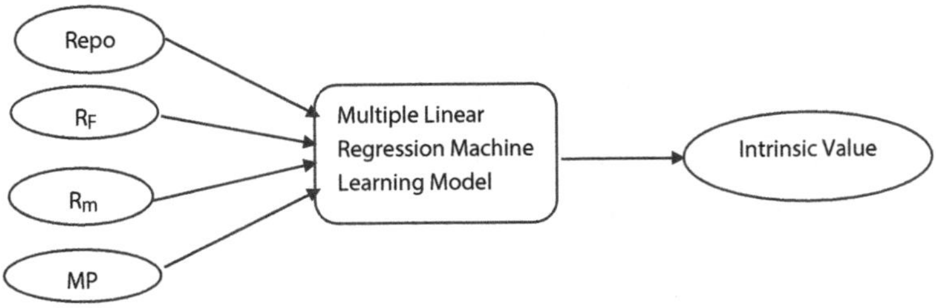

Figure 11.4 Architecture of refined capital asset pricing model using multiple regression ML approach.

11.7 Analysis—Checking the Valuation Accuracy of Revised and Refined Models Using Machine Learning Approach

This section covers checking the accuracy of the revised and refined three superior valuation models. First, three equity valuation models such as P/E, P/B, and CAPM models are selected and revised, substituting the model with the most appropriate feature that improves its accuracy. Then, the revised model is refined using a multiple regression machine learning model. Finally, the revised and refined model is tested for its accuracy in valuation.

Figure 11.5 shows the RMSE of the revised and refined models for Sensex stocks. The mean RMSE of the refined price-to-earnings model (P/E) is 1.71. It was found that the refined price to earnings model that resulted in the least RMSE with the machine learning algorithm was adjudged as one of the best models that can provide accurate predictions. The RMSE of Sensex stocks decreased significantly after using the multiple regression ML algorithm. This proved that regression is more accurate than other methods. Power Grid and ITC have lower RMSE values under the refined price to earnings model bringing more accuracy to the intrinsic value of those stocks.

Table 11.2 shows a comparison of the RMSE values of the refined P/E, P/B, and CAPM models. There was a significant decrease in the RMSE value from the base models to the refined models. This indicates the impact of the variable repo on the valuation models and their accuracy. The mean RMSE of the refined P/B model is 2.12, and for CAPM it is 3.15. These values are much lower when compared to the RMSE of the base models.

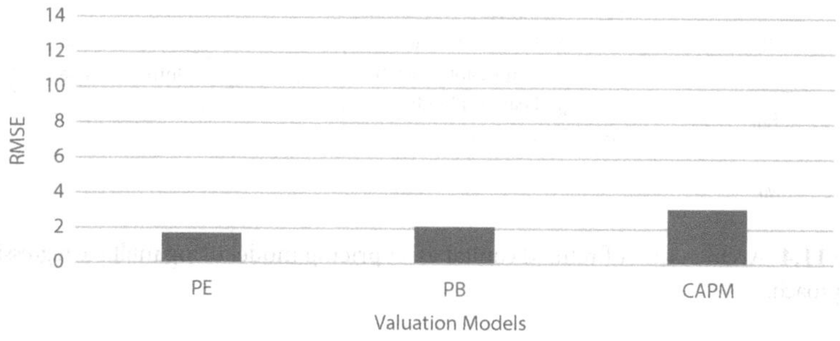

Figure 11.5 Comparison of select three revised and refined equity valuation models for Sensex Stocks in India based on RMSE.

Table 11.2 RMSE comparison of revised and refined equity models.

Stocks	Refined P/E model	Refined P/B model	Refined CAPM
Asian Paints	3.01	3.19	10.20
Axis Bank	1.07	1.75	3.28
Bajaj Auto	1.66	1.94	2.54
Bajaj Finance	4.22	22.41	2.54
BharathiAirtel	0.55	0.63	0.44
Coal India	0.61	0.42	0.60
HCL Tech	0.73	0.95	0.90
HDFC	2.19	1.07	2.10
HDFC Bank	3.86	2.45	4.69
Hero Motors	2.09	2.72	4.86
HUL	0.59	0.69	3.06
ICICI Bank	1.64	0.92	3.26
IndusInd	0.78	0.69	4.89
ITC	0.22	0.20	0.40
Kotak Bank	0.86	1.10	4.89
LT	2.29	2.56	1.47
Maruti	3.20	2.33	16.60
MM	1.91	0.57	2.15
NTPC	0.14	0.14	0.20
ONGC	0.64	0.33	1.92
Power Grid	0.10	0.15	0.38
Reliance	1.09	2.13	1.43
SBI	5.44	3.24	6.42
Sun Pharma	2.16	2.00	1.73

(Continued)

Table 11.2 RMSE comparison of revised and refined equity models. (*Continued*)

Stocks	Refined P/E model	Refined P/B model	Refined CAPM
Tata DVR	0.46	0.26	0.62
Tata Motors	2.83	2.78	1.04
Tata Steel	1.11	0.11	2.68
TCS	1.87	2.89	4.95
Vedanta	0.74	1.45	0.48
Yes	3.19	1.67	3.87
RMSE	1.71	2.12	3.15

* *Results computed using R-4.0.2*

It was found that the RMSE of the refined P/E model works very well for Sensex stocks due to the predictive power of the variables in the model.

Figure 11.6 compares the RMSE of the P/E model to that of the revised and refined P/E model. The plot shows that the RMSE of the stocks, which had a range from 0 to 30 for the 30 Sensex stocks reduced to 0–10 with the help of the multiple regression machine learning models. The P/E model gave an RMSE of 6.65 (Reference Table 3.15), whereas the refined PE model had an RSNE of 1.71. The RMSE of 93% of the stocks was reduced except for HDFC Bank and Tata Motors. The Sensex returns and the stock returns of these are highly correlated; hence the market risk represented by beta is highly significant for these stocks.

Figure 11.7 compares the RMSE of the P/B model with that of the refined P/B model. The plot demonstrates that the RMSE of the refined P/B model was significantly reduced after refining the model. The RMSE, which initially reached 25.04 was brought down to the range of 0–5 except for Bajaj Finance.

Figure 11.8 provides a comparison between the CAPM and the refined CAPM model. The RMSE values, which were originally in the range of 0–40, have been reduced to 0–10. However, it is worth noting that Maruti Suzuki is an outlier with a value of 16.6. This indicates that market risk is the primary factor that influences the price movement of this stock.

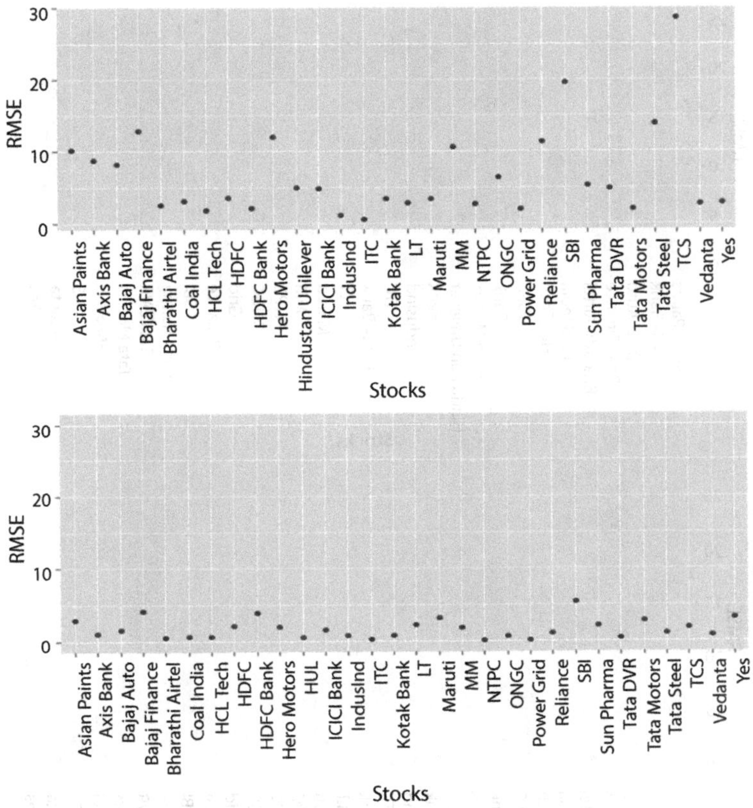

Figure 11.6 RMSE of the P/E model and refined PE model.

Consequently, when predicting the performance of Maruti Suzuki, Tata Motors, HDFC, and Bajaj Finance, it is advisable to use the traditional models.

Figure 11.9 shows the overall RMSE values of the three refined models. The RMSE value was reduced significantly, demonstrating the importance of the substituted variables. In certain sectors, such as the automobile industry and financial firms, market risk is a highly significant variable. However, it is important to note that considering such variables may sometimes lead to unexpected adverse results, as illustrated by the outliers shown in the plot.

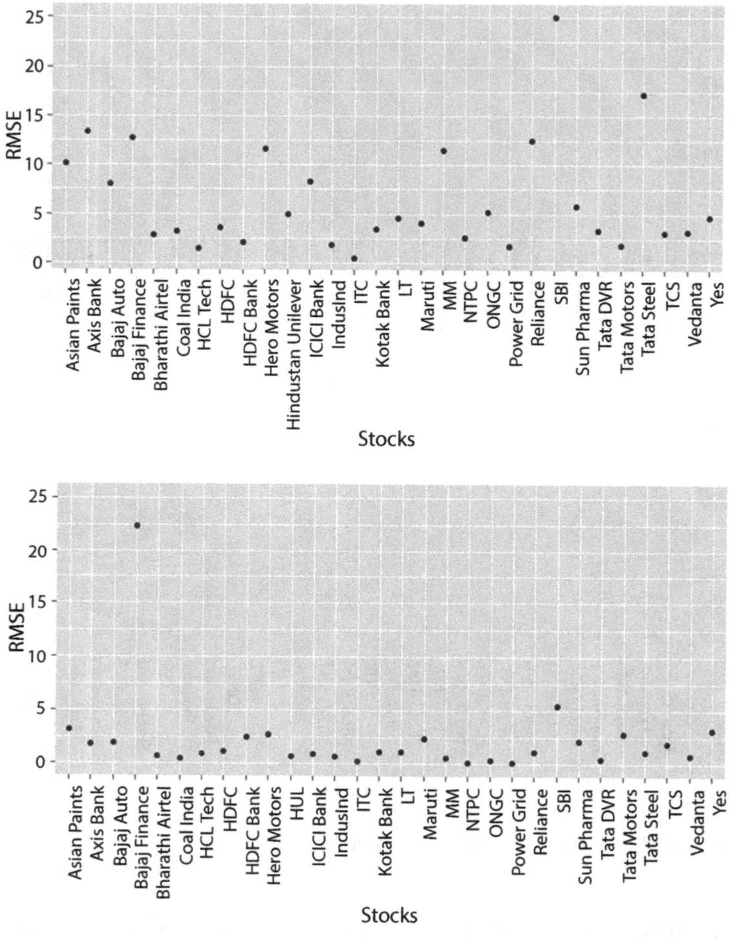

Figure 11.7 RMSE of the P/B model and refined PB models.

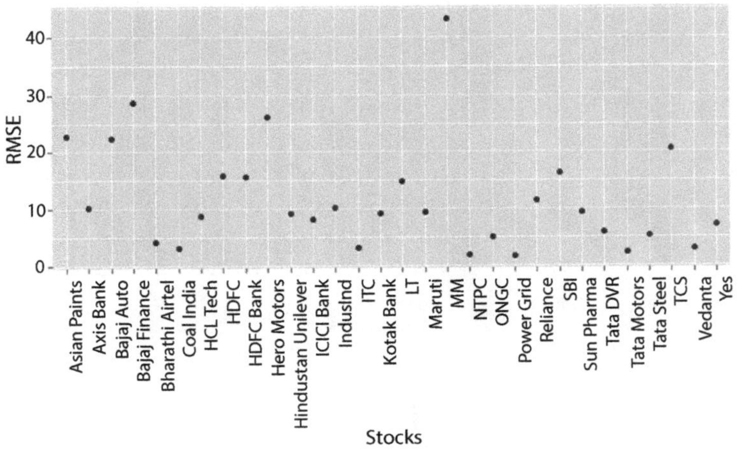

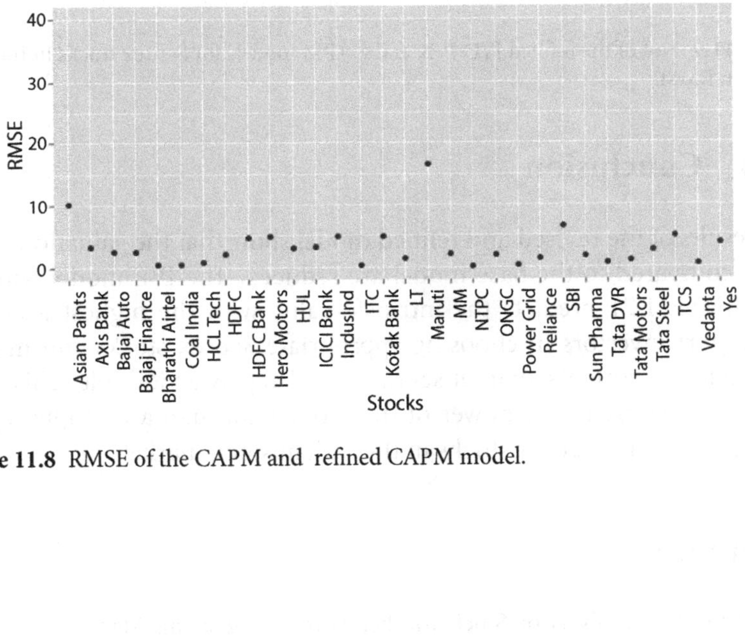

Figure 11.8 RMSE of the CAPM and refined CAPM model.

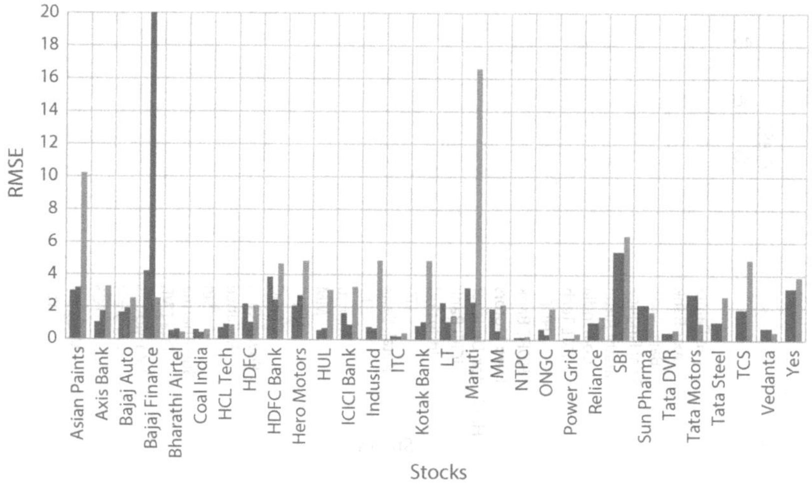

Figure 11.9 Plot of the refined P/E, P/B, and CAPM models for Sensex stocks in India based on RMSE.

11.8 Conclusion

The results of the revised and refined model show that the valuation errors when compared to the base model are reduced. The P/E model with the least RMSE 1.71 predicts the intrinsic value with the highest accuracy. To support investors in choosing appropriate Sensex stocks and making profitable investments, market sentiments also play a vital role. This study improved the predictive power of the models through a multiple regression approach for Sensex stocks in the Indian stock market.

References

1. Patel, K., Analysis of Stock Market Forecasting using Machine Learning Mechanism. *J. Appl. Sci. Comput.*, 6, 112–119, 2018. http://www.jetir.org/papers/JETIR1904I65.pdf.
2. Patel, R., Stock Market Prediction Using Sentiment Analysis: Testing the Method's Accuracy and Efficiency. *IJLTEMAS*, 5, 143–145, 2016. https://www.ijltemas.in/DigitalLibrary/Vol.5Issue6/143-145.pdf.
3. Das, D., Hybrid Clustering-GWO-NARX neural network technique in predicting stock price. *IOP Conf. Ser. J. Phys. Conf. Ser.*, 5, 1–14, 2017. https://www.researchgate.net/publication/333673096_Hybrid_Clustering-GWO-NARX_neural_network_technique_in_predicting_stock_price.

4. Das, S., Real time sentiment analysis of twitter streaming data for stock prediction. *Procedia Comput. Sci.*, 2, 956–964, 2018. https://doi.org/10.1016/j.procs.2018.05.111.
5. Henrique, B.M., Stock price prediction using support vector regression on daily and. *J. Finance Data Sci.*, 4, 183–201, 2018. https://doi.org/10.1016/j.jfds.2018.04.003.
6. al Augby, S., Stock Market Prediction Using Sentiment Analysis based on Social Network: Analytical Study. *J. Eng. Appl. Sci.*, 11, 2388–2402, 2018. https://www.researchgate.net/publication/326146699_Stock_Market_Prediction_Using_Sentiment_Analysis_Based_on_Social_Network_Analytical_Study.
7. Wang, C., *Novel Approaches to Sentiment Analysis for Stock Prediction*, vol. 11, Github repository, pp. 1–12, 2019, doi: DOI: 10.1007/978-981-99-9037-5_9.
8. Atkins, Financial News Predicts Stock Market Volatility better than Close Price. *J. Finance Data Sci.*, 3, 120–137, 2018. https://www.researchgate.net/publication/323013379_Financial_News_Predicts_Stock_Market_Volatility_Better_Than_Close_Price.
9. Naik, R.L., Prediction of Stock Market Index Using Genetic Algorithm. *Comput. Eng. Intell. Syst.*, 3, 162–172, 2012. https://core.ac.uk/download/pdf/234644513.pdf.
10. Nyman, R., News and narratives in financial systems: exploiting big data for systemic risk. *Journal of Economic Dynamics and Control (JEDC)*, 127, 104119, June 2021, https://doi.org/10.1016/j.jedc.2021.104119.
11. Lima, L., *Big Data for Stock Market by means of Mining techniques*, vol. 7, Algoritmi Research Centre, University of Minho, Portugal, pp. 1–14, 2013.
12. Ding, X., Deep Learning for Event-Driven Stock Prediction. *Proceedings of the Twenty-Fourth International Joint Conference on Artificial Intelligence (IJCAI 2015)*, vol. 2, pp. 2327–2333, 2013, https://ijcai.org/Proceedings/15/Papers/329.pdf.
13. Liu, W., EPSO-GHSOM Stock Selecting and Trading Strategy on Big Data. *Int. J. Intell. Inf. Syst.*, 6, 7–20, 2017, doi: DOI: 10.11648/j.ijiis.20170602.11.
14. Kaushik, B. and Sharma, S., Quantitative Analysis of Stock Market Prediction for Accurate Investment Decisions in Future. *J. Artif. Intell.*, 3, 48–54, 2018, doi: DOI:10.3923/jai.2018.48.54.
15. Wanzala, R.W., Estimation of market immediacy by Coefficient of Elasticity of Trading three approaches. *J. Finance Data Sci.*, 6, 139–156, 2018. https://www.researchgate.net/publication/327253544_Estimation_of_Market_Immediacy_by_Coefficient_of_Elasticity_of_Trading_Three_Approach.
16. Wanzala, R.W., Market resiliency conundrum: is it a predicator of economic growth? *J. Finance Data Sci.*, 4, 1–15, 2017. https://doi.org/10.1016/j.jfds.2017.11.004.
17. Kanade, V., Stock Market Prediction: Using Historical Data Analysis. *Int. J. Adv. Res. Comput. Sci. Software Eng.*, 8, 267–270, 2012. https://www.

researchgate.net/publication/356191515_Analysis_and_Prediction_of_Healthcare_Sector_Stock_Price_Using_Machine_Learning.
18. Liu, W. and Stock Selecting, EPSO-GHSOM, and Trading Strategy on Big Data. *Int. J. Intell. Inf. Syst.*, 9, 7–20, 2017.
19. Bach, M.P., Text Mining for Big Data Analysis in Financial Sector. *Sustainability*, 10, 1–27, 2019. https://doi.org/10.3390/su11051277.
20. Kavitha, S., A Review on Big Data Analytics Via Social Media. *Int. J. Sci. Res. Comput. Sci. Eng. Inf. Technol.*, 18, 35–45, 2017. https://www.academia.edu/44791260/A_Review_on_Big_Data_Analytics_Via_Social_Media.
21. Kavitha, S., Big Data Analysis in Financial Market. *Int. J. Res. Eng. Technol.*, 4, 422–427, 2015. https://ijret.org/volumes/2015v04/i02/IJRET20150402057.pdf.
22. Yablonsky, S., Modern Advanced Analytics Platforms and Predictive Models for Stock Price Forecasting: IBM Watson Analytics Case. *Proceedings of the 50th Hawaii International Conference on System Sciences*, vol. 5, pp. 1083–1092, 2017, http://hdl.handle.net/10125/41281.
23. Bibasadia, K., Stock market prediction using machine learning algorithms. *Int. J. Eng. Adv. Technol.*, 8, 25–31, 2019. https://www.ijeat.org/wp-content/uploads/papers/v8i4/D6321048419.pdf.
24. Er. Hari, K.C., Performance Analysis and Prediction of Nepal Stock market (Nepse) for Investment Decision Using Machine Learning. *Int. J. Comput. Sci. Eng.*, 4, 15–27, 2018.
25. Umer Ghani, M., Stock market prediction using MACHINE LEARNING ALGORITHMS. *Adv. Distrib. Comput. Artif. Intell. J.*, 5, 97–116, 2019, doi: DOI:10.14201/ADCAIJ20198497116.
26. Suchitha, B., Study of market predictions using machine learning. *Int. J. All Res. Educ. Sci. Methods*, 9, 971–977, 2021. https://www.ijaresm.com/study-of-stock-market-predictions-using-machine-learning.
27. Aryendra, S., An empirical research and comprehensive analysis of stock market prediction using machine learning and deep learning techniques. *IOP Conf. Ser. Mater. Sci. Eng.*, 10, 1–12, 2020, doi: DOI: 10.1088/1757-899X/1022/1/012098.

12

Hyper Automation and its Applicability in Automation Finance

Pushpendra Pal Singh[1]*, Rakesh Kumar Dixit[1] and Rajesh Kumar Dhanaraj[2]

[1]G.L. Bajaj Institute of Management, Greater Noida, India

[2]Symbiosis International (Deemed University), Pune, Maharashtra, India

Abstract

The term "hyper automation" is quickly becoming one of the most frequently used expressions within the realm of information technology. It is possible that the introduction of the new technological phenomenon known as hyper automation will lead to intelligent automation processes. This can be achieved through the utilization of various technologies, including robotic process automation (RPA), artificial intelligence (AI), machine learning (ML), and others. These technologies may be instrumental in accomplishing this goal. Many big information technology companies and start-ups are investing significantly to take advantage of the potential benefits that hyperautomation may offer in the future. This is because hyper automation can be applied in a wide range of business contexts. This conceptual paper aims to provide an explanation of the vocabulary, concepts, technologies, and models associated with hyper automation. In order to achieve this objective, it is recommended to provide such an explanation. Additionally, the study focuses on the significant advantages that hyper automation provides, particularly in the banking and finance industry. This is one of the subjects being examined by researchers. Furthermore, the study presents a few instances of industrial test cases to explain the extent of hyper automation adoption observed in various countries worldwide.

Keywords: Hyper automation, finance, robotic process automation, artificial intelligence, machine learning, operational efficiency, cost reduction

**Corresponding author*: pps2907@gmail.com

Deepa Gupta, Mukul Gupta, Rajesh Kumar Dhanaraj, Balamurugan Balusamy and Parth Mukul Gupta (eds.) Computational Intelligence for Autonomous Finance, (243–268) © 2025 Scrivener Publishing LLC

12.1 Introduction

As a consequence of the development of various technologies, every aspect of human life has become much easier. Business tycoons are always introducing new technological advancements, products, and services, and often accompanied by new terminology. Once such concept is hyper automation, which is a relatively new term that has recently gained attention worldwide. These examples represent the exciting technologies that are being generated [15]. Additionally, there is a lot of enthusiasm surrounding its new counterpart, referred to as Hyper automation. However, Hyper automation is still in its early stages, having been introduced only a few years ago and developing slowly. Consequently, only a few people are currently discussing hyper automation due to its recent emergence. As a result, there are only a limited number of publications available on this topic, including books, research articles, white papers, and annual reports [8]. Nevertheless, a few companies focusing on hyper automation have started publishing blog posts, news articles, short novels, videos, as well as designing, coding, and developing new hyperautomation-related technology. This has been happening for quite some time. The academic community, including students, researchers, and technology enthusiasts, has also engaged in discussions on hyper automation. Furthermore, manufacturers have begun making significant investments in an attempt to capture the next commercial market [3]. This industry includes numerous startups, such as "UiPath, Automation Anywhere, Blue Prism, Pegasystems, Work Fusion, Antworks, KOFAX, Softomotive, Datamatics, Assistance Systems, SAP, IBM, and many more. Consequently, we can learn about the top-selling automation solutions that are currently available, including UiPath RPA, Blue Prism, Automation Anywhere-RPA, Laserfiche, Appian, Pega Platform, WinAutomation (Softomotive), and Automate RPA [26].

Furthermore, in light of the fact that robotic technology is going to alter the world in order to increase its efficiency and effectiveness, a number of major firms have been given financing in 2021, as indicated by Apoorva Komarraju on 17 July 2021. This is because the world is going to be reshaped that way. Real Time Robotics, Verve Motion, Seoul Robotics, Fetch Robotics, and a considerable number of additional businesses are included in this group of enterprises. To add insult to injury, new enterprises are concurrently obtaining investment from a wide range of stakeholders to enhance their operations [29]. As of right now, the hyperautomation business has a market worth of $4.2 billion, and it is projected that the market will expand at a compound annual growth rate of 18.9% during the forecasted time period (2019–2027). By the end of 2027, this market is predicted to have achieved a performance of more than $23.7 billion. It is therefore of utmost importance that we take the necessary steps to ensure that technological breakthroughs continue to increase at an exponential pace. This expansion should include the development of a broad variety of applications specifically adapted to meet the demands of the modern-day business environment [32]. Technologies considered cutting-edge include artificial intelligence and machine learning, both of which are examples of technologies used in hyper automation. Consequently, the skills of human talent are supplemented by these technologies, which are used to automate corporate operations, procedures, and services. Hyper-Automaton is a system and model that, as stated by [20], has the main purpose of augmenting the World Wide Web by offering a hypermedia service. This is the fundamental definition of Hyper-Automaton. This goal can be achieved through the use of fundamental ideas inherent to the discipline of Computing Science, particularly Automata Theory, Category Theory, and Hyper Docs technology. When it comes to the influence it will have on the technical front [22], the hyper-automation technology that will be produced in this technological era will be nothing less than a savior. Hyperautomation is a strategy that tries to automate and convert as many business and information technology operations as possible. It does this by using a broad variety of automation approaches [23]. All of this is made possible through the use of machine learning and artificial intelligence strategies. This definition has developed over the last several years in response to the demands placed on organisations as well as the breakthroughs that have occurred in technological growth [1].

12.2 Background

It is already common knowledge that robots have taken over the tasks that were formerly performed by humans in the back offices of businesses. We have been able to serve clients in a wide range of sectors by providing them with considerable benefits as a result of our innovative approach to intelligent automation. These advantages consist of increased production, decreased cycle time, higher accuracy and compliance, enhanced service, and therefore reduced costs. As a result, robotic process automation is the next revolution in terms of productivity [6]. There is a widespread consensus among industry professionals that robotic process automation (RPA) will be yet another game-changer due to the fact that it will enhance service

Table 12.1 RPA vendors: client market and source of revenue.

S. no.	Key vendors	Key clients	Source of revenue by industry
1	Automation Anywhere	Deloitte, Accenture, AT&T, GM, J P Morgan Chase	Banking, Financial Services, and Insurance (BFSI)
2	UiPath	Atos, AXA, BBC, Capgemini, CenturyLink, Cognizant, Middlesea, OpusCapita, and SAP	BFSI, healthcare, telecom and media, and retail
3	Blue Prism	BNY Mellon, RWE npower, and Telefonica O2	BFSI, health and pharmaceuticals, retail and consumer, telecom and media, manufacturing, public sector, travel, and transportation
4	WorkFusion	Thomson Reuters, Infogroup, Citi Bank, and Standard Bank	BFSI sector, followed by the retail and consumer sectors
5	Thoughtonomy	Atos, Fujitsu, CGI, Unite BT, and Business Systems	BFSI, public sector, telecom, healthcare, retail, and consumer sectors
6	KOFAX	Arrow Electronics, Delta Dental of Colorado, Pitt Ohio, Audi	BFSI, retail, consumer, travel, transportation, public sector, manufacturing, and healthcare

Source: [34], Learning robotic process automation, packet publishers, Birmingham—Mumbai (India).

quality and, therefore, customer satisfaction. In layman's terms, robotic process automation (RPA) refers to the use of software that mimics human behaviors [12] to interact with computer programs and carry out operations defined by rules. This is accomplished by incorporating automation software. Sometimes, it is necessary to read from and type, or click on pre-existing applications used to carry out assigned responsibilities [34]. To do this, it is sometimes necessary to read from and write [14].

In addition to this, the market for these technological solutions is also seeing substantial expansion in the Asia Pacific Countries (APAC) area [2]. There is a huge demand for robotic process automation (RPA), particularly in industries that need deployment on a large scale. The retail industry, the healthcare and pharmaceutical industries, the telecommunications industry, and the banking and financial services industry are now among the most significant sectors for robotic process automation. Because of this, with a particular focus on Table 12.1 [31]. It is feasible to reach the conclusion that robotic process automation (RPA) will bring about a significant change in the manner in which we do our jobs, interact with one another, and live our lives. This is shown by a specific group of RPA providers, the clientele they serve, and the revenue streams they generate. The use of this technology by a number of Fortune 500 and global corporations, like Citi Bank, Fujitsu, Audi, and SAP, among others, is enabling these firms to take advantage of the benefits that the technology offers for their respective operations [19].

According to [11], robotic process automation (RPA) is still in its infancy as a technology, and the literature that is now available does not cover a particularly wide range of issues. The difficulty, as stated by Abid *et al.* [1], is a loss of connection, which may be solved by incorporating autonomous technologies that make it possible for ground-based autonomous vehicles to land or hover in a safe manner [21]. As a result of this, the firms started looking for a new and innovative solution, which ultimately turned out to be none other than hyperautomation.

12.3 Hyper Automation: Evolution, Technologies, and Impact in the Digital Era

Father of Hyper automation: Gartner (Global research and advisory firm)
Year of Hyper automation Coined: 2019
Alias for Hyper automation: Intelligent Automation, Digital Process Automation

Definition: Hyper automation is an advanced technological process for automating both routine-and non-routine business tasks using intelligent technologies such as RPA, AI, ML, and NLP among others. These technologies are integrated into a single system to ensure round-the-clock operational efficiency.

Technologies:

- Robotic Process Automation
- Artificial Intelligence
- Machine Learning
- Natural Language Processing
- Computer Vision
- Optical Character Recognition
- Cognitive Process Automation
- Low-Code Application Platforms
- iBPMS, etc.

Programming Languages:
Almost all programming languages can be used to develop different hyper automation applications including C, C++, C#, Python, Java, PHP, R, Ruby, Julia, Go, and so on.

Advantages:

- Wise technologies in workforce 24/7
- Complete business process automation
- Advanced data analytics
- Instant more accuracy results
- Greater compliance-cum-risk reduction
- Boost employee productivity
- Growth of team collaborations
- Increases the workers knowledge
- Better customer support
- Save operational cost

In accordance with [16], all contemporary companies have effectively incorporated themselves into the digital environment. This digital ecosystem contains a wide variety of the most current technologies, including, but not limited to, the Internet of Things (IoT), artificial intelligence (AI), machine learning (ML), blockchain, robotic process automation (RPA), and hyperautomation, to name just a few. When it comes to hyperautomation, there is no precise operational definition that can be found out there. On the other hand, working definitions were developed by specialists in the field based on the collected practical information and advancements they have made about this phenomenon. Because the phenomenon has not yet achieved its full potential, it is possible that it will take some time before one can establish definitions that are adequate for practical purposes.

Hyperautomation, on the other hand, was defined by a different author as a set of communication processes that include specific characteristics. In an effort to make the concept easier to understand, this definition was provided to enhance comprehension [13].

In the context of hyperautomation, the true capabilities of software robots are becoming more apparent due to their integration with a wide range of tools and approaches. In the year [20], it is not surprising that forward-thinking businesses will increasingly rely on self-sufficient robots equipped with artificial intelligence to assume trained professional labor and larger responsibilities. According to the findings of [24], the use of hyper automation has the potential to significantly reduce production expenses, especially when combined with advanced digital technology capabilities [10]. This service aims to automate processes by combining robotic process automation (RPA) with artificial intelligence (AI). The term "automation" refers to the use of technology to manage processes or perform activities with minimal human involvement [18]. Automation and advanced intelligence technologies have the ability to enhance the user experience, and increase consumer satisfaction simultaneously. While hyper automation can be applied to any industry, the ones mentioned here are just a few that could benefit from its implementation. In the following section, we will conduct a more detailed investigation of the frameworks associated with hyper automation [20].

12.4 Automation-(2)-Hyper Automation: Gartner

The next phase in the automation process is hyper automation, which is an advanced form of automation that follows robotic process automation as the next step. According to a study released by Gartner, tracing back the roots of hyper automation reveals its progression from basic automation to the highly sophisticated hyper automation seen today. Initially, corporate firms developed Task Automation, a process where event processing was carried out with software assistance. This started with the establishment of Task Automation [28]. Detailed rule development and specialized tasks

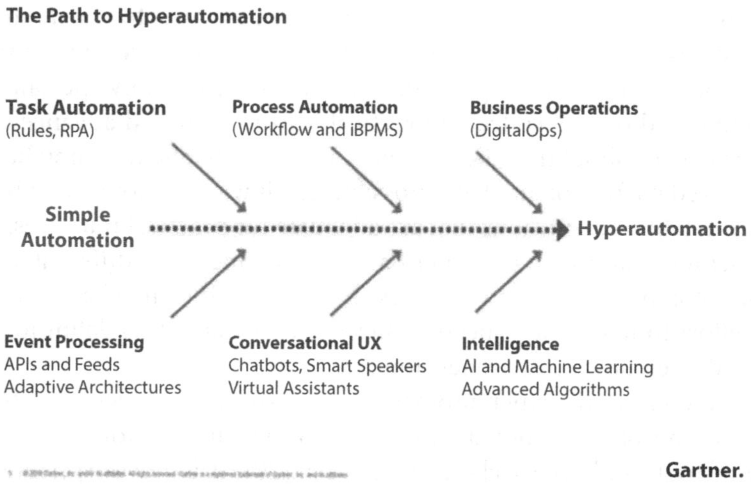

Figure 12.1 Path to hyper automation. Source: https://appian.com/resources/learn/what-is-hyperautomation.html.

were used for this automation. A robust supply of Application Process Interface (API) and flexible designs are necessary for this type of automation. An example of this is the automation of procedures that involve robotics [30]. Process Automation is the next category, encompassing the entire workflow of company operations and executed through software. This category includes applications that provide a Conversational User Experience, such as chatbots like Apple's Siri, Amazon's Alexa, and Microsoft's Cortana, which are all examples of smart speakers. Figure 12.1 illustrates the progression of Hyper automation technology over time in a straightforward and comprehensible manner. This model was developed by Gartner (research and consulting) based on the results of an empirical study conducted over a period of time [34].

12.5 Could Hyper Automation be a Name for AI Plus RPA?

Researchers from all over the world have already established that Hyperautomation technology is nothing more than a combination of Robotic Process Automation (RPA), Artificial Intelligence (AI), Machine Learning (ML), and other intelligent sister technologies used to automate complicated operations. This is the main idea behind Hyperautomation technology.

A significant number of researchers from around the globe have come to this conclusion. It was prior to the invention of the technology now known as hyper automation that researchers made this assumption [5]. A visual representation of Figure 12.2 can be found at this location. Throughout the presentation, the author [23] has used a distinct approach when addressing hyper automation. She has mentioned that the phrase "hyper-automation" refers to the combination of artificial intelligence with robotic process automation, and that this combination is not only feasible but also practical.

In line with the author's understanding, the answer is yes. The author believes that the automation process can be divided into two distinct categories: process-driven automation, which can be further subdivided into (a) robotic desktop automation, which is distinguished by the fact that the automation process is carried out only at the desktop level, even with some human interventions [7]. The author also believes that the automation process can be broken down into two distinct categories. The next version of Robotic Desktop Automation is called Robotic Process Automation, and it is the one that should be considered the following version. This kind of automated self-service facility is available at any time of the day or night, thanks to the help of digital triggers that have been pre-programmed ahead of time. Data-Driven Automation is the second category, and it is once again separated into two categories: (a) Machine Learning and (b) Artificial Intelligence. Together, these two categories make up the second category. This is because these tools enable managers to make better decisions. When this occurs, it eventually leads to managers making

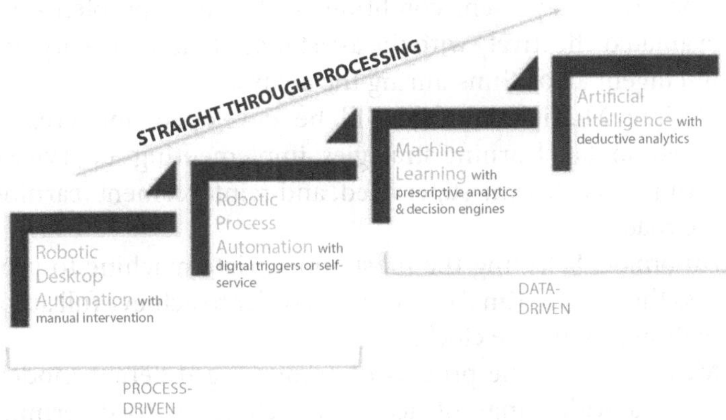

Figure 12.2 Could hyper automation be a name for AI plus RPA? Source: https://www.automationanywhere.com/company/blog/rpa-thought-leadership/could-hyperautomation-be-a-name-for-ai-plus-rpa.

the proper choice at the appropriate time and in the suitable place, which ultimately results in enhanced profitability and growth for the company [4]. At the present time, there is a substantial quantity of demand in the market across a wide range of different industrial sectors. In addition, the approach of automation that is based on artificial intelligence is the one that is at the forefront of the present state of affairs. For the purpose of producing deductive analytics, this method is used. According to McIver *et al.* (2018), a theory-driven deductive technique begins with a hypothesis that is either something that has never been seen before and is completely original or one that has been the focus of research attention in the scientific literature in the past. The conclusion that robotic process automation (RPA) and artificial intelligence (AI) are the components that make up hyperautomation is viable.

12.6 Sophistication of the Automation

The blog post authored by [x]cube LABS and published on 1 December 2020, titled "Hyperautomation and its Role in Digital Transformation across Industries" makes reference to the complexity of hyper automation. Specifically, the following topics are covered in the journal (see Figure 12.3):

1. Find out: The first step in the process involves identifying the things, equipment, people, organizations, and processes that are connected to the relevant surroundings.
2. Analyze: The present conditions of business problems are evaluated effectively with the assistance of high-capacity and intelligent algorithms during the analysis.
3. Design: Multiple models will be developed and created based on data learning strategies, implementing supervised, unsupervised, semi-supervised, and reinforcement learning approaches.
4. Automate: Selecting the most appropriate machine to process the most optimal outcomes in order to achieve full automation around the clock.
5. Measurement: The process of comparing different models using a wide range of accuracy techniques to determine which model is more accurate.
6. Step 6: This involves the ongoing monitoring of the whole process, starting from the beginning of the process and

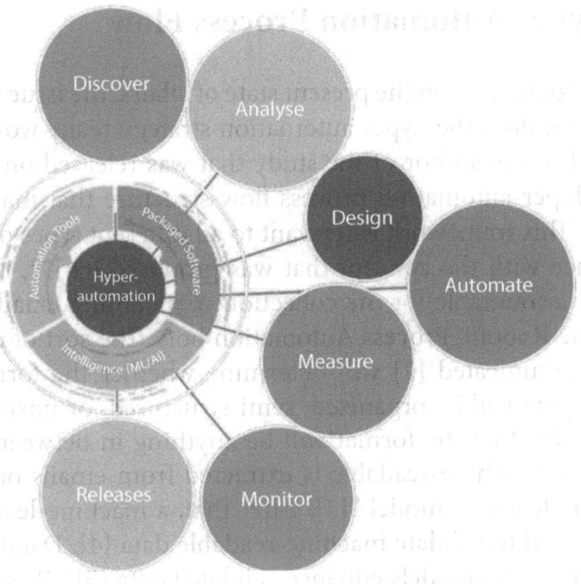

Figure 12.3 Sophistication of the automation. Source: https://www.xcubelabs.com/blog/hyperautomation-and-its-role-in-digital-transformation-across-industries/.

continuing through training, testing, and validation of the outcomes, to ensure the best possible results are achieved [3].

7. Release: This is the final level, which is not the least significant one, and it represents the Hyper automation stage.

Furthermore, the authors argue that hyperautomation makes use of a broad range of cutting-edge technology in its operations. These technologies include Digital Operational Tools and other equivalent to technologies. "Robotic Process Automation, Artificial Intelligence, Intelligent Process Discovery, Intelligent Document Processing, and Advanced Analytics" are all included in this category of technologies [5]. When it comes to hyperautomation, it is crucial to possess the appropriate technology and tools; hence, it is essential to make use of such instruments. There are several factors that have a significant impact on the decisions made about these tools. These factors include the company's strategy, the decision-makers and teams within the organization, and the competences of the individuals involved. In the next portion of the book, an analysis of the hyper automation approach will be presented.

12.7 Hyper Automation Process Flow

Taking into consideration the present state of affairs, the issue that arises is, to what degree does the hyper automation strategy really work? In accordance with [7], the author of the study that was released on 5 July 2021, there is a Hyper automation process flow structure that may be seen in Figure 12.4. This framework is relevant to all different types of businesses. In accordance with the concept that was proposed by [7], the individuals who are accountable for the collection of incoming emails and documents are the Robotic Process Automation bots. The sort of material that is being communicated [2] will determine whether the format of these emails or papers will be organized, semi-structured, or unstructured [6]. It is conceivable that the format will be anything in between. The information that is machine-readable is extracted from emails or documents by a machine-learning model "[3]. After that, a machine-learning model or rules are used to validate machine-readable data [4]. Database lookups or machine learning models enhance validated data [5]." If the confidence level of the machine-learning model is low, the output can be reviewed by a human using software that allows for human-in-the-loop review [5]. The data that has been vetted and enhanced such that it is readable by machines is then transferred to the subsequent system of record [10]. In the field of hyper automation, some of the most noteworthy examples include the administration of accounts payable and accounts receivable, travel and expenditures, purchase order management, customer support operations, anti-money laundering, and the production of leads from anonymous site users. These are just a few examples.

A Platform for Hyperautomation Through the Use of Quixy Through the Use of No-Code: Getting "started with no-code automation for

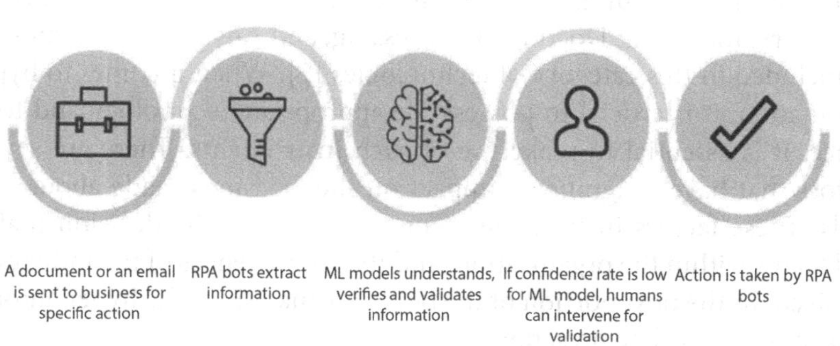

Figure 12.4 Hyper automation process flow (document-based process). Source: AI Multiples: https://research.aimultiple.com/hyperautomation-examples/.

hyper-automation is made easier with the assistance of Quixy. With the support of the Quixy High-Performance Application Platform as a Service (hpaPaaS) [13], businesses are able to construct complicated bespoke software applications more quickly, all while maintaining a better level of quality and spending less money. Using Quixy, businesses are able to enhance their flexibility and agility, which allows them to better deal with fluctuations in their business needs. According to Quixy, the most significant technologies are included in the section that is next to this one.

12.7.1 Technologies

The term "hyper automation" was first documented by Gartner in their publication. Additionally, the consulting company Gartner believes that hyper automation will have the most significant impact in the coming years. Businesses can enhance their degree of automation and digital transformation through the use of hyper automation, which includes technologies such as robotic process automation (RPA), process mining, machine learning, and other similar technologies. In 2020, Gartner stated that hyper automation is expected to be the most important technical advancement with a global impact [18]. According to Jacoby and Uslander's 2020 research, this term encompasses all automation initiatives deployed throughout an entire business and is closely linked to the concept of Industry 4.0. Over time, the process of hyper automation is shifting from fixed automation to processes that are rely on perception. According to [20], robotic process automation (RPA) becomes the key technology enabling hyper automation when combined with artificial intelligence and machine learning. It is conceivable that multiple writers may support the same notion in different ways [19].

Intelligent and strategic process optimization is achieved by the integration of automation tools that coordinate various types of workers—both human and artificial—with low-code and no-code application authoring tools in "hyper automation" systems [6]. However, hyper automation—which is facilitated in part by AI, big data, and robots—has the potential to enhance productivity and shorten production times in the industrial sector [25]. This might occur when all three of these technologies are used simultaneously. Similar to how AI and ML drive hyper automation and process and interface improvement, [26] found that the potential value of data rises exponentially. This is because these two technologies are revolutionizing how we use data. The Internet of Things (IoT) is only one of several technologies used by hyper automation. An extensive analysis of these technological advancements follows [24].

12.7.2 Robotics Process Automation (RPA)

Gartner was the first company to introduce the phrase "hyper automation" in their book. Additionally, the consulting firm Gartner believes that hyper automation will have the most significant impact in the coming years. This is their opinion. Businesses have the opportunity to enhance their level of automation and digital transformation through the use of hyper automation. This can be achieved by utilizing technologies such as robotic process automation (RPA) [21], process mining, machine learning, and other similar technologies. These technologies enhance the value of data. They are the main drivers of data consumption, which is why this is the case. One conclusion that can be drawn is that hyper automation combines various technologies, including the phenomenon known as the Internet of Things. In the next part, there will be a discussion of these technological advancements.

12.7.3 Artificial Intelligence (AI)

At the moment, Artificial Intelligence (AI) has been completely interwoven into our everyday lives as well as our professional lives in a way that has never been seen before. The artificial intelligence (AI) technology is another ancient technology that has received a lot of attention in the last decade. This is due to the fact that the industry has taken an interest in new advancements. Enormous amounts of data have been created from a variety of sources [20], high processing power is readily available in today's world, and there are more applications of AI in our day-to-day lives. There is a connection between the history of artificial intelligence and the white papers written by McCarty and Turing in the year 1955. 1980, which was designated as the Year of Artificial Intelligence, gradually established the foundation for AI.

On the other hand, the real scientific work did not begin until the year 2000. Because of this, John McCarty is considered to be the "father" of artificial intelligence. Technology that imitates human intellect is referred to as artificial intelligence (AI). By thinking, seeing, hearing, and perceiving in the same way that humans do [23], and eventually acting in the same way that humans do, scientists first built electronic machines with the intention of supporting humans in their job and therefore making their lives more pleasant. There are now applications of artificial intelligence that are not very powerful. These applications allow AI to perform certain tasks, such as autonomous vehicles, financial bots, text translations, and speck identification, to name a few examples. Additionally, scientists believe that we will be using AI in our everyday lives in the coming years. In the future, these apps will be integrated into our daily lives in virtual-cum-real-time environments, and their AI cognitive level will be on par with that of a human. However, many believe that beyond the current societal applications, the next level of General A—which is essentially Super AI—will be able to out-think humans in terms of intelligence and might present a danger to human existence on Earth. Therefore, in order to achieve a harmonious future where humans and robots coexist, numerous tech companies are focused on developing technologies and applications that utilize weak, general, and super artificial intelligence. They are also aiming to create responsible AI, which essentially means ethical AI [26].

12.7.4 Machine Language (ML)

According to [28], the field of artificial intelligence has been focused on machine learning since it was first introduced in the 1950s. Academic researchers, techies, and tech giants are now engaged in substantial discussions on the latest breakthroughs in machine learning. These developments include designs, algorithms, libraries, packages, and programs that utilize a variety of languages such as Python, Julia, JavaScript, C, C#, and many more high-level languages. Moreover, corporations are increasing their financial investments to capitalize on the new commercial prospects associated with machine learning software breakthroughs. Machine learning is a strategy that aims to address the question of how to teach computers to improve over time. In addition to being at the crossroads of computer science and statistics, this ever-evolving area of research is considered crucial to data science and artificial intelligence according to [15]. Machine learning is an emerging field of computer algorithms that, as described by El Naqa and Murphy [28] describe it, seeks to learn from context in order to imitate human intelligence. Machine learning, abbreviated as ML, is an emerging field within AI. In today's IT and MIS industries, it is not uncommon for engineers to conduct software engineering requirement studies in addition to designing, developing, building, and testing new software packages for corporate applications. One exciting aspect of this technology is that computers can learn from datasets using algorithms developed by CS and domain experts. The continuation of this trend may lead to the eventual development of intelligent machines. Most licensed and open source software applications are built using one or two of the most popular programming languages. Numerous machine learning methods, such as supervised, unsupervised, semi-supervised, and reinforced supervised learning algorithms, are now available to the general public. These algorithms are accessible to the public.

12.7.5 Optical Character Recognition (OCR)

Academics from around the globe have dedicated a significant amount of time and energy to studying optical character recognition (OCR) and writing about it over the past hundred years. Optical character recognition is a crucial aspect of converting pixel-based images into editable and searchable text. Numerous Artificial Neural Network (ANN) models have been developed in an effort to find solutions to challenges that require intellect comparable to that of a human [22] described a successful implementation of optical character recognition using an artificial neural network technique. According to [14], it involves breaking down a digital document image into its individual characters. Optical character recognition is one way to describe the optical patterns found in digital images. Character recognition can be achieved through the three phases outlined by [8]: segmentation, feature extraction, and classification. Identifying and categorizing visual characters is the most fundamental form of visual character recognition. OCR strengthens the relationship between handwriting and machine code (H-2-M).

12.7.6 Language Understanding Intelligent Service (LUIS)

The ability to express ourselves verbally is fundamental for interacting with others and achieving our goals and requirements. Whether it is through a combination of natural talent and formal study, most people can speak more than one language fluently. Due to the exponential expansion of globalization over the past several decades, many countries will eventually need to contact and communicate with each other. Because of this, there has been a dramatic increase in the employment of software engineers who specialize in developing translation tools and who utilize complex mathematical techniques to translate across languages. Information technology professionals are coining terms like "natural language processing" and "language understanding intelligent service" to describe this emerging trend. In particular, [27] attests to our strong reliance on the LUIS system, an NLU system. Because it allows us to apply the basic concepts of purpose classification and entity extraction, it offers a powerful tool for education. The LUIS AI system is said to be able to anticipate human wants by interpreting natural language, according to research by Banu and Patil in 2020. The use of hyperautomation is widespread in systems that handle NLP. Natural language processing (NLP) refers to the study of how computers can understand and use written and spoken language for practical purposes [10]. Many people are familiar with chatbots, which are a kind of machine learning. The fact that it stays true to the text's initial intent is the approach's most appealing feature. Moving from spoken to written or written to spoken word may be a part of the specific process of translating across languages. "Chatbots" are computer programs that use text-to-speech technology to mimic human conversation.

12.7.7 Hyper Automation Technological Ecosystem

According to the writers, Lawton and Bernstein, in their blog titled "Hyper automation" and as seen in Figure 12.5, they investigated the fact that the hyper automation technology environment can be broken down into three distinct groups. Identifying Potential Opportunities for Automation: [29]. These technologies are used to determine which automation operations should be prioritized and to identify them. Specifically, this refers to the major technologies that are necessary at the preliminary stage of identifying potential for machinery automation. Among the technologies that

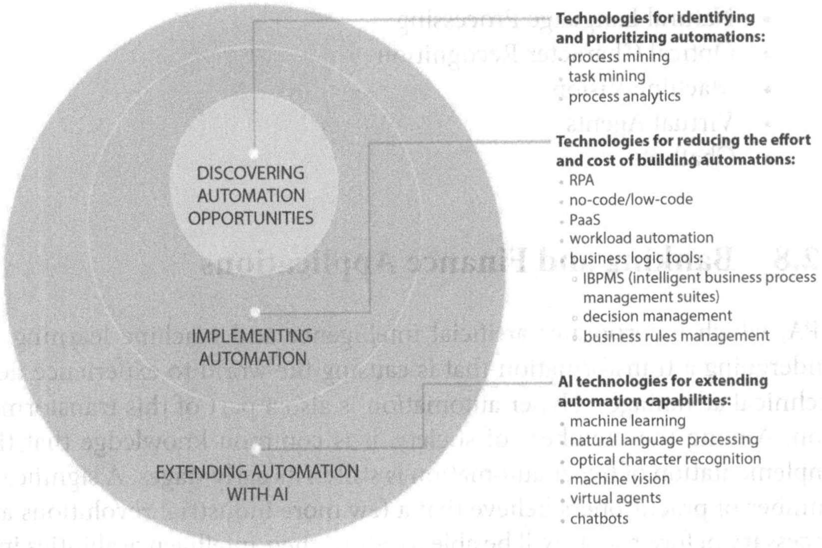

Figure 12.5 Ecosystem of hyper automation technologies. Source: https://searchcio.techtarget.com/definition/hyperautomation.

provide prospects for automation discovery include, but are not limited to, the following: (1) Process Mining:

1. Task Mining
2. Process Analytics

Implementing Automation: The second category of technologies is meant to reduce the effort and cost of building automation at different firms' levels. These technologies include

- Robotic Process Automation (RPA)
- no-code/low-code
- Platform as a Services (SaaS)
- Workload Automation
- Business Logic Tools
- intelligent Business Process Management Suites (iBPMS)
- Decision Management
- Business Rules Management

Extended Automation with AI: The third category includes AI technologies for extending automation capabilities:

- Machine Learning
- Natural Language Processing
- Optical Character Recognition
- Machine Vision
- Virtual Agents
- Chatbots

12.8 Banking and Finance Applications

RPA, which incorporates artificial intelligence and machine learning, is undergoing a transformation that is causing the world to experience new technical advantages. Hyper automation is also a part of this transformation. Among the members of society, it is common knowledge that the implementation of hyper automation is still in its early stages. A significant number of practitioners believe that a few more industrial revolutions are necessary before robots will be able to adjust their intelligence abilities in a more significant manner. On the other hand, there are some organizations that are processing the companies with the assistance of hyper automation of the business processes [30]. The manufacturing or packaging industry, the insurance industry, and the health sector are the only ones that have hyper automation, which refers to the capacity of machines to think and process autonomously. Despite this, even its implementation has gained widespread acceptance in the financial sector. I would like to talk about some examples of how automation may be used in the banking and financial industry. Many major businesses are showing a significant amount of interest in robotic process automation. It plays a crucial part in the process of making informed choices and serves as a means of coping with the various problems that are present in the business process. Sets of loans, deposits, and a great deal of other financial criteria are produced by the banking and finance industry each and every day [1]. Errors caused by humans in the process of manually analyzing data provide significant challenges for financial institutions. The sector is enjoying a significant decrease in the costs associated with consultations as a result of the use of robotic process automation. Using hyper automation, the following are some important areas in which the industry has the potential to undergo a significant shift in the way it serves its customers.

12.8.1 Marketing

The marketing department plays an essential role in bringing products to end users, particularly given the rapidly evolving technological landscape. The process of responding to emails and providing product-related information through human participation is not only time-consuming but also inefficient in terms of cost [7]. By utilizing hyper automated software, financial institutions can deliver personalized goods to specific customer groups in a shorter time frame. Additionally, the response time for customer requests is reduced. By analyzing consumer product needs, the program can identify client interests. Financial institutions can identify the data patterns indicating a customer's intention to purchase a product through the use of chatbots.

12.8.2 Sales and Distribution

Additionally, since they have access to essential information, financial institutions are able to simply covert the percentage of excellence into target groups. The delivery and distribution methods of banks are expected to undergo significant transformation in the not too distant future, according to a consultancy firm based in Boston [12]. Banks are attempting to reduce the number of services they provide at their branches in order to focus on providing consumers with digital channels of service, as the adoption rate of digital channel continues to rise. Through the use of the app, users can experience banking in a digital format.

12.8.3 Regulatory Reporting

With the use of robotic process automation, financial institutions are able to process information around the clock. Additionally, this assists financial institutions in simplifying the regulatory reporting process within their own institutions. The use of robotic process automation is helpful in comprehending and resolving the extreme complexity that is present in the data, as well as understanding the patterns that are present in the data. Because of this, banks are able to have honest reporting since there are fewer mistakes made by humans [14]. Along with all of these use cases, a great number of other industries are undergoing rapid transformations as a result of hyper automation. Additionally, hyper automation's ability to recognize patterns in transactions contributes to its ability to manage and eliminate instances of corruption. Each and every one of them is an essential sector in which hyper automation has transformed and will continue to change the face of the banking business. The next part will provide an overview of the two case studies that pertain to banking applications.

12.8.4 ICICI Bank

Industrial Credit and Investment Corporation of India, more often referred to as ICICI, is a well-known financial corporation worldwide. As a financial institution, ICICI provides a wide range of services to its clients. The organization carries out various activities through its branches, which are located across the globe. These activities account creation, deposits, withdrawals, loan processing, and investments. To track cash flows and identify business trends, ICICI utilizes software robots. The implementation of these robots helps identify and explain the connections between different transactions in various segments. ICICI currently uses this software robot to manage human resources and make informed judgments when applying for retail and agricultural services. Additionally, ICICI is renowned in India for integrating blockchain transactions into its corporate operations.

In addition to the use of robots in the internal processes of banks, ICICI has also introduced robotics on the retail end of the customer service department. Bank client transactions have become simpler in the modern world as a result of technological advancements. Additionally, the fast proliferation of mobile devices has made it possible to complete transactions with just a single click. ICICI has taken this a step further by allowing voice instructions to be programmed into the software. To make this service available to customers, the bank has included Apple's Siri speech assistant, which allows customers to complete transactions using just their voice [16]. Furthermore, this financial institution has introduced a service known as "Smart Vault," which allows customers to use lockers with minimal assistance from a human being. The Smart Vault is equipped with a robotic arm that, with the assistance of sophisticated radiofrequency waves, can both seal and unlock the vault. Additionally, ICICI has incorporated the use of artificial intelligence to provide consumers with information about investments [2]. The application known as Mobile Coach, which is programmed using the robotic algorithm, was released by the company. With a single click, this provides the user with the necessary documents to start a Demat account, and it also makes recommendations about the mutual fund with the best performance. With the goal of running and performing its business in a more effective and efficient manner, ICICI has been focusing on improving its software framework in line with the best standards in artificial intelligence and machine learning. This has fundamentally changed how it serves its customers and has made hyper automation possible for better internal decision-making. While the benefits of hyper automated technologies and procedures in increasing efficiency and production are well-known, these benefits are rarely objectively or scientifically measured. Businesses are therefore rethinking their operations in response to this adoption, with the aim of achieving overall greater efficiency.

12.8.5 Softbank

In the world of banking and finance, SoftBank is a well-known and respected company. Its headquarters are located in Japan. The company is well-known for the substantial investments it has made in a variety of industries all around the world. SoftBank comprises a subsidiary that is known as the SoftBank Robotic Group, which is the robotic section of SoftBank. The robotics organization known as SoftBank has brought about a revolution in the sector of robotic production. With the names Nao and Pepper, the two humanoid robots are gaining popularity in a number of different nations [32]. Humanoid robots have the ability to comprehend how humans are feeling and reacting to them. Both intriguing and efficient algorithms are used in the development of these humanoid robots. The majority of these purchases are taking place in Japan, and hotels are quite excited about the prospect of using these robots to provide superior service to their customers. Nevertheless, SoftBank is now focusing its efforts on increasing income through the production of robots that are intended for commercial usage [30]. Most businesses operating in the industrial industry are using robots to carry out job procedures. Robotic arms are becoming more popular in manufacturing facilities, particularly those that produce automobiles, as a means of improving production quality and efficiency. There are a few nations in which SoftBank's robots are not accessible, but even in those countries where they are, they come at a very high price. As a means of addressing this issue, the SoftBank Robotics Group [33] is forming partnerships with local robot manufacturing businesses to capitalize on the opportunities presented by the robotics sector. In addition, SoftBank developed a robot for floor cleaning and named it "Whiz." This robot was of assistance to the firms at times when sales of the two humanoid robots were slow. In the future, the SoftBank Robotic Division is exploring the possibility of increasing the company's profits through the purchase of robots.

12.9 Conclusions

Despite the fact that the phenomenon of hyper automation has applications in various industries, including the ocean and commercial operations, as well as our everyday lives, there is a need for collaborative efforts from all stakeholders. This includes academics, researchers, students, industrial giants, and consultants. It is particularly crucial for any nation to have backing from the bureaucracy in order to create new goods and apps that improve the quality of services and benefit human existence. As a result, many new start-ups are utilizing this phenomenon to launch their businesses, alongside well-established multinational corporations such as Microsoft, IBM, SAP, Capgemini, Infosys, and Wipro, to name a few. Additionally, companies like Uipath, Automation Anywhere, Blue Prism, Pegasystems, Workfusion, Antworks, and KOFAX, are well-known in this niche market. Therefore, it is of utmost importance for all parties involved to make extensive use of these technological advancements to improve the quality of our lives. However, stakeholders must also be patient and wait for total hyper automation to be achieved for the sake of future quality of life in their day-to-day lives.

References

1. Abid, M.E., Austin, T.L., Fox, D.C., Hussain, S.S., *Drones, uavs, and rpas: an analysis of a modern technology*, Journal of Information Systems and Technology Management, 2014.
2. Aratrika, D., ICICI Bank Gets Innovative, Deploys Robotic Arms to Sort Notes, URL accessed. *Journal of Information Systems and Technology Management*, 19, 2022, e202219009, June 25, 2022, https://www.analyticsinsight.net/icici-bankgets-innovative-deploys-robotic-arms-to-sortnotes/.
3. Banu, S. and Patil, S.D., An Intelligent Web App Chatbot, in: *2020 International Conference on Smart Technologies in Computing, Electrical and Electronics (ICSTCEE)* IEEE, October 2020.
4. IOP Publishing, Big Data. *J. Phys. Conf. Ser.*, IOPscience, Nov 2023.
5. Bornet, P., Barkin, I., Wirtz, J., *Intelligent Automation: Welcome to The World of Hyperautomation &Learn How to Harness Artificial Intelligence to Boost Business & Make Our World More Human*, Intelligent Automation: Welcome to the World of Hyperautomation, 2021, https://doi.org/10.1142/12239|.
6. Calkins, M., Ward-Dutton, N., Westerman, G., Fernandes, S., Lakshmi, N., Wei, A., Heneghan, L., Skinner, C., Blake, D., *Hyperautomation*, Bookbaby, Nov. 2020.
7. Dilmegani, C., Top 11 Hyperautomation examples. Accessed July 2021, https://www.research.aimultiple.com/hyperautomation-examples/.
8. Chaudhuri, A., Mandaviya, K., Badelia, P., Ghosh, S.K., Summary and Future Research, in: *Optical Character Recognition Systems for Different Languages with Soft Computing*, Springer, Cham, 2017.
9. Chen, Y., Research on Convolutional Neural Network Image Recognition Algorithm Based on Computer Big Data. *J. Phys. Conf. Ser.*, IOP Publishing, 2744, 2021, 022096, February 2021.
10. Chowdhury, G.G., Natural language processing. *Annu. Rev. Inf. Sci. Technol.*, 37, 1, 51–89, 2003, https://doi.org/10.1002/aris.1440370103.
11. Doguc, O., Robot process automation (RPA) and its future, in: *Handbook of Research on Strategic Fit and Design in Business Ecosystems*, IGI Global, Hershey, Pennsylvania, USA, 20202020, doi: 10.4018/978-1-7998-1125-1.ch025.
12. El Naqa, I. and Murphy, M.J., What is machine learning?, in: *Machine Learning in Radiation Oncology*, Springer, Cham, 2015, https://doi.org/10.1007/978-3-319-18305-3_1.
13. Hofmann, P., Samp, C., Urbach, N., Robotic process automation. *Electron. Mark.*, 30, 1, 14, 99–106, 2020, https://doi.org/10.1007/s12525-019-00365-8.
14. Islam, N., Islam, Z., Noor, N., A survey on optical character recognition system, *A Survey on Optical Character Recognition System*, 2017, arXiv preprint arXiv:1710.05703, http://arxiv.org/pdf/1710.05703.pdf.

15. Jordan, M., II and Mitchell, T.M., Machine learning: Trends, perspectives, and prospects. *Science*, 349, 6245, 255–260, 2015, https://doi.org/10.1126/science.aaa8415.
16. Kaelble, S., Robotic Process Automation For Dummies, NICE Special Edition, in: *Robotics Process Automation for Dummies-NICE RPA, Steve Kaelble*, Google Books, 2018.
17. Koubâa, A. (Ed.), *Robot Operating System (ROS): The Complete Reference*, vol. 625, SpringerLink, New York City, 2020.
18. Kroll, C., Bujak, A., Darius, V., Enders, W., Esser, M., Robotic Process Automation-Robots conquer business processes in back offices. Capgemini Consulting, 2016, https://doi.org/10.1007/s12525-019-00365-8.
19. Lasso-Rodriguez, G. and Winkler, K., Hyperautomation to fulfil jobs rather than executing tasks: the BPM manager robot vs human case. *Rom. J. Inf. Technol. Autom. Control*, 30, 3, 7–22, 2020, https://doi.org/10.33436/v30i3y202001.
20. Machado, J.P., Notare, M.R., Costa, S.A., Diverio, T.A., Menezes, P.B., Hyper-Automation System Applied to Geometry Demonstration Environment, in: *International Conference on Computer Aided Systems Theory*, Springer, Berlin, Heidelberg, February 2001, https://doi.org/10.1007/3-540-45654-6_36.
21. Madakam, S., Holmukhe, R.M., Jaiswal, D.K., The future digital work force: robotic process automation (RPA). *J. Inf. Syst. Technol. Manage.*, 16, 2019, e201916001, 2019, https://doi.org/10.4301/S1807-1775201916001.
22. Mani, N. and Srinivasan, B., Application of artificial neural network model for optical character recognition, in: *1997 IEEE International Conference on Systems, Man, and Cybernetics. Computational Cybernetics and Simulation*, IEEE, October 1997, https://doi.org/10.1109/ICSMC.1997.635312.
23. Nabi, M., Could Hyperautomation Be a Name for AI Plus RPA?, *Industrial Automatic Control Systems and Controllers*, Automation Anywhere, pp. 08–17, January 20, 2021.
24. Остроух, А.V. and Колбасин, А.М., Гиперавтоматизация предприятий по производству строительных материалов и конструкций. Промышленные АСУ и контроллеры, 2020.
25. Park, S.C., The Fourth Industrial Revolution and implications for innovative cluster policies. *AI Soc.*, 33, 433–445, 2018, https://doi.org/10.1007/s00146-017-0777-5.
26. Robertson, J. and Parsons, C., What's Next?, in: *Building the Network of the Future*, Chapman and Hall/CRC, United Kingdom, 2017.
27. Rozga, S., Language Understanding Intelligent Service (LUIS), in: *Practical Bot Development*, Apress, Berkeley, CA, 2018, https://doi.org/10.1007/978-1-4842-3540-9_3.
28. Shavlik, J.W., Dietterich, T., Dietterich, T.G. (Eds.), *Readings in machine learning*, Morgan Kaufmann, San Francisco, CA, 1990.

29. Srivastava, A., Kumar, A., Damle, M., Hyperautomation in Transforming Underwriting Operation in the Life Insurance Industry. *PalArch's J. Archaeol. Egypt/Egyptol.*, 17, 6, 2020, http://dx.doi.org/10.4301/S1807-1775202219009.
30. Crowe, S., *Softbank Robotics Europe cutting workforce 40% in shake-up*, June 24, 2021, https://www.therobotreport.com/softbankrobotics-europe-cutting-workforce-40-inshake-up/.
31. Stoudt-Hansen, S., *Predicts: barriers fall as technology adoption grows*, A Gartner Trend Insight Report, Boston, 2020, https://www.gartner.com/en/documents/3978529.
32. Tarafdar, M. and Beath, C.M., *Wipro limited: developing a cognitive DNA*, 2018, https://aisel.aisnet.org/icis2018/education/Presentations/3.
33. Taulli, T., *The Robotic Process Automation Handbook: A Guide to Implementing RPA Systems*, Apress, New York City, 2020, https://link.springer.com/book/10.1007/978-1-4842-5729-6.
34. Tripathi, A.M., *Learning Robotic Process Automation: Create Software robots and automate business processes with the leading RPA tool–UiPath*, Packt Publishing Ltd, Birmingham, 2018.
35. Zyubin, V.E., Hyper-automaton: A model of control algorithms, in: *Siberian Conference on Control and Communications*, IEEE, Tomsk, Russia, April 2007, https://doi.org/10.1109/SIBCON.2007.371297.

13

Pre- and Post-COVID Autonomous Finance: Global Perspective

Shikha Singh[1]*, Deepa Gupta[1], Roshan Kumar[2] and Balamurugan Balusamy[3]

[1]*GL Bajaj Institute of Management, Greater Noida, UP, India*
[2]*Banaras Hindu University, Banaras, UP, India*
[3]*Shivnadar University, Greater Noida, UP, India*

Abstract

The effects of the coronavirus disease 2019 (COVID-19) pandemic on financial services and customers' decision to utilize financial technology (FinTech) for financial services are examined in this research. Research on how the pandemic has affected financial services is still lacking, and little is known about the role that Fintech has played in crisis situations. We examine the opportunities and challenges faced by Fintech and fintech-enabled services in this article, with an emphasis on the advantages and disadvantages for Fintech firms. Aside from the unexpected but crucial impetus for the adoption of technology in financial services provided by the COVID-19 lockdowns, several additional factors have contributed to the growth story of FinTech. These elements include government support for a digital economy, the dependable and quick processing capacity of mobile devices, and the expansion and speed of internet connection. FinTech's ascent and expansion are further supported by the growing need for accessible financial services, rising client demands, and a fiercely competitive financial services industry. India gained attention in 2021 for its FinTech accomplishments, which mirrored the industry's global pace. The government along with regulators' nurturing initiatives, the robust Venture Capital (VC) ecosystem and funding climate, the undeniably enormous demographic opportunities, the high adoption of FinTech, and the availability of talent and technology for the entrepreneurs constructing the new India are all contributing factors to this growth. The collaborative ecosystem that exists between financial institutions and insurance companies is the foundation of the innovative spirit of FinTech. Traditional financial services (FS) companies and Fintech companies are forming symbiotic relationships that

**Corresponding author*: shikha.singh@glbim.ac.in

Deepa Gupta, Mukul Gupta, Rajesh Kumar Dhanaraj, Balamurugan Balusamy and Parth Mukul Gupta (eds.) Computational Intelligence for Autonomous Finance, (269–288) © 2025 Scrivener Publishing LLC

leverage the preparedness for safe data sharing and revenue generation. There are further issues that reflect a lack of financial literacy and awareness, IPO underperformance, global geopolitical and macroeconomic events that make institutional investors wary of big investments, data security and privacy risks in partnership scenarios, and the rate at which regulatory policies change, which keeps FinTech companies on their toes. The report finds that India leads the globe in FinTech development and has witnessed a huge increase in its utilization. Our findings show that FinTech partially mitigated the COVID-19 pandemic and boosted consumer adoption of FinTech.

Keywords: COVID 19, Autonomous finance, financial technology, venture capital ecosystem, collaborative ecosystem, financial literacy

13.1 Introduction

The Indian FinTech sector has grown to become one of the largest FinTech markets in the world and has emerged as a powerful global force. FinTech is now a widely used term to describe technological innovation in the financial services industry. We are witnessing a growing amount of cooperation and innovation in the market from established banks, well-known digital companies, and even regulatory bodies [1, 45]. The Indian Financial System has undergone changes due to the expanding Indian economy, new innovations, and advancing technologies. The conventional wisdom about how to operate and deliver financial products and services has been transformed by fintech. Today's FinTech buzz has evolved into a highly adaptable strategy and a competitive ecosystem for established financial institutions. In terms of FinTech Hubs, the Indian market currently dominates the global market. Over the past few decades, the impact of the financial industry and its role as a catalyst for economic growth has become a global concern [2, 9, 33]. Indian FinTech firms are heading in the right direction, as evidenced by one of the largest digital payment ecosystems in terms of value and volume, remarkable developments in digital credit access for consumers and SMEs, and significant retail investor participation in the stock market [4, 8, 13, 31]. However, this responsibility has gradually shifted to FinTech businesses, which work to promote economic growth by reducing costs and risks such as credit risk, transaction risk, financial risk, and convenience cost [3, 22]. Vijai claims that "India's fintech sector is changing the financial services sector and is currently the fastest-growing in the world," and that "Over the past two years, FinTech usage in India has experienced a considerable surge" [6, 8, 11].

After the US and the UK, India is the third-largest FinTech market, home to several FinTech unicorns, companies, and financing [14, 19, 29, 37]. India has established itself as a technologically advanced and rapidly developing country. The development and evolution of the FinTech industry have been positively impacted by India's entrepreneurial ecosystem [4], which has fostered new consensus, customer support, and financial inclusion [18, 21, 28]. This environment enables the FinTech industry to prosper and become an important part of the Indian financial system. India's transformation into a progressive FinTech country is not an overnight success. According to a 2019 Medici report, it followed the implementation of a four-point plan. This architecture has driven India's FinTech revolution. The key approaches include: (i) Employee identification with Aadhaar [5, 16, 21], (ii) the use of bank accounts through the PMJDY government initiative, (iii) the development of scalable digital systems like IMPS and UPI, and (iv) innovating by combining fintech and banking. According to data from EY's FinTech Adoption Index 2019, India's adoption of FinTech has risen from 52% in 2017 to 87% in 2019, making it a major player in the field and ranking second out of 27 economies worldwide [25, 30, 31].

13.2 Literature Review

The report by [1, 2] states that one of the biggest threats to the global economy and financial markets is the ongoing spread of COVID-19. Globally, the Indian economy is thought to be evolving quickly. The COVID-19 epidemic has affected the growth and richness of developing nations like India [22, 40, 47]. The pandemic has spread faster throughout Indian markets and the economy than any other macroeconomic cause. Initially causing an economic slowdown, the pandemic crisis has more recently resulted in a stagnant economic market [6, 8, 19]. Nonetheless, the banking and finance industry is one that is growing during a pandemic. India has emerged as a major player in the global FinTech market, with FinTech usage rising faster than anticipated [7, 23, 27, 31]. Consequently, India now leads the world in the adoption of FinTech, surpassing developing countries like Colombia, United Kingdom, and Russia [20, 27, 35]. Furthermore, the average actual adoption rate of fintech increased from 33% in 2017 to 64% in 2019, according to global statistics [25, 32, 33, 43, 49]. There is a great deal of awareness about the usage of fintech services in India. As per [33, 45, 47] 99.5% of clients in Russia and India possess knowledge about the FinTech services available for processing payments and money transfers [8].

The government's announcement in 2017 of its intention to decrease the amount of paper money in circulation has contributed to the increasing awareness in India [34, 40, 46].

According to the financial hub regional race to the top, India is currently the leading financial hub in Asia, despite the size and growing recognition of China's digital ecosystem platforms [27, 50]. Compared to China, India's 11 cities are tracked by the Index. As per the Global FinTech Index of 2020 [9, 12], Bangalore is ranked seventh, Mumbai is ranked tenth, and New Delhi is ranked sixteenth among the top 20 FinTech hub cities in the world. In the study's list of wagers, India comes in first as well [10]. According to a 2017 Deloitte research by Anand and Bhatia, "Indian finance technology companies have the potential to transform the ecosystem of financial services in three ways": (i) FinTech firms are likely to cut costs and raise the quality of financial services. (ii) The FinTech sector will create original and cutting-edge methods for evaluating risks. (iii) The financial services industry will become more diverse, safe, and stable thanks to FinTech. Furthermore, while "FinTech in India is still an emerging sector," the sector is expanding swiftly, according to the Yes Bank Initiative study [11, 19]. FinTechs in India are split equally between 21% and 27% at the conception, prototype, early revenue, and firm expansion stages [36, 45]. Given the average age of these companies, it is rather remarkable that 7% of the FinTech enterprises have already turned a profit [12, 28]. With time, the newest trends in technology are evolving. "The FinTech ecosystem in India is currently at an important juncture where we have start-ups, some of the reputable technology industry players, incubators and accelerators, and government task forces who can quantify the significant possibilities," assert [13]. These can be in the form of insurtech, blockchain, risk analysis, and financing, among other things. The report also shows that India can maintain its position as the global hub for equitable growth and development.

Prior to the COVID-19 pandemic, the Indian FinTech ecosystem had seen an increase in FinTech funding activity; this trend persisted during the pandemic, after it ended, and during the recovery period [14]. Given the increasing need for technological and contactless financial service delivery, FinTech opportunities are abundant in the current environment, even though firms are working nonstop to overcome challenges and adapt to the new normal. It encapsulates the changing dynamics occurring both inside and beyond the industry [15]. "In the post-COVID era, there is a dire need to move towards entirely digital, paperless, and presence-less end-to-end processes," the research also stated. The remarkable rise in FinTech adoption and penetration has helped the Indian financial system [16, 43, 50].

13.2.1 Objectives

The following are the study's objectives:

- To examine how FinTech has changed the established financial system, specifically as it relates to India.
- To investigate the impact of the COVID-19 pandemic on Indian financial services' capacity to adopt innovative financial technologies.

13.2.2 Research Design

The qualitative method was used in this study since it is more appropriate and enables for the acquisition of deeper knowledge. The knowledge gleaned from the available literature forms the foundation of the study, which examines how adaptable FinTech was during COVID-19. A thorough investigation is also derived from the literature's deficiencies brought on by the novelty of FinTech's influence [17, 35]. As a result, the topic is transformed into an exploratory qualitative research study.

13.2.3 Data Collection

Journal articles, manuals, book chapters, organizational reports, reports from consulting firms, newsletters, and websites are additions to the list of secondary data sources. Most of the secondary data comes from statements and scientific papers, which offer insightful data, particularly regarding industry patterns.

13.3 Factors Behind the Digitalization of Financial Services During the COVID Pandemic

The COVID-19 pandemic's outbreak over the projected timeframe played a significant role in the market's expansion [7, 18, 23]. Digital banking services and contactless payment methods became increasingly popular as more individuals stayed home. The global outbreak of COVID-19 has resulted in a decline in consumer interaction and negatively impacted regular business operations across all industries [19, 24, 46]. Everything from academics to the workplace to ordering groceries has accelerated due to COVID-19. This also applies to the financial services sector, where financial technology, or FinTech, is essential in lowering the risk of contracting the corona virus from exchanging cash, assisting small- and medium-sized businesses, and promoting financial inclusion in developing nations both during and after the pandemic [11, 19].

COVID-19 accelerated several developments already in motion, such as the adoption of digital payments and modifications to the purchasing and selling practices of retail consumers and sellers [20, 28]. A significant portion of the economy shifted to relying on technology, giving businesses with well-established platforms, digital strategies, and sizable client bases an edge. COVID-19 expedited the uptake of digital technologies and transformed consumer behavior. Non-cash payments increased significantly between the fiscal year (FY) 2020 and 2021, with a 75% year over year increase in UPI transactions [25, 29]. Using digital lending applications (DLAs), nonbank financial businesses (NBFCs) disbursed more than 60% of their loans in FY21 [21]. The number of Demat accounts increased by 63% from 55 million in FY21 to approximately 90 million in FY22, due to the addition of approximately 35 million new accounts in FY22 (up to November 21) [21, 39, 46].

The pandemic may benefit current Fintech businesses engaged in insurance, investing, and leadership services. The global use of digital technology has accelerated due to the COVID-19 [29, 30]. Financial regulators responded to COVID-19 by enacting policies that were both fintech-specific and sector-wide, aiming to minimize risks and maximize opportunities presented by technologically enabled financial innovation. Additionally, COVID-19 created internal difficulties for regulators regarding Fintech [22].

Numerous macroeconomic factors contribute to the growth of the Indian fintech market, including India's rapidly expanding economy with growing disposable income, a sizable population of unbanked people, initiatives from government and regulatory bodies, an increasing number of young individuals, improved internet access, widespread smartphone adoption, and a rapidly expanding e-commerce marketplace [26, 33, 49]. Additional macro factors include:

1. **Capital Availability/Funding:** FinTech start-ups must have access to capital from venture capitalists and private equity companies to expand. India secured more than $7.8 billion in 363 venture capital fintech transactions in 2021 [23, 44]. In the first half of 2022, fintech funds totaled $2.47 billion, with $0.5 billion in loans and $0.3 billion in payments leading the way [43, 47]. Additionally, participants in the wealth, insurance, and neo-banking sectors are rapidly developing

from their early stages to a critical mass of adoption, promising potential investments for investors [24, 30, 44]. While spending was restricted due to the COVID-19 shutdown, certain households, especially those with higher incomes, saw a significant rise in bank balances. Regarding investments, a low interest rate environment and rising savings may have prompted ordinary investors to put money into riskier crypto-assets like shares and bitcoins [18, 19].

2. **Regulatory Environment for FinTech's:** Because of the nature of their services and the way the financial services supply chain is segmented, FinTech's may occasionally be subject to fewer financial regulatory requirements than banks. This could have given new competitors more room to expand [25, 29]. Additionally, during the pandemic, several established financial institutions were subject to prudential constraints that did not apply to FinTech's, such as prohibitions on stock buybacks and dividend payments. Regulators governing financial services have acted as engines for the expansion of the FinTech industry in the nation [3, 26, 31]. Government initiatives have also contributed to the growth of FinTech and the industry of digital financial services in general. However, a great deal of well-established financial organizations benefited from central bank liquidity [27, 45]. Adjustments in the delivery of digital financial services during the pandemic were influenced by governmental regulations and the digital maturity of institutions. These frequently resulted in disparate performance from various financial service providers, particularly during the pandemic's height [28, 37]. Among these important previous and current programs and policies are: new mutual fund licenses; the RBI innovation hub; the new FinTech division of RBI the digital lending framework; the National Strategy on the Blockchain; regulatory sandboxes by RBI and IRDAI for FinTech's; e-RUPI, the payment infrastructure development fund; the National Common Mobility Card (NCMC), digital banking infrastructure with 75 new digital banking units; Developing digital infrastructure with digital KYC, e-signatures, and major digital India program objectives; the recognition of P2P lenders as NBFCs; and the rollout of 47 initiatives aimed at strengthening the e-payment ecosystem [29, 35, 50].

3. **Technology and Industry Partnerships:** Using innovative and cutting-edge technologies like blockchain, artificial intelligence, machine learning, and cloud infrastructures, the financial services industry is undergoing a significant transition [4, 30, 45]. Due to institutions' existing digital infrastructure and their digital readiness and established digital infrastructure, new companies, as well as certain established financial institutions, were able to quickly satisfy customer demands and carry on with business as usual. Likewise, companies with pre-pandemic remote labor practices saw a more seamless shift [31, 39, 40]. The financial services sector has evolved from generic goods and services to specialized, data-driven service offerings. Some of the oldest banking institutions in India collaborate with digitally native FinTech businesses to provide the finest digital customer experience, recognizing the synergistic impact of digitization and customer engagement [32, 44]. Partnerships between established companies in the financial services industry and emerging FinTech companies are prevalent, facilitated by the widespread adoption of application programming interfaces (API) and data sharing guidelines [7, 20, 33]. Banks appreciate that FinTech start-ups may only enter the market through partnerships, as there are not many new licenses available [46]. Government agencies are eager to cooperate with FinTech firms to develop better identity verification solutions, enhancing the efficacy and transparency of direct benefit transfer processes [17, 34, 37]. To support the development of digital infrastructure, initiatives like Digital India, Jan Dhan-Aadhaar-Mobile (J-A-M) linkages projects, and India stack have been introduced. Scheduled Commercial Banks are also establishing Digital Banking Units. Reduced transaction costs are forcing retailers to adopt digital payment methods across all areas [12, 35, 45]. The pandemic has expedited the uptake of digital financial services and products among small and medium-sized enterprises (SMEs) in India, resulting in increased demand for FinTech software as a service (SaaS) solution, including app-based bookkeeping and accounting, no-code payment aggregation, and equity cap administration. Big Tech companies like Google, Amazon, and WhatsApp have also adjusted their products to offer customized services like

Google Pay, Amazon Pay, and WhatsApp Payments in India [7, 36, 45].

4. **Adoption of Emerging Technologies:** From the standpoints of consumer trust and regulator data compliance, authentication and verification technologies have been among the most important facilitators of digital-only financial services. Customers feel more secure when using biometric identity verification technology like voice, face, and iris scanning. According to EY's FinTech Adoption Index 2019 research, India has one of the highest rates of FinTech adoption globally [37]. FinTech acceptance has been made possible by the simplicity of opening accounts, customization to meet individual needs and goals, and the availability of several user-friendly features [40]. FinTech offers a wide range of business potential because it is native to smartphones and typically operating system agnostic [21, 38]. The foundation for digital-native financial services is being built by industry and regulatory adoption of modern infrastructures and cutting-edge technologies, including blockchain technology, e-KYC, Internet of Things, artificial intelligence, digital authentication through encrypted signatures, and account aggregation infrastructures [19, 26, 38]. Increased regulatory encouragement and a supportive digital public infrastructure are major factors accelerating the adoption of digital technology. The largest success story in this regard is UPI, which processed 6.3 billion transactions in July 2022—the highest number of exchanges since its introduction six years ago [39, 40]. The COVID-19 period has seen an acceleration of this digitization. Anecdotal and formal data point to a dramatic drop in customers' inclination or capacity to visit bank branches as the reason behind the rise in internet banking during the pandemic [40, 43]. Most businesses and people modified their demands for financial services in response to pandemic mitigation measures. The demand for digital and contactless payments has clearly shifted [13, 41]. The majority who paid less in cash during the pandemic indicated they would do so after crisis is over. Retail behavior was altered by the COVID-19 pandemic due to a significant rise in remote labor, e-commerce, and digital payments. As a result, companies increased their digital presence, and customers relied more on online platforms for daily tasks

[26, 42, 49]. Over time, these shifts may become fundamental as people engage in more digital activities and corporations invest in their online platforms.

Banks and FinTech can create new applications and services tailored to their consumers' needs by providing secure access to consumer data through application programming interfaces (API) with licensed and authorized service providers [38]. The implementation of an account aggregator framework is anticipated to enhance consumers' trust in the managed exchange of data, leading to improved financial services and a comprehensive understanding of their financial status [13, 43].

Technology firms and financial institutions emphasize that the "search for convenience" by customers is a major factor driving the platformization trend in all industries, including finance [44, 50]. The COVID-19 pandemic has expedited this trend by encouraging consumers to access goods and services online rather than in person. Convenience is further increased by the round-the-clock availability of these services, setting them apart from brick-and-mortar financial service providers with set hours [33]. Freemium pricing models have proven popular with new and experimental clients who prefer to get the most for their spending [41, 45].

5. **Access to Qualified Talent:** India continues to be one of the world's leading centers for tech talent, fostering the advancement and better use of emerging technologies in Indian companies' problem-solving processes, including FinTech. FinTech firms have also had success attracting highly qualified personnel from traditional financial services, e-commerce, consulting, and professional services sectors [46].
6. **Significantly Underserved Market:** The Telecom Regulatory Authority of India (TRAI) reports that as of April 2022, there were 1,142 million wireless subscribers in India, with 518 million customers in rural areas and 624 million in urban areas (TRAI, 2021) [23, 47]. By 2030, India will have 21 million high-income and 140 million middle-class households by 2030, fueling demand and expansion in the country's fintech industry. Beyond the traditional target population, India presents enormous prospects for FinTech businesses in underserved demographic segments in tier-II and tier-III towns [26, 48].

Low insurance penetration is another significant issue that must be resolved. The World Inequality Report 2021 states that in India, the richest 10% of the population possessed 57% of the nation's revenue in 2021, and the richest 1% took home more than one-fifth (21.15) of the nation's total income, while the poorest 50% only made 13.1%17 [31, 49].

13.4 Challenges/Barriers for FinTech

FinTech faces several significant obstacles. Below are some of the most critical problems and difficulties the sector is currently encountering, particularly in the Indian FinTech industry.

1. **Volatilities in Geopolitics:** According to a report from Pareto Economics and Fintrail, geopolitical unpredictability hinders the growth potential of the global FinTech business [34, 37]. This issue affects their potential for growth outside of their home markets, attracting capital from investors while considering Fin Crime mandates, policy constraints on the funding source, embargoes and bans, and outsourcing limitations that might restrict B2B tech providers [33, 50]. These hazards have become more apparent in the past year than ever before. Large FinTech businesses can still manage these risks because to their specialized compliance, Fin Crime, and risk teams, but smaller FinTech companies looking to expand internationally are likely to be more negatively impacted [19, 32].
2. **Growing Risks Associated with Data Security and Privacy:** Data and related innovations are the foundation of FinTech. However, fraud, information theft, platform outages, and data leaks have increased the hazards that FinTech must contend with. Traditional financial services organizations are not the only ones facing the growing financial and reputational costs of security breaches [36, 49]. It is crucial to have a robust data protection strategy, and players will need to make significant investments in procedures to manage this risk and adhere to legal obligations for data security.
3. **Speed of Regulatory Updates:** One of the main issues facing India's FinTech sector, given its enormous ecosystem, is the speed at which regulatory authorities issue updates [45, 48]. It is crucial to strike a balance between protecting

customers and fostering innovation in the financial services sector while carefully supporting innovation.

4. **Low Financial Knowledge and Awareness:** The use of FinTech platforms is primarily concentrated in urban areas, whereas over 70% of India's population resides in villages [26, 47]. Furthermore, just 27% of Indians are financially literate, according to SEBI research, which poses a significant barrier to onboarding new, knowledgeable clients. It is anticipated that FinTech will spread to smaller towns and cities, innovating for these populations and raising awareness and financial literacy along the way [23, 33].
5. **Diverse Adoption with Pockets of Underbanked and Overbanked Segments:** MSMEs, which make up most of the Indian business environment, are generally undecided about digital adoption. But the length of the pandemic has given us a push [16, 46]. A recent CRISIL poll indicates that about 65% of MSMEs surveyed had either improved or accepted the use of digital media. Another issue facing customers is the disparity in technology usage between urban and rural consumers [23, 28, 30]. Remarkably, 58.2% of rural Indians have access to telecom, compared to 134.7% of urban Indians [16, 45]. FinTech lacks its fundamental infrastructure in areas without telecom penetration.

13.5 Advantages and Disadvantages of Market Structure Modifications Towards the Digitalization of FinTech Services

Despite delays brought on by the pandemic, 2021 was a great year for the global FinTech sector's expansion. The core services of today's contactless, remote, and digitally native FinTech landscape include payments, lending, financial investment advisory, insurance distribution, and many other services that formerly required physical or in-person interactions [33, 45]. FinTech's real-time, transparent, and effective products throughout value chains have permanently disrupted the financial services sector's status quo. At international FinTech events, India's significant contributions to the industry in terms of start-up numbers, investment values, user base, and transaction volumes are regularly showcased as a bright point. Today, India exports not only manpower but also ideas and the greatest financial innovations to the world [15, 44, 50].

13.5.1 Advantages

- **Increased Inclusivity:** By offering a wider range of financial services, financial innovation can lessen vulnerabilities and maintain stability during adverse shocks. Enhancing access to financial services is another way that financial innovation can promote inclusiveness [26, 43]. Today, people who live far from bank offices can still use computers and mobile devices to obtain financial services.
- **Reduced Fixed Cost:** Digital innovation has the potential to reduce fixed costs associated with a provider's absence of physical presence, which can then be passed on to the customer. Creative applications of digital technology can result in financial services that are more effectively and affordably delivered [44]. This is partly because they reduce the cost of providing financial services by eliminating the need for physical infrastructure and replacing labor intensive, paper-based procedures with automated operations.
- **Increased Market Contestability:** Financial technology can increase market competition by making it easier for businesses to enter and exit markets [10, 42]. For example, online banking has made the market for time deposits more competitive and reduced fixed costs for some bank products.
- Increased market contestability can encourage competition and result in lower prices for customers. However, it may also lead established financial institutions to prioritize sales and market share over operational profit [5, 17, 43]. Additionally, many financial sector operations are now conducted remotely due to higher rates of digitalization, enabling operational continuity even during disruptive events like the COVID-19 pandemic [8, 41]. Benefits from the use of FinTech services, such cloud computing, include lower costs, more flexibility and scalability, improved security, and increased operational resilience.
- **Maintain Financial Stability:** When financial institutions' solid business models are supported by competitive incentives and impact overall efficiency improvements in both the real economy and the financial system, contestability can help maintain financial stability [32, 40]. Additionally, there are other ways that financial innovation might promote financial stability.

- **Monetary Steadiness:** In the interim, the monetary stability risks from FinTech's might become increasingly significant. From a regulatory perspective, the risks associated with the complexity and opacity of FinTech's activities in certain jurisdictions are more challenging to assess when such firms work outside the regulatory border [7, 22, 39]. FinTech companies often have platform-based business models which enable them to operate globally and access a worldwide retail client base, challenging national regulators.

13.5.2 Disadvantages

- **Increased Vulnerabilities:** Digitalization's increased dependence on technology might lead to new risks, such as being more susceptible to cyberattacks. Malicious activities (such as fraud, phishing, or cyberattacks) or operational issues (such as computer system failure) may cause this [11, 38, 47]. They might, in any event, lead to interruptions in the delivery of payment and financial services. Additionally, changes in market structure might bring about vulnerabilities that could affect financial stability.
- **Increased Regulatory Arbitrage:** The rapid expansion of financial service offerings by FinTechs raises the possibility of potential regulatory loopholes [2, 37, 44]. Consequently, some governments have already taken measures to address regulatory scope. Many financial service companies have transitioned to digital platforms, increasing complexity and opacity and presenting regulatory challenges. FinTechs collaborate with numerous incumbent enterprises to enhance their online presence [9, 36]. Similar collaborations are emerging in other jurisdictions. Moreover, FinTech lending platforms often collaborate with incumbents, creating complex regulatory challenges for regulators and supervisors to assess potential risks due to business arrangements [7, 35]. When FinTech's provide services outside of their primary jurisdiction, achieving transparency can be even more challenging. Additionally, it remains unclear whether regulatory arbitrage plays a role in specific FinTech collaborations and business arrangements.

- **Increased Risk-Taking Behavior:** A related concern is that competition from Big Tech and FinTech competitors might create incentives for incumbent financial institutions to increase risk-taking. For example, under pressure from existing business models, incumbent banks and insurers could engage in riskier lending or investment activities to preserve market share and profits [10, 15, 34]. They may need to carefully assess the viability of incumbents' business models and the prudence of their responses to industry and competitive challenges posed by FinTech firms.
- **Data Gaps:** Data gaps remain a significant concern. Reporting requirements related to financial management, credits, insurance, and payments may vary depending on the specific business model of FinTech operations [17]. The extent and composition of FinTech operations are often poorly documented in officially central bank and regulatory statistics [27, 33]. These data gaps can make it challenging to assess the financial risks or potential systemic relevance introduced by new entrants. This creates a "Catch 22" situation where only institutions within the regulatory perimeter have access to the necessary data to evaluate critical factors such as risk and systemic importance, crucial for determining whether adjustments to the regulatory perimeter or enhanced surveillance are necessary [32, 39].

13.6 Conclusion

This study presents promising insights into understanding the FinTech landscape from a financial crisis perspective. The findings and results can be valuable and significant in various sectors and investments. The pre- and post-pandemic COVID-19 global outbreak has influenced the adaptability and adoption rate of FinTech ventures. Additionally, government initiatives have a profound impact on the development and resilience of FinTech. However, India's weak regulatory framework may potentially hamper the progress of FinTech ventures.

Globally, the Indian economy is considered a rapidly developing one. The COVID-19 outbreak has impacted the growth and development of emerging countries like India. India gained attention in 2021 for its FinTech accomplishments, which mirrored the industry's global pace [18, 30]. After the US and the UK, India is the third-largest FinTech market, home to several FinTech unicorns, companies, and significant financing. Initially, this pandemic crisis resulted in an economic downturn and, subsequently, a sluggish financial market. However, the banking and finance has been one of the growing industries during a pandemic. Despite the challenges, India has emerged as a prominent global player in the FinTech sector. According to a bulletin by [25, 29], "One of the biggest threats to the global economy and financial business sectors is the ongoing spread of the coronavirus." Like other countries, India is taking steps to mitigate the impact of the COVID outbreak. It is anticipated that the measures will mitigate the pandemic's impact on the Indian financial and economic sectors [22, 27]. FinTech is not an unusual business; in fact, the unfavorable impacts of the COVID-19 pandemic are affecting significant areas of the Indian economy, with manufacturing, auto, retail, avionics, and hospitality enduring the worst part of the lockdown. According to a PwC report (2020), there is an urgent need to transition to extremely sophisticated, paperless, and presenceless end-to-end operations in the post-COVID future. The Indian financial framework has been significantly altered by the rise of FinTech's presence and acceptance. However, there are several concerns. A lack of financial literacy and awareness, IPO underperformance, global geopolitical and macroeconomic events making institutional investors wary before big investments (reflected in the first half 2022 funding trends), data security and privacy risks in partnership scenarios, and the rapidly changing regulatory policies that keep FinTech companies on their toes are just a few of the issues [2, 22]. According to the study's findings, FinTech development is leading the world in India, and the country has seen a significant increase in the use of the technology in recent years.

The message from [6, 26] conveys the harsh reality that "The FinTech area ends up at an enunciation direct as the world go on toward tackle the financial aftermath of the Coronavirus emergency." In a powerful climate, FinTechs can acquire opportunities for rethinking the monetary plans of action [19]. The steady development of the FinTech area is reflected in investor opinions. Before the COVID-19 outbreak, the Indian FinTech ecosystem saw a positive trend in FinTech financing activity and follows a similar pattern during and after the pandemic or in the recovery period [23]. While organizations are working nonstop to acclimate to the new normal and address the challenges, there are numerous potential opportunities for FinTechs in the ongoing situation, given areas of strength for the digital and contactless delivery of monetary services.

References

1. Daluwathumullagamage, D.J. and Sims, A., Blockchain-enabled corporate governance and regulation. *Int. J. Financ. Stud.*, 8, 2, 36, 2020, https://doi.org/10.3390/ijfs8020036.
2. Zhao, X., Ai, P., Lai, F., Luo, X., Benitez, J., Task management in decentralized autonomous organization. *J. Oper. Manage.*, 68, 6, 649–674, 2022, https://doi.org/10.1002/joom.1179.
3. Ha, T. and Lee, S., Examination of Bitcoin exchange through agent-based modeling: Focusing on the perceived fundamental of Bitcoin. *IEEE Trans. Eng. Manage.*, 69, 4, 1294–1307, 2022, https://doi.org/10.1109/TEM.2020.2983416.
4. Caselli, S., Governance and strategy within the financial system: Tradition and innovation. *J. Manage. Gov.*, 14, 3, 241–271, 2010, https://doi.org/10.1007/s10997-010-9149-y.
5. Toporowski, J., International business and the crisis, in: *Critical Perspectives on International Business*, vol. 5, pp. 162–164, 2009, https://doi.org/10.1108/17422040910938776.
6. Pérez-Castro, MA., Montero-Alonso, MA., Abderrahman-Azaar, A., Bankarization in the first European cities with an equal number of Muslim and Christian inhabitants: Melilla and Ceuta. *Int. J. Islam. Middle East. Finance Manage.*, 10, 4, 554–580, 2017, https://doi.org/10.1108/IMEFM-02-2017-0033.
7. Harwick, C. and Caton, J., What's holding back blockchain finance? On the possibility of decentralized autonomous finance. *Q. Rev. Econ. Finance*, 84, 420–429, 2022. https://doi.org/10.1016/j.qref.2020.09.006.
8. Yihua, L., Beibei, L., Huanhong, G., Measurement index of fiscal decentralization and the revaluation of the economic growth effect. *China Finance Econ. Rev.*, 4, 4, 39–57, 2015, https://doi.org/10.1515/cfer-2015-040405.
9. van Rijnsoever, F.J., Intermediaries for the greater good: How entrepreneurial support organizations can embed constrained sustainable development startups in entrepreneurial ecosystems. *Res. Policy*, 51, 2, 104438, 2022, https://doi.org/10.1016/j.respol.2021.104438.
10. Hawkes, D., Against financial derivatives: Towards an ethics of representation. *J. Interdiscip. Econ.*, 31, 2, 165–182, 2019, https://doi.org/10.1177/0260107918812535.
11. de Cock, C., Baker, M., Volkmann, C., Financial phantasmagoria: Corporate image-work in times of crisis. *Organization*, 18, 2, 153–172, 2011, https://doi.org/10.1177/1350508410388681.
12. Mundo Neto, M., Donadone, J.C., Alves, P.V.B.F., Financial intermediation and innovation: Linking international agents and local investors. *J. Risk Financ. Manage.*, 15, 1, 108–117, 2022, https://doi.org/10.1590/1806-9649-2022V29E3622.

13. van der Zwan, N., Making sense of financialization. *Socio-Econ. Rev.*, 12, 1, 99–129, 2014, https://doi.org/10.1093/ser/mwt020.
14. Sun, J. and Yano, G., Finance and enterprise performance: Does ethnicity make a difference? *Hitotsub. J. Econ.*, 56, 2, 197–212, 2015, https://doi.org/10.15057/27573.
15. Kaal, W., Reputation as Capital—How Decentralized Autonomous Organizations Address Shortcomings in the Venture Capital Market. *J. Risk Financ. Manage.*, 16, 5, 263, 2023, https://doi.org/10.3390/jrfm16050263.
16. Lacity, M.C., Blockchain: From Bitcoin to the Internet of Value and beyond. *J. Inf. Technol.*, 37, 4, 326–340, 2022, https://doi.org/10.1177/02683962221086300.
17. Bay, C., Catasús, B., Johed, G., Situating financial literacy. *Crit. Perspect. Account.*, 25, 1, 36–45, 2014, https://doi.org/10.1016/j.cpa.2012.11.011.
18. Saito, Y. and Rose, J.A., Reputation-based Decentralized Autonomous Organization for the non-profit sector: Leveraging blockchain to enhance good governance. *Front. Blockchain*, 5, 1083647, 2022, https://doi.org/10.3389/fbloc.2022.1083647.
19. Azzutti, A., Ringe, W.-G., Stiehl, H.S., Machine learning, market manipulation, and collusion on capital markets: why the "black box" matters. *J. Int. Law*, 43, 1, 79–135, 2021, https://doi.org/10.15779/Z38S33S.
20. Zhang, J. and Qian, F., Digital economy enables common prosperity: Analysis of mediating and moderating effects based on green finance and environmental pollution. *Front. Energy Res.*, 10, 35–45, 1080230, 2023, https://doi.org/10.3389/fenrg.2022.1080230.
21. Pauly, L.W., Managing financial emergencies in an integrating world. *Globalizations*, 6, 3, 353–364, 2009, https://doi.org/10.1080/14747730903141951.
22. Pelagidis, T. and Kostika, E., Investigating the role of central banks in the interconnection between financial markets and cryptoassets. *J. Ind. Bus. Econ.*, 49, 3, 481–507, 2022, https://doi.org/10.1007/s40812-022-00227-z.
23. Botta, A., Caverzasi, E., Russo, A., When complexity meets finance: A contribution to the study of the macroeconomic effects of complex financial systems. *Res. Policy*, 51, 8, 103990, 2022, https://doi.org/10.1016/j.respol.2020.103990.
24. Beltrame, F., Grassetti, L., Bertinetti, G.S., Sclip, A., Relationship lending, access to credit and entrepreneurial orientation as cornerstones of venture financing. *J. Small Bus. Enterp. Dev.*, 30, 1, 4–29, 2023, https://doi.org/10.1108/JSBED-07-2021-0281.
25. Chugunov, I., Sidelnykova, L., Sosnovska, O., Zhytar, M., Navolokina, A., Tools for Assessing the Level of Adaptivity of the Financial Architecture of Economy to Financial Globalization Conditions based on the Capacity of Banks, Non-Banking Financial Institutions and Stock Market. *WSEAS Trans. Bus. Econ.*, 19, 1075–1084, 2022, https://doi.org/10.37394/23207.2022.19.94.

26. Dholakia, N., Finanzkapital and consumers: How financialization shaped twentieth century marketing. *J. Hist. Res. Market.*, 4, 3, 453–461, 2012, https://doi.org/10.1108/17557501211252989.
27. Peng, G., Han, M., Yuan, H., Artificial Intelligence Drives the Coordinated Development of Green Finance and the Real Economy: Empirical Evidence from Chinese Provincial Level. *J. Knowl. Econ.*, 1–39, 2023, https://doi.org/10.1007/s13132-023-01506-3.
28. Pinto, J.C.V., Aguilar, J., Suescún, E., Román, J.A., Montoya, A.C., Restrepo, M.F., Córdoba, L.S., An intelligent financial management system for optimal resource allocation in an organization. *Int. J. Appl. Decis. Sci.*, 16, 5, 565–586, 2023, https://doi.org/10.1504/IJADS.2023.133145.
29. Ziegler, C. and Zehra, S.R., Decoding Decentralized Autonomous Organizations: A Content Analysis Approach to Understanding Scoring Platforms. *J. Risk Financ. Manage.*, 16, 7, 330, 2023, https://doi.org/10.3390/jrfm16070330.
30. Grabel, I., Global Financial Governance and Development Finance in the Wake of the 2008 Financial Crisis. *Fem. Econ.*, 19, 3, 32–54, 2013, https://doi.org/10.1080/13545701.2013.798021.
31. Menon, S. and Jain, K., Blockchain technology for transparency in agri-food supply chain: Use cases, limitations, and future directions. *IEEE Trans. Eng. Manage.*, 71, 106, 120, 2024, https://doi.org/10.1109/TEM.2021.3110903.
32. Cennamo, C., Marchesi, C., Meyer, T., Two Sides of the Same Coin? Decentralized Versus Proprietary block chains and the Performance of Digital Currencies. *Acad. Manage. Discov.*, 6, 3, 382–405, 2020.
33. Werbach, K., *The block chain and the New Architecture of Trust*, MIT Press, Cambridge, MA, 2018.
34. Liu, Y., Lu, Q., Zhu, L., Paik, H.-Y., Staples, M., A systematic literature review on block chain governance. *J. Syst. Softw.*, 197, 111576, 2023, https://doi.org/10.1016/j.jss.2022.111576.
35. Gudgeon, L., Werner, S., Perez, D., Knottenbelt, W., DeFi Protocols for Loanable Funds. *Proceedings of the 2nd ACM Conference on Advances in Financial Technologies*, 2020.
36. Sorkin, A.R. *et al.*, *The New 'Shadow' Banks*, The New York Times, New York, USA, 2021, Retrieved from https://www.nytimes.com/2021/09/08/business/dealbook/crypto-bitcoin-regulation.html.
37. Szabo, N., Smart contracts: building blocks for digital markets. *EXTROPY: J. Transhumanist Thought*, 18, 2, 28, 1996.
38. Beck, R., Müller-Bloch, C., King, J.L., Governance in the block chain Economy: A Framework and Research Agenda. *J. Assoc. Inf. Syst.*, 19, 10, 1020–1034, 2018, https://doi.org/10.17705/1jais.00518.
39. Jentzch, C., *Decentralized Autonomous Organization to Automate Governance*, 2017, Available at: https://lawofthelevel.lexblogplatformthree.com/wp-content/uploads/sites/187/2017/07/WhitePaper-1.pdf.

40. Buterin, V., *DAOs, DACs, DAs and More: An Incomplete Terminology Guide*, Ethereum Blog, p. 6, 2014, Retrieved February 12, 2021, from https://blog.ethereum.org/2014/05/06/daos-dacs-das-and-more-an-incompleteterminology-guide/.
41. Polanyi, M., *The Logic of Liberty: Reflections and Rejoinders*, University of Chicago Press, London, 1951.
42. Qin, K., Zhou, L., Afonin, Y., Lazzaretti, L., & Gervais, A., CeFi vs. DeFi–Comparing Centralized to Decentralized Finance, 2021. Retrieved from https://arxiv.org/abs/2106.08157.
43. Carlisle, K. and Gruby, R.L., Polycentric Systems of Governance: A Theoretical Model for the Commons. *Policy Stud. J.*, 47, 4, 927–952, 2017, https://doi.org/10.1111/psj.12212.
44. Ostrom, E., *Understanding Institutional Diversity*, Princeton University Press, New jersey, USA, 2005.
45. Ostrom, E., Coping with Tragedies of the Commons. *Annu. Rev. Polit. Sci.*, 2, 1, 493–535, 1999, https://doi.org/10.1146/annurev.polisci.2.1.493.
46. Taleb, N.N., *Skin in the game: Hidden asymmetries in daily life*, Random House Trade Paperbacks, New York, USA, 2018.
47. Ostrom, V., Tiebout, C.M., Warren, R., The Organization of Government in Metropolitan Areas: A Theoretical Inquiry. *Am. Polit. Sci. Rev.*, 55, 4, 831–842, 1961, https://doi.org/10.1017/S0003055400125973.
48. Murray, A., Kuban, S., Josefy, M., Anderson, J., Contracting in the Smart Era: The Implications of block chain and Decentralized Autonomous Organizations for Contracting and Corporate Governance. *Acad. Manage. Perspect.*, 35, 4, 622–641, 2019.
49. Bartoletti, M., Chiang, J., Lluch-Lafuente, A., *SoK: Lending Pools in Decentralized Finance*, 2020, Available at: https://arxiv.org/abs/2012.13230.
50. Oliveira, L., Zavolokina, L., Bauer, I., Schwabe, G., To Token or Not to Token: Tools for Understanding block chain Tokens. *39th International Conference on Information Systems*, San Francisco, 2018.

14

Emerging Trends and Future Directions in Artificial Intelligence for Next-Generation Computing

Rafael Vargas-Bernal

Departamento de Ingeniería Electrónica, DICIS, Universidad de Guanajuato, Salamanca, Guanajuato, Mexico

Abstract

The progress of artificial intelligence depends on new hardware infrastructures being developed to overcome the constraints of conventional computers, such as the von Neumann bottleneck. Two-dimensional materials can emulate artificial neural networks (ANNs) with high performance to develop devices with artificial synaptic behavior using low power consumption through memristor configurations. New materials and devices must be proposed to exploit artificial intelligence, and the options that have shown greater efficiency and versatility are linked to the application of two-dimensional materials. In this way, nanotechnology can be exploited in basic research to implement applications based on new emerging materials. Among the two-dimensional materials that have been used for the implementation of memristors are graphene, phosphorene (BP), hexagonal boron nitride (*h*-BN), transition metal dichalcogenides (TMDs), MXenes, etc.The purpose of this chapter is to review the advances achieved so far and predict the technological and scientific trends that will enable the practical implementation of neuromorphic computing to exploit artificial intelligence in high-speed computing and large amounts of data.

Keywords: Artificial intelligence, neuromorphic computing, memristor, nanomaterials, transition metal dichalcogenides (TMDs), nanotechnology, two-dimensional materials, phosphorene

Email: r.vargas@ugto.mx; ORCID: 0000-0003-4865-4575

Deepa Gupta, Mukul Gupta, Rajesh Kumar Dhanaraj, Balamurugan Balusamy and Parth Mukul Gupta (eds.) Computational Intelligence for Autonomous Finance, (289–312) © 2025 Scrivener Publishing LLC

14.1 Introduction

With the advent of the digital world, increasing amounts of data are produced, stored, and used by multitudes of users around the world [1]. In the last two decades, this growth has been estimated at 300 times. Thus, non-volatile memory technologies must be developed to increase the speed of operation during storage, reading, and processing so that the data can be effectively utilized by artificial intelligence (AI). Technologies such as magnetic random-access memories (MRAMs), resistive random-access memories (RRAMs), phase change memories (PCMs), and others have offered practical implementations with outstanding advantages in both the amount of information stored and the speed of data processing. Conventional neuromorphic devices have a metal/oxide/metal structure, which presents problems with vacancy and ion migration.

To artificially simulate the computational neuromorphic advantage of neurons in the human brain, researchers around the world have developed artificial synaptic devices to emulate biological processes, such as pre-neuron-post neuron junctions, to transmit, learn, and store information [2]. The first synaptic devices were based on silicon to make them compatible with the semiconductor manufacturing industry [3]. For example, it was feasible to implement neural networks containing 2,400 silicon neurons to achieve reconfigurable synapse-based connectivity that is programmable. An artificial neural network (ANN) uses random access memories for event routing on a 3 mm × 3 mm chip using 0.5-micron CMOS technology. Unfortunately, these systems were not feasible due to their excessive power consumption and high complexity, making them unsuitable for large-scale integration.

Memristors, which are two-terminal memory electronic devices whose resistance states are non-volatile and reversibly switched, are capable of high-performance neuromorphic computation and information storage [1, 4]. Conventional implementations of memristors based on oxides in the form of thin films and solid electrolytes have leakage currents that degrade their performance by preventing guaranteed state switching. Due to these shortcomings, researchers have found that two-dimensional materials can overcome these obstacles by using them as electrodes as well as the resistive switching (RS) layer for the implementation of memristors used in neuromorphic computing to develop artificial intelligence. Due to the nanoscale dimension of two-dimensional materials, their scalability is feasible, allowing for high densities in devices within a small physical space.

The purpose of this chapter is to study the advantages offered by two-dimensional materials in the development of synaptic devices for neuromorphic computing, thereby increasing the efficiency of artificial intelligence. The chapter is divided into six sections: *Section 14.2* describes the fundamental concepts associated with neuromorphic computing to emphasize its role in artificial intelligence for handling large amounts of data. The advantages that two-dimensional materials bring to neuromorphic computing are analyzed in *Section 14.3*. In *Section 14.4*, a study of the contributions of two-dimensional materials to implement synaptic devices as hardware elements for artificial intelligence is presented. Future research directions are discussed in *Section 14.5*. Finally, the chapter conclusions are given in *Section 14.6*.

14.2 Concepts of Neuromorphic Computing, Artificial Intelligence, and Memristor

Neuromorphic computing is defined as a method for modeling or implementing computational elements like those used by the human brain and nervous system, based on hardware and software [5]. To implement the hardware and software for neuromorphic computing, it is necessary to use disciplines such as biology, physics, mathematics, electronic engineering, and computer science. Neurons transmit information to different sectors of the brain and nervous system using electrical and chemical impulses through synapses that connect them, as illustrated in Figure 14.1. An input

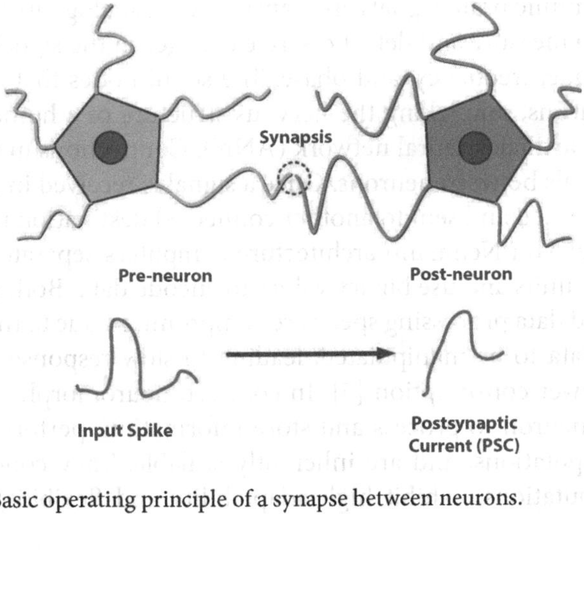

Figure 14.1 Basic operating principle of a synapse between neurons.

signal or spike is supplied to the pre-nerve cell or pre-neuron and communicated to the post-neuron to produce a post-synaptic current (PSC). The synapse can be defined as a structure in the neuron's dendrites (nerve terminals) that transfers a chemical or electrical signal to another neuron. During this transmission, the initial neuron passes the signal to the target neuron. In the transfer process, the molecular machinery of both neurons holds them together while the signaling process takes place. In many cases, the synaptic part is located on an axon while the postsynaptic part is located on a dendrite. This architecture makes neural processes much more versatile, adaptive, and energy-efficient than conventional computing systems.

This type of computing is an emerging field of scientific research from the last four decades, being developed in universities, research centers, companies, government entities, and the military. Among the technological products that will benefit from neuromorphic computing are next-generation semiconductors and transistors, particle accelerators, autonomous systems such as drones, robotics, and self-driving cars, as well as deep learning and artificial intelligence. Neuromorphic processors are expected to offer an alternative to comply with Moore's Law, which recent technology has struggled to maintain [5]. In the case of artificial intelligence, when applied to computers, it will allow systems to achieve understanding and learning like a human being.

Through hardware that mimics the structures, processes, and capacities of the neurons and synapses of a human brain and nervous system, neuromorphic computing processes and maintains data using artificial synaptic devices. These devices model or simulate neuronal activity [5]. Electrical signals that mimic brain signals are transferred by analog rather than digital circuits to measure and detect discrete changes in the signals related to their amplitude, frequency, and phase. The set of nodes that connect the artificial neurons, mimicking the nervous structure of a human being, is known as an artificial neural network (ANN). Connections in the synapse transmit signals between neurons. Once a signal is received in a neuron, it must be processed and sent to another connected destination neuron.

Traditional Von Neumann architecture computers separate processing and memory units and use binary values to encode data. Both power consumption and data processing speed are compromised due to the increased amount of data to be manipulated, leading to slow response speeds and increased power consumption [5]. In contrast, neuromorphic computers utilize each neuron to process and store information, perform massively parallel computations, and are inherently scalable. They conduct event-driven computations, exhibit high adaptability and flexibility, and have significant fault tolerance. However, neuromorphic computing faces issues such as precision problems, high costs and complexity, limited algorithms and software, low accessibility, lack of standards, and incomplete knowledge of brain processes. Due to the poor reliability and repeatability of conventional materials and the technical problems associated with excessively large-scale production, researchers continue to search for novel materials and topologies to overcome these challenges.

Artificial intelligence is defined as the set of both cognitive and intellectual capabilities achieved by hardware and software to imitate human intelligence and perform tasks optimized through exhaustive use of information [6]. The goal of artificial intelligence research is to achieve human-like computational capabilities using machines through neuromorphic computing. Without the development of hardware to implement neural networks, artificial intelligence (AI) systems—capable of performing numerous parallel operations in a repetitive manner—would not be possible [7]. The fundamental operations of a neural network are addition, multiplication, and calculation of the activation function. The weights or multiplicative factors between the input and output values are stored in random memory cells. During computations in a neural network, the following events occur: data retrieval from memory, data transfer to the computational core, computation performance, and sending the results to memory via the data bus. These events, applied to large data sets stored in memory, lead to excessive power consumption and reduced computational speed. Massive amounts of data must be stored and computed during processes such as virtual reality, the Internet of Things (IoT), and autonomous driving.

The memristor, as a passive circuit element, can convert the electric charge circulating in it into a magnetic flux, resulting in a variable resistor behavior controlled by the electric charge that can be retained without power [1]. The electrical conductivity of a memristor is a function of the voltage and/or current applied across its terminals. In the past decade, researchers worldwide have discovered that many nanometer-sized materials exhibit memristive properties through different physical mechanisms for switching their electrical conductivity [7]. These mechanisms involve nanomechanical memory, phase change memory, thermochemical effect, valence change effect, electrochemical metallization cell, electrostatic effects, ferroelectric effects, and magnetoresistive memory effects.

The use of the memristor in neuromorphic computing offers two options: for peak neural networks or as a vector–matrix multiplier in memories [7]. To achieve a change in electrical resistance in conventional memristors, functional layer materials are regularly used for data storage.

These materials are generally based on traditional oxide materials including titanium dioxide (TiO_2), hafnium oxide (HfO_x), tantalum oxide (Ta_2O_5), tungsten oxide (WO_x), and titanium nitride (TiN)-hafnium zirconium oxide-indium gallium zinc oxide (IGZO) (TiN/ZHO/IGZO) [1]. In an artificial biological synapse, the computational weight influences the resistive change produced in the memristor [4]. Reducing the thickness of a conventional dielectric in a memristor to the nanometer range results in a loss of stability due to the leakage currents.

14.3 Advantages of Two-Dimensional Materials Used in Neuromorphic Computing

Since the application of mechanical exfoliation as a graphene synthesis process in 2004, two-dimensional materials have attracted researchers to exploit their physicochemical properties and electronic structure in various technological and scientific fields [1, 4]. Depending on their electrical properties, two-dimensional materials can behave as conductors, semiconductors, or insulators. These materials, including graphene and its derivatives, transition metal dichalcogenides (TMDs), carbonitrides (MXenes), phosphorene or black phosphorus (BP), bismuthene, hexagonal boron nitride (*h*-BN), and organic 2D materials, are being used to implement vertical and lateral memristor devices with promising operational results. For the implementation of memristors, the most commonly used transition metal dichalcogenides are tungsten disulfide (WS_2), molybdenum sulfide (MoS_2), tungsten diselenide (WSe_2), and molybdenum ditelluride ($MoTe_2$) [8]. The primary functions of two-dimensional materials in memristors are as electrodes or as dielectric materials to perform resistive switching (RS), which depends on the electrical properties of the material used to optimize the best operation of the van der Waals (vDW) layers, placed either vertically or laterally [1]. The switching mechanism can be based on the use of ionic filaments, entrapment and detrapment, or atomic vacancy. The main two-dimensional materials used for the implementation of neuromorphic devices are shown in Figure 14.2.

Tungsten disulfide (WS_2), a transition metal dichalcogenide, exhibits a bandgap with tunable semiconductor properties and operates under vacancy mechanisms of its constituent elements that make up the functional and electron-hopped material to produce resistive switching (RS) [1]. Molybdenum ditelluride ($MoTe_2$) utilizes its polymorphism to exploit the conductive phase shift when subjected to electric fields, also resulting in

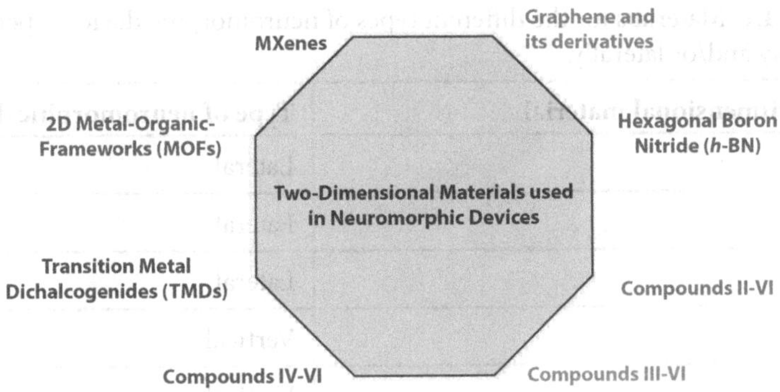

Figure 14.2 Two-dimensional materials for neuromorphic devices.

resistive switching [1]. Hexagonal boron nitride (*h*-BN) is used in memristors to decrease power dissipation in memory devices, facilitate mechanical bending, protect the device from ambient moisture, increase transparency, and prevent diffusion of oxygen. Phosphorene or black phosphorus can be leveraged due to its conduction bands induced by mechanical deformation, negative Poisson ratio, perpendicular topological behavior, and outstanding optical response [1]. Two-dimensional gallium selenide (GaSe), with its direct and indirect bandgaps, can generate terahertz signals and be used in optoelectronic devices and nonlinear optics to produce memories with large switching ratios, long retention times, high wear resistance, and low electric field threshold. Some two-dimensional materials with a perovskite structure based on organic lead halides exploit the simplicity and low costs of the processes, high charge mobility, and high light absorption coefficient to generate and fracture ionic filaments polarized by electric fields to produce resistive switching required by neuromorphic computing devices [1]. Hybrid and organic two-dimensional materials offer better flexibility and compatibility than their inorganic counterparts and are therefore preferred for wearable electronic devices and even for replacing biological-type neural networks [4]. Out-of-plane polarization leads to neuromorphic devices operating vertically, while in-plane polarization allows devices to be implemented laterally. Table 14.1 summarizes the two-dimensional materials used in vertical and lateral neuromorphic devices.

Two-dimensional materials offer a novel technological alternative to reduce power consumption and device thickness in neuromorphic computing [1, 2, 4]. These materials provide high performance in achieve resistive switching compared to conventional materials, prompting numerous research groups worldwide to optimize memristor design based on

Table 14.1 Materials for the different types of neuromorphic devices operating vertically and/or laterally.

Two-dimensional material	Type of neuromorphic device
GaSe	Lateral
SnS	Lateral
SnTe	Lateral
SnSe	Vertical
WS_2	Vertical
WTe_2	Vertical
d1T-$MoTe_2$	Vertical
MoS_2	Vertical
$CuInP_2S_6$	Vertical
BA_2PbCl_4	Lateral
α-In_2S_3	Lateral and/or Vertical
β'-In_2S_3	Lateral
2H α-In_2S_3	Lateral and/or Vertical
Phosphorene	Vertical
Graphene	Vertical
MXene	Vertical
h-BN	Vertical
2D-Metal-Organic Frameworks (MOFs)	Lateral

two-dimensional materials. Researchers continuously propose various alternatives for both electrodes and the switching layer, ranging from simple monolayers to heterostructures with different bandgap values and optical properties capable of producing multiple states during the resistive state transition through very diverse mechanisms [1, 2, 4, 8–24]. Examples of memristor structures include Ag/MoS_2/Ag, Ag/*h*-BN/Au, Pd/WS_2/Pt, Ag/MoS_2/Pt, Ag/SnS/Pt, Pd/Cr/Si/graphene/Cr/Pd, Au/$HfSe_2$/Ti, and Ag/BP/ITO [24]. While most memristors implemented to date are two-terminal devices, multi-terminal devices are also possible, increasing the versatility of applications made possible by innovative designs using two-dimensional materials.

Lateral resistive random-access memories (RRAM) consist of three layers in a sandwich structure made up of a metal layer, a functional material layer, and another metal layer using a planar geometry like that of a hybrid transistor as, illustrated in Figure 14.3 [1]. Two-dimensional materials are used as the functional layer due to their high optical transparency, high mechanical flexibility, and low manufacturing cost. When two-dimensional materials like graphene are used in a multilayer system with high electrical conductivity, they can serve as electrodes in memristors. The possibility of functionalizing two-dimensional materials is even considered a way to increase electrical conductivity. The use of two-dimensional heterogeneous layered structures is feasible for producing durable, repeatable bipolar resistive switching at high operating temperatures. Thanks to two-dimensional materials, it is possible to achieve memristors that are tunable, stable, and present reliable resistive switching (RS) [4]. So far, two-dimensional materials allow memristor on/off ratios comparable to traditional memristors. Researchers are investigating the possibility of increasing these ratios to optimize synaptic devices for processing large amounts of data at high speeds. Conventional memristors exhibit better retention and endurance than their counterparts based on nanometric Van der Waals layers. However, the use of hybrid materials containing organic and inorganic components, as well as 2D/3D and 2D/2D heterostructures, promises to improve the poor performance of monolayer versions of the two-dimensional materials.

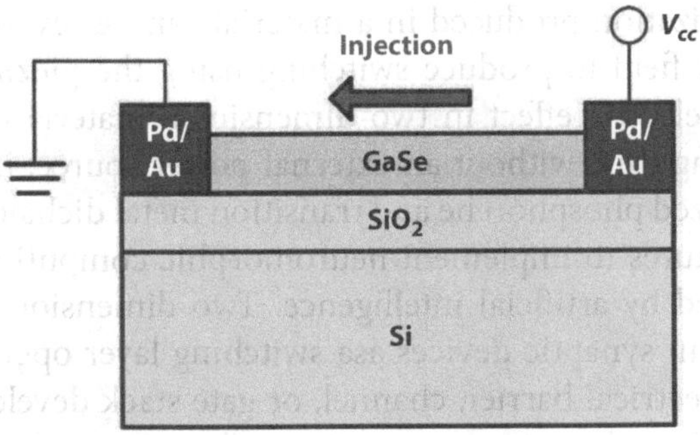

Figure 14.3 Cross-section through a lateral-operated resistive random-access memory (RRAM).

14.4 Devices Implemented with Two-Dimensional Materials to Evolve Artificial Intelligence

The von Neumann architecture was suitable for initial investigations into developing neuromorphic computing through conventional technologies for basic artificial intelligence applications. However, due to the demands on both speed and size of information structures, it is no longer feasible to continue using conventional materials [8]. In the implementation of next-generation artificial neurons and synapses for neuromorphic computing, two-dimensional materials are used as functional materials in the design of transistors, memories based on ferroelectric materials, and resistive switching memristors.

Among the significant advances so far is the design of artificial neurons using Gaussian heterojunction transistors (GHeTs) with dual gates [9]. These transistors use heterojunction switching material based on a chemically deposited molybdenum disulfide monolayer with an embedded array of carbon nanotubes to emulate ion channels that generate the input signals for neurons. These devices, with full tunability of the transfer curve, can generate peak responses, including delayed peaks, phasic peaks, and tonic bursting, which are useful for the implementation of neural networks in artificial intelligence. Two-dimensional ferroelectric materials can serve as semiconductor materials in the implementation of field-effect transistors, acting as a channel layer to improve the integration density of the devices despite their low spontaneous polarization and large area requirement [10].

Through two-dimensional ferroelectric materials in non-volatile memories, it is possible to implement artificial synapses for neuronal emulation [8]. Ferroelectric materials exploit the possibility that the spontaneous electrical polarization produced in a material can be reversible under an applied electric field to produce switching using the piezoelectric effect. Since the ferroelectric effect in two-dimensional materials can be maintained for a long time without an external power source, it is possible to use functionalized phosphorene and transition metal dichalcogenides with distorted structures to implement neuromorphic computing devices that can be exploited by artificial intelligence. Two-dimensional ferroelectric materials used in synaptic devices asa switching layer operate as a polarization layer, electrical barrier, channel, or gate stack developing synaptic plasticity based on long-term potentiation/long-term depression (LTP/LTD), spike-timing-dependent plasticity (STDP), paired-pulse facilitation/paired-pulse depression (PPF/PPD), excitatory postsynaptic current

(ESPC), short-term synaptic plasticity (STP), spike-amplitude dependent plasticity (SADP), spike-rate-dependent plasticity (SRDP), or induced pluripotent stem cell (iPSC). The main two-dimensional materials with ferroelectric properties are tungsten ditelluride (WTe_2), *alpha* phase-indium selenide (α-In_2Se_3), copper indium thiophosphate $CuInP_2S_6$ (CIPS), and molybdenum ditelluride ($MoTe_2$).

Through ferroelectric materials in non-volatile memories, it is feasible to achieve extremely low power consumption, multiple states of stable polarization, higher density, fast switching speeds, and ultra-fast write and/or speed, which are required for neuromorphic computing applications [11]. Two-dimensional materials contribute to high compatibility with CMOS technology and electronic tunability. These materials that are not inherently ferroelectric can be converted to ferroelectric through defect engineering, surface modification, strain engineering, and doping. The advantage of converted materials lies in their ability to integrate into substrates through strong intralayer coupling and weak interlayer interaction. In addition, they can avoid the degradation caused by charge trapping in conventional materials, which reduces the performance of neuromorphic devices used in neural networks for artificial intelligence.

The use of heterostructures based on three layers: metal, insulator, and metal, has allowed the implementation of memristive devices, which have become the fundamental design block of artificial neural networks (ANN). Two different types of memristors using two-dimensional materials can be designed: lateral memristors and vertical memristors. The type of memristor implemented depends on the stacking order of the van der Waals layers used as well as the location of the electrodes in the device [4]. In the case of lateral devices, it is possible to control the field effect through a gate terminal that is available due to the implementation of the device. Through a vertical memristor, it is possible to use low switching voltages due to the reduced distance between electrodes on the order of nanometers or below nanometers thanks to the use of thin films, such as two-dimensional materials. To achieve reliable and stable resistive states, it is necessary to use ultra-low set and reset voltages in vertical memristors. To date, implementations for the design of memristors has been based on the integration of heterostructures between two-dimensional materials, two-dimensional and three-dimensional structures, and two-dimensional hybrid structures. Using two-dimensional materials, it is feasible to implement devices and systems that allow the development of essential neural functions, including spike time-dependent plasticity (STDP), short- and/or long-term memory (STM/LTM), and paired-pulse facilitation (PPF) [2].

Graphene is used to implement electrodes and a protective material was placed between them and the switching layer to provide stability to the memristor [2]. The switching layer is based on molybdenum disulfide (MoS_2) functionalized with molybdenum oxide (MoO_3), which functions as a variable resistor. The resistor was deposited on a sandwich formed by two layers of dielectric material based on hexagonal boron nitride (*h*-BN) with graphene as a semi-metallic interlayer. This material is deposited on a thin film of silicon dioxide (SiO_2) that separates the memristor from the rest of the devices mounted on a silicon wafer. Figure 14.4 illustrates the cross-section of a neural device with lateral and vertical operations, where a set of multiple layers is used to implement the device.

A two-dimensional material that has recently been introduced for use in neuromorphic computing is the metal-organic framework [12]. These materials mimic the learning and memory functions of the nervous system because of their ability to trap charge due to their multiple accessible active sites, stable crystalline structure, and high specific surface area. Among the stimulus signals to achieve synaptic behaviors in these neuromorphic devices are long-term memory, short-term memory, excitatory postsynaptic current, and paired-pulse facilitation. Metal-organic frameworks (MOFs) are crystal lattices composed of organic bonds as well as clusters and/or metal ions. MOFs as resistive switching layers allow memristors to have higher erasure speed, better endurance, improved mechanical flexibility, proper compatibility, etc. [25]. The possibility of combining organic and inorganic properties makes it possible to synergistically combine the advantages of self-assembly as well as that of ions or clusters for excellent

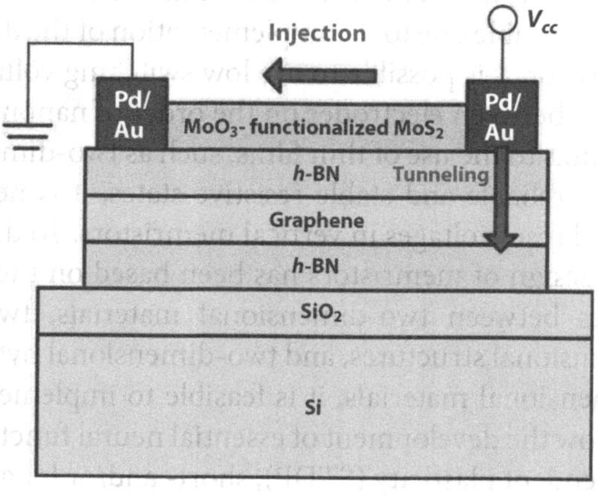

Figure 14.4 Cross-section of a vertical/lateral synaptic device using two-dimensional materials.

performance in memristor design. Some expected qualities of memristors fabricated using MOFs are long-term stability, resistive state regulation, and low power consumption. Using MOFs, it is possible to obtain conduction mechanisms such as spatial conduction by π conjugation, conduction by chemical bonds, and organic conduction. In addition, MOFs offer unique properties such as void filling of the structure to increase electrical conductivity, which allows for smooth pathways for selective ion penetration and migration.

Artificial neural networks (ANNs) through previously described neuromorphic devices based on transistors, memristors, and ferroelectric memory devices implemented with two-dimensional materials can perform high-level and low-level information processing [12]. Neuromorphic devices allow full control of freedom and facilitate the implementation of various complex neural and synaptic functions. Therefore, a system that mimics both the architecture and the operating principle of the brain should be based on such neuromorphic computing devices. Therefore, the hardware developed to emulate a neural system can use synaptic modulation techniques to perform neuromorphic computation. The term synaptic plasticity refers to the relationship between the information storage and learning functions of two adjacent neurons in the human brain. In the trained neural network, a supervised learning algorithm is used because the data are properly labeled.

In the implementation of artificial synapses for neuromorphic computation, the use of van der Waals heterostructures allows tuning of neural functions [13–16]. The metallic materials regularly used in the implementation of electrodes in these nanometric devices are silver (Ag), gold (Au), palladium (Pd), and platinum (Pt) [14]. The use of more than one two-dimensional material in the functional material of the neuromorphic device allows the possibility of achieving band modulation that can be used as a means of wireless transmission through the potentiation and depression of voltage in the form of pulses applied to the device electrodes. This effect can be exploited in resistive random-access memories (RRAM) to store information at artificial synapses for ANNs. The complex biological functions where associative learning and long-term memorization are used imply that it is necessary to modulate interneuron actions where more than two nerve signals are executed through plasticity based on multiple heterogeneous synapses. In a heterostructure, it is feasible to use two or more layers of different two-dimensional materials stacked to increase the functionality of neuromorphic devices for various applications. Heterostructures based on two-dimensional materials exhibit electron confinement in at least one dimension, depending on their chemical composition and crystal structure [16]. These structures have applications in neuromorphic electronics, spintronics, and optoelectronics. Through two-dimensional materials, it is possible to implement computation-in-memory as well as memristors for neuromorphic computing applications, making them suitable for integration into silicon CMOS processes, which have been widely used for many decades by the global electronics industry [15].

Resistive random-access memories (RRAMs) store data by reducing power consumption, low cost, high-switching speed, high endurance, and high information retention [17]. Because the size of transistors is already in the nanometer range and tends to be subnanometer, it is important to design devices in which the use of quantum properties, such as quantum tunneling, is feasible. It is expected that two-dimensional materials will overcome the great challenges of traditional materials in terms of bandwidth, power consumption, retention time, data storage, endurance, and switching speed. During resistive switching, the dielectric material must change its resistance from low to high (OFF/ON) and vice versa (ON/OFF) using the electric field applied between its terminals at the operating speed of the non-volatile memory. Thus far, both transition metal oxides and dichalcogenides (TMDs) have optical and electrical properties suitable for the implementation of artificial synapses. Doping ferroelectric materials reduces the power consumption by controlling the number of carriers during state transitions, where the electric current increases or decreases suddenly. The use of TMDs facilitates light-controlled resistive switching, which is useful for image recognition performed by humans, making it feasible to achieve 98.6% accuracy using two-dimensional materials.

The strategic advantages from the artificial biological synaptic point of view of two-dimensional materials in the implementation of neuromorphic computing devices are their thickness at the atomic level and the reduced flickering effect, both of which modulate neural stimuli [18]. Artificial intelligence applications such as big data processing, feature extraction, image recognition, pattern recognition, reinforcement learning, and machine learning require energy-efficient neuromorphic devices designed using two-dimensional materials. In a neural network, each neuron has the possibility of connecting with thousands of different neurons through dendrites; thus, the synaptic connection represented by the neuromorphic devices must react to stimuli coming from the transistors that will be sent to be stored and processed through non-volatile memories and memristors and processors, respectively. With the application of two-dimensional ferromagnetic materials that control spin in the gate and two-dimensional ferroelectric materials that experience polarization under electric fields, the implementation of heterosynaptic devices is feasible.

The applications of artificial intelligence with a focus on large amounts of data are, among others, entertainment, security, medicine, transportation, and the Internet of Things (IoT) [19]. Implementing artificial intelligence requires not only the design of neuromorphic computing devices but also digital electronics and Boolean algebra devices compatible with the speed, compatibility, and capabilities of two-dimensional material-based designs. In short, future computing systems will be supported by electronic circuits, spintronics, and memristors designed with van der Waals materials. Feasibly it is possible to appropriate the coexistence and complementarity with other emerging technologies and with conventional systems to make devices based on synaptic devices a technology that will be adopted for commercial application in various technological sectors with high added value.

The possibility of exploiting the optical properties of memristors allows the application of photonic integrated circuits with active tuning, as well as their adjustment and reprogramming without continuous power consumption [12]. An optical memristor switches between nonvolatile states by modulating the light amplitude applied to its switching layer. Optical memristors increase the storage, retrieval, and processing speeds, which are geared toward parallel processing and reduce power consumption. These devices are feasible for developing both human brain-like systems and artificial synapses with non-volatile storage capabilities and non-linear output replicas that offer long-term plasticity for synapses, leading to replicas more like natural biomimetic versions. Optical memristors exploit the high bandwidth and ultra-high operating speed of light for information processing in neuromorphic computing, artificial intelligence, and machine learning.

The multifunctionality associated with two-dimensional materials allows more than two physical properties to be used synergistically in the design of optical memristors. For example, a memristor modulated by light modulation can produce a photo response and provide data storage capability [21]. Phosphorene possesses broad-spectrum light absorption capacity in the visible range as well as a natural forward band, so it can be used in the design of light-modulated multi-color memristors. This memristor is made of a sandwich of outer layers of indium tin oxide (ITO) and an inner layer of a composite material based on polystyrene (PS) and black phosphorus (BP) or phosphorene nanosheets, as shown in Figure 14.5. The device exhibits a transmittance greater than 75% for light in the range of 350–1,100 nm. The voltage that biases the memristor is applied between the ITO layers. A functional composite material that operates as a resistive switch has no initial preforming, exhibits a long retention time, and operates

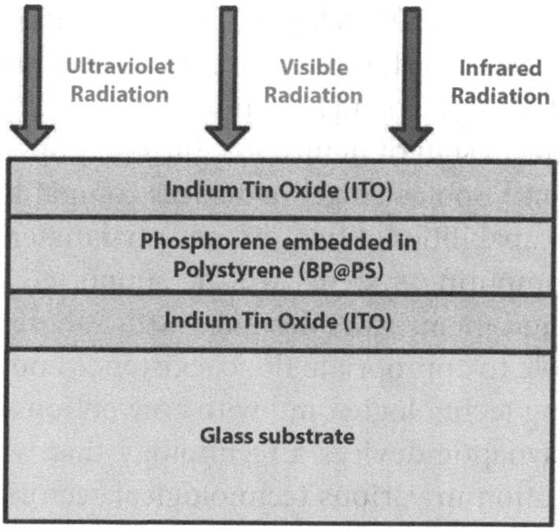

Figure 14.5 Memristor based on light modulation using phosphorene.

at low voltages. During the high-resistance state, the device behaves like an Ohmic contact, whereas in the low-impedance state, it behaves like a Schottky contact. Under ultraviolet radiation, there is low resistance, and as the optical spectrum is covered, the resistance increases, which reduces power consumption and reset voltage. The insertion of phosphorene as a functional material increased the on/off ratio of the memristor. In this way, modulated light as an input stimulus allows it to operate under different resistive states, which leads to the possibility of multi-level data storage in the same neuromorphic computing device depending on the applied wavelength. These operational advantages make memristors multifunctional devices and reduce electronic circuitry and power conversion losses from optical to electrical and vice versa. The use of almost transparent materials also enables the use of these devices in applications that require touch screens by not using opaque conductors.

An important task of artificial intelligence is unsupervised learning, which requires fast and reliable neuromorphic devices [22]. For this type of activity, it is required to perform resistive switching as well as multiple accumulation operations, which can be implemented using crossbar arrays of MXene-based memristors. In turn, this type of design allows the development of target tracking using average displacement algorithms that are applicable to neuromorphic computing. In unsupervised learning, the use of unlabeled data leads to the neuromorphic computing system having to identify specific features and unknown patterns. For the implementation of neuromorphic computing systems, crossbar arrangements are used that require a non-volatile and continuously modifiable memory device at each crossing point to perform accumulation and weight application operations for learning algorithms. Among the main building blocks of such computing systems are charge trapping and ion gate transistors, ferroelectric devices, phase-change memories, and memristors. The most recent systems use memristors as elements for training and accumulation operations, as shown in Figure 14.6. They support CMOS fabrication technology, and the presence of multiple resistance states or operating points.

Xenes are functional materials with unique physical, chemical, optical, and electronic properties. The application of Xenes (antimonene (Sb), arsenene (As), bismuthene (Bi), borophene (B), germanene (Ge), phosphorene (P), silicene (Si), stanene (Sn), and tellurene (Te)) with intrinsic oxidation layers in the design of memristors has the potential to extend their dynamic range as well as multi-bit storage [20]. They can be used in the energy, electronics, healthcare, and environmental sectors. As with other two-dimensional materials, its technological applications have expanded because of the possibility of tuning its electrical properties through the control of its band gap and the use of functional groups on its surface. Their versatility is increased when used in conjunction with other

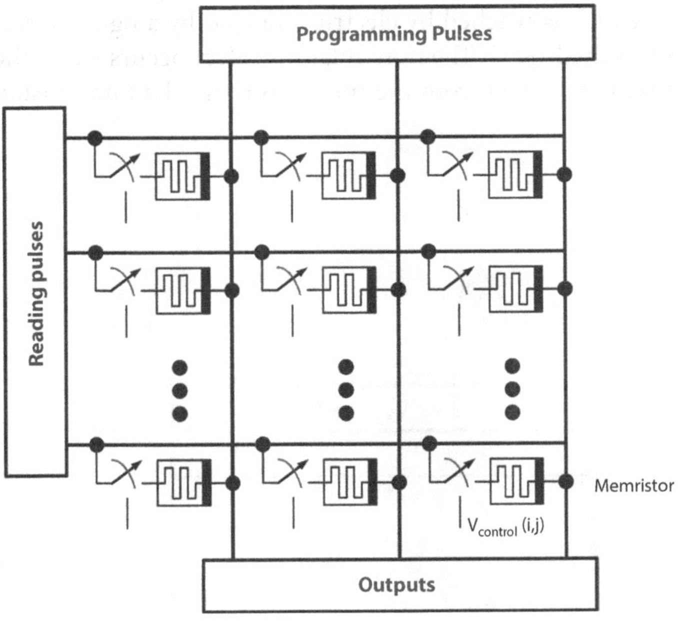

Figure 14.6 A crossbar based on memristors.

two-dimensional or functional materials when applications take advantage of specific heterostructures, expanding the individual intrinsic properties of each component, and giving rise to unique synergies.

MXenes are attractive functional materials due to their unique crystalline structure and useful electrochemical behavior for electronic applications [23]. For energy storage applications, MXenes can be easily functionalized, and their tunable interlayer spacing. Vanadium carbide (V_2C) is a two-dimensional material that has been used to fabricate a memristor with a structure based on silver-vanadium carbide-titania-tungsten ($Ag/V_2C/TiO_2/W$), as illustrated in Figure 14.7. Among the advantages of V_2C are the introduction of a volatile switching threshold, low-set-voltage, low-reset-voltage, and low cycle-to-cycle and device-to-device variations. In this device, the main switching mechanism is associated with a current limitation caused by the spatial electrical charge, which can be stored in two-dimensional and dielectric materials. The possibility of tuning the direct electrical bias current allows implementation of volatile or a non-volatile devices using the same materials. In these neuromorphic devices, it is possible to emulate different behaviors depending on the sign of the applied polarization, either to boost (positive) or depress (negative) neuronal activity.

The basic transition states of a memristor can be high (HRS) or low (LRS) resistance, which is reached by electrical bias or by a light source applied across its terminals [24]. The non-volatility effect occurs when the bias or illumination is removed from the memristor and the low-resistance state

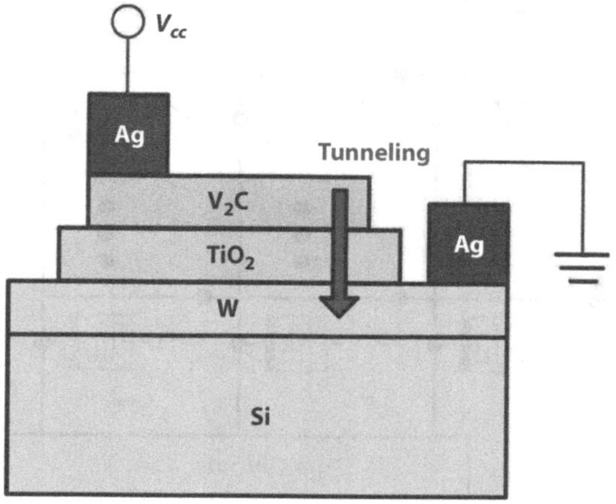

Figure 14.7 Cross-section of an MXene-based memristor used in a low-power synapse.

is maintained, which allows the use of a "1" and "0" scheme of operation as in a digital device. During the operation of a memristor as an artificial synapse, it should be possible to achieve short- or long-term plasticity for artificial intelligence applications. Through the heterostructures, potential barriers can be tuned, more dielectrics can be inserted to introduce gates, and even layers can be included to store electrical charges, which is not feasible in the case of monolayers. Care must be taken because the inclusion of multiple layers can lead to chemical contamination from the stacking and transfer processes of the layers. Despite all the advances achieved thus far, no device to date has achieved all the desired operating parameters; thus, new devices should achieve the highest number of ideal performance parameters presented in Table 14.2.

Neuromorphic computing is expected to improve the performance of smart devices, self-driving cars, and advanced robot control in the coming years. Humans will use computers to think like us and solve very complex problems to establish a new era of technological development and offer innovative solutions for artificial intelligence. It is expected that computing move from neuromorphic to cognitive to exploit images, audio, and text in databases, which will make artificial intelligence a reality without data types. Through this innovation, it is hoped that activities will be developed without human intervention and that humans will have other capacities not inherent to human beings. The latter will lead to increasing processing capabilities, improving efficiency, and reducing costs by using AI in all technological sectors.

Table 14.2 Ideal parameters for a memristor based on two-dimensional materials.

Parameter	**Ideal value**
On/off ratio	$>10^{11}$
Set voltage	<0.05V
Retention	$>10^{5}$ s
Endurance	$>10^{7}$ cycles
Switching speed	>0.67 GHz
Power consumption	<1 fW
Energy consumption	<8.8 zJ

14.5 Future Research Directions

Innovation in memristors designed with two-dimensional materials should be directed at increasing performance through good endurance and retention, lowering the switching voltage, increasing the switching ratio, lowering the power consumption, as well as setting/reset voltages and expanding the applications, as shown in Figure 14.8. Although significant advances have been made, technological research and development associated with optimizing memristor performance will ensure that both neuromorphic computing and data storage can be developed for high-density applications, which are required for the practical application of artificial intelligence.

Although advances in the implementation of artificial intelligence using electronic devices designed using two-dimensional materials have been achieved, enormous challenges must be overcome to achieve the expected performance in neuromorphic computing systems [4]. In particular, the need to synthesize high-quality, large-area two-dimensional monolayers or heterostructures makes it imperative that these characteristics are achieved through optimized synthesis processes and transfer technologies, which are still in the development stage. One of the great challenges that the application of two-dimensional materials presents is to achieve ideal interfaces between the layers that make up the electronic device because its performance is reduced by not transferring or confining available electrons from one layer of material to another. The use of doping in devices with increasingly smaller thicknesses requires the development of new models to estimate the most appropriate strategies to achieve effective and stable contributions to physical performance in the operation of nanoscale devices. The enormous variability in performance that can occur in

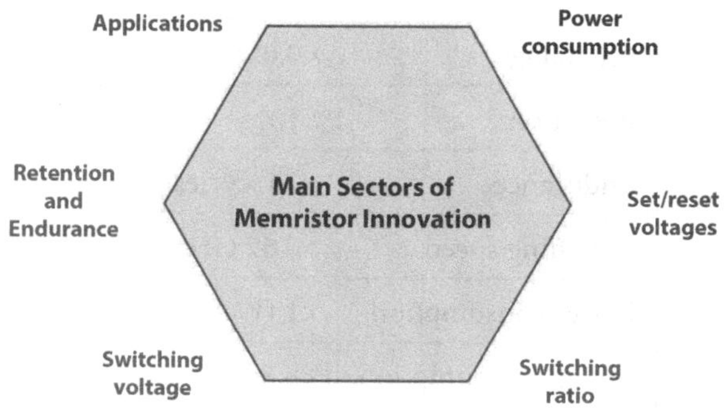

Figure 14.8 Main sectors of memristor innovation.

memristive materials for resistive state switching must be reduced or eliminated to bring the implementation of these devices to a commercial level. These aspects are expected to be achieved in this decade. Achieving the operation and performance of biological synapses requires scientists to develop high-speed, energy-efficient, multiterminal, and multifunctional synaptic devices. Additionally, the compatibility of devices synthesized using two-dimensional materials with the manufacturing processes of traditional semiconductor technology continues to be a challenge to its widespread use in commercial processes. The improvement of the previous aspects will allow the application of two-dimensional materials for the design of electronic systems and circuits in high-density applications. In addition to hardware for the design of artificial neural networks (ANN), the structure and corresponding algorithm must also be optimized to be adapted to novel synaptic devices developed using two-dimensional materials to implement artificial intelligence applications.

In the case of memristors, either optically modulated or fully optically controlled, they can be used in high-speed applications, but their implementation is still at laboratory test levels, so research must be matured to reach biological synapses that allow the mimicry and implementation of neural networks with the capacity to handle large amounts of data. Through the implementation of optical memristors, it is feasible to develop neuromorphic devices that can be applied to artificial intelligence, machine learning, and broad-bandwidth neuromorphic computing; therefore, new materials and new topologies of these devices should be implemented in the following decades. However, scalability in memory devices and neuromorphic computing devices remains a challenge because it is difficult to guarantee large-scale reliability and repeatability, power consumption, programming speed, and high storage density. The use of optically operating devices should exploit the multi-gate tuning design for applications in the implementation of neuromorphic vision systems, which could broaden the possibilities of artificial intelligence applications.

14.6 Summary

In this chapter, an overview has been provided of the advantages of implementing neuromorphic devices using two-dimensional materials to design artificial neural networks as hardware for AI-based solutions. Depending on the use of injection or tunneling currents, devices can be designed to operate laterally or vertically, using either a monolayer of two-dimensional materials or a vertically stacked Van der Waals heterostructure.

Two-dimensional materials with ferroelectric properties enable the design of transistors, memristors, or non-volatile memories as neuromorphic devices, offering significant advantages over conventional materials. These materials allow the combination of optical capabilities with current and future information processing techniques, increasing the feasibility of previously unimaginable devices that will make AI applications a reality in countless high-value-added solutions. Despite the significant advances provided by two-dimensional materials, their application in artificial intelligence needs optimization, both in novel and optimized designs based on materials and topologies, to achieve large-scale, commercial physical implementation. In the coming decades, researchers worldwide will continue to optimize the performance of neuromorphic devices using two-dimensional materials for various AI applications that handle large amounts of data.

Acknowledgments

The author is grateful for the support of the Universidad de Guanajuato in the development of this scientific research and thanks his family for their support during the time required to complete it. He also appreciates the support of the researchers who shared their articles for this study.

References

1. Zhao, Q., Xie, Z., Peng, Y.-P., Wang, K., Wang, H., Li, X., Wang, H., Chen, J., Zhang, H., Yan, X., Current Status and Prospects of Memristor based on Novel 2D Materials. *Mater. Horiz.*, 7, 6, 1495–1518, 2020.
2. Pan, X., Zheng, Y., Shi, Y., Chen, W., Surface Charge Transfer Doping Enabled Large Hysteresis in van der Waals Heterostructure for Artificial Synapse. *ACS Mater. Lett.*, 3, 2, 235–242, 2021.
3. Vogelstein, R.J., Mallik, U., Vogelstein, J.T., Cauweberghs, G., Dynamically Reconfigurable Silicon Array of Spiking Neurons with Conductance-based Synapses. *IEEE Trans. Neural Netw.*, 18, 1, 253–265, 2007.
4. Liao, K., Lei, P., Tu, M., Luo, S., Jiang, T., Jie, W., Hao, J., Memristor based on Inorganic and Organic Two-Dimensional Materials: Mechanisms, Performance, and Synaptic Applications. *ACS Appl. Mater. Interfaces*, 13, 28, 32606–32623, 2021.
5. Ham, D., Park, H., Hwang, S., Kim, K., Neuromorphic Electronics based on Copying and Pasting the Brain. *Nat. Electron.*, 4, 635–644, 2021.

6. Russell, S.J. and Norvig, P., *Artificial Intelligence: A Modern Approach*, Fourth Edition, pp. 19–23, Pearson, Harlow, United Kingdom, 2021.
7. Ivanov, D., Chezhegov, A., Kiselev, M., Grunin, A., Larionov, D., Neuromorphic Artificial Intelligence Systems. *Front. Neurosci.*, 16, 959626, 2022.
8. Bian, J., Cao, Z., Zhou, P., Neuromorphic Computing: Devices, Hardware, and System Application Facilitated by Two-Dimensional Materials. *Appl. Phys. Rev.*, 8, 4, 041313, 2021.
9. Beck, M.E., Shylendra, A., Sangwan, V.K., Gaviria Rojas, W.A., Yoo, H., Bergeron, H., Su, K., Trivedi, A.R., Hersam, M.C., Spiking Neurons from Tunable Gaussian Heterojunction Transistors. *Nat. Commun.*, 11, 1565, 2020.
10. Zhang, Z., Yang, D., Li, H., Li, C., Wang, Z., Sun, L., Yang, H., 2D Materials and van der Waals Heterojunctions for Neuromorphic Computing. *Neuromorph. Comput. Eng.*, 2, 3, 032004, 2022.
11. Chen, L., Pam, M.E., Li, S., Ang, K.-W., Ferroelectric Memory based on Two-Dimensional Materials for Neuromorphic Computing. *Neuromorph. Comput. Eng.*, 2, 2, 022001, 2022.
12. Liu, D., Shi, Q., Zhang, J., Tian, L., Xiong, L., Dai, S., Huang, J., 2D Metal-Organic Framework based Optoelectronic Neuromorphic Transistors for Human Emotion Simulation and Neuromorphic Computing. *Adv. Intell. Syst.*, 4, 11, 2200164, 2022.
13. He, C., Tang, J., Shang, D.-S., Tang, J., Xi, Y., Wang, S., Li, N., Zhang, Q., Lu, J.-K., Wei, Z., Wang, Q., Shen, C., Li, J., Shen, S., Shen, J., Yang, R., Shi, D., Wu, H., Wang, S., Zhang, G., Artificial Synapse based on van der Waals Heterostructures with Tunable Synaptic Functions for Neuromorphic Computing. *ACS Appl. Mater. Interfaces*, 12, 10, 11945–11954, 2020.
14. Liu, P., Luo, H., Yin, X., Wang, X., He, X., Zhu, J., Xue, H., Mao, W., Pu, Y., A Memristor based on Two-Dimensional MoSe2/MoS2 Heterojunction for Synaptic Device Application. *Appl. Phys. Lett.*, 121, 23, 233501, 2022.
15. Lemme, M.C., Akinwande, D., Huyghebaert, C., Stampfer, C., 2D Materials for Future Heterogeneous Electronics. *Nat. Commun.*, 13, 1392, 2022.
16. Liang, S.-J., Li, Y., Cheng, B., Miao, F., Emerging Low-Dimensional Heterostructure Devices for Neuromorphic Computing. *Small Struct.*, 3, 10, 2200064, 2022.
17. Asif, M. and Kumar, A., Resistive Switching in Emerging Materials and Their Characteristics for Neuromorphic Computing. *Mater. Today Electron.*, 1, 100004, 2022.
18. Cao, G., Meng, P., Chen, J., Liu, H., Bian, R., Zhu, C., Liu, F., Liu, Z., 2D Material based Synaptic Devices for Neuromorphic Computing. *Adv. Funct. Mater.*, 31, 4, 2005443, 2021.
19. Joksas, D., AlMutairi, A., Lee, O., Cubukcu, M., Lombardo, A., Kurebayashi, H., Kenyon, A.J., Mehonic, A., Memristive, Spintronic, and 2D-Materials-based

Devices to Improve and Complement Computing Hardware. *Adv. Intell. Syst.*, 4, 8, 2200068, 2022.
20. Tao, W., Kong, N., Ji, X., Zhang, Y., Sharma, A., Ouyang, J., Qi, B., Wang, J., Xie, N., Kang, C., Zhang, H., Farokhad, O.C., Kim, J.S., Emerging Two-Dimensional Monoelemental Materials (Xenes) for Biomedical Applications. *Chem. Soc. Rev.*, 48, 11, 2891–2912, 2019.
21. Zhou, Y., Liu, D., Wang, J., Cheng, Z., Liu, L., Yang, N., Liu, Y., Xia, T., Liu, X., Zhang, X., Ye, C., Xu, Z., Xiong, W., Chu, P.K., Yu, X.-F., Black Phosphorus based Multicolor Light-Modulated Transparent Memristor with Enhanced Resistive Switching Performance. *ACS Appl. Mater. Interfaces*, 12, 22, 25108–25114, 2020.
22. Wan, X., Xu, W., Zhang, M., He, N., Lian, X., Hu, E., Xu, J., Tong, Y., Unsupervised Learning implemented by Ti3C2-MXene-based Memristive Neuromorphic System. *ACS Appl. Electron. Mater.*, 2, 11, 3497–3501, 2020.
23. He, N., Zhang, Q., Tao, L., Chen, X., Qin, Q., Liu, X., Lian, X., Wan, X., Hu, E., Xu, J., Xu, F., Tong, Y., V2C-based Memristor for Applications of Low Power Electronic Synapse. *IEEE Electron Device Lett.*, 42, 3, 319–322, 2021.
24. Duan, H., Cheng, S., Qin, L., Zhang, X., Xie, B., Zhang, Y., Jie, W., Low-Power Memristor based on Two-Dimensional Materials. *J. Phys. Chem. Lett.*, 13, 31, 7130–7138, 2022.
25. Shu, F., Chen, X., Yu, Z., Gao, P., Liu, G., Metal-Organic Frameworks-based Memristors: Materials, Devices, and Applications. *Molecules*, 27, 8888, 2022.

Index

Account reconciliation, 11
Accountability and transparency, 58–59
AI governance, 195, 196
AI in finance, 167, 168
Algo trader, 37
Algorithmic trading, 119
AmiBroker India, 34–35
Analytical models, 184, 188
Analyzing information, 94
Anti-money laundering (AML), 54, 116
APAC expension, 247
Appian, 244
Application areas, 169, 170
Application programming interface, 132, 276–278
Artificial intelligence (AI), 10, 65–77, 84, 109, 120, 142, 151, 155, 157, 160, 254, 287–291, 296–297, 300–302, 305–308
Artificial intelligence in Fintech, 124, 127, 128, 133
Artificial neural network (ANN), 289–290, 292, 299, 301
Assessment, 98
Augmentation and optimization, 114
Augmented analytics, 153–155
Automated financial services, 124, 125
Automatic civilization, 1
Automatic contact recognition, 113
Automation anywhere, 244, 246, 264
Automation gaps, 91–92
Automation in banking, 82
Automation startups, 244
Automation technology, 245, 250, 259
Autonomous finance, 1, 163–165, 168, 170, 199–199, 201

Bank reconciliation, 88
BankTech, 108
Base model, 240
Bibliometric, 66, 69–70
Big data, 93, 103, 107, 108, 179, 180
Biometrics, 176, 177
Bitcoin, 104–105, 275
Blockchain, 66, 104–105, 116, 120, 161–162, 176, 175
Blockchain technology, 10, 124, 128, 129, 132, 133, 277
Building trust, 61–62
Business tycoons, 244

Catch 22, 283
Chatbot automation, 84
Chatbots, 175, 176
Chief financial officer (CFO), 3
Cloud banking, 143–144
Cloud computing, 3, 155, 159, 162
Cloud computing in Fintech, 130
CMOS processes, 290, 299, 302, 305
Cognitive process automation, 243, 245
Consumer protection, 54–55
Core privacy and security issues, 46
Credit allocation, 118
Credit checks, 85

Credit Rating Information Services of India Limited (CRISIL), 280
Credit scoring, 68, 184, 188
Crypto-assets, 275
Cryptocurrency, 104
Cryptocurrency development, 125
Customer behavior analysis, 117
Customer lifecycle, 173, 174
Customer onboarding, 173, 174
Customer relationship management, 158
Customer security and privacy, 134, 135, 136
Cyberization, 145
Cybersecurity risks, 48–49

Data preprocessing, 231
Data privacy, 194, 195
Data privacy and security regulations, 53–54
Data security, 120
Data vulnerability, 47–48
Datascience, 101–102, 108–111, 114–115
Decision making, 66
Decision trees, 187, 188
Deep learning, 114, 200–202, 204
Deep learning using python, 38
Delinquency management, 176, 177
Demat accounts, 274
Deploy RPA, 97
Detecting fraud, 86–87
Digital financial inclusion, 129, 130
Digital lending application (DLA), 274
Digital process automation, 247
Digitization, 93
Discriminant analysis, 186, 187
Discrimination, 195
DSAI, 111–112, 114

EcoFin, 111–116
e-KYC, 277
eKYC, 176, 177
Enablers, 178, 180
Ensuring fairness, 51–52
Enterprise resource planning, 144
Equity financing, 107
e-RUPI, 275
eSignal, 30–31
Establish workflows, 97
Ethical considerations, 52
Ethics, 196, 197
Executing plan, 99

Ferroelectric materials, 293, 298–299, 310
Financial exchange ventures, 226
Financial modeling, 116
Financial services sector, 68
Fintech, 65–66, 70, 72, 101–115, 118–120, 269–288
Fintech applications overviews, 124, 125, 126, 127
Fintech ecosystem, 272–284
Fraud detection, 181, 182
Fraud prevention, 116
Freemium pricing model, 278
Fundamentals of operational risk, 55–56
Funding for Fintech, 134

Generative artificial intelligence, 144
Graphene, 289, 294–297, 300

Heterostructures, 296–297, 299, 301, 306–308
High-speed computing, 289, 297, 303, 309
Hybrid work, 95
Hyper automation, 244, 245

Impact, 176, 177
Information technology, 83
Insurance organizations, 83
InsureTech, 105
Insurtech, 272
Integrated model, 222

Intelligent automation, 245, 247
International operations and compliance, 55
Internet of Things, 66, 144, 148, 163
Investar, 29

Jan Dhan-Aadhaar-Mobile (J-A-M), 276

Key components, 172, 173
Key ethical issues, 57–58
KNN, 186, 187
Know your customer, 88
KOFAX, 244, 245, 264
KYC processes, 131, 135, 136

LendTech, 105
Linear regression, 229
Logistic regression, 184, 186

Machine learning, 14, 257
Machine learning approach, 221
Magnetic random-access memories (MRAMs), 290
Market growth, 244, 245, 259, 261, 263
Marketable distinction, 6
Marketplace, 145–148
Markov decision process, 204–208
Masterswift, 24
Maturity stages, 177, 179
MCA, 75
Memristors, 289–290, 293–310
Meta, 148–149
Metal-organic frameworks (MOFs), 295–296, 300
Metatrader, 25–26
Microfinance, 168, 170
ML in finance, 167, 168
Mobile payments, 104, 106
Money laundering, 84
Mortgage processing, 85–86
Motive wave, 27
Multiple regression, 222
MXenes, 289, 294–296, 304, 306

NARX neural network algorithm, 225
Natural language processing, 117, 153, 154, 158
Navigating legal frameworks, 52–53
NCMC (national common mobility card), 275
Neo-banking, 132
Neural network, 200–204, 208–213, 215–216
Neuromorphic computing, 289–295, 298–305, 307–309
NinjaTrader, 33
NonBanking Financial Companies (NBFC), 274–275
Non-volatile memory technologies, 290, 298–299, 302, 305, 310

OCR, 180, 181
OCR technology, 85
Onboarding, 87–88
Operation bloomsdale, 193, 194
Operation moonwalk, 190, 192
Operation sunshine, 192, 193
Optical character recognition, 258
Optimize resources, 83

P2P lending platforms, 66
PayTech, 105
Personalised marketing, 119
Phase change memories (PCMs), 288, 291, 303
Phosphorene, 289, 294–296, 298, 303–305
Portfolio, 222
Potential and risks, 45–46
Pradhan Mantri Jan Dhan Yojana (PMJDY), 271
Precautions, 193, 194
Predictive analysis, 119
Predictive analytics, 167, 168
Profit source platform, 36
Protection of personal privacy, 49–50

Random forest classifier, 222
Readiness, 171, 173
Reconciliation, 87
Refining, 236
RegTech, 105, 116
Regulatory compliance, 59, 197, 198
Reinforcement learning, 200, 203–204, 208–209, 214
Repercussions of bias in finance, 51
Report management, 89–90
Resistive random access memories (RRAMs), 290, 297, 301–302
Resistive switching, 290, 294–295, 297–298, 300, 302, 304
Response synthesis, 113
RichLive Trade, 25
Ridge regression, 186, 187
Risk analysis, 117
Risk management, 155, 181, 182
Risks in autonomous finance operations, 56–57
Roadmap, 188, 190
Robo-advising, 107
Robotic, 81
Robotic process, 143, 146, 150, 159, 162
Robotic process automation, 13, 66, 246, 247, 248, 250
Robotics in banking, 124, 129
Robotics process automation, 159
RPA, 181, 182
RPA in finance, 83

Scopus, 66, 69
Sensex stocks, 223
Sentiment analysis, 203, 211–214
Significance, 171
Social media analytics, 76
Societal marketplace, 145
Solution drivers, 173, 176
Spider stock market software, 28
Stock price prediction, 223
Success factors in Fintech, 137, 138
Supervised or unsupervised, 222
Supply chain management, 144, 152, 161
Support vector regression, 225
Surveillance, 195
SVM, 185, 188

Team work, 93
Technology acceptance model, 136, 139
Technology dependency and infrastructure, 57
Technology drivers, 172, 174
Technology investments, 259
Telecom Regulatory Authority of India (TRAI), 278
Thematic map, 73
Trade tiger, 31–32
Trader guide, 33
TradeTech, 105
Traditional model, 237
Transition metal dichalcogenides (TMDs), 289, 294–296, 298, 302
Two-dimensional materials, 291, 294–295, 297–299, 301–303, 305–310

Understanding algorithmic bias, 50–51
Underwriting, 90
Unlabeled data, 222
Unsupervised learning, 222
UPI, 176, 177
User education and transparency, 60–61

VectorVest, 35
Venture capital (VC), 269–274
Virtual assistants, 175, 176
Von Neumann architecture, 289, 292, 298

WealthTech, 107
Web science, 66, 69
Work fusion, 244

XGBoost, 187, 188

Printed in the USA/Agawam, MA
September 16, 2026

910661.093